THE MEYERSON SYMPHONY CENTER

Building a Dream

Morton Meyerson

LAURIE SHULMAN

UNIVERSITY OF NORTH TEXAS PRESS

THE
MEYERSON
SYMPHONY
CENTER

—ↄ⌀ↄ—

Building a Dream

Permissions:

University of North Texas Press

PO Box 311336

Denton TX 76203–1336

The paper used in this book meets the
minimum requirements of the American National
Standard for Permanence of Paper for Printed
Library Materials, z39.48.1984. Binding materials
have been chosen for durability.

Library of Congress Cataloging-in-Publication Data

Shulman, Laurie C., 1951–

The Meyerson Symphony Center: building a dream /
by Laurie Shulman.—1st ed.

    p. cm.

Includes bibliographical references and index.

ISBN 1–57441–082–2 (cloth: alk. paper)

1. Morton H. Meyerson Symphony Center—History.

2. Music—Texas—Dallas—History and criticism.

3. Dallas Symphony Orchestra—History. I. Title.

ML200.8.D22 M67   2000

784.2′06′07642812—dc21

99–054375

This book is dedicated to all the people who worked so tirelessly to bring the Meyerson Symphony Center to fruition and especially to the memory of those I did not have the privilege of interviewing:

Jack Evans
Charles Brenton Fisk
Lloyd H. Haldeman
Louise Wolff Kahn
Eduardo Mata
William H. Seay
Annette Strauss
Buck J. Wynne III

Publication of this book was made possible in part through the generosity of:

Anonymous

A. H. Belo Corporation Foundation

Centex Corporation

The Eugene McDermott Foundation

John G. and Nancy P. Penson

Howard E. Rachofsky

CONTENTS

PART 3: 1982–1985

PART 4: 1985–1989

FOREWORD

THIS BOOK preserves the history of the conception and building of a new symphony hall in Dallas. I love history and think that without its study we are destined to repeat mistakes that are avoidable. Therefore I applaud this comprehensive historical account of the building. It will be a reference tool for other communities that take on the enormous task of planning a concert hall.

Our principal goals in building the symphony hall were to create an environment for music that was aesthetically pleasing and acoustically as perfect as we could make it. I think we succeeded reasonably with both those goals. That story is now part of the past. The legacy of the symphony hall lies in the present and the future.

In the next decades, the Meyerson Symphony Center will be judged as much for what takes place within it as for the building itself. Our Dallas hall, now ten years old, is itself an instrument that embraces us with great classical music. The hall also bears witness to our human reaction to the music. In the broadest sense, as a temple for high art, a concert hall has the potential to help us educate ourselves about life and emotion. The experience of hearing great music in a great hall nourishes the soul.

The future is especially important. The prospect of tomorrow energizes many of us. What does that mean for a symphony hall? The future is about artistic excellence: matching the superior caliber of the acoustics and the architecture with superior music-making. Meeting the highest standards, both in the artists and repertoire who perform in the hall and in their performances. If we combine success in these challenges within this wonderful hall, we will achieve all our goals. The concert hall committee reached a major destination in its long journey with the opening of the hall in 1989. The decade since then has given rise to a new set of goals that were in the embryonic stages during planning, design, and construction.

We have a responsibility to educate our children about the virtues and values of classical music. This is a task that originates at the local level, but ultimately has an impact on the larger community. How do we achieve this goal? We must expand the audience for great music and find new venues for delivery. Finding a way to use digital electronic means to communicate with classical music will be fundamental to our success. Each live performance is unique, but by using electronics and the internet, we can create an interactive environment that will supplement live performances and reach a wider public. Electronic transmission of music has the potential to encourage a global community. It can open up the concert venue to the world and transcend geographic barriers. In short, we can have as much future impact on the culture of Dallas as we have had by creating our symphony hall.

In order to accomplish that, we must first nurture our orchestra and its leaders. We need to find the best orchestra players to ensure the ensemble's continued artistic strength in the future. We need to work hard on creative and imaginative programming that will expand the experience of our established audience and draw in new listeners. The Dallas Symphony is already one of the best orchestras in the United States. With focus and determination and hard work, it can become one of the greatest in the world, perhaps even the very best. This ambitious goal is within our reach if we have the will and invest the effort it will entail. When the Meyerson Symphony Center was inaugurated, it was evaluated by the highest artistic and architectural standards. That is as it should be. So too should the Dallas Symphony Orchestra continue to strive to achieve the utmost in artistic excellence, and live up to the splendid building it calls home.

Ultimately, success will be measured one hundred years from now and beyond. If we are active and vibrant, develop and maintain a top-ranked orchestra, cultivate an expanded audience, and enrich the lives and souls of our listeners, then we will have done our part for our community.

MORTON H. MEYERSON

ACKNOWLEDGMENTS

WHEN I BEGAN work on this project late in July 1996, I never anticipated that it would become such a consuming passion for me, nor that it would develop into a book. Because the cast of characters that brought the Meyerson Symphony Center to completion is so extended, I am indebted to a large group of individuals. My first debt of thanks is to the many persons who granted me interviews in order to share their recollections of the hall's history. Their individual and collective passion for the project was contagious, repeatedly reinforcing my conviction that the story of the Meyerson Symphony Center deserved to be told. Dozens of my interviewees read portions of the manuscript at various times and made helpful corrections and suggestions to improve it. Their diplomatic and constructive contributions have strengthened the integrity and accuracy of the text. Any factual errors are mine. A complete list of the persons I interviewed is included as part of the bibliography.

Artec Consultants partially funded the first eight months of my research. The Dallas Symphony Association sponsored my work during summer 1998. I am indebted to Eugene Bonelli, Dolores Barzune, and the Dallas Symphony Orchestra for believing in this project and helping to make it possible for me to complete the first draft during those torrid months. The entire Dallas Symphony staff has been extremely helpful in making archival sources available to me. They have also been most gracious about accommodating my impromptu requests for work space on the premises.

Mary McDermott Cook retained all her records from the concert hall planning committee and related matters from 1980 to the mid-1990s, and made them available for my use. Her documents were invaluable in establishing precise chronology and providing rich detail about key meetings in the evolution of the Meyerson.

Nicholas Edwards and David Kahn of Acoustic Dimensions made helpful suggestions to focus my steep learning curve in the science of acoustics. Their bibliographic recommendations and thorough answers to my dozens of questions were essential not only to my overview of acoustics in chapter 8, but also my broader understanding of the Meyerson's significance. Nick Edwards's editorial guidance and substantive contributions to the chapter on room acoustics were invaluable.

Several individuals who were not involved in the evolution of the hall were kind enough to take an interest in the manuscript, looking over excerpts and, in three cases, entire drafts. In particular, Keith Evans, Jessica Stewart Freeman, Daniel Margulis, Gigi Sherrell Norwood, and William Allin Storrer brought both objectivity and a level eye to my revision process.

My personal editor, Althea Romaine Welch, maintained both razor-sharp humor and unfailingly keen perception in her role as the grammar and style police. Her always-constructive criticism enhanced the clarity of my writing and added felicity of phrasing. Stephanie Radway Lane and Steve Wilson copy-edited the manuscript for University of North Texas Press. Mark McGarry, of Texas Type & Book Works, worked his magic to lay out type and illustrations, transforming the manuscript into a handsome volume.

My husband, Bill Barstow, has been unflagging in his support, enthusiasm, patience, and love. I could not have written this book without him.

DRAMATIS PERSONAE

KEY INDIVIDUALS WITH A ROLE IN THE HISTORY OF THE HALL

Dallas Symphony Association Board of Governors

The Dallas Symphony Association (DSA) is the governing body of the Dallas Symphony Orchestra (DSO). It raises money, sets policy, hires and fires, and oversees the organization's finances. The Dallas Symphony Orchestra consists of the performing musicians. Both the musicians and members of the orchestra administrative staff are employed by the association. Throughout this book, the acronym DSA is used to denote the association, and DSO to denote the orchestra.

David Stretch, president, 1968–71 [deceased]

Jack Vandagriff, president, 1971–74

Henry S. Miller, Jr., president, 1974–76; chairman of the board, 1976–78

Robert E. Glaze, chairman of the board, 1974–76; later treasurer

Philip R. Jonsson, vice chairman; later chairman of the board

Richard I. Galland, vice chairman; later chairman of the board, 1981–82

Robert W. Decherd, president, May–December 1979

Donald J. Stone, president, January 1980–1982

William H. Seay, president, May 1982–May 1984 [deceased]

Liener Temerlin, president, May 1984–May 1986; later co-chairman of grand opening fortnight

William L. Schilling, president, May 1986–May 1988

Dolores G. Barzune, president, May 1988–May 1990; also Stradivarius patron chair from 1985

Richard A. Freling, president, May 1990–May 1992

Howard Hallam, president, May 1992–May 1994

Dallas Symphony Staff

Kenneth Meine, general manager in 1974

Lloyd H. Haldeman, president and managing director, November 1974–December 1978 [deceased]

Sydney Reid-Hedge, director of volunteer services

Al Milano, development director from July 1977; then managing director, 1981–82

Leonard David Stone, general manager from June 1979; later executive director until 1993

Melissa McNeil, marketing director in 1979; then director of concert hall planning to 1986

John Luther Adams, secretary to Melissa McNeil until 1986; then concert hall coordinator to 1989

Victor Marshall, artistic administrator since 1981

Douglas Kinzey, marketing director, 1981–98

Martha Blaine, operations manager, 1981–1986

Willem Brans, development director August 1981–October 1984

Domenick Ietto, associate director of development from March 1984; then director of development, September 1985–1988

Warren Gould, fund-raising consultant; later development director

Fred Hoster, general manager, 1982–93

Mark Melson, public relations director from 1986; later operations manager

JoLynne Jensen, Stradivarius patron coordinator; later associate director of development

Dan Ellinor, box seat sales, 1986–90

Mort Meyerson's Concert Hall Committee: The "Smaller Unit"

Morton H. Meyerson, president, Electronic Data Systems

Stanley Marcus, chairman of Neiman Marcus Department Stores, chair of architecture subcommittee

Dr. Eugene Bonelli, dean, Meadows School of the Arts, Southern Methodist University, and chair of acoustics and organ subcommittees; later president of the Dallas Symphony

Louise Wolff Kahn, Dallas Symphony Board member, patron, volunteer, and donor [deceased]

Mary McDermott Cook, Dallas Symphony Board member, patron, volunteer, and donor

Richard Levin, attorney with Akin, Gump, [Strauss], Hauer & Feld

Nancy Penson, Dallas Symphony Board member, patron, volunteer, and donor

City of Dallas Personnel

Wes Wise, mayor, 1973–75

George Schrader, city manager, 1966–September 1981; later administrative construction manager for the DSO, serving as liaison to the City of Dallas and J. W. Bateson

Robert Folsom, mayor, April 1977–April 1981

Jack Evans, mayor, April 1981–April 1983 [deceased]

Starke Taylor, mayor, April 1983–April 1987

Annette Strauss, mayor, April 1987–April 1991 [deceased]

Steve Bartlett, mayor, April 1991–April 1995

Cliff Keheley, director of public works

Victor C. Suhm, assistant city manager

Louise Reuben [Elam], city architect

Robert M. Wilkinson, assistant director, building services

Construction Personnel

Joe Walker, CEO of J. W. Bateson Company (now Centex Construction Company)

Coy Porter, construction manager

Laurie Dale, Porter's assistant

Paul Lyons, quality control

Bob Lemke, assistant project engineer

Glenn Redmond, architect's representative subcontracted through Bill Hidell & Associates

Design Team: Architectural

I. M. Pei, architect

George Miller, project architect with I. M. Pei & Partners (now Pei Cobb Freed & Partners)

Charles Young, architect with I. M. Pei & Partners; principal designer of McDermott
Concert Hall interior

Ralph Heisel, senior associate at I. M. Pei & Partners

Theodore Amberg, head of I. M. Pei & Partners' Dallas office

Ian Bader, architect

Perry Chin, architect

James Langford, architect

Abby Suckle, architect

Design Team: Acoustics and Performance Equipment

Russell Johnson, acoustician, and principal of Artec Consultants

Robert Wolff, theatre consultant

Nicholas Edwards, acoustician

Robert Essert, acoustician

David Kahn, acoustician

Other Consultants

Peter Wexler, stage designer

Leslie E. Robertson, structural engineer

Dan Cecil, structural engineer

Edison Allen, C. W. Shaver Company, fund-raising

Stewart Donnell, cost consultant with Hanscomb Roy Associates, Toronto

Hoffend & Sons, canopy builders

Don Reynolds, LWFW Associates

Randy Thueme, Sasaki Associates

Dvora Lewis, international press relations

Dallas Symphony Orchestra Music Directors and Musicians

Anshel Brusilow, music director, 1970–73

Max Rudolf, artistic adviser, 1973–74 [deceased]

Louis Lane, principal guest conductor; then music director, 1973–78

Eduardo Mata, music director, 1977–94 [deceased]

Andrew Litton, music director since 1994

Douglas Howard, principal percussion and chair of players' committee

Eric Barr, principal oboe and member of players' committee

Kalman Cherry, principal timpani and member of players' committee

Gregory Hustis, principal horn and member of players' committee

John Kitzman, principal trombone and member of players' committee

Clifford Spohr, principal bass and member of players' committee

Lois Vornholt, second violin and member of players' committee

Wilfred Roberts, principal bassoon and contractor of musicians

Fortnight Committee and Participants
(see also DSA Board list)

Karla and Liener Temerlin, co-chairs

Clara Hinojosa

Jane Holahan

Wolford McCue

Bette Mullins

Meyerson Symphony Center Staff and Volunteers

Ted DeDee, building manager

Sharan Goldstein, coordinator of docent program

Bruce MacPherson, assistant manager; later Meyerson Symphony Center manager

Lamar Livingston, sound engineer; later technical director

Art

Margaret McDermott

Linda Marcus

Bill Booziotis (also architect for corporate suites and education center, including Horchow Hall, completed in 1998)

Organ

Charles Brenton Fisk, founder of C. B. Fisk, Inc. [deceased]

Virginia Lee Fisk, C. B. Fisk, Inc.

Steven Dieck, project manager at C. B. Fisk; now president

Charles Nazarian, visual designer at C. B. Fisk

Gregory Bover, vice president for operations at C. B. Fisk

David Pike, executive vice president and tonal director at C. B. Fisk

Robert Cornell, senior design engineer at C. B. Fisk

Dr. Robert T. Anderson, professor at Southern Methodist University, chairman of organ selection subcommittee

1982 Bond Election

Philip O'B. Montgomery III, chair

Buck J. Wynne III, campaign director [deceased]

Nela Wells [Moore], staff coordinator

Amanda Dealey, vice chairman

Pat McBride, volunteer chair

Philip Seib, political consultant

Judy Bonner Amps, political consultant

Enid Gray, political consultant

John Weekley, political consultant

PROLOGUE

The Music Hall at Fair Park, because of the miserable acoustics, was also forgiving. If we played together, it didn't really change much. If we played apart, that was OK, too. If it was soft, you couldn't hear the music anyway.[1]

DALLAS SYMPHONY CELLIST MICHAEL COREN

The sound in the Meyerson Symphony Center is absolutely wonderful. It is one of the best concert halls in the country—and that includes both new and old structures. A great concert hall is absolutely necessary to enjoy live music on the highest level. The citizens of Dallas are lucky indeed.[2]

COMPOSER JOHN CORIGLIANO

A SYMPHONY hall is a building for the ages. In any given city, a new one comes along perhaps once a century. Each community that erects such an edifice intends that it will serve the citizenry forever—or at least for a half-dozen generations. In a way, performance halls are cathedrals for our time. Music and the institution of symphony orchestras lend both permanence and dignity to our culture. At the same time, any public building serving a civic purpose in American society must respond to community needs beyond those of a single user.

In the middle years of the twentieth century, architects and city planners sought to solve the problem of multiple needs in a single building by designing multi-purpose performance venues. They built larger halls to accommodate larger crowds. A single structure was intended to serve the needs of opera, symphony, theatrical performances, inspirational speakers, high school graduations, and rock concerts. In America, bigger was better, and newer was also better. Flexibility was an asset, and the new large halls appeared to serve the needs of a growing public and a healthy economy.

The problem was that they didn't sound very good. Aural and visual aesthetics often took a back seat to function.

Like many large cities, especially newer American cities—ones that could not trace their lineage back to the thirteen colonies—Dallas had no venerable bastion of music like New

York's Carnegie Hall or Boston's Symphony Hall. That changed in September 1989, when the Morton H. Meyerson Symphony Center opened to universal acclaim as an architectural jewel and an acoustical masterpiece. The inauguration of the Meyerson was the culmination of more than twelve years of hard work and planning. During that period, a remarkably diverse group of individuals participated in the process: architects and acousticians, engineers and construction workers, musicians, board members and symphony staff, business and political leaders, arts patrons and volunteers.

The story of the Morton H. Meyerson Symphony Center in Dallas is inextricable from the history of the orchestra itself. The ensemble known today as the Dallas Symphony Orchestra was founded in 1900 as the Dallas Symphony Club, under the direction of Hans Kreissig, a pianist and conductor who had emigrated from Germany to the United States. That comparatively ancient birth date lends Dallas the distinction of having the eighth oldest major symphony orchestra in America. (Only the New York Philharmonic, Boston Symphony, St. Louis Symphony, Cincinnati Symphony, Oregon Symphony, Pittsburgh Symphony and Chicago Symphony were formed earlier.)

Despite the prestige the Dallas Symphony accrued through a series of distinguished music directors—including Antal Dorati, Walter Hendl, and Georg Solti—the ensemble had not found a satisfactory home. For years the orchestra played in Fair Park Music Hall, a large fan-shaped auditorium on the Texas State Fair grounds east of downtown Dallas. During the early 1960s, the DSO moved for a decade to McFarlin Auditorium on the campus of Southern Methodist University, but parking and other logistics proved problematic. Furthermore, McFarlin was not much of an improvement on Fair Park Music Hall from the standpoint of acoustics. So, in 1972, after the music hall had been renovated, the Dallas Symphony returned to Fair Park. Inadequate though it remained, people knew how to get there, and it was a place to perform. Within two years, however, the orchestra management was forced to suspend operations because of a financial crisis that had been long in brewing.

"What Sank the Dallas Symphony Orchestra—After 74 Years?" screamed a *New York Times* banner headline on the front page of the Sunday arts and leisure section. Robert Finklea, a *Dallas Morning News* reporter writing on a freelance basis for the *Times,* asked: "How could this have come to pass? Especially, how could it happen in one of the richest cities in the world? Dallas, after all, has nearly four thousand individuals and families (out of a population of 800,000) with annual incomes in excess of $50,000, and, according to local sources, no fewer than 400 millionaires."[3] The city had pretensions of greatness, yet despite a period during which federal, state and philanthropic funding for the arts was at an all-time high, it could not sustain a cultural institution like an orchestra. The article stung. Eleven years after November 22, 1963, Dallas was still deeply mired in negative fallout from the Kennedy assassination. Now additional humiliation, this time cultural, came from the nation's premier daily newspaper.

Echoes continued to rebound throughout that chaotic year. In November 1974, *D Magazine* published an overview of the orchestra's demise. Writer John Merwin's title, "High Culture, Low Politics: The Death of the Dallas Symphony" was emblazoned on the popular new city magazine's cover. For a month, grocery shoppers who may have been oblivious to the fact that the orchestra was going through a major crisis absorbed the message implied by that headline. In late 1974, just a couple of months after Richard Nixon had resigned in disgrace, much of America had a poor opinion of politics. Any rejuvenation of the Dallas Symphony would necessitate major rehabilitation on the public relations front as well.

Sadly, similar scenarios have recurred numerous times in the last quarter of the twentieth century. Between 1985 and 1998, eight orchestras shut their doors. The San Diego Symphony suspended its orchestra operations for eighteen months in May 1986, in the wake of a musicians' strike. They resumed performances in November 1987, only to declare bankruptcy in 1996. The Oakland Symphony Orchestra went under in September 1986. New Orleans cancelled its season in January 1987. (They were later replaced by the Louisiana Philharmonic.) Less than a month later, Nashville was forced to lay off its musicians and suspend all operations. Oklahoma City, Denver, Orlando, Birmingham, Detroit, and Sacramento have been through similar crises.

Not all the *dénouements* have been so sweet as Dallas', and Dallas took a long time to achieve its current enviable status: an economically and artistically healthy orchestra with one of the finest halls in the world to call its home. The story of the Morton H. Meyerson Symphony Center is a classic tale of triumph over adversity. It is also a story of remarkable cooperation and collaboration: between the public and private sectors, between artists and management. Most of all, it is a saga of commitment to an ideal and of determination to see a dream through to completion.

Part One

1970–1979

Chapter One

DEBACLE

BETWEEN the late 1960s and the early 1970s, the Dallas Symphony's total costs for musicians' salaries, fringe benefits, and artist fees increased by ninety-nine percent. Other concert expenses, such as rental of Fair Park Music Hall, promotions, printing of programs, and the like, more than doubled. As these and other budget items such as administrative staff salaries rose, earned income dropped. The orchestra took out loans. By 1970, more than a decade of weak board leadership and internal management problems had led to an annual operating deficit that threatened the continued viability of the organization.

The Dallas Symphony Association Board of Governors was grabbing at straws. At the end of the 1969–70 season, they decided to replace Music Director Donald Johanos, who had led the orchestra since 1962. Board President David Stretch called his friend Carlton Cooley, the retired principal violist of the Philadelphia Orchestra, to ask Cooley's advice about an interim conductor for Dallas. Cooley recommended Anshel Brusilow, a violinist who had been concertmaster of the Philadelphia Orchestra from 1959 to 1966. Brusilow's conducting experience was limited—he was founder-conductor of the Philadelphia Chamber Orchestra and, later, the Chamber Symphony of Philadelphia—but he had studied with the great French conductor Pierre Monteux for ten years. Furthermore, he had charm, good looks, and what appeared to be innovative ideas.

Stretch contacted Brusilow, who flew to Dallas in summer 1970. "I met with David, [immediate past president] Ralph Rogers and some others, and consummated a contract as interim conductor for one year," recalls Brusilow, who is still active in North Texas musical life three decades later. After Brusilow's first concert, Stretch met him backstage beaming and declared, "We want you to be the regular conductor."

Within a few days, they met to discuss specifics. Brusilow told Stretch, "From what I understand, the orchestra is in such bad shape, not musically, but financially, I would like to know everything that's going on."

"Would you be happy being executive director as well?" Stretch asked.

"Yes. I want to have my hand in all aspects of it, from ticket sales to publicity. I don't want to control it; I just want to know." Thus for the first and only time in the orchestra's history, the artistic and administrative functions were led by the same individual.[1]

—⁊—

BRUSILOW'S brief tenure was dogged by problems from the start. At a cool outdoor Cotton Bowl concert on October 18, 1970, the musicians invoked a clause in their contract about performances in conditions with temperature extremes. "There was a slight revolt," recalls Brusilow drily. "I insisted that we play, but the orchestra was *very* upset." The orchestra members voted against their conductor. Instead of hearing the Dallas Symphony that night, the Cotton Bowl audience listened to an Army Band and taped music while they watched dancing on the field.[2] It was an inauspicious beginning for the new music director.

Shortly afterward, Brusilow learned of plans to renovate Fair Park Music Hall. He stated publicly that the remodeling was a waste of money. "That was another reason I got into trouble with our Board, the Park Board, and the newspapers," he recalls. "I thought they ought to take that money, add funds to it, and build a concert hall. *Everyone* jumped on me."[3]

In reviewing the orchestra's financial records, Brusilow grasped that the orchestra was in serious trouble. He decided to borrow an idea from the Boston Symphony. "It's no secret that the Pops sold the Boston Symphony," he says today. "I thought, that's the direction the Dallas Symphony has to go, whether they like it or not, because that's where we can raise funds and attract new audiences. We came up with the idea of DallaSound. The Philadelphia Orchestra had the Philadelphia Sound. This would be the DallaSound."

Brusilow geared the new series to lure the disaffected younger generation by introducing a popular element to a symphony environment that some perceived as stodgy. "We were one of the first to perform the musical *Jesus Christ Superstar*. We advertised, and within a day we had a line of people queued completely around McFarlin Auditorium to get tickets. We sold out 10,000 seats. We did concerts with the Fifth Dimension, and with Sonny and Cher. This was all DallaSound. They were extremely successful."[4]

The orchestra was unimpressed. "I'm from Philadelphia," says DSO principal timpanist Kalman Cherry, who joined the orchestra in 1958. "They always talk about the 'Philadelphia

Sound.' When I first heard the term 'DallaSound,' I thought it would be like that: the Dallas Symphony Orchestra has a certain sound. Instead what turned out was mediocre arrangements of popular tunes. I just felt it was pretty low class."[5] Cherry's opinion of Brusilow's experiment was widely shared among the orchestra. "He hired expensive arrangers from Philadelphia," recalls Dorothea Kelley, then associate principal viola. "What we got was a carnival of pop players out in front. The orchestra played whole notes while the featured players changed the harmony. It was terribly boring for us."[6]

Then as now, ticket sales did not cover the cost of presenting concerts. Despite the sellouts for some of the big-name stars, the orchestra was burdened with the high cost of engaging the rock 'n' roll performers and handling the amplification equipment they required. An ill-conceived and expensive orchestra tour of Nicaragua in September 1972 exacerbated the symphony's financial problems. The deficit mounted, and morale plummeted within the orchestra. By mid-February 1973, the executive committee of the orchestra's board saw the need to apply for a line of credit from Republic National Bank for $350,000; one month later, the bank authorized an increase of that amount to $400,000.[7] According to long-time board member Henry S. Miller, Jr., "The leadership did the easy thing [*i.e.*, borrowing], instead of balancing the budget or raising the money through contributions."[8]

Brusilow's stint as music director lasted three years. For classical repertoire, he enjoyed artistic success. Principal double bass Clifford Spohr declares him "the best conductor I've ever played for. He has a magical quality of being able to set the right tempo. He made playing the music so easy."[9] Unfortunately, Brusilow's tenure proved to be financially catastrophic for the Dallas Symphony. His vision for a pops series was a good idea at the wrong time. Later iterations of the DallaSound concerts—Summertop, Starfest, and Dallas SuperPops—would prove to be the orchestra's bread and butter. But the timing was off in the early 1970s because of the orchestra's precarious fiscal position. "I saw all the monthly financials and monitored ticket sales," Brusilow insists. "Yes, there were problems. It was no surprise that the orchestra was in the red, but I never saw anything to indicate that it might go out of business."[10] Too late, the board recognized its mistake in neglecting its fundamental artistic mission. It dismissed Brusilow in favor of Max Rudolf, a naturalized German from the old school who boasted Metropolitan Opera experience and the music directorship of the Cincinnati Symphony Orchestra among his credentials.

Brusilow believes he was a sacrificial lamb. "[Board President] David Stretch died suddenly, during my second year, and Jack Vandagriff was named president," he remembers. "Immediately after that I realized there was no way I would be able to continue. I was Ralph Rogers and David Stretch's boy."[11] On a June evening in 1972, Vandagriff came to Brusilow's home to inform him that the DSA would not be renewing his contract beyond the 1972–73 season.[12]

At the time of Max Rudolf's appointment in Dallas as artistic adviser in February 1973, he was head of the opera and conducting departments at Philadelphia's Curtis Institute of Music. During the fleeting eleven months he held his position with Dallas Symphony, Rudolf was able to restore a measure of dignity and artistic integrity to the demoralized ensemble. He is reputed to have said, upon his arrival, that there were a few musicians who were really good, but it was clear that he wanted to clean house. The musicians called him "Max the Axe." Rudolf's stumbling block, however, did not turn out to be the orchestra personnel. He rapidly lost patience with a board that, in his view, lacked artistic knowledge and musical sensitivity. His contract was due to expire on January 14, 1974. He resigned at a stormy press conference coinciding with his contract expiration, lambasting both the board and the Dallas business community for their lack of support. Privately, Rudolf recommended appointing Louis Lane as acting music director. A native Texan who had a long-standing relationship with George Szell and the Cleveland Orchestra, Lane accepted the Dallas appointment with the proviso that all hiring and dismissal of orchestra personnel be subject to his authority.

In the short term, that issue proved to be moot. The January forecast for end of season indicated indebtedness between $950,000 and $1 million. Payroll delays to orchestra members began on January 21. Within two months, money to pay the orchestra members had run out, and the orchestra's accumulated deficit was escalating at an alarming rate. The symphony board held out hope that a $600,000 bequest from the estate of Mrs. Alex B. Camp, a DSO benefactor, might bail them out. The Camp monies were expected to become available in April, at which point the orchestra could eradicate its debt.

Board Chairman Henry S. Miller, Jr., met with the Dallas Citizens Council Executive Committee on February 14 to request approval to borrow more money and to appeal for assistance in providing leadership to the floundering organization. The Citizens Council was a group of top business and professional leaders in the community. It had been formed in 1936 by R. L. Thornton, a four-term Dallas mayor who was instrumental in getting the state fairgrounds at Fair Park renovated and expanded for the Texas Centennial Exposition. According to Dallas historian Patricia Evridge Hill, "While publicly extolling the virtues of rugged individualism and nurturing his image as a 'self-made' man, Thornton formed the Dallas Citizens Council—a private agency within which competition was minimized so that a small cadre of business leaders could amass unprecedented civic power."[13] The Citizens Council grew increasingly strong during the decades following the Second World War. It guided city policy and growth, placing its members in the mayor's office with ease until the early 1970s, and helping to preserve a council-manager form of government that was losing popularity elsewhere in the United States.[14] Henry Miller observes, "As an organization, the Citizens Council didn't make monetary contributions, but they controlled so many important companies, their backing was essential."[15]

William L. Schilling, the managing partner of Peat Marwick Mitchell's Dallas office from 1971 to 1990, was a member of the Citizens Council for a long time. "It comprised the heads of the major corporations in Dallas, and fostered activities considered to be beneficial to the city," Schilling says. "Back at that time, I truly think it was altruistic. The business leaders wanted Dallas to prosper, and they constituted the real power base of the city. Collectively, their companies employed many thousands of people, controlled millions of dollars of corporate wealth and generated billions of dollars in economic activity."[16]

As an organization, the Citizens Council was not particularly concerned with the arts. Some of its individual members—notably Henry Miller, who was CEO of a Dallas real estate empire, and Stanley Marcus of the Neiman Marcus luxury retail empire—clearly were, but they went about their philanthropic activities as individuals, not as representatives of the council. According to Schilling, "I would say that if the Citizens Council had listed its agenda, the arts would have been very low on the list. It may not have been on the list at all. The Citizens Council was more interested in matters like bond issues, which of course affected the symphony."[17]

Miller perceived that the Citizens Council would likely be less concerned with the embarrassment of a suspended symphony season than with the economic ramifications of any such suspension. In his presentation to the Citizens Council, Miller pointed out that the DSO risked losing both the Camp monies and a sizeable grant from the Ford Foundation if the season were curtailed.

The Ford Foundation had undertaken a major initiative in 1966 to support symphony orchestras nationwide. As one of the beneficiaries, the DSO was eligible to receive a grant in the principal amount of $2 million, provided that it could be matched by local funds—and provided that the orchestra continued its regular operations and did not suspend its activities for a significant length of time during a ten-year period. The Ford Foundation's New York–based office forwarded interest payments to the Dallas Symphony and its other beneficiaries annually, but it retained the principal amount as an incentive to recipient organizations to build endowment. The $2 million was scheduled to be paid to the DSO in 1976, if the orchestra were still alive to receive it.

The Citizens Council powers—Lee Turner of Dallas Power & Light, John Stemmons of Industrial Properties, Dewey Presley of First National Bank, Jim Keay of Republic National Bank, David Fox of Fox & Jacobs, and Joe Dealey of *The Dallas Morning News*—listened politely and attentively to Miller's plea. At the next meeting of the symphony's executive board, which was now in a crisis mode and convening weekly, Miller reported that "they [the Citizens Council] did not seem to be enthusiastic at any point." As a condition of providing leadership for a fund drive, the Citizens Council asked the Dallas Symphony Association to finalize a new contract with its musicians. It was hardly what Miller and his symphony board colleagues wanted to hear. They had hoped to secure the imprimatur of the Citizens Council as a basis for rallying corporate support for the symphony.

Republic Bank forced the issue in early March 1974 by terminating the symphony's

$600,000 loan, which the bank had agreed to make with the Camp bequest as collateral. "We had two reasons for cutting off the loan," Republic's Board Chairman Jim Keay later told *D Magazine*. "One was to underscore the seriousness of the symphony's situation, and the other was to make it clear to symphony trustees that they must do something toward reaching a financial solution to the orchestra's problems."[18] On March 8, General Manager Kenneth Meine cancelled a special *Messiah* performance planned for April and announced that the orchestra could not meet its payroll without an emergency bank loan of $75,000.

Four days later, DSA Board President Jack Vandagriff officially suspended operations. In addition to the Republic Bank loan, the DSA had accumulated $200,000 of other debt in unpaid artists' fees and to creditors such as printers.[19] Eight hundred thousand dollars in the hole, with the musicians unpaid, the orchestra's board of governors was effectively declaring bankruptcy—the first such occurrence in the history of an American symphony orchestra.

—

LATER than preferred, Henry Miller received the strong statements of support he had needed from Dallas Citizens Council members John Stemmons and former Mayor Erik Jonsson. The Dallas Chamber of Commerce called on the Dallas business community to increase its financial support of the financially beleaguered orchestra. Of course the chamber cited recovery of economic balance and resumption of the suspended season. The big carrot was the Ford Foundation grant. "Under the circumstances," advised a Chamber of Commerce press release, "it would be unwise to let the Symphony disband."[20]

The symphony, however, was already disintegrating. Concertmaster William Steck jumped ship on April 3 and signed a contract with the Atlanta Symphony. During the next few months more than a dozen other players would follow his example, including the assistant concertmaster, principal clarinet, and principal trombone, all accepting positions elsewhere with orchestras that were on firmer footing. Attempting to stem the exodus, Vandagriff on April 5 announced an influx of contributions totaling $135,000. He was confident that if he could secure $65,000 in additional donations, the season could resume.

In closed session, the symphony's executive board acknowledged that the crisis "was not of recent vintage, but has really been coming on for a number of years and has just now come to a head."[21] Grimly, they reviewed requests from violinist Kyung-Wha Chung, conductor Charles Mackerras, and pianist Rudolf Serkin to be released from contractual commitments to appear with the Dallas Symphony the following season. Holes were springing in the dike faster than they could be plugged.

Hoping to raise some money, the players agreed to perform a free outdoor Easter concert. In a formal statement, the musicians said, "We hope that our intended display of good faith and desire to aid the Symphony during these difficult times will awaken in the Symphony management a similar good faith toward the musicians."[22] The event drew 7,500 people, at that time the largest outdoor crowd in the orchestra's history. No tickets were sold, and volunteers passed the solicitation envelopes for contributions, following the announcement that the twelve-week Summer Sound series had been cancelled. Dallas Mayor Wes Wise spoke between musical works to implore support from the community. Holding up a copy of an out-of-state newspaper discussing the DSO's plight, he told the audience, "I'm afraid I have to agree with this article. We've gotten too used to Dallas brags and not enough to Dallas action."[23]

Negotiations between the board of governors and the musicians that week resulted in the players voting, by a narrow margin, to perform one outdoor concert at Fair Park and three pairs of subscription concerts in May to conclude the subscription season. One pair of the subscription performances did not take place, because Itzhak Perlman's contract was cancelled as a result of the financial crisis. Isaac Stern's May 23 and 24 concerts were also cancelled, but Stern agreed to honor the contract when the orchestra pulled together for his scheduled weekend. Once again, the musicians performed without pay. Such an arrangement was a violation of their union contract, but these were emergency circumstances.

The players believed that any monies taken in would either come to them or be applied toward the rejuvenation of the orchestra. Instead, what funds were raised were directed toward administration and debt retirement. Members of the orchestra remained unpaid, frustrated, and without any prospect of summer season income, except for those who played in the pit orchestra for the Dallas Summer Musicals. For many of them, disillusionment and bitterness were setting in. "When the orchestra folded, we felt like the rug was pulled out from under us," recalls second violinist Janet Cherry. "We realized how much of our lives we had invested in the orchestra. We had to think about what else we wanted in our lives."[24]

In his capacity as board chairman, Henry Miller fired Kenneth Meine on April 23—the official announcement stated that Meine had resigned—and recruited Lawrence Kelly, general manager of the Dallas Civic Opera, on the board of which Miller also served, to assume responsibility as the symphony's acting manager. The crisis seemed about to be alleviated by the prospect of collecting the Camp estate bequest of $600,000. The monies were combined with the contributions that had been trickling in. Lawrence Kelly was able to clear the outstanding debt to Republic Bank; however, there was not enough money to pay the musicians.

—❧—

FOLLOWING its financial collapse, the Dallas Symphony did not resume regular performances until January 1975. During the intervening months, a number of important changes occurred that planted the seeds for the orchestra's renaissance.

In spring 1974, several Dallas business leaders approached Chairman Henry Miller and asked him to take over the more active role of board president from Jack Vandagriff and try to get the symphony association back on track. A gentle, soft-spoken man with a deliberate manner, Miller took his time. "I told them I would think about it. I went home and told Juanita, my wife. She told me to do it, so I did."[25]

With Lawrence Kelly in place as acting general manager, Miller shifted into recruiting mode. He commandeered a group of four to assist him in rebuilding the orchestra and helping it to regain credibility: Philip R. Jonsson, a media executive who owned several radio stations; Alan Gilman, chairman of the board of the Sanger-Harris department store; Robert Glaze of Trammell Crow Company; and Richard Galland of American Petrofina.

Jonsson, president of KRLD Corporation, was already a board member. As the son of Erik Jonsson, a former Dallas mayor, co-founder of Texas Instruments, and a revered city patriarch, Philip Jonsson had name recognition and precisely the sort of prestige Henry Miller was hoping to associate with his board. Jonsson later acknowledged that a phone call he received from Margaret McDermott in the summer of 1973 convinced him to serve. She and her husband, Eugene McDermott, another co-founder of Texas Instruments, had established the Eugene McDermott Foundation. The foundation has been a major supporter of education, health, and medical institutions as well as Dallas arts organizations. Margaret McDermott was closely associated with the Dallas Museum of Fine Arts (as it was then called) and widely known as a collector and generous patron of the visual arts in Dallas. As one of the orchestra's senior board members, she also had a strong interest in the welfare of the Dallas Symphony.

"Philip, I want you to go on the board of the Dallas Symphony. They need your help," she announced.

Taken aback, Jonsson protested, "But Margaret, I'm not even a subscriber to the symphony!"

Sternly, she replied, "Philip, I didn't call you to hear your problems! I want you to go on the board!"

He backed down. "Yes, Ma'am." He wasn't about to say no to her. In September 1973, he was unanimously elected to the board of governors.[26]

Margaret McDermott understood that it was time for Philip Jonsson to live up to his family's legacy. When Henry Miller identified him as a key member of the rebuilding team, Jonsson was quick to perceive the initial difficulty after a six-week suspension of performances. The community and the city leadership had no confidence in the symphony. That confidence had eroded because the organization had always teetered on the edge financially, and this time it had been forced to shut down operations altogether. In the mid-1970s, the city's business leadership was even more important to Dallas than it is today. "The trunk of the power tree was, and is, the big downtown banks, Republic and First National. The chief executives of the big banks sit at the Big Table regardless," *D Magazine* wrote in 1974.[27] Jonsson recognized that the bankers also sat on the boards of charitable foundations and other community organizations, wielding power, influence, and money.

As Philip Jonsson embarked on his campaign to identify and secure business support, he understood better why Margaret McDermott had identified him as an effective board member. "We had a terrible credibility problem. *The Dallas Morning News* was carrying quotes from business leaders saying, 'We don't need the symphony.' Henry Miller put me in charge of building the board. At first, I couldn't get anybody to come on the board. 'The symphony? No, I don't believe I could do that. Thanks for asking me.' or 'I'll let you know.' I thought the key was to get some bankers." Why bankers? "I thought they could help us get *more* bankers."[28]

One of his first appointments that spring was with Jim Keay, the chairman of the board of Republic National Bank, which was the symphony's largest creditor. It was also where Jonsson banked. The visit was unsuccessful. Unfortunately, Keay said, his schedule was so busy that he doubted if he would be able to fit in the DSO Board. Jonsson left the door open, urging Keay to think about it. Next stop was Republic National Bank's principal competitor, First National. En route to see First National's president, Harry Shuford, Jonsson dropped by his father's office and inquired, "Do you have a few minutes? Would you walk over with me? I want to ask Harry Shuford if he'll serve on the symphony board." Erik Jonsson agreed.[29]

Jonsson remembers the ensuing interview clearly. "We walked there, and I asked Harry Shuford to serve on the board, with my father sitting there. He said yes, which I'm sure would have been 'no' *without* him sitting there! At that point I was able to go back to Jim Keay at Republic National Bank, and ask, 'Jim, have you decided yet? Harry Shuford's going to join us.' And Jim was able to reach a decision."[30]

Before long, Henry Miller had an active board again, whose membership comprised a number of prominent civic leaders. Using a combination of gentle persuasion backed by the prestige of the right bankers, Jonsson, Miller, and their colleagues were armed to enlist corporate leaders who had borrowed millions of dollars from the big banks on behalf of their companies. Jonsson turned the symphony board into a bandwagon. He launched the process of rebuilding by approaching the community's foremost citizens, adding their names to the masthead, and soliciting energy, money, and corporate support to strengthen this rejuvenation. As soon as they secured a few of those prominent names, they had credibility again, which is what the symphony needed. At that point, Jonsson knew, he could invite pretty much anyone they wanted, without any further apprehension that the offer would be declined. Shuford and Keay, the two bank presidents, spearheaded a special gift announced in early August, pledging to underwrite two regular season concerts during the symphony's 1974–75 season.

One of Jonsson's invitations was tendered to Bob Glaze, chief financial officer of the Trammell Crow Company. Glaze says, "One day, at my office, Harry Shuford, Henry Miller, and Philip Jonsson walked in. One of them announced, 'We want you to be chairman of the symphony board.' I said, 'Now, fellas, come on. I've never even served on the board of the symphony. I've never been on a committee. I have no background at all, no intimate connection with the symphony. Maybe I've given them a little money from time to time, but I don't have any knowledge of how the symphony really works. If you want me to dive in, why don't you invite me to be treasurer?' They replied, 'No, that's not what we want. We want you to be chairman of the board, because we need to transform the business community's image of the symphony into an image of financial responsibility.' We talked quite a long while. I finally said, 'I'll give it a go. I'll do the best I can.'"[31]

It was a difficult time for Glaze to take on the responsibility. The symphony was broke and not performing. Glaze knew many people in town, and his reputation was good, but he didn't have the prestige or name recognition of a Henry Miller or a Philip Jonsson. Although he lacked nonprofit board experience, like any experienced and capable financial planner—and like the solid business thinker Shuford, Miller, and Jonsson knew him to be—Glaze took a good, hard look at the symphony's books and rapidly reached some conclusions.

He applied his energy where his strengths lay: in immediate and long-range planning for fiscal stability. "I was there to see to it that the direction we were headed for the year to come was reasonable, that we carried out what we planned to do, and that we didn't engage in processes that were impossible," Glaze says. Yes, it would be nice to go to Carnegie Hall, but that would mean a lot of expensive plane tickets and hotel rooms. Sure, having six more violinists in the orchestra would improve the sound of the string section, but one more violinist would fall better within budget projections.

Seeking colleagues who would share his philosophy, Glaze directed his recruiting to the financial community. He decided to approach William L. Schilling, managing partner of Peat Marwick's Dallas office. Without hesitation, Schilling agreed to join the board as treasurer. Except for a one-year rotation off the board to comply with a bylaws limitation, he would remain on the DSA Board of Governors continually for nearly fifteen years, including a stint as president from 1987 to 1989.

Miller and Philip Jonsson knew that if the kind of collapse they'd just experienced ever happened again, the business community would desert them. Glaze shared their perspective, initially, at the expense of artistic goals. His message was simple: "You [at the symphony] all are so interested in the artistic quality levels of community life; fine, go do it. But we're not going to contribute if you can't maintain fiscal responsibility." Eventually leaving the chairman's spot to serve several terms as board treasurer—a progression defying organizational norms—he remained a fiscal conservative and a voice of caution, with the memory of the 1974 catastrophe always fresh in his mind.

ANOTHER Henry Miller recruit to assist in the symphony's financial resuscitation was Richard Galland, then president and CEO of American Petrofina, Inc. Initially, Galland had sent a contribution in his own name, in response to Miller's plea for assistance. Miller had a more active role in mind. By mid-May, Galland was officially a member of the board's executive committee, and Miller had appointed him chairman of the symphony's fund drive. The program was called SOS (Save our Symphony). Its goal was to raise $500,000 to restart the orchestra. American Petrofina soon supplemented Galland's personal donation with a substantial corporate gift.

Dallas had an expanding economy that spawned a feeling that the city could do anything it set its mind to. Changes in banking laws allowed for the financing of a great deal of real estate, and the downtown skyline started to alter as skyscrapers were erected. Optimism was nearly omnipresent, if not uniform good taste. After the Yom Kippur war in October 1973, when Israel was attacked by the Arab states, the Arabs had exercised their economic muscle by seeking to deprive the West of the abundant oil reserves in the Middle East. Consequently, the price of oil rose, and Dallas benefited. Although the stock market was down in 1974, the petroleum business was thriving.

Henry Miller remembers, "The Arab states' oil embargo had adversely affected our economy, so the economic times were tough, but the oil industry prospered because the price of oil soared. Dick Galland had all those connections, so he was able to raise a considerable

"Save our Symphony" was the slogan adopted by Henry Miller and Dick Galland to spearhead their initial fund-raising campaign after the orchestra suspended operations in spring 1974. (*Courtesy Henry S. Miller, Jr.*)

amount of money from oil companies and oil men, among others. We had ordinary symphony lovers out on the streets with buckets, or baskets, raising money. We had billboards,
and we had buses covered with posters reading 'Save our Symphony.' It was a great community effort. The newspapers were very supportive."[32]

Philip Jonsson had approached his recruiting by focusing on major Dallas banks. Galland
concentrated his fund-raising within the oil community, soliciting colleagues he knew professionally. It was fortunate for the city and the orchestra that these and other city fathers recognized that it might be a source of considerable embarrassment if Dallas no longer had a
symphony orchestra. Galland told them, "I don't think we can look each other in the eye at
the Petroleum Club if we lose our symphony."[33] The men he contacted immediately came
through with contributions. The formal development drive, begun in June, reached its initial
$500,000 goal by August. The orchestra's debt to Republic Bank had been satisfied by the SOS
campaign funds and the Camp estate bequest.

As Philip Jonsson remembers it, Henry Miller presided over a full symphony board but
used his smaller working group, comprising Glaze, Jonsson, Galland, and sometimes other
members of the executive committee—Alan Gilman, Irvin Levy, Alan May, and William Moss
—to get things done quickly. "The board was a larger organization that couldn't be involved in
day-to-day decisions," Jonsson recalls. "As we recruited these people, we were really recruiting
the executive committee. We'd meet for breakfast, at first weekly, but the meetings quickly
became monthly. That executive group made most of the decisions."[34]

The executive board did not always see eye to eye with the musicians, and labor negotiations were testy. The players were holding out for a longer season of forty-two weeks; the
board of governors recited a mantra emphasizing the need for fiscal responsibility. Miller's
executive committee felt that the symphony could afford to offer them only thirty-three
weeks of employment: a twenty-six-week concert series, six weeks of opera season, and one
week of paid vacation. For the musicians, that package meant a twenty-four-percent salary
cut instead of the eleven-percent-cost-of-living increase they had expected. More than a dozen
of the players had simply looked elsewhere after the shutdown in the spring, and the ranks
were decidedly thinner.

As a group, the orchestra members threatened in early June to sue the Dallas Symphony
Association for eleven weeks of unpaid back wages, claiming in a contentious formal statement that "many of us have been financially humiliated by non-payment of wages . . . and
while our wages go unpaid the orchestra management uses available funds to pay off nearly
all other debts."[35] Players' committee spokesman Merle Clayton asserted that the orchestra
members never received official notification that the summer season was cancelled, and
therefore showed up for their first summer rehearsal pursuant to their contract. The board
insisted that the musicians must forfeit their summer pay and agree to a truncated twenty-

five-week season for 1974–75. Battle lines had been drawn, and the divide between the two parties' stances underscored the tension and mistrust that had arisen.

Negotiations between the DSA and the players' committee continued through July, as the fund-raising program approached its goal. Henry Miller found new support for the symphony, with an important condition. "When corporations, business organizations and individuals are approached and learn how crucial their support is to the very life of the symphony, they respond," he said, "but without exception they have placed one prime condition on their support: that the DSA commit itself to a fiscally responsible program."[36] The musicians countered with an accusation that the association was "destroying the orchestra under the guise of 'fiscal responsibility.'" Spokesman Clayton said, "The musicians think Dallas deserves the quality of cultural life a major symphony brings and have vowed not to take a step backwards musically. We also expect a living wage."[37]

In early August 1974, negotiations reached a crisis point when Local 147 of the American Federation of Musicians, the musicians' union, placed the DSO on a blacklist, alleging that the symphony had failed to negotiate in good faith. Henry Miller was astonished, because he was about to announce that ninety-seven percent of the fund-raising goal had been reached as a result of Dick Galland's big push. "I can't believe they have the power to prevent Dallas from having a symphony orchestra if the people want it. Based on that premise, we will continue our fund raising," he told *The Dallas Morning News*.[38] Such continuation was blind faith on the part of the board, for the union "bad list" precluded any musician from performing with the DSO until the contract dispute over the curtailed 1973–74 season was settled. Miller told his board of governors that, if the musicians' demands for a longer season could not be resolved, there was a chance the DSO would be forced to cancel its 1974–75 season. He reiterated that the DSA Board of Trustees had been doing everything possible to assist the musicians and voted to pay a week's salary to each musician to help ease the financial burden.[39]

The divide was narrowing. Nevertheless, the musicians were demoralized. Few of them had independent means. Among those who remained, ten new players were not even eligible for unemployment benefits. "We were in dispute over our salary, because they had broken the contract," recalls violinist Janet Cherry. "If you tried to go work in the dime store or something, you would have automatically lost it. So we sat around wondering if we were going to get anything. We were a test case for everybody, because the situation was so unusual. We weren't on strike. We weren't exactly fired."[40]

Under pressure, the symphony board agreed to arbitration, which took place in mid-August 1974. The ruling awarded the musicians full salary for eight weeks of their cancelled summer season, plus three weeks of vacation pay. Henry Miller stated that the DSA did not plan to appeal the decision, even though it had expected to pay at most a compromise amount. "These developments simply mean that we now must raise additional funds and sell more tickets," he stated.[41] On August 30, the Dallas Symphony Association made its first payment in accordance with the arbitration rulings, but the quarrel continued throughout the autumn. The season remained suspended, with no symphony performances inaugurating the 1974–75 season; however, in early October the DSA announced it would begin its subscription drive on November 1.[42] Through a second court-appointed arbitrator, the dispute was resolved in late November 1974. The symphony settled the unpaid wages issue from the prior season, and the parties agreed that talks would begin in early December for a speedy opening of the delayed 1974–75 season.

Chapter Two

PICKING UP THE PIECES: A NEW MANAGER

In February of 1975, the orchestra did the most amazing recovery act since Lazarus, coming back from zero to community support and artistic strength it had not known for a decade. . . . The current success story of the Dallas Symphony can be explained in two words: Lloyd Haldeman. . . . With the zeal of a sinner who had found religion, and with obvious relish for a seemingly impossible situation, he effected a settlement, launched massive fund drives which erased accumulated deficits and stabilized the orchestra's finances.[1]

JOHN ARDOIN,
The New York Times, October 4, 1981

ACTING General Manager Lawrence Kelly, who had been battling phlebitis and cancer, had scaled back his involvement with the orchestra in July. At the time, the executive committee elected to keep information about his condition confidential; however, Kelly's declining health became public knowledge in August. He was forced to resign in late August for medical reasons and died just a few weeks later. Still wrestling with fund-raising and labor negotiations, the symphony embarked on a search for a permanent general manager. Philip Jonsson chaired the search committee. In the interim, the board appointed John DeFord as acting general manager with responsibility for a continuing development program and a subscription drive. In late October, they engaged Lloyd Haldeman, a forty-one-year old Pennsylvanian with both managerial and development experience, as president and managing director of the orchestra. The dual title was unusual and indicated the broad spectrum of powers the board was granting him.

At the time of his appointment, Haldeman was a Cincinnati-based vice president of New York's C. W. Shaver & Company, the preeminent arts fund-raising company in North America. He had started his orchestral career in California as manager of the Fresno Philharmonic Orchestra, moving first to the Vancouver Symphony, then to Cincinnati. He became the manager of the Cincinnati Orchestra in 1963, forming a very successful relationship with music director Thomas Schippers that included a European tour. Haldeman left the Cincinnati Orchestra in 1971 and went into the private sector, joining fund-raising expert Carl Shaver's organization.[2]

Henry and Juanita Miller had a good friend in Cincinnati, Mrs. Fred Lazarus III, of the Lazarus department store family. She was a prominent member of the Cincinnati Symphony Board and also active in the American Symphony Orchestra League. When the Millers contacted her to inquire about Haldeman's managerial qualifications, she told them, "If you're able to get Lloyd Haldeman, you'll be the most fortunate symphony organization in the country." That was enough for Henry Miller. Philip Jonsson confirmed Haldeman as a solid candidate, and Haldeman was tendered an offer.[3]

Miller later said, "We pretty much gave Lloyd a free hand. He had to be accountable to the symphony's executive board." Haldeman had his work cut out for him. The musicians had no contract; the orchestra had no season. Still, he was ambitious, announcing at the time of his hiring, "My long term objectives for the institution are to build an orchestra of the highest musical standards featuring the world's great musical artists and with the capability to present a broad range of subscription, educational and pops concerts throughout the entire North Texas area."[4]

His first act as managing director was to resume meetings with representatives of the symphony's musicians. The issues were salary and length of season. By mid-December, when matters reached another impasse, the board and musicians were still about fifteen weeks apart on proposed season length. Just after the first of the year, Haldeman issued a confidential memo to the board's labor finance committee, explaining what had held up settlement thus far and predicting a deficit. He wrote: "The attached forecast shows a bottom-line deficit that is very substantial and beyond the level we all would like to see. We are, however, after six weeks of intense negotiation, at the point where we either settle promptly, within the next weeks, or face the danger of risking our Ford Foundation grant, a cancellation of this Season, the loss of our key musicians, and the probable loss of the fall of 1975."[5]

Haldeman's communiqué sent a blunt message: it's now or never, and let's get a contract in place. Within a week, on January 14, 1975, the musicians finally approved a partial season, by a squeaker vote. They accepted a twenty-seven-week proposal, beginning with youth concerts in January and a series of ten subscription pairs starting in mid-February. The contract included two weeks of vacation and a curtailed summer season, for a total of ninety concerts. Louis Lane would be artistic advisor and principal guest conductor for 1975. Haldeman told the press, "Obviously, I am delighted to have this matter resolved. The Board of Trustees have worked diligently to put together this final economic package which the musicians have accepted. Now we can all begin the process of rebuilding our orchestra."

The Dallas community was evidently ready to embrace its orchestra again. Public school concerts resumed on January 22 to full houses. A subscription renewal campaign launched in late January reported more than a thousand renewals in the first four days. A volunteer phone bank staffed by the DSO Women's League, DSO Men's Guild, Dallas Jaycees, and other civic organizations fielded questions and took subscriber orders for more than two weeks, with enthusiasm fueled by Haldeman's announcement that Jacob Krachmalnick had accepted an appointment as the new concertmaster. The community heaved a collective, nervous sigh of relief as opening night drew nigh.

With the new season underway, Henry Miller recognized the need to sustain momentum. On February 10, with board members Dick Galland, Jim Keay, and William Seay at his side, he called on Joe Dealey of *The Dallas Morning News*—a Dallas Citizens Council member—to ask him to chair the symphony's March 1975 fund-raising campaign. Dealey accepted, with Galland, Harry Shuford, Keay, and Seay as his co-chairmen. The business community was behind the symphony again. By the first week in March, the orchestra had a reinstated credit line at Republic National Bank, First National Bank, and Mercantile National Bank. For the first time in several years, it appeared that the symphony association's annual meeting in May might be a pleasant occasion.

Toward the end of the partial season in spring 1975, Henry Miller asked Philip Jonsson if he would succeed him at the symphony's helm. Jonsson thought about it and finally said, "Henry, I just don't know enough to do this. I would not be a good president. But, if you'll do it for another year, and you choose to ask me again, the answer would probably be different."[6] Miller took Jonsson at his word and continued in his capacity as president for another year. Meanwhile, he named Jonsson first vice chairman and appointed him to every committee and planning group there was, including the chairmanship of the executive committee, determined that he acquire the experience to take over. Jonsson remained active for years, eventually serving as chairman of the board 1979–80. (He never served as president because Lloyd Haldeman assumed that title.)

—⁂—

HALDEMAN was instrumental in revamping the organization's business processes. He gave the orchestra and its board direction, seeking out new blood in both areas. Getting the orchestra back on track financially was his chief priority, but he clearly perceived the orchestra's artistic potential and had wished to rebuild the orchestra artistically. Philip Jonsson remembers Haldeman as a great salesman who was ambitious for the orchestra and very hard working. "There was only one area where Haldeman and I had problems. He was not nearly as concerned with the financial stability of the organization as I was. He was much more interested in the artistic betterment, at whatever cost."[7] Artistic growth was well and good, but under no circumstances was the board shooting for anything other than a bottom line that was solidly in the black. The organization required both artistic vision and the practical, money-conscious balance of people like Bob Glaze, Philip Jonsson, and the newly recruited banking establishment.

Haldeman's personal artistic vision for the Dallas Symphony included two major components. The first was new artistic personnel; the second, a new performing facility. The personnel changes meant hiring a dynamic music director and a young complement of new talent within the orchestra so that it could fulfill its musical potential. New talent was the easier part of that two-pronged task. Douglas Howard, principal percussionist of the Dallas Symphony, was one of a sizeable group of players who joined the orchestra in calendar 1975. "The real focus was to rebuild," he remembers. "A lot of us—[principal clarinet] Steve Girko, [principal English horn] Steve Lickman, [principal bass clarinet] Chris Runk—came in that year. The finances were still dicey, but they pulled it together pretty well."[8]

The following season brought additional instrumental strength to the rehabilitating artistic ensemble, including cellist Yuri Anshelevich, a new concertmaster, Eliot Chapo, and trumpeter Bert Truax. Gregory Hustis, principal horn of the DSO since 1976, was hired in the spring of that year and moved in late summer to Dallas to start the new season with his wife, Barbara Hustis, who joined the DSO viola section. Greg Hustis credits Haldeman with bringing the orchestra from regional management style to major orchestra style. "I had a sense from the players here that the orchestra was on the way up, or I never would have come here. I didn't want to move to Dallas unless I felt I had some future here. I always felt that Lloyd was very astute. His style was extremely tough. In negotiations, he didn't want to give an inch. On the other hand, if I can easily outfox a manager, then we don't have a very good manager. I don't expect him to play the horn, either! With Lloyd, it was always business. He was going to cut the best deal he could. He did it with me, and with the board, and with the city. That's one of the reasons things got better."[9]

According to Al Milano, who became the DSO's development director in 1977, Haldeman's strengths did not lie in fund-raising. "When Henry Miller brought in the Shaver Company [in 1974] to save the symphony, they put together a three-year campaign. Lloyd Haldeman was one of the guys Shaver sent to Dallas to help work with Louis Lane on programming, to help make it more appealing. Because Shaver sent him, the people in Dallas thought he was a Shaver fund-raiser and that he could run Shaver's three-year campaign. Of course he couldn't; he was personally unsuited for that kind of work. They decided they needed a professional fund-raiser. Lloyd conducted the search for a development director under pressure from Philip Jonsson."[10] He found Milano, who left a position as development director of the New York Public Library and moved with his family to Dallas.

Haldeman clearly made distinctly different impressions on those who worked with him in various capacities. According to both his daughter and his former wife, he felt tremendous pressure to achieve a great deal in a very short time, in budget stabilization, fund-raising, marketing, and artistic excellence.[11] Attracting a new music director was the greatest artistic challenge. Leonard Stone, Haldeman's eventual successor, recalls, "Lloyd committed to the board that he would bring on a major European conductor to lead the orchestra. Philip Jonsson and Lloyd went to New York to visit the legendary Ronald Wilford of Columbia Artists Management, Inc. [CAMI], the largest classical music management agency in the world, to inquire who might be available. 'Why should I give you one of our conductors?' Wilford asked them with incredulity. 'You've just come out of bankruptcy, you don't have a large audience, you don't tour, you don't record. You don't have a great hall.'"[12] Wilford's dig about Fair Park stuck in Haldeman's craw. Dallas was the only major city in the United States without a hall specifically designed for its symphony orchestra. Haldeman understood that the Dallas Symphony could not be one of the nation's premier orchestras *without* its own home.

Ultimately, Haldeman realized that he was not going to be able to secure a great European conductor to lead the Dallas Symphony. To satisfy the wish to have a big-name conductor on a permanent basis, he created the position of principal guest conductor, reasoning that contracting with a great European for that position was a considerably easier thing to accomplish than signing a permanent music director with a big name. Although the principal guest position did not materialize for a number of years, Haldeman did succeed in bringing in Kurt Masur, now music director of the New York Philharmonic, as a guest conductor for two seasons.[13]

Philip Jonsson chaired the symphony's committee to identify and recruit a new music director. He and Haldeman went to a handful of cities around the country, including St. Louis, Cleveland, and Washington D.C., to hear performances in their concert halls. "Of course," Jonsson remembers wryly, "Lloyd took the opportunity to point out to me what nice halls we were in, like the Kennedy Center. We met with music directors or visiting conductors, people we might be able to hire away. Eduardo Mata turned out to be the one that we went for." Mata was an exciting young Mexican conductor with an excellent reputation in Europe and a substantial number of recordings already under his belt. According to Gregory Hustis, "Lloyd was willing to take a chance on Eduardo, as young and relatively unknown as he was, rather than some tired old guy who had been rehashed a million times. He felt that Eduardo had charisma."[14]

Jonsson remembers that Haldeman was one of the first to voice the need for a permanent home for the orchestra. "He kept talking about it, so I appointed a committee to start working on a hall. At that time, in my mind, it was not the highest priority. My number one priority was strengthening this organization and making sure that we didn't get into financial trouble that would ruin our credibility again." Nevertheless, Haldeman succeeded in organizing a facilities committee that, by July 1977, had interviewed two acoustical consultants, Cyril Harris and Christopher Jaffe, and evaluated a third candidate, the firm of Bolt, Beranek & Newman.[15] By the end of July, the committee had voted to retain Harris, provided that his $25,000 retainer fee could be raised.[16] The arrangement was never consummated. The following month,

Haldeman described an offer by H. Ross Perot to build a full concert hall facility, at no cost to the DSO, on Perot's Electronic Data Systems campus in North Dallas. The choice of architect and acoustician would be left to the DSO.[17] That prospect also failed to come to fruition, partly because of homeowner opposition in the EDS neighborhood. Equally important was a growing conviction on the part of the symphony leadership that fund-raising would hinge on the support of the business community, which meant a downtown location. Although Jonsson subsequently stated that his hall committee accomplished little and that he didn't have enough time to stay on top of it, in many respects his and Haldeman's early efforts were farsighted. Jonsson credits a later board president, Robert W. Decherd, with having put steam into the project.[18]

Philip Jonsson and Bob Glaze had recruited Robert Decherd to the symphony board in 1976. A scion of the family that publishes Texas' largest newspaper, *The Dallas Morning News,* Decherd had returned to his hometown in 1973 after graduating from Harvard. "The symphony seemed like a good way for me to find involvement in the community," Decherd explains. "As a matter of civic necessity, it seemed abundantly clear to me that Dallas needed to have a strong symphony. Perhaps more from the standpoint of local pride than anything else, Dallas needed to overcome the embarrassment of the orchestra having failed financially. I had virtually no history with the Dallas Symphony. My immediate family hadn't been involved per se. The extended Belo 'family,'[19] of course, had been involved for a long time. I've always been interested in cities and how they worked. Instinctively I've been curious about, and drawn to, the way communities and organizations function, how you influence people and institutions for the public good. I see the visual and performing arts as a part of this."[20] Jonsson and Miller were happy to put Decherd's youth and energy to work on behalf of the orchestra.

They continued to focus their own efforts on financial stability. When the Ford Foundation money became available in 1976, Jonsson was responsible for its being set aside as a nest egg through the establishment of the Dallas Symphony Foundation. He instructed the symphony's attorneys to set up the foundation so that interest was available to the orchestra for operations, touring, or other costs, but principal would remain intact. That sum was seed money for the Dallas Symphony's endowment, which had its birth at this time.

By late-1999, the DSO boasted an endowment well in excess of $65 million, with a goal of $100 million by the year 2000. While still modest in comparison to the hefty endowments enjoyed by the "Big Five" orchestras of Boston, Philadelphia, New York, Cleveland, and Chicago, the Dallas Symphony's endowment is one of the healthier orchestral endowments in the United States. In retrospect, Jonsson's contribution to the DSO was indirect in terms of the evolution of the Meyerson Symphony Center but crucial to the long-range financial health of the Dallas Symphony, which allowed the Meyerson dream to come to fruition.

Chapter Three

ARTS DISTRICT VISION

I had been mayor about four or five months. It was pretty obvious to me that, to be a major city in this country, we were lacking in two areas: a downtown sports arena and an arts program. I was trying to help downtown Dallas. We needed to start a cultural area within downtown.[1]

MAYOR ROBERT FOLSOM

F AIR Park Music Hall epitomized everything that was wrong with oversized, multi-purpose American halls built in the twentieth century. Its most distinguishing feature was appalling acoustics. People in the balconies joked that they were sitting in a different zip code from the performers on stage. The orchestra could hear itself, but the sound was dead and flat in the hall.

Acoustics were not the only problem. Scheduling strictures at Fair Park placed an unusual burden of inconvenience on the orchestra, which was forced to present several miniature seasons within each official season. The DSO was low on the totem pole at Fair Park. The Metropolitan Opera, Dallas Summer Musicals, and the Dallas Opera all had precedence for booking the facility. When the orchestra returned from its ten-year stint at McFarlin Auditorium to a newly refurbished Fair Park Music Hall in December 1972, it slipped to fourth on the priority list for scheduling. The symphony was obliged to store its equipment in a warehouse in Dallas' Deep Ellum area about a mile away. Johnny Gutierrez, the orchestra's senior stage manager, ran a shuttle service between the warehouse and music hall for each performance. Stage management was a nightmare, with added costs for constant moving of equipment and large instruments.

Operating with Fair Park as its home, the Dallas Symphony was compelled to inaugurate its subscription season earlier than any other major orchestra in the country, once even in late August. In the early autumn, when the searing heat was just beginning to moderate and the audience would have just started getting into the rhythm of the season, the last of the Dallas Summer Musicals would return with a production concurrent with the Texas State Fair, and the symphony would be booted out. Right on the heels of the musicals came the Dallas Civic Opera season. For three months each year, the orchestra was effectively exiled from the music hall. The DSO players comprised the opera's pit orchestra—but it wasn't the symphony. The DSO's limited access to the music hall forced it to adopt a convoluted schedule, with another few intense months of performances in the spring. Visiting conductors leading the orchestra mid-season observed that the disruption of the season affected precision and polish within the ensemble.

Robert Decherd, who became board president in May 1979, recognized that the problems were not simply acoustical. "It was a matter of having access to the venue on a schedule basis that enabled us to maximize earned revenue from orchestral events. The operating arrangements that existed at the time made heavy demands on the music hall. It was impossible for Lloyd or anyone to schedule the classical series through the most desirable months of the year in a way that was orderly and could be marketed on an effective basis. We needed access to a hall with an adequate number of seats and with enough schedule flexibility to push earned income up to a level that would represent a threshold of financial stability."[2]

Dick Galland, again serving as chairman of the fund drive, chaired more than a dozen breakfast meetings with the DSO fund-raising group, moderating discussions about the feasibility of a new concert hall. His committee consisted primarily of Dallas business people and major donors to the orchestra. Not all of them approved of the idea. Objections to the idea of a new hall were myriad: the orchestra was too small and too elite. Its audience was limited. DSO constituents lacked diversity. (This was long before the concepts of political correctness and ethnic diversity had taken hold.) And the nagging question remained, cast by the long shadow of the 1974 demise: "How could we possibly finance any such option as a new concert hall when we are having trouble meeting our budgets?"[3] At the close of the 1976–77 and 1977–78 seasons, Lloyd Haldeman reported deficits, reduced from prior years, but deficits nonetheless.

Countering these arguments was the reminder at every concert of Fair Park's unsuitability. As Robert Decherd recalled, "Once that issue began to be more sharply focused, it immediately spilled over to strategy considerations. Other than financial stability, it was topic A: 'How do we gain access to a venue which will enable this orchestra to be financially viable?'"[4]

Ambition at City Hall

Robert Folsom, a North Dallas real estate developer, was elected mayor of Dallas in April 1974, after Mayor Wes Wise retired to run for U.S. Congress. Folsom had built Bent Tree Country Club in Far North Dallas and was a part owner of the Chaparrals, then the local professional basketball team. City Manager George Schrader knew that Folsom's public image was that of a guy who was interested in athletics and commercial real estate. He discovered that Folsom was also very ambitious for the City of Dallas.

Shortly after Folsom's election, Schrader scheduled a lunch appointment with the mayor, preparing a list of current projects and other items Folsom might want to consider. After lunch, things got quiet. Schrader queried, "You ran for mayor. Do you have some particular interests you wanted to get the council to consider? Tell me what they are." Folsom demurred, "Oh, I guess I don't have any in particular. The city has been so good to me; I just think those of us who have had good fortune ought to be able to reinvest back into the community. Do you have anything, George?"[5]

Schrader retorted, "You don't think I'd come out here without my list, do you?" He handed Folsom an 8½-by-11-inch sheet of paper with programs and ideas written on both sides. The list included a new library, a new museum, a new indoor sports arena, along with numerous other suggestions. He expected Folsom to identify three or four.

The mayor took a moment to look over the sheet, reviewed both sides, then looked up at Schrader and smiled. "Looks good to me. Let's do 'em all!"

Schrader was aghast. "You've got to be kidding me! They'll ride us out of town if we do that!" But he agreed to think about it for a while. He and Folsom both knew a bond program was on the horizon, probably two or three years out. In a subsequent meeting a week later, Schrader outlined his thinking. "You know what I'd really like to do? Think of a public/private program for the arts, and let's define 'arts' as the sports arena and the library and our cultural facilities."

Folsom understood. "You mean, expand the definition to include more activities, gearing it toward a wider public."

"Exactly. Some people like basketball, others like Monets. The biggest issue won't be the program itself, but some of your friends will go to war if we start talking about building facilities outside of Fair Park."

"That's all right," replied Folsom. "Where do you think we should build them?"

"I think we ought to go through a research and planning process to decide where they ought to go. We need to offer everybody a chance to be a part of it, but if they want to participate, they have to pay a share of the consulting fees. We ought to bring in independent planning consultants. Let's invite the library board, the museum board, the symphony board, the theater center board and say, 'We want to help you get new facilities. We know you'd like to have some public financing, and we'd like to help—but we want it limited, planned.'"[6]

Schrader's instincts told him that Folsom was ideal to lead the program, precisely because his known interest in both basketball and country club development made him an unlikely standard bearer. That very fact would enable the program to garner broader support.

Schrader asked Folsom to write a letter calling a meeting with representatives of each prospective beneficiary organization and the Dallas Park Board. He knew that if the mayor requested their participation, no one could refuse.

Folsom also recognized that Fair Park presented problems as a location for cultural facilities. "It was evident that, as long as we had the museum in Fair Park, we would never have a great museum. People didn't think of Fair Park as an arts center. It was an entertainment area: the midway, rides, food, and all the other things that go along with an annual fair."[7]

—◦—

AS EARLY as autumn 1976, Mayor Folsom, Dallas Park Board President Sid Stahl, and representatives from nine Dallas cultural organizations met to discuss the feasibility of building new arts facilities. Schrader remembers the meeting, which took place in the basement of the old public library. Mayor Folsom said, "I've called this meeting to tell you we're going to put a plan together. We will engage a consultant, and the city will bear a certain percentage of the cost; we're asking you to bear the rest of it. If you want to be included in this plan, you'll have to spend and invest as part of it."[8] Dallas Symphony representatives told the arts committee that municipal aid must be available to build a downtown performing arts center.[9] Mayor Folsom later said, "I never had a meeting that was so universally accepted! They knew they needed an arts program."[10]

Because Fair Park fell within the park board's purview, Folsom and Schrader felt obliged to involve that agency. (The parks themselves are a part of the City of Dallas, but the park board is independent.) According to Schrader, "We wanted the park board's help; we certainly didn't want to offend them, so we made them an integral part of this planning process. The way we worked, the city gave [Dallas Park Board President] Sid Stahl and the park board a lot of pride in having a part of it, instead of them being crosswise and mad about it."[11] Schrader and Stahl explored the possibilities, including a trip to New York to interview candidate firms. Schrader had met Kevin Lynch, then chairman of the department of urban and regional planning at Massachusetts Institute of Technology, at a seminar, and knew that Lynch also did consulting work with Steve Carr through Carr, Lynch Associates of Cambridge, Massachusetts. The firm had experience in identifying locations for urban arts programs, exactly what Dallas was looking for. Carr, Lynch won the consulting assignment.

In its October 1977 report, "A Comprehensive Arts Facilities Plan for Dallas," Carr, Lynch identified the need for a new museum, an outdoor theatre, two small theatres, and several performing halls. They recommended the creation of a downtown arts district grouping new facilities in a designated geographical area slightly northeast of the central business district. In a different era, such an ambitious proposal might have been dismissed as economically unfeasible. The city's economy was healthy and improving, however. Dallas had experienced steady growth spurts for several decades, and city fathers saw no reason that the Carr, Lynch recommendations could not be implemented.[12]

"Dallas appears to be at a special moment of growth to cultural excellence," the report observed. Its authors noted that interaction among arts groups had grown steadily in recent years. The report focused on four principal concepts for the City of Dallas to embrace: a coherent, predictable public policy of support for the arts; relocation of significant arts organizations to a central location downtown; the conservation and revitalization of Fair Park; and action in local neighborhoods to sustain cultural activity.[13]

The area they recommended downtown was occupied mostly by small offices and warehouses. Its primary value lay in the land itself, not in the buildings that sat on the land. That meant that the demolition of existing structures to make way for new construction would be comparatively simple. Carr, Lynch recommended a plan for a "loose" arts district. Their concept mandated that the area not be restricted to arts facilities with museum, symphony hall, and theatre all situated on one block. Instead, they recommended that Dallas implement landscaping, offices, and shops as part of the district.

Both Folsom and Schrader believe that identifying the downtown area as the locale for the Arts District was a bold political move. The State Fair Board was made up of the most influential business people in the community, most of whom were dead set against any arts facility being moved out of Fair Park or any sports facility being built anywhere other than near the Cotton Bowl. The museum and symphony representatives were concerned that, if they were going to attract audience and donors, their building should be located where their patrons were willing to go.

Philip Jonsson, as chairman of the DSA facilities committee, was exploring the feasibility of a new concert hall and meeting with representatives of the city. In July 1977, he reported to the DSA Executive Board that in order to receive financial support from the city, the facility would have to be located in downtown Dallas. Henry Miller remarked that in a recent conversation, Dallas City Councilman William Nicol stated that both the concert hall and the new museum could be built at the same time. The City of Dallas was developing a strong commitment both to its long-range plans for cultural facilities and to the reclamation of downtown.[14]

As the policy was being developed for the proposed public-private sharing of costs, a group of six prominent bankers requested a meeting with Mayor Folsom. For several of them, it was the first time they had been to city hall. They expressed their concern about the policy. "You know that we're going to have to raise the money," they told him. "The museum will come to us for the money, then the symphony will do the same thing. The way we figure, that's about $120 to $150 million, which is more than we can finance. You're saddling us with a huge fund-raising job." Folsom held his ground. "This is all the city can afford; you'll just have to do it!"[15]

"Nobody likes to go face to face with friends," comments George Schrader. "Bob was simply heroic. He was a customer of all these banks; he owed them all money. He was on the board at Mercantile! When they told him, 'We can't pay more than that,' he said, 'You're going to have to!' And he knew that they would be coming to him for some of that money, too. It was an extraordinary performance on his part."[16]

Under the terms of the proposed arts policy, an organization desiring to build would be responsible for raising forty percent of the cost of capital construction. The city would foot the bill for the remaining sixty percent. Further, the city would absorb seventy-five percent of land cost, with the remaining twenty-five percent to be covered by the private sector. Such a public-private partnership presumed that supporters of the building organization would raise its portion from corporations, foundations, and individuals—entirely from the private sector. Responsibility for operational and maintenance costs would be absorbed by the public, with a tenant-landlord format. Dallas City Council formally adopted the policy on December 19, 1979.[17]

—❧—

SHORTLY after the release of the Carr, Lynch report, Philip Jonsson told his board colleagues that city officials were open to the possibility of the art museum, public library, and concert hall being on a bond election for spring 1978. Doubtless influenced by Lloyd Haldeman's enthusiasm, Jonsson favored a single-purpose hall, rather than multi-purpose. He argued that a single-purpose hall would produce better acoustics for symphonic music, would cost less than a multi-purpose facility, and would allow the Dallas Opera and the Dallas Ballet to expand their seasons at the Fair Park Music Hall. Mayor Folsom had appointed an arts facilities committee to study the city's needs. That committee's stated preference for a downtown location worked well with the symphony argument: that both the orchestra's ticket sales and its artistic development had a brighter future outside Fair Park.

Eduardo Mata had just inaugurated his first season as music director, catalyzing a significant increase in season ticket sales that was helping to mitigate the previous season's deficit. Mata addressed the symphony board in its September quarterly meeting, explaining that Fair Park Music Hall was beautiful but its acoustics were bad. Although he was doing the best he could with the facility, the dashing new young music director would clearly have been happier with the prospect of a permanent new home.

His opinion certainly carried weight. Shortly after Mata's first concerts, President Jimmy Carter invited Mata to come to Washington to perform for a meeting of the Organization of American States. Cultural diversity was evolving as a politically expedient concept in Washington, and Carter recognized the significance of Mata being the first Mexican to lead a major American orchestra. That national exposure, in turn, bolstered Mata's credibility and prestige in Dallas.

The city had made it clear that it expected private money to be raised before any city money would be forthcoming. Its proposed funding policy would require partial private funding to be in place in order for the city to underwrite the structures. Jonsson told his colleagues that the Dallas Symphony Association's presence on a city bond election required city council approval in January (it turned out to be later than that by several months), which in turn would require planning and action by the executive committee and the board of governors. Honorary Board Chairman Bob Glaze, ever the cautious fiscal conservative, suggested securing commitments from private donors to cover a substantial share of the cost before proceeding further. Dick Galland therefore instructed each member of the board's fund-raising steering committee to provide Development Director Al Milano with the names of five people they thought would be major donors toward the hall.[18]

By November 1977, Jonsson had made a presentation to the city council on the need for a new concert facility and secured the volunteer services of a local architect, E. G. Hamilton, to advise the symphony with regard to land requirements, construction costs, and other aspects of a new hall. Hamilton thus became the first architect to be associated with the project, albeit in an advisory capacity. A native Texan and a prominent member of Dallas' architectural community, he was a close friend of *The Dallas Morning News'* Robert Decherd, and his firm, Harrell & Hamilton (Omniplan), eventually designed the downtown headquarters building for A. H. Belo Corporation, parent company of *The Dallas Morning News*. Hamilton also joined Jonsson and Haldeman on a trip to Minneapolis to tour and hear performances in the newly opened Orchestra Hall, home to the Minnesota Orchestra.

Hamilton made a slide presentation to the DSA Executive Committee and discussed a tentative schedule: selection of a site before the 1978 bond election; design of the facility by May 1978; start construction early in 1979; and open the facility on August 27, 1980, to inaugurate the DSO's 1980–81 subscription season. Hamilton estimated, optimistically, that the site would require three-and-a-half to four acres. He speculated that the City of Dallas would provide or build an adjacent parking garage.[19]

Hamilton had also consulted a local construction firm, J. W. Bateson Co., with respect to cost. Bateson estimated design and construction costs at $16,852,000, with additional land acquisition costs of $3 million. Their estimates did not address architect's or acoustician's fees. In retrospect, Hamilton's time schedule and the Bateson budget seem absurdly optimistic. Anything seemed possible in 1977, and no one could have foreseen the detours and challenges that lay ahead.

1978 Bond Election

After an area on the north side of downtown was designated for the Arts District, the Dallas Museum of Art approached the city and asked to be placed on the next bond program.

Mayor Folsom later said, "The museum went first, because they went to work and were able to raise the money first for their share of the public-private partnership. It was exciting to see them that motivated."[20] George Schrader recalls that the museum also began assessing the real estate market for property owners' willingness to sell.

While the museum oiled its fund-raising machine, Dick Galland was obtaining discouraging results on the symphony front. Initial responses from prospective large donors in regard to underwriting a new concert hall were disappointing. The city had indicated that the DSA could be on the bond issue, but it wouldn't release funds until the private sector monies were received. The city council was scheduled to vote in March whether to include the new concert hall officially on the forthcoming bond election.[21]

Early in March, at the request of Mayor Folsom, Board Treasurer Bill Schilling agreed to chair the Citizens' Information Committee campaign for the city bond election, which was scheduled for June 10, 1978. By early May, the city had tentatively approved a massive $285 million bond program. The ballot's seventeen propositions encompassed a broad spectrum of projects ranging from Trinity River Greenbelt improvements, preliminary development of Town Lake, and extension of floodway levees to a buses-only transitway on North Central Expressway. Also included were funds for what is now the Erik Jonsson Central

The bumper sticker from the 1978 bond campaign. (*Courtesy William L. Schilling*)

Library, Dallas' flagship public library.[22] Collectively, they constituted the biggest bond program in Dallas history. Lumped together as Proposition 5—$45 million for public cultural facilities—were proposals to purchase land for a new museum and symphony hall, renovate the Majestic Theater, and expand the Dallas Theater Center.

Schilling spearheaded a fund-raising campaign that secured $300,000 from the corporate community to inform citizens about the bond package. "We felt the best thing was to keep a low profile, but we still had a message to get out to encourage voter support. That meant brochures, bumper stickers, yard signs. Historically, Dallas had passed bond programs with little controversy. Accordingly, the strategy of the campaign was to promote the benefits of city improvements that could be implemented without increasing taxes. The campaign slogan was 'Tell Dallas You Love Her. Vote Yes on June 10.'[23] Our campaign strategists gave serious consideration to mobilizing the arts community to support Proposition 5, but opted not to do so in order to avoid an elitist backlash."[24] The elitism issue—that the symphony served the needs and interests of a wealthy minority—would continue to haunt supporters of a new hall. On a short-term basis, the strategy worked. The only organized opposition targeted Proposition 4: the Trinity River Greenbelt and Town Lake project.

What proved far more important was the timing in terms of national events. Dallas' 1978 bond election took place just four days after the passage of Proposition 13, California's revolt against property taxes. Anti-tax crusader Howard Jarvis succeeded in passing Proposition 13, which amended the California state constitution to cut state property tax revenues by $7 billion. The Citizens' Information Committee had conducted some private polling locally before the California vote. The polls indicated that all of Dallas' propositions were favored handily by Dallas citizens likely to vote in the bond election. But California's anti-tax referendum received major national media coverage. Locally, the two Dallas dailies debated the effect of the California vote. The *Dallas Times Herald* observed that the passage of Proposition 13 had "injected a note of uncertainty into an election that looked like a shoo-in two months ago."[25] City officials were worried; the timing was extremely unfortunate for supporters of the election, because there was insufficient time to counter the adverse publicity.

Capitalizing on a growing anti-tax sentiment, the publicity played the issue close to Dallas voters' hearts and turned the election around. People selected individual propositions to vote down and, on June 10, 1978, they rejected the arts proposal along with several other major items. It was only the second time in Dallas history that part of a bond program had been defeated. Ironically, the total of projects approved, $194 million, was still larger than any prior bond program.

The bond defeat was a major blow to symphony supporters. "People had been talking about a better hall for years," recalls DSO principal percussion Douglas Howard. "Everyone

For Summertop, the DSO performed under a giant tent at NorthPark Shopping Center. The musicians nicknamed it "Saunatop." (*DSO archives*)

recognized what a terrible place [Fair Park] Music Hall was for orchestral music. The 1978 bond election was the first time I became aware that anyone really wanted to do something about it. After that first election failed, I don't think any of us really had much optimism that Dallas would actually build a hall."[26]

The failure was a wake-up call. DSO cellist Michael Coren says, "In the 1978 bond election, we just assumed, because we were the DSO and they were the Dallas Citizens Council, that they would succeed. I think the whole city was shocked. In a way, the whole political process woke up the morning after the bond election to find that the world was different, and they had missed the boat that had already set sail."[27] *The Dallas Morning News* architecture critic David Dillon agrees. "It woke the arts groups up," he declares. "They were incredibly complacent, I think, about how the public would support the arts. Bond issues simply didn't fail in Dallas. There was a lot of self-congratulatory discussion and not much hard politicking, very little political common sense applied to it. It was simply assumed that it was a slam dunk, it was going to pass, and things would move on."[28]

"I was absolutely devastated," recalls former City Manager George Schrader. "It's probably one of the few times I was that discouraged. We absolutely could not, *should* not let this voter decision kill the project forever. It was just too good a chance." Schrader asked for a *post mortem* meeting with key museum supporters, whose proposal had gone down the drain along with the symphony's. "I called John Murchison, Margaret McDermott, and museum director Harry Parker. I thought the best therapy for me was to be therapeutic to them, to lift their spirits. We met, and they said, 'We came down here to encourage *you* not to give up!' I said, 'Funny thing, I called to pump *you* up!'" They agreed that land in the Arts District needed protection. Schrader counseled them to take options on land for the museum. If the public approved bonds for the museum in a future election, they could bring their purchases to city hall and the city would then buy the property.

Schrader and Mayor Folsom had a similar conversation with symphony representatives, but the election had taken the wind out of Lloyd Haldeman's sails. "He told me later that was the primary reason that he decided to leave the Dallas Symphony," recalled his successor, Leonard David Stone.[29] Haldeman was having financial disagreements with the symphony board, which understandably was extremely cautious about maintaining financial stability. Although the board had renewed his contract in March 1978, they declined to give him a raise. He submitted a resignation letter to the board on September 5, 1978, three months after the failed election.

The board appeared to be stunned. Board members Dr. Bryce Jordan and Alan May called Haldeman and asked him to reconsider for twenty-four hours. He told them that he had been approached by other orchestras but he had decided to leave the arts altogether. His resignation was made public two days later, after an announcement to symphony staff. Haldeman agreed to remain in a consulting capacity until February 1, 1979, at which time the orchestra hoped to have a new manager in place.

During the Lloyd Haldeman era, the Dallas Symphony offered its players what was then the largest contract increase in the history of major American orchestras. The orchestra's musicians credit Haldeman with the vision for recognizing that a full-year season was essential. "We were pushing for a full-year season," recalls principal timpanist Kalman Cherry. "Naturally we wanted the stability and the security. He was able to stir up interest in the outlying communities. We played in places like Greenville, Graham, Duncanville, Lewisville, in horrible high school auditoriums. For us, the runouts were a pain in the neck—but it was work. I'd rather work than not work."[30]

Principal oboe Eric Barr, who joined the orchestra in autumn 1973 just months before the financial crisis, agrees. "I thought Lloyd was a very creative guy," he says. "He initiated our electronic media program, and also the concept of splitting the orchestra into smaller units. We would subdivide into small orchestras going out to different cities to play concerts, using those as services [a contractual term designating a rehearsal or performance] instead of sending the entire orchestra. Lloyd could get three performances a week out of the orchestra [using each player only once] and call it one concert in terms of our contract. His ideas gave us work flexibility, and got the most for the money out of the orchestra, because he got us out to the community as cheaply as he could. He was a tough negotiator, but I think he did it with humor and humaneness, which is not always the case these days. In meetings you would get irked at him, but you couldn't really dislike him."[31]

The final piece in Lloyd Haldeman's crown was to have been the hall. With the June 1978 rejection of the bond issue by the citizens of Dallas, his personal vision was also defeated. He resigned from the Dallas Symphony and went to work at Electronic Data Systems, taking his executive assistant and marketing director with him. He convinced H. Ross Perot and Morton H. Meyerson to set up a division of EDS called Innovision, intended to provide computer online services. The venture was not successful financially, and Haldeman eventually left the Dallas area.

Philip Jonsson initiated the search for a new managing director, benefiting from the *pro bono* services of Roland Stuebner, a vice president of the international executive search firm Korn Ferry & Associates. To ensure a smooth transition, the board appointed staff member Paul Stapel as interim managing director, because it seemed unlikely that a new manager would be able to step in as soon as February 1979, Haldeman's scheduled departure. By early December, Stuebner had identified six candidates to invite to interview with the board in January 1979. They chose Leonard David Stone, who had recently taken a position with the Syracuse Symphony in upstate New York.

Leonard Stone's Background

A native of Canada, Leonard Stone had begun his career in 1959 as director of the Winnipeg International Film Festival. He entered the orchestra management business in 1967 with the Winnipeg Symphony, taking it from 56 musicians and 700 subscribers to 70 musicians —then the fourth largest orchestra in Canada—and 5,700 subscribers. During his ten years in Winnipeg, he had been intimately involved with the fund-raising and construction of a new concert hall. Stone left Canada in February 1978, to become general manager of the Syracuse Symphony Orchestra.

Leonard David Stone (*DSO archives*)

Six months after the Dallas bond election had failed, in mid-December 1978, Marty Stark of Columbia Artists Management, Inc., telephoned Leonard Stone in Syracuse. "Leonard, Lloyd Haldeman is leaving the Dallas Symphony. He just called me and said, 'Marty, you guys keep in touch with all the orchestras around North America. You know all the managers. I want you to recommend two guys you think we should put on the short list to find my successor.' We've had a meeting here in the office. We've tossed out your name and a couple of other names. We want to recommend one person, and we want it to be you. But we don't want to recommend you if you won't go."

Stone protested, "Marty, I've got a three-year contract with Syracuse. I just got here. I haven't even unpacked."

"We didn't ask you if you've unpacked yet. We want to know would you go to Dallas?"

"Let me call you back." Stone discussed the opportunity with his wife. Years later, he said, "We decided that Syracuse was not the end-all and the be-all of the world. We threw our hat in the ring. I called Lloyd, whom I had met at American Symphony Orchestra League conventions. He gave me Philip Jonsson's name, and I wrote a letter to Philip expressing my interest."[32]

Within two weeks, in late December 1978, Roland Stuebner of Korn Ferry called Stone to arrange a first meeting. Stone moved to Stuebner's short list and traveled to Dallas in late January 1979 to interview. He can still picture the people around the table at the Sheraton when he was ushered into the conference room: Philip Jonsson, Robert Decherd, Sis Carr, Bob Glaze, Catherine Fikes, Bill Schilling, and Roland Stuebner. After his interview was over, the panel asked him to go downstairs for a cup of coffee in the hotel coffee shop. About a half-hour later, Jonsson and Decherd joined him downstairs and said, "We'd like to talk to you about a three-year contract."

"I thought I had died and gone to heaven," Stone said later. He moved his family to Dallas, beginning work on June 1, 1979.[33] He was to remain at the administrative helm of the Dallas Symphony for fourteen years.

"The first we ever heard of Leonard Stone was when they put the newspaper article announcing his appointment on the DSO bulletin board," remembers principal timpanist Kalman Cherry. "We didn't think too much of it. We had a lot of different people over the years. Here comes another one, we thought. But our first impression was favorable. He seemed to be knowledgeable, and he exuded an air of confidence. More than most managers, he understood the musicians' point of view. Not to say he always agreed with it!"[34]

⸺ℯ⸺

Leonard Stone's first artistic project was Summertop, the summer series that Lloyd Haldeman had established under tents at NorthPark Shopping Center. The musicians nick-

Leonard Stone converted Summertop into Starfest, which became immensely popular in a new home in North Dallas on the grounds of Electronic Data Systems. (*DSO archives*)

named it "Saunatop." Stone converted the Summertop concert series into Starfest, which became enormously successful in a new North Dallas location on the EDS grounds.

A mixed bag of challenges faced him almost immediately. Some were artistic. He remembers, "I arrived just in time to find out that Kurt Masur was not going to honor the last two years of his contract as a guest conductor. An English agent called me and ran off three or four choices. One was Gunther Herbig. I'd never heard of Herbig. The agent mentioned Berlin. I made a mistake. I thought Berlin Philharmonic. I should have known better, because that was Von Karajan. It was the Berlin Symphony. East Berlin. But Berlin sounded pretty good. If you were heading up an orchestra in Berlin, you had to be good. So I said, 'Great!' That's how Herbig came to Dallas!"[35] More than twenty years later, Herbig is still a regular guest conductor with the DSO.

Other matters were mundane but equally pressing. "The subscription campaign was in shambles," he says. "Box office and subscriber records were maintained in a shoebox. The organization had no computerized capability. Its fund-raising records were in recipe containers with little tabs." But Stone was pleased with the people he worked with in Dallas. He struck an immediate and solid rapport with Bob Glaze, then the board treasurer, and with music director Eduardo Mata.[36] Stone also inherited Al Milano, Haldeman's development director. According to Milano, marketing was the new managing director's strong suit. "Leonard's major contribution in the first year was a tremendous marketing drive, which really did start an upturn in the symphony's marketing fortunes."[37]

1979 Bond Election

By the time Stone arrived in Dallas, the machinery for a new ballot initiative was underway. The 1979 election was a special bond program. According to George Schrader, "The 1978 election was consistent with the established rhythm of every three or four years. We came back with a special program for 1979, one with no street improvements, fire station, or library. It was scheduled to provide the funding for the arts."[38]

This time, museum and symphony proponents had learned their lesson. The museum hired Phil Seib, an associate professor of communications at SMU, as a political consultant to organize its campaign. Schrader says, "From my perception as an observer, the museum had more tangible support earlier for a new facility. They wanted to be on a bond program, but they didn't want anybody else on it! My sense was, if any arts facility were going to be built by the city, we had to get all-encompassing arts support from the community and tell them, 'Y'all help each other. If you don't, the gravel-haulers, the folks who want to build streets and water lines, are going to beat you! They'll say your facilities are elitist and don't serve the community.'"[39] His argument swayed museum backers, and the pro-bond effort became multi-organizational.

At the symphony, Stanley Marcus assumed the board's committee chairmanship to oversee passage of the bond issue. William Bennett Cullum, an attorney and member of a prominent Dallas family, worked on nuts and bolts as vice chairman of the bond election steering committee. With the help of Amanda (Mandy) Dealey, a Dallas native and civic volunteer,

Lloyd Haldeman, Henry S. Miller, Jr., and Philip Jonsson worked in the mid-1970s to rebuild the Dallas Symphony artistically and financially. (*DSO archives*)

Cullum assembled a team of twelve hundred volunteers to canvas fifty precincts beginning the first of October. The public relations campaign included fliers and brochures as well as broadcast television and radio ads supporting Proposition 5. Philip Jonsson was a major dollar contributor, giving $75,000 to the bond campaign. Robert Decherd and Bob Glaze also supported it financially. Richard Levin, an attorney with the law firm of Akin, Gump, Hauer & Feld, became bond election treasurer. At monthly meetings, DSA President Decherd urged his executive board members to telephone or write to city council members to garner support. His message was simple and direct: without a permanent facility, we cannot maintain the revenue base for the orchestra we aspire to have. In August, city council approved Proposition 5—land for a new concert hall—for inclusion on the November ballot.

Symphony staff and board had the sense that momentum for a new concert hall was building all through 1979. "There was a lot of revisionism about what happened [in the 1978 election] and what could have been done differently," Decherd says. "We were reviewing all the choices for the association and the venue question, when the museum, in early 1979, decided to go ahead on its own. Their concern was that voters wouldn't support a broader program. We had a series of meetings. We decided that whither goest the museum, so go we, because it was our conclusion that we might not have a chance to come back a year or two later. It might be the end of a serious pass at an arts facility bond issue for the foreseeable future. As it turned out, we were right. Therefore, much to the dismay of the museum leadership, we decided to go it on our own, beginning in February or March. Once we sorted out the politics and began to understand a little bit better how to get a vote out, how to achieve a plurality in this vote, there was a lot of momentum that carried through to the bond issue, then clear on to the next year."[40]

A Dallas Museum of Fine Arts study identified East Dallas as the pivotal area that would determine passage of the bond issue. The orchestra musicians, many of whom lived in East Dallas because of its proximity to Fair Park, joined the volunteer forces. "When the second bond election came up, and we had an opportunity to purchase the land, the orchestra really got involved in the political process," says principal percussion Doug Howard. "A lot of us went door to door. I remember delivering fliers in East Dallas, urging people to vote in the bond election."[41] Another important component of the orchestra's public relations effort was a series of free concerts presented to the public.

The entire 1979 bond issue was more modest than the 1978 slate, because the program was a special election specifically designed to secure approval for the cultural arts. The Dallas Museum of Fine Arts remained on the program for $24.8 million, a sum believed to be sufficient for its entire new home. The Dallas Symphony sought $2.25 million to acquire land for its concert hall. Polling at the end of October indicated that the vote would be close. The canvassing continued, and in November 1979, Dallas voters approved the bond issue. By then, the symphony had received another $750,000 in private donations, which was also earmarked for land acquisition. The association had also secured pledges for an additional $1.5 million to finance the architectural design for the building. While it seemed like a lot of money, the long-range plan would clearly call for a future bond proposal to underwrite the largest cost of all: construction.

On many levels, the 1979 bond program was an easier sell than its predecessor seventeen months earlier. The symphony argued persuasively that the orchestra needed a home of its own. Pro-bond publicity trumpeted impressive statistics from the 1978–79 season: 328 concerts performed, a fifty-two-week season and six recording sessions for RCA. Best of all, the DSO had earned fifty to sixty percent of its annual budget through earned income via ticket sales, which had doubled from the prior year. And, in Eduardo Mata, the orchestra had an exciting young music director who proved an eloquent spokesman in favor of the proposed hall. "The real difference between 1978 and 1979," says George Schrader, "was that both groups were better organized, and worked harder. They got beat once, and they weren't going to get beat again."[42]

Part Two

1979–1982

Morton H. Meyerson (*DSO archives*)

Chapter Four

MORT FORMS A COMMITTEE

Each member of the small group had a distinct personality. It was like having different species of humans. Working closely with this committee was like cooping up a jury for six months. At the end of it, you know everything except for their sexual habits! I think that happened in our group. I feel that I have an intimate personal relationship with every member of the smaller unit that is radically different from anything I had experienced with any board member before. It still lives today.[1]

MORT MEYERSON

WHEN Philip Jonsson and Bob Glaze invited Robert Decherd to join the Dallas Symphony Association Board in 1975, Lloyd Haldeman had been general manager for less than a year. As Decherd remembers, "The orchestra's ability to overcome its financial and labor problems depended on assembling a new group of civic leaders to support and amplify the people who had traditionally been the leaders of the symphony association."[2] Decherd became involved right away, joining the executive committee shortly after joining the board. "Philip [Jonsson] and Bob [Glaze] and others had their hands full. They needed as many capable people as they could assemble on the executive board. Specific expertise was far less important than the ability to become actively engaged in the management of the symphony association, not the orchestra per se, but the symphony association, and address all of the orchestra's challenges. Foremost among them was the income stream, from concerts as well as non-concert activities. Labor negotiations were a critical issue at the time. There were a number of balance sheet issues, pre-existing obligations of the orchestra. The image was of an organization that had failed. We faced enormous marketing challenges, building the symphony into a new and exciting attraction in a fairly competitive arts and cultural environment."[3]

At the first meetings Decherd attended, the board discussed the problems that Fair Park

Music Hall presented to the association. "I'd never been to—and never since been to—so many breakfast meetings in my life! It seemed as if we had breakfast four days a week for four years! I might exaggerate a little bit, but the key was that, in Philip Jonsson, we had someone who was totally committed to making this work, and was willing to devote his expertise and time to a degree that inspired the rest of us to make significant commitments of our own time. I was amazed at the number of hours that Philip, Dick [Galland], Bob Glaze, and others were devoting routinely to this and other symphony matters. I found a way to devote the same or greater numbers of hours as I moved up into leadership positions. It was a pace they had established and the turnaround Lloyd achieved. I was thrilled to be there."[4]

Decherd Appoints Meyerson

Decherd emerged rapidly as one of the bright young stars who could bring energy and new ideas to the organization. By spring 1979, the executive board officers were tapping on his door to ask him to assume the presidency. "It was either a desperate need on the part of the orchestra or lack of other viable candidates," Decherd chuckles in retrospect. "I was twenty-eight years old! The symphony had taken a risk in appointing someone from my generation. The collective wisdom of the executive board was that I was up to the task. My age profile tended to draw new people in. I wasn't as intimidating to my peers in age as someone in his mid-fifties or sixties would have been in the same role. Particularly in the [1979] bond election, I think that was an important factor enabling us to attract a lot of leadership, an effective team through my contacts and people they knew. Many of those people stayed involved with the association in various roles for a number of years afterward."[5]

Talk about a new performing facility was buzzing more loudly when Robert Decherd became DSA president, yet the organization still sported a hefty annual deficit exceeding $300,000. The long-range plan mandated an increase in earned income and an increase in fund-raising and development activities. Decherd recognized that part of his role as president would be to help the symphony association appear more accessible to new and younger volunteer participants and future leaders. "It wasn't the only factor, but it helped in recruiting some key people. I was able to do that because I knew different individuals: people like Phil Montgomery and Bennett Cullum, who are my contemporaries. These are not people who would have occurred to Bob Glaze. He didn't know their skills the way I did."[6] Montgomery is the oldest son of Dr. Philip O'Bryan Montgomery and Ruth Ann Montgomery, long-time civic leaders. He and Cullum would later play critical roles in the 1982 bond election.

DURING early discussions about the possibility of a new hall, real estate developer Trammell Crow had his house architects generate some preliminary sketches for a concert hall.[7] Philip Jonsson sent the Crow schematics to Donald L. Engle, former president of the Minnesota Orchestra, for his review. During his tenure in Minneapolis, Engle had overseen the construction and opening of Minnesota's Orchestra Hall, with acoustics by Cyril Harris. After retiring from the Minnesota Orchestra, he became a private consultant. He addressed the symphony trustees at the May 1979 annual meeting, urging the need for a new hall but shooting down the Crow Company's design.[8]

Decherd needed someone within the symphony association to focus on the planning for the concert hall. Initially, it was unclear who would be the chair. "As the bond election approached and we accelerated the site selection process, it became obvious to all of us that we would appoint this committee sooner rather than later," Decherd recalls. "The fundraising for the hall was already beginning." He decided to ask local businessman Morton H. Meyerson, president of Electronic Data Systems, to chair the committee to oversee planning for a hall.

Stanley Marcus had been the initial catalyst for Meyerson's involvement in the Dallas Symphony. Marcus called Meyerson in 1975 because the board was uncertain how to approach H. Ross Perot for a contribution.

"Contribution for what?" Meyerson asked.

"For the Dallas Symphony."

"How much are you asking for?"

"$1,500."

Meyerson thought a moment, and was silent. Fifteen hundred dollars was not an enormous sum, and Ross Perot was a busy man. "Why don't you *not* call him, and we'll just give it to you?" He had expected that the symphony wanted big money! No, they didn't, Stanley Marcus assured him. Meyerson said, "Great." The symphony received its donation. Several months later, Meyerson was tendered an invitation to join the board.[9]

For the first couple of years, Meyerson was a name on the roster. "Frankly, I wasn't too enthused about the board meetings," he says. "They were big meetings with as many as seventy people. An organization like the symphony has many constituencies, the league and the this and the that and the other. For somebody like me, who is somewhat impatient and used to working on things in quick time, it was very slow. Board meetings were painful because of the 'make nice' that you have to do in an organization like that. In that phase of my life, I was much more about substance and less about containers."[10]

Meyerson's strengths and potential for leadership were clear to Robert Decherd, who had a task that required someone with unwavering focus and a no-nonsense approach. Late in summer 1979, he decided that Meyerson would be the best candidate to head the concert hall committee. Coincidentally, Meyerson was also the leading candidate in Leonard Stone's mind and in the minds of the officers of the executive board. "Mort represented all of the most important attributes for a person to fill this chairmanship," remembers Decherd. "He was, and is, someone who loves classical music and understands it in a sophisticated way. He was, and is, a very astute businessman. His skills at organizing, pursuing, and completing a complex process are beyond dispute. He is personally engaging, but he is also very tough-minded and decisive when necessary. In my judgment, the process would not have been well served by someone who was engaging but lacked decisiveness. Mort is a person with very high standards and expectations. It was our hope and assumption that he would apply those kinds of high standards to this task. And, he was objective. He didn't bring to the position years of history with the orchestra, or any agenda such as: 'I want acoustics no matter what.' 'I want architecture first.' 'I want a hall with 3,600 seats because. . . .' None of that existed in Mort's case. It was a nearly perfect fit of one person's strengths and what we deemed to be the needs of the association."[11]

Having identified his preferred candidate, Decherd called Meyerson in October 1979 and said he would like to have breakfast at EDS. Meyerson asked him what he wanted to talk about. Decherd was cagey and close-mouthed. He told Meyerson he had a very important subject he wanted to discuss but declined to specify what it was. Meyerson did not press him, and they agreed on a date.[12]

Meyerson remembers the ensuing conversation clearly. "Robert started the breakfast by saying that as president he'd been talking with the board's executive committee. They had decided it was mandatory that the symphony get out of Fair Park, and that, to ever become what we should become, we'd have to get a new symphony hall. I replied, 'That's nice.' He said that they really didn't know what to do with that idea; that was the whole idea. That was the beginning and the end."

Then Decherd dropped the bomb. "I'm here to see if you will chair the committee that figures out what to do, and then goes and does it."

Meyerson thought, that's the whole thing? Figure out what to do, get the people to do it, supervise their doing it. Then he thought again.

"I don't think that you're talking to the right person."

"Why not?"

"Well, number one, I've just become president of EDS, and I've got my hands full. Number two, and most important, I am very non-political. I'm used to working in an environment where we get things accomplished. We spend little time on pomp and ceremony. We spend most of our time trying to do something. Everything that I know about symphony politics and what you have to do, and you have to get the players, and you have to get the city council, all this stuff, is going to require a dance, which I am not emotionally or intellectually suited to do."

Decherd asked, "Why is that?"

Meyerson replied, "Because I'm too impatient. I think I would come at it with too big a force."

He said, "You have just described why I have asked you."

"What do you mean?"

"We don't think that we can take the normal, politically safe chair and give it to him or her, because there's too much at risk here. Nobody knows what this is. Nobody knows what the purpose is, other than we can't stay in Fair Park. And, we think this project will be big and complicated. We thought [of you because of] your background with computer systems, etc., plus your personality, plus you happen to know music."

"How do you know that?" Meyerson demanded, taken aback.

Decherd said, "Well, I've done a little background checking, and I know that you play classical piano, and that your mother is a pianist, and that you've sung in choirs, that you were a choral singer at University of Texas. So you know classical music, therefore you would be sensitive."

Meyerson said, "OK, so you're willing to take the risk. You don't mind if I'm going to be hard-nosed about it?"

He said, "No. If you were other than that, I wouldn't have selected you."

"What do you think it entails?" Meyerson asked.

"You'll be the chairman of the committee. You form a committee, you select the members, you work together, you meet twelve, fifteen, eighteen times over the next few years. That's it."

"Oh, I bet it takes more than that."

He said, "It might take a little more."

"OK," said Meyerson, "I'll do it." Right then on the spot. "OK, you got a deal." And they shook hands. Decherd thanked him and departed. Meyerson returned to his office and said to himself, "What in the name of God have I done?" Because he didn't have a clue what he'd been asked to do.[13]

AT FIRST, the attraction of the project for Meyerson was the sense of fulfilling a civic responsibility. He thought the goal was important and that he could do some good for Dallas. "I had never worked on anything on a civic basis, and I felt that I was old enough and that EDS was mature enough that EDS should become more participative in the city and that I, representing the firm, should do it. Plus, I love music. If Robert had come to me a year before, I would not have done it. If he had come to me three years later, I couldn't have done it. He happened to have come at the right time. It was not the right time for me in my position; it was the right time for me psychologically. I wanted to do something like that. So I accepted."[14]

Meyerson began to educate himself. "I went to the computer and got a list of old symphony hall and acoustical articles. I had my secretaries pull articles from *The New York Times* on the [acoustical] failure of Philharmonic Hall in New York, going back to the early 1960s and the Lincoln Center opening, in an effort to determine what went wrong and what errors could be avoided. I wanted to know, number one, 'What did they do?' and number two, 'Why did it fail?'

"I learned that you can't give responsibility to an architect and to an acoustician, each of whom is going to do what he wants to do. The alternative is to have tight supervision and be a very active client, which we were. You have to form a collaboration. The collaboration we ultimately formed was among the players, the symphony board members-at-large, and the committee, among the city, the architects, the acousticians, and the contractor. In the later stages, the contractor became very important. We had to get all of those people singing in unison, so that they were an ensemble. Failure to have all of them singing together meant you had an unbalanced group. That's how we approached it."[15]

Not realizing that he was undertaking a ten-year project, Meyerson met with Leonard Stone to discuss who would be invited to serve on the committee. "Where do we start?" Meyerson asked.

Stone replied with another question. "Whom do you want on the committee?"

Meyerson said, "I want Stanley Marcus for aesthetics, because he's built great stores, he has great taste and he loves the symphony. I want Gene Bonelli for acoustics because he's a great musician, he loves the symphony, and he's a professional. I'd like to recruit them as my informal vice chairmen; then we'll get other people we need."

Leonard Stone nodded with approval. Marcus, the patriarch of the Neiman Marcus department store empire, was legendary for his impeccable taste. He was also well versed in architecture. Eugene Bonelli was dean of the Meadows School of the Arts at Southern Methodist University and held a doctorate in music. Both men were already members of the symphony board and had lengthy history with the orchestra. Stone expressed his agreement, then told Meyerson, "Well, Louise Kahn would really like to do it."

Meyerson hesitated. "You sure about that?" Louise Kahn was a long-time symphony board member with a reputation of being opinionated, strong-willed, and difficult.

Leonard Stone said, "Yes, I'm sure." He continued with names that board President Robert Decherd had suggested. "Mary McDermott and Richard Levin have expressed some interest, too." McDermott was the daughter of Eugene and Margaret McDermott. Levin was an attorney with a strong interest in music and architecture.

Mort Meyerson said, "I don't know Levin that well. I know Mary and Madame Kahn. Okay, that's about as many people as you can really get to work on something." As far as he was concerned, the committee was complete.

Doggedly, Stone persisted. "Well, I've worked with that many, too, but we've also got Al Casey and Nancy Penson." Casey was the chairman of American Airlines; Penson was another long-time symphony patron, board member, and major donor. Stone ran through a list of additional people he wanted to involve, including Dick Galland, Bob Glaze, Philip Jonsson, Raymond Nasher, Henry Miller, and Don Stone.

Meyerson was not happy. He preferred working with small groups. He suggested, "Why don't we have two committees? The big committee can be everybody that you need for political reasons and who has shown any kind of interest at all. But then, give me a small committee, an executive committee. I will take that small group and we will come up with what you really do, then we'll pass it through the large group and let the large group pass it to the board."

Leonard Stone acquiesced, and the beginnings of the machinery were formulated. They agreed that the smaller unit would handle the nuts and bolts, meeting regularly and frequently to do whatever it took to get the ball rolling. They would take their recommendations to the larger committee, which would meet infrequently, and which Meyerson would also chair. Full votes for major issues, such as budget determinations, would still be subject to approval by the symphony's board of governors.

When word first circulated in symphony circles as to the makeup of Meyerson's small group (which became known as the "smaller unit" of the concert hall committee), Louise Kahn presented herself in Leonard Stone's office to tell him how offended she was that she had not been invited to join. In the few months since his arrival, Stone had quickly come to understand the feistiness of Louise Kahn's personality. He also knew she was highly intelligent and well educated, with a degree from Smith College. Further, she possessed enormous financial resources, knew architecture, and had interior design experience. Louise Kahn would bring commitment, energy, time, and passion to the project. Stone urged Meyerson to add her to the smaller unit.

By February, Mort Meyerson had completed his recruiting. He announced the eighteen members of his large committee to the symphony's executive board and advised that the committee had approached E. G. Hamilton's firm to be professional consultants for the project. His subcommittee chairs were Stanley Marcus for architecture and taste, Eugene Bonelli for acoustics, Richard Levin for finance, Nancy Penson for public space, and Robert Decherd for community impact.

MEYERSON had assembled a remarkable and diverse team—each member brought specific talents and experience to the table. Stanley Marcus was the elder statesman, the experienced guru of elegance and taste. A former president of the DSA in the 1940s, he had been involved with the orchestra for decades. In his capacity at the helm of luxury retailing giant Neiman

Marcus, he had built many architecturally distinguished stores and consequently knew many of the world's great architects. Mort Meyerson remembers, "The most surprising of the people was Stanley. Given his age [Marcus was already seventy-five in 1980] and his prestige, it was amazing to me that he actually stayed engaged in the whole thing. His involvement was more in line with the architecture aspect, which was essentially over after the first two or three years. But he stayed right in there. I was quite amazed."[16]

Eugene Bonelli was a highly trained musician with community stature because he held the Meadows School deanship at Southern Methodist University. He knew music and acoustics, and his eloquence had given him a reputation as a superb public speaker. In committee meetings, he kept his eyes and ears open. As Meyerson recalls, "Bonelli carried a tremendous load, and he was kind of a middleweight talker. He would talk when necessary."[17]

Nancy Penson was an elegant lady whose family, the Pensons and the Penns,[18] had been generous supporters of the orchestra for a long time. An excellent listener, she absorbed things well and had a sense of balance. Wellesley educated and well traveled, she brought reason and experience to the group. According to Meyerson, "Nancy Penson didn't say much in committee meetings, but she was very active. She was an absolute jewel to work with. Fabulous woman."[19]

 Richard Levin, an attorney with Akin, Gump, Hauer & Feld, was an aficionado of both architecture and music who knew a great deal about opera and symphony and who would later served on the Board of the Salzburg Festival. As Meyerson remembers it, "Levin was good at being organized. He's very academic, and he was very helpful from a process and legal structure standpoint."[20]

Mary McDermott's family had a long-standing involvement with great art and architecture, and she had studied art history at University of Texas. From all reports, however, she was a passive participant in the early meetings, perhaps because she was the junior member of the group. Meyerson's assessment was, "Mary had a reputation of never saying anything. Especially at first, she was the most studious and quiet." As she gained confidence and assurance, she became a more vocal and contributing member.[21]

Louise Kahn had nearly as much history with the orchestra as Stanley Marcus. Her husband, Edmund J. Kahn, had accumulated an enormous fortune in cotton, oil, and other ventures. Eddie Kahn was primarily interested in education. Louise shared his interest, but her great passion was music, and she focused her energies on the Dallas Symphony. Leonard Stone's predecessor, Lloyd Haldeman, had declared Louise Kahn *persona non grata* at the symphony offices. According to Al Milano, Haldeman's development director, the friction between them arose because of artistic disagreement. Milano says, "Louise had been very supportive of Louis Lane, the former artistic director, and was very close to him. Lloyd spent considerable time trying to get rid of Louis Lane, because he needed to have a great, young, upcoming conductor. That's why he brought in Mata. He wanted to dump Louis Lane. Louise fought him tooth and nail."[22]

Nine years after the hall opened, Meyerson wryly observed of his smaller unit, "Louise was the biggest talker." He confirms that Louise Kahn and Mary McDermott were originally only on the large committee. "They both lobbied to be on the smaller committee. I didn't know either one of them very well, but Louise had a larger-than-life reputation as being a pain in the ass. Leonard pressed me to include them, and I acquiesced."[23]

Louise Kahn, who died in 1995, had her own issues with Meyerson. "Louise gave as good as she got," recalls Dolores Barzune, an active DSO volunteer since the 1960s and subsequently president of the DSA. "She had very negative, strong feelings about Mort, I think because he was kind of a dictator. He ran his committee like a military operation, and Louise wasn't in an army. She was giving, and giving generously, not only of her time, her money, and her intelligence, but also giving through her love of an institution, an art form, and a discipline. She was a straight shooter. Whatever she told you was exactly what she thought."[24]

Meyerson later observed, "One of the reasons that Louise and I clashed so much in the beginning is because a lot of my own characteristics were the same as hers. Our backgrounds were similar. My mother's entire family was from Germany. These are highly sophisticated, highly cultured, musically oriented, well-read, intellectual, I-know-the-way-to-get-it-done German Jews. That's who Louise was. I'm partly the product of that same culture."[25] Initially, that similarity caused them to throw sparks off one another. In time, it led to mutual respect.

As for Meyerson himself, all the assets Robert Decherd had counted on came into play. Leonard Stone opines, "In Mort, you had a guy who knew how to make things happen. He knew how to move things off a dime. I think the genius of Meyerson was the way he put the committee together and the reasons that he invited certain people. You had academics, people who knew music, the quintessential administrator: Mort. You had the elder statesman: Stanley Marcus. You had two ladies—Nancy [Penson] and Louise [Kahn]—who were diametrically opposite; one demure and ladylike, the other strong as battery acid. It made for interesting chemistry. What was good was that Mort did not fashion a group of people who were going to be 'yes men.' Certainly there was no way Louise was going to fulfill that! And Mort allowed dialogue. He allowed give and take."[26]

Al Milano, speaking from the development standpoint, admired Meyerson's savvy in identifying the heart of his donor base on the committee. "The key thing to me was [fundraising consultant] Carl Shaver's first recommendation to most clients: allow the donors to participate in things like the building committee, architectural selection, and so on," Milano says. "Mort put together a really fine committee of potential seven-figure-and-above donors to form the building committee, to hire the architect. That's where the real electricity started from donors."[27]

THE first meeting of the smaller unit was a brainstorming session over breakfast in Meyerson's private conference room at EDS. According to Meyerson, "We talked about the hall and what it could mean, why we needed to leave Fair Park. Primarily, we discussed how one goes about planning a concert hall. I passed out an article from *The New Yorker* about acoustician Cyril Harris. He was the second person to try to fix Avery Fisher Hall and fail. Before we did anything, I challenged everybody to obtain their own reading material, find books at the library, read up on acoustics, symphonic music, and hall building [if there were such a thing], articles like the one in *The New Yorker*. I also suggested that we start attending symphonies outside of Dallas to see what other halls were like."[28]

Leonard Stone recommended pulling in Peter Wexler, a New York–based producer and designer with whom Stone had previously worked in Canada, as a consultant to Meyerson's committee. Wexler had some architectural experience as well as extensive experience in production and design for music, opera, and theatre. Meyerson was already acquainted with Wexler through his work in conjunction with the DSO's outdoor summer concerts on the EDS grounds in North Dallas.

Wexler remembers, "I got a call from Leonard, saying, 'Mort has formed a committee. The committee needs to know a lot about how to go about getting started on our concert hall.' I think primarily they wanted to talk about how to select an architect. 'Would you accept a certain fee to be an adviser and come to a meeting of the concert committee?' I did."[29]

The committee asked Wexler, "Where do we start?" He told them, "First, I think, you need to know what we theatre folk and the architects think we know about opera houses, theatres, and concert halls."[30] Wexler also assisted in developing a preliminary reading list for Meyerson and the other members of the smaller unit. Subsequently, Wexler participated in discussions about what to look at during their visits to other halls, such as what the musicians would require. The committee queried him as to what worked and did not work in his experience with other facilities, and what they should look for in terms of possible other uses for a hall. Eventually, that inquiry evolved into the commissioning of an independent economic impact study.

Simultaneously, Stone and Meyerson realized that the musicians of the Dallas Symphony must have a voice in the selection of the acoustician. Stone brought up the issue. "What are we going to do about the musicians?"

Meyerson said, "Let's include them."

"Well, you know you're buying a pack of trouble, because they're moody."

Meyerson told him, "They'll be *more* moody if we don't include them. So, I'd rather include people and let them be moody with me than be moody outside, in a way, because they can throw rocks in from the outside, but it's hard to do it on the inside."[31]

They asked the players to provide representatives. Doug Howard remembers, "I got a letter from Leonard Stone, asking me to put together a group of musicians to help with the planning process. I had been chairman of the players' committee in orchestra negotiations the year before. We'd worked pretty well together on that. He was fairly new here at that point, but he knew me and had worked with me, so he asked me to do it."[32] Thus the players' concert hall committee was born and undertook its own meetings. The cast of characters involved in planning a new home for the Dallas Symphony was expanding.

The first meeting of Meyerson's large committee took place early morning, May 7, 1980, at the Hilton Inn at Mockingbird Lane and Central Expressway, adjacent to the affluent neighborhoods of Highland Park, University Park, and North Dallas where the symphony's constituents were concentrated. Mary McDermott walked in and recognized a number of prominent Dallasites, but at first saw no one she knew personally. Then she spotted Louise Kahn and sat with her. "Mort Meyerson ran a very autocratic meeting," recalls McDermott. "I didn't know who Mort Meyerson was from a hill of beans. He told the group that he had been asked to chair this committee and that the large group present at the meeting represented the broad community support that the symphony felt it needed for this project; however, he had assembled a small committee of five, and they would do all the work."[33] The select five were Meyerson, Marcus, Bonelli, Levin, and Penson. The rest of the large group, McDermott and Kahn deduced, were expected to be rubber stamps, with no more involvement beyond garnering support for the project. Meyerson explained the general process they proposed for architect and acoustician selection, then thanked everyone for being there and dismissed them.[34]

McDermott and Louise Kahn made a beeline for Meyerson as people started to disperse. Nearly in unison, they announced to him, "We don't want to be on this big committee. We're not good rubber stamps. You either let us off the big committee or put us to work on the small group."

Unfazed—though he later described the incident as "like having a buzz saw come at me" —Meyerson considered the two women confronting him. "I'll have to think about it." Later, he called each of them to ask, "What good would you be?"

McDermott replied, "I was an art history major, I studied architecture in college, and I've been around architects all my life. I could help with the architect selection. I don't think I could help on the acoustics at all, but I'd be interested in the architect search."

Robert Decherd, Leonard Stone, and Margaret McDermott had all urged Meyerson to involve Mary McDermott as much as possible. "Well, come on then; you'd be good at the interviews for the architects," he conceded. In a later telephone conversation with Louise Kahn, she declared her passion for the symphony, and Meyerson made the same decision. "I was impressed with what they both said. I was still skeptical, but I put them on," he says. Both Kahn and McDermott participated in the final review of architectural candidates in November and December 1980. Meyerson did not formally add them to his "working committee"—the smaller unit of the concert hall committee—until March 1981.

Chapter Five

ROLE MODELS: VISITING OTHER HALLS

The top of the list, no question, the two concert halls you've got to see and hear are the Musikvereinssaal in Vienna and the Concertgebouw in Amsterdam. Every musician tells me that these are the best halls in Europe. In America, the best halls I know are Carnegie Hall and Symphony Hall in Boston.[1]

PETER WEXLER, TO THE SMALLER UNIT, 1980

MEYERSON set about educating himself and charged the smaller unit of the concert hall committee with the same tasks: reading about halls, about acoustics and architecture—and listening. The members realized that, if they were going to adequately assess proposals for a new hall, they would have to hear music in other venues domestically and internationally. Over a period of about two years, Meyerson, members of the small group, Leonard Stone, and a small handful of other persons would hear some fifty halls among them, primarily in North America.

One of Meyerson's first trips early in 1980 was to San Francisco's Louise Davies Hall, scheduled to open in September 1980. "I had called ahead and arranged to spend a half-day with Samuel Stewart, the man who chaired their committee," Meyerson recalls. "He was a retired Bank of America executive who had been kept on the bank's payroll to work on this as a public service. Of course I asked him the normal questions: How did you do it? What were the problems? What would you do over? He talked about San Francisco politics and the difficulty of working with a city-managed program, people on the committees, and the labor unions, which he said were a nightmare.

"Then he told me, 'Young man, you have a big challenge in front of you.' 'How long do you think it will take?' 'It will take you ten years. I spent about ten percent of my time over ten years working on it.' I shot back, 'I'm sorry, I don't *have* ten years. Besides, we don't have strong labor unions in Texas. We don't have that much contention at city hall,' which I later learned was incorrect. 'And we have a can-do attitude. I think we'll be finished in six years.' Sam started laughing. 'You'll never do it.' I said, 'Well, I'll invite you to the opening,' which I did—ten years later!"[2]

The committee was hard at work formulating a program brief that would summarize its goals for the new symphony hall. The brief would eventually address all parameters of the public lobbies, stage and backstage areas, office space, and exterior space, in addition to the music chamber. In its early stages, it furnished the guidelines for initial solicitation of proposals from architectural firms.

As chair of the acoustics subcommittee, Eugene Bonelli developed a list of four essential criteria to be used in assessing each hall. These criteria were incorporated as an addendum to the program brief. They specified excellent bass response providing a rich, full foundation sound; brilliance in high frequencies and clarity of orchestral lines in combination; good blend and mixture of sounds without losing clarity; and stage acoustics that allow musicians to hear one another well, without forcing. In addition, his acoustics brief stated that visual and aural intimacy between audience and orchestra was a priority. The committee wanted excellent sight lines for the audience so that no listener's view of the stage was obscured.

Implicit in all these criteria was the concept of a single-purpose hall designed exclusively for the Dallas Symphony. Characteristics more general to the concert-going experience included a comfortable environment for listening to music and an overall aesthetic appearance within the music chamber to complement the sound and contribute to a sense of physical pleasure and well being. With these stringent, ambitious guidelines in mind, and soon to be committed to paper for reference, individual members of the concert hall planning

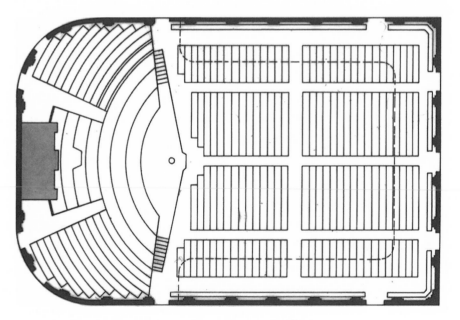

A plan of orchestra level, Concertgebouw, Amsterdam. (*DSO archives*)

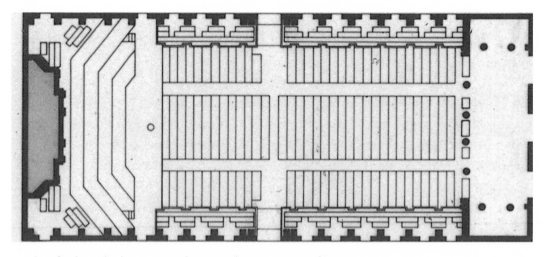

A plan of orchestra level, Grosser Musikvereinssaal, Vienna. (*DSO archives*)

committee began to add concerts to their itineraries in various cities. Each of them wanted to hear orchestral music in as many venues as possible.

———— ❧ ————

PHILIP Jonsson stepped down as chairman at the time of the DSA's annual meeting in May 1979, assuming the role of honorary chairman. Robert Decherd succeeded him as president; Bob Glaze was treasurer. E. G. ("Bill") Hatfield was still the nominal chairman of the facilities committee, which was reporting monthly to the executive board. The board discussed the need for a full-time staff member to assist on the new hall. Initially, Meyerson asked Leonard Stone's executive assistant, Julia George, to keep track of the data and paperwork relating to the hall. Meyerson and Stone soon realized that they could no longer delay hiring an administrator specifically responsible for matters concerning the proposed hall.

Because most of the early committee meetings were taking place in Meyerson's office at EDS, it made sense to situate the concert hall planning office at EDS as well. Initially, Stone staffed the satellite office with Peter Ryan, a DSO employee. Ryan and Meyerson were not a good mix. Stone proposed Mary Sullivan as an alternative. Sullivan worked on EDS premises for six months in 1980, but Meyerson was still dissatisfied.

Neither Ryan nor Sullivan had struck the right chemistry with Meyerson. "We were going nowhere with a staff liaison to the project and to the committee," recalls Stone. "The committee needed arrangements for its trips and its visits and its meetings. These were all high-powered people who were used to having things done in a very professional way with no slip-ups. I recognized this as an important need."[3] In March 1981, Stone shifted his marketing director, Melissa McNeil, into a newly created staff position: director of concert hall planning.[4]

Stone's guess that McNeil would be able to handle Mort Meyerson's powerful personality was a good one. "I presented Melissa with the challenge, and she accepted it. Melissa could get along with Mort," Stone later said. "The problem with Mort was he was so damn intelligent, and so driven, and so focused. He needed somebody he could relate to." Peter Wexler concurs with Stone's assessment of Meyerson. "Mort is a brilliant guy," Wexler says. "He once said to me that one reason for his prominence at EDS was that he understands the way a computer 'thinks.' He operates similarly, in that he can store an enormous amount of information and process it systematically. He also knows how to interview people and determine what people can and cannot provide."[5] Meyerson recognized that McNeil could handle this job, and then some.

Stone had hired McNeil in October 1979 as director of marketing.[6] A Wellesley College and University of Texas undergraduate with an MBA from Southern Methodist University, she came to the symphony from Methodist Hospitals of Dallas in Oak Cliff, where she had been director of marketing services. In that capacity, she had overseen the renovation of hospital facilities and thus had hands-on experience administering a large construction project. She turned out to be a multi-talented individual with many strengths, although initially she lacked experience in the business of symphony orchestras. Stone found McNeil bright, with a fertile, receptive imagination. During her first year in the marketing slot, the DSO succeeded in a campaign to double its subscribers, to almost eight thousand. Former Development Director Al Milano remembers, "Melissa came from hospital marketing, which wasn't the right background for a symphony. It was clear that she was on a learning curve working for an orchestra. Leonard needed somebody on staff to administer the concert hall project, because there's an awful lot of paperwork. The shift to concert hall coordinator was a good one. She was a terrific person, and she brought her assets to this other important activity. I think everyone felt that was for the better. She was brought in to the concert hall project to manage the internal documentation and meetings in relation to the concert hall."[7]

McNeil's marketing department secretary, John Adams, came with her into the newly created department of concert hall planning. Adams had his own set of academic credentials, holding master's degrees in both musicology and library science. His strong sense of organization and attention to detail complemented McNeil's administrative and people skills nicely. The two of them proved to be an effective team. McNeil began to interview all the constituents of the hall—musicians, staff, acoustician, architect—to define what spaces the hall required. She incorporated this information into the draft program brief the smaller unit had begun.

One of McNeil's first actions was to reestablish the concert hall planning office at Fair Park, rather than at Meyerson's EDS offices in North Dallas. "This was an important first issue for my job," she recalls. "My predecessors had been out at EDS. I felt strongly that we should be in a central location available to all constituents participating in the design on this hall, starting with the musicians and Eduardo Mata. They were the reason we had undertaken this project. I wanted an open-door policy, to make sure they felt they had free access at any time. Same thing with staff members, who knew about operations, backstage matters, ticket selling and public spaces. I needed to be accessible to board members and volunteers who would drop by to share thoughts and ideas."[8] Meyerson agreed with her reasoning after she reassured him that if he needed to see her she could be at EDS within twenty minutes.

Doug Howard, chair of the players' committee, was an immediate beneficiary of McNeil's proximity. "She involved us more than someone else might have. I'd walk by her office at Fair Park Music Hall two or three times a week. She'd spot me going past the door and call, 'Come on in; I want you to look at something and tell me what you think.'"[9] As a result, Howard reviewed design ideas regularly, passed them along to members of his committee, and provided McNeil with their feedback.

Concurrently, the smaller unit crystallized its thoughts as to what parameters a new hall should have. "We made several crucial decisions from the beginning," Eugene Bonelli recalls. "First, we had been challenged to build a world-class hall; the city wanted that. It was a boom time, and everyone was very optimistic. We were told to build the best. We determined that it would not be the best unless the acoustics were great. Second, we felt we wanted a great organ. That plan was part of our process from the first."[10]

Equally important was the balance of power issue. The committee decided to hire the acoustician and the architect on an equal footing. Samuel Stewart, the San Francisco gentleman who had chaired the Davies Hall committee, had counseled Meyerson about working with

The interior of Grosser Musikvereinssaal, Vienna. (*DSO archives*)

major consultants. "He told me about the tensions that arise between architect and acoustician," Meyerson remembers. "He predicted I would have great difficulty. He said, 'Hire the architect, get the architect to hire the acoustician, and be done with it.' I decided not to do that. I declined his advice because I didn't want an aesthetically pleasing hall that was not very good acoustically. I knew that if we had the architect hire the acoustician, he would have been beholden to the architect, and the architect would win all the arguments. I was prepared to moderate, in order to get what we wanted, which was as close to perfect acoustics as is humanly possible, in an aesthetic package that was beautiful. We knew that this would be difficult, but I thought it was possible. So we established

that as our target."[11] The decision to give acoustician and architect equal authority proved to be the most momentous of the entire project.

In spring 1980, members of the committee, both large group and smaller unit, toured halls in the eastern United States, attending concerts to assess acoustics and patron amenities. In July, at Eduardo Mata's suggestion, a group traveled to Mexico City to visit the campus of the National University. It was clear that they needed to acquaint themselves with the legendary European halls as well. By late summer they were making plans for a trip to Europe at their own expense. Marcus's office made many of the advance arrangements and hotel reservations; Meyerson's staff attended to airline reservations. An assistant in Levin's office prepared information packets for each venue the group would visit. The European tour, which took place from the last week in October through early November 1980, was a memorable journey and a pivotal educational experience as the committee approached its selection of the architect and acoustician.

Europe 1980

The travelers comprised Nancy Penson, Louise Kahn, Henry and Juanita Miller, Mort and Marlene Meyerson, Richard Levin, Eugene Bonelli, plus Leonard Stone, Mary Sullivan, and Julia George from the DSO staff. They flew coach class but stayed at the best hotels: Claridge's in London, the Amstel in Amsterdam, the Crillon in Paris, the Imperial in Vienna.

London was the first stop. Leonard Stone was treasurer for the trip. "That meant I was to take care of all the expenses, maintain a log, then we were to divvy them up. We arrived at

The interior of Symphony Hall, Boston. (*DSO archives*)

Claridge's. Louise's great concern was that her room would always be ready. In some places she insisted that she pay for the night before so that the room was available when she got there, because occasionally the rooms were not ready. I had with me the DSO's credit card and US$20,000 in traveler's checks. I looked at the rates at Claridge's and started calculating: eleven people times four nights at those rates. I was going to go through my stash pretty darn quickly! I went downstairs to inquire, 'Which credit cards does Claridge's honor?' The concierge drew himself up and replied, 'Claridge's *prides* itself, Mr. Stone, that it doesn't take *any* credit card.' I guess Visa and MasterCard weren't as readily accepted in those days! I had to wire back to Dallas, I think for $40,000 more. That was just the start of the trip!"[12]

At Royal Festival Hall, the manager of the hall took the Dallas entourage to a private office to discuss the hall's strengths and weaknesses. Meyerson was concentrating on what they were seeing and hearing. "It became startlingly clear that the London hall, Royal Festival Hall, was terrible. They had electrical boosts on the bass. The maintenance was terrible. The layout was ugly. It was hard to find your way around. It was just a disaster."[13] In addition to hearing a performance at Royal Festival Hall, the group toured the still-incomplete Barbican Centre.

Each member of the committee was assigned a particular area of concern to observe and critique in addition to overall reactions to the concert experience. For Bonelli, it was acoustics; for Levin, architecture. Nancy Penson took responsibility to assess patron amenities such as rest rooms and handicapped facilities. Others concentrated on backstage layout, seating configuration, coat check, ingress and egress, parking availability, and other practical considerations. These were areas of concern the committee had pinpointed that needed significant improvement over Fair Park. In each hall, the group met with local musicians and staff. They compared notes after each concert and kept careful records of their observations.

Everywhere they went, the rest of the committee would ask Nancy Penson if she had checked out the bathrooms. "At Rotterdam, they sent me to inspect the facilities. I went charging in, and there was a man standing at the wash basin. I said, 'Oooh! Excuse me.' He didn't speak English, but he indicated that it was a unisex bathroom, which completely threw me. They had stalls with doors that extended all the way up and down, and the only togetherness was at the wash basins, but it was still kind of a shock!"[14]

On the continent, they heard performances at Rotterdam's De Doelen Hall, the Muziekcentrum Vredenberg in Utrecht, Amsterdam's Concertgebouw, Pierre Boulez's underground IRCAM Studio beneath the Pompidou Centre in Paris (not exactly a performance; clarinetist Richard Stoltzman was recording at the time of their visit) and, finally, the Musikvereinssaal in Vienna.

For much of the committee, an epiphany took place when they heard Eugen Jochum conduct the Royal Concertgebouw Orchestra in Amsterdam in what was to be one of the last concerts of his distinguished career. Meyerson remembers talking to Bonelli after the performance. "We were both moved to tears listening to Bruckner in the Concertgebouw. I had never heard Bruckner sound that way. Now, it was Jochum conducting, which helped, although he was older than Methuselah. But when I heard Jochum and the Concertgebouw Orchestra play in there, that was the first time that I knew that there was a big difference. I had heard Carnegie, which was good. I had heard Boston's Symphony Hall, which was good. I had heard good halls, and I knew the difference between good and not so good, but I had never tasted exquisite. The European halls I had heard previously were intermediate, mediocre halls. This was the first time that I knew that there was the possibility, that we were not talking academic talk, that there was something to this."[15]

Of all the European cities and halls, Vienna stands out most clearly in Eugene Bonelli's memory. "The experience of music in the Musikvereinssaal was the high point of the whole trip. More than any other concert, I think that convinced the committee that there was a real difference in the way a room made orchestral music sound, and that we needed to commit to build this kind of hall in Dallas. In a way, the whole purpose of the trip was to show the committee what the ideal was, so that we had backing for the decisions that could produce such an acoustical ideal, including such things as a smaller hall, as well as the shape and the kind of materials. People had tears in their eyes when they heard Riccardo Chailly conduct a visiting London orchestra in the Musikvereinssaal. It was phenomenal from the standpoint of the resonance and the richness of that sound. Everyone came away from there knowing that we had never *really* heard the Dallas Symphony in the acoustical environment at Fair Park. *This* was the ideal."[16]

Meyerson confirms the reaction. "We knew the Musikvereinssaal was held up as an icon. Then we heard Tchaikovsky in the Musikvereinssaal. When I felt the notes, the bass fiddles, go up my feet through my nose—I mean, I literally could feel the vibration in my nose! I looked down and noticed the wooden floor with the reverb under it. After the concert, I went to the stage and saw where the cellos and double basses had stuck their pins into the stage to establish the connection for vibration. I'd never seen that. The combination of the Concertgebouw Bruckner performance and the Vienna Tchaikovsky performance changed how I listen to an orchestra. Both experiences were much more than just visits to a symphony hall."[17]

—❧—

SUBSEQUENTLY, in spring 1981, different groups (this time including some DSO musicians) visited halls in the United States, Canada, and Mexico. Meyerson says, "Every hall that we visited, we talked to the musicians, the conductor, and the professionals. We would ask, 'What are the shortcomings of the hall? If you had to do it all over again, what would you do?' In Avery Fisher, they took me backstage and showed me that the distance between the back wall of the stage and the back wall of the building was so narrow that you couldn't carry a double bass through it. Itzhak Perlman told me, when I talked to him, that there was no consideration of

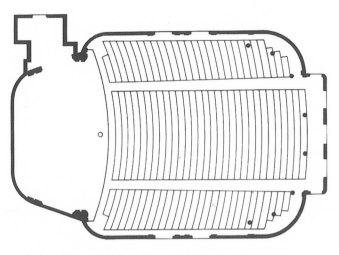

A plan of Carnegie Hall, orchestra level. (*DSO archives*)

handicapped artists in the backstage areas or dressing rooms. This was New York, but Itzhak observed that the same situation existed all over the country. For halls that were built at the turn of the century, it's understandable. For those built in the '60s and '70s, I don't know why they didn't provide handicapped access. It was a design flaw. Every hall we went to had bad bathrooms. The problem, if you think about it, is really very simple. You have people who are cooped up in a place for an hour to an hour and a half. At the intermission, they all want to go to the bathroom at one time. If you built a bathroom that accommodated everybody at once, it would be so enormous that the bathrooms and the hall would be about equal size. So, you've got to be really smart about where you place them. That's why Nancy [Penson] got into that, because we identified bathrooms and handicap access as needs and problems."[18]

―☙―

EACH trip to hear other halls yielded more information that could be put to use in the new hall. On the heels of their return from Europe, Bonelli reported to the executive board that the administrator at the newly opened Barbican Arts and Conference Center, new home of the London Symphony, had "graphically illustrated to the committee the shortcomings of their hall due to the fact that they, the users, were not consulted prior to construction."[19] The message was clear: Stone, his staff, and the musicians must be an integral part of the design and planning process.

On a trip to Boston, Meyerson heard the Boston Symphony perform in its legendary home, Symphony Hall. He discovered that (a) the seats were too hard; (b) they were too narrow; (c) the aisles were too chopped up; (d) the access was poor; and (e) it wouldn't meet the fire codes of today. "It took me two hours to figure all that out. We did a tour of the hall. There were no public areas. The lobbies were terrible. Then we listened to the Boston Symphony. It was superb. The acoustics were spectacular. I learned a very valuable lesson: What is eye-appealing doesn't have much to do with the acoustics. You can live with the hardness of the seat if the music sounds good enough. Everything revolves around acoustics as being the principal consideration. If you get in enough halls and listen, you discover, hey! acoustics is the name of the game. Not only what the audience hears but how the players hear each other. To be in an ensemble, you've got to hear each other. You can't have something that projects all the sound out and it sounds great. The sound up and down has to be there too. It's pretty complicated, when you think about all these considerations. We learned these a piece at a time."[20]

It became clear that two European halls and two American halls provided superior listening, appearing consistently at the top of everyone's list. Vienna's Musikvereinssaal, Amsterdam's Concertgebouw, New York's Carnegie Hall, and Boston's Symphony Hall were the committee's undisputed favorites. The principal characteristics they shared were relatively limited seating—1,680 in Vienna,[21] 2,037 in Amsterdam, 2,625 in Symphony Hall, and 2,804 in Carnegie Hall—high ceilings, and a rectangular, or shoebox, shape with parallel side walls.

—⁂—

In March 1980, DSA Board President Decherd was promoted to executive vice president of *The Dallas Morning News*. He wished to avoid any appearance of conflict of interest in terms of his community involvement. He was particularly concerned that he not jeopardize the Dallas Symphony's relationship with the city with respect to land acquisition for the new concert hall. Consequently, he resigned from all civic boards and committees but agreed to remain on the DSA Board in his capacity as immediate past president.

He was succeeded by Donald J. Stone, the CEO of Sanger-Harris Department Stores. Stone moved to Dallas early in 1975 from Foley's, another division of Cincinnati-based Federated Department Stores. "When I moved to Dallas, there was no orchestra," he recalls. "It was out in bankruptcy and was revived shortly thereafter. I became involved with the symphony because I was chairman of Sanger-Harris at the time, and if you were the chairman of the largest department store in town, you were automatically asked to be on the board of various different organizations."[22]

Meyerson's position as chairman of the concert hall committee had no specific term or time limit. Meyerson says, "Theoretically, the symphony board could have voted me out at any particular time. Since it now was a ten-year project and not a three- or four-year, you might logically think that they even wanted to pass it around the board. When Don Stone became president, he asked, 'Look, Mort, I want you to stick with the concert hall. Will you continue?'"[23] At the time, Meyerson was happy to do so. He had a functioning committee; they'd done some traveling. Now they needed to decide on experts who could design the best concert hall for Dallas, inside and out.

Chapter Six

SELECTING AN
ARCHITECT

ONCE Meyerson assumed responsibility for the concert hall committee, discussions about process and schedule became more focused. Early in 1980, local architect E. G. Hamilton provided Meyerson and his smaller unit with a basic, broad architectural overview, delineating between general and specific responsibilities of the city, the committee, and the consultants. Hamilton also helped with the "footprint" of the site, which ultimately took several years to develop.

In the architecture world, news of plans for a large civic building travels rapidly. Expressions of interest from architects interested in designing the concert hall began to arrive in Dallas from around the country and from some international architects. Word about Dallas' long-range plans circulated in orchestral circles as well. In a visit to Los Angeles in February 1980, Leonard Stone and Peter Wexler met with Norman Pfeiffer of Hardy Holzman Pfeiffer Associates and with Frank O. Gehry. Both architectural firms had an international reputation and experience with performing arts facilities. Knowledge of those meetings spread around Los Angeles. Ernest Fleischmann, the venerable executive director of the Los Angeles Philharmonic, got wind of the fact that Dallas was considering building a new hall. He sent an unsolicited letter in April 1980 to Peter Ryan at the DSO, recommending Frank Gehry and pointing out that Gehry had recently renovated the Hollywood Bowl. Other unsolicited proposals from architectural firms began to trickle in from around the country.

Meyerson asked each member of his building committee to submit a list of architects he or she felt would design an outstanding symphony hall. Suggestions from the smaller unit included many prominent architects. Some of them already had a significant presence in Dallas, most notably I. M. Pei. In addition to Dallas City Hall, the firm of I. M. Pei & Partners had been responsible for a downtown skyscraper, One Dallas Centre. Another office tower was under construction: the Allied Bank Tower on Ross Avenue (now called Fountain Place). Pei's firm had also designed a research laboratory in suburban Farmers Branch.

The most passionate response to Meyerson's request came from Louise Kahn in June 1980, in support of Enslie ("Bud") Oglesby of The Oglesby Group, Dallas. She wrote: "I know Bud Oglesby personally and have worked with him on my own home as well as professionally for clients. He listens, he hears, and much of the prize-winning work of the firm is impeccable. Bud has been interested in music all his life, and when travelling has gone to performances all over this country and abroad. . . . My strong personal hope is that, for once, Dallas might have the building of a major institution designed by a Dallas architect—that decision, of course, resulting from stringent research and comparison. There should be no sacrifice of professional capacity."[1]

Leonard Stone remembers calling Oglesby to request that he send his credentials. "He immediately asked, 'Oh, am I going to be the token Dallas architect?' I replied, 'No, Bud, you have a champion on this committee. Her name is Louise Kahn, and you are admired and respected by Dallasites, and you're wanted.'"[2]

The committee initially sent a letter to a large group of established architects in addition to those recommended by its own membership, inquiring as to whether they would be interested. Some of the most prominent firms initially declined to submit presentations, including Kevin Roche/John Dinkeloo Associates; Gwathmey & Siegel; Charles Bassett of Bassett & Reiner; Gerald McCue of Harvard University School of Design; Geddes, Brecher, Qualls, Cunningham Architects; E. G. Hamilton of Omniplan Architects in Dallas (presumably declining because of conflict of interest, because Hamilton had served the project in an advisory capacity), Welton Becket Associates; and I. M. Pei of I. M. Pei & Partners.

Pei's name was thus the most conspicuously absent from the list of applicants. Eason Leonard, the administrative partner at Pei & Partners, wrote to Stanley Marcus declining the project because of the DSO's selection process that had been described.[3]

Portfolios and letters of interest, both solicited and unsolicited, continued to stream into the symphony offices. Some of the submissions came in as simple letters, others with marketing kits, models, or videocassettes—quite cutting-edge in 1980—or slide carousels. The first cut yielded a list of thirty-five candidates. Leonard Stone remembers, "We all gathered at EDS in one of their media rooms. We passed around information. We made a sheet on each of these architects. Who were they, where were they, what had they done, had they done a concert hall? Then we looked at slides."[4]

After another look at the first-cut group, the committee sent thirty architects a letter of interest. Twenty-six responded that they would still like to be considered for the project. In two days of intense meetings on September 26 and 27, the committee, plus Peter Wexler and Robert M. Wilkinson, assistant director of the City of Dallas' building services department, reviewed twenty-six sets of slides. By the evening of the 27th, they had narrowed the candidates to a list of six finalists. Those six architects were invited to Dallas for an interview, with the opportunity to make a formal presentation to Stanley Marcus's architecture subcommittee.

The interviews were scheduled for Friday, November 14, and Saturday, November 15, five days after the conclusion of the crucial tour to Europe when members of the smaller unit had heard concerts in European halls. The symphony forwarded information to the finalists about two sites currently under consideration. Each one was allotted ninety minutes to discuss his ideas and concepts of what a great music hall should be and how he might work with his concept of those two sites, taking into consideration factors such as access, parking, and landscaping. The committee also wanted to know what recent buildings were each architect's favorites, as well as his thoughts about existing concert halls. Given the fact that the new symphony hall would follow both Dallas City Hall and the new museum, there were other questions. Did the candidate have any thoughts about relating it to either of those buildings. How reliably could he work within a budget and avoid costly redesign? What other commitments did he have that might interfere with the early design stage? Who would be assigned to the design team?

Once again, the group convened in the board room of Meyerson's company, EDS. The finalists were as follows:

1. Enslie ("Bud") Oglesby, of the Oglesby Group, Dallas, which had a strong presence in the Dallas/Fort Worth metroplex, with buildings at Richland and El Centro Community colleges, St. Marks School of Dallas, the McDermott Library at University of Texas–Dallas, and Fairway Plaza in nearby Las Colinas. At the time of Oglesby's proposal to the symphony, his firm was engaged in the renovation of downtown Dallas' Majestic Theatre. As Leonard Stone remembers, "Bud Oglesby gave us a pleasant presentation—this was a good, old home boy. He didn't have the body of work. He'd never designed a hall."[5] Marcus is more blunt. "Oglesby didn't get much support other than the fact that he was local. There are a lot of things that would have been advantageous to using a local architect. I just don't think many of us felt we should have a local artist just for the sake of saying, 'This building was designed by someone local.' I don't think Bud Oglesby had a big enough vocabulary."[6]

2. Gunnar Birkerts, born in Riga, Latvia, in 1925, was educated at Stuttgart's Technische Hochschule, and came to the United States upon graduation in 1949. He worked in the offices of Eero Saarinen and Minoru Yamasaki for ten years until he established his own practice. At the time of his submission to the Dallas concert hall committee,

Birkerts was head of Gunnar Birkerts and Associates in Birmingham, Michigan, and held a professorship teaching architecture at University of Michigan. His buildings included the Federal Reserve Bank of Minneapolis, Contemporary Arts Museum in Houston, and the South Addition to the Detroit Institute of Arts.

Leonard Stone says, "There was no certain front runner [among the architects], but if anybody had an early edge, it was Gunnar Birkerts, because of the stunning Federal Reserve Building in Minneapolis."[7] Mary McDermott found him well prepared and forceful. She was impressed by his observations that newer halls lacked the grace of older halls in their surroundings, and by his prior experience working with acousticians.[8]

3. Leandro Locsin of Leandro Locsin Partners in Manila, Philippines, had been an architect for Ferdinand Marcos. The committee had seen slides of his Cultural Center in Manila and loved the building. Furthermore, Stanley Marcus knew him well. Locsin was added to the list because during the initial interviewing process with Russell Johnson, one of the acoustician candidates, Johnson had shown some slides of a Locsin hall in Manila for which he did acoustics work. "They were stunning photographs," recalls Leonard Stone. "I can't imagine in real life the hall looks that glorious, but the setting in the bay in Manila looked just fabulous. All I wanted for Dallas [as landlocked as it is] was to create a big lake in the center of the city and put the hall in the middle of that lake! Locsin was championed by Imelda Marcos, so whatever money he needed to do the project [would be there]. Everybody loved him, and they loved his work, but I remember what Stanley said: 'You will have a big problem with him. He thinks in metric terms, and we think in feet. There will be mistakes made.'"[9] Marcus confirms the remark, adding that he also felt Locsin simply lived too far away —literally the other side of the world—to be a practical choice.[10]

4. Aldo Cossutto of Cossutto & Associates, New York, had previously been chief design architect for the I. M. Pei office. He had designed the Mormon Church in Boston and was at work on a major project in Lyon, France. Later, he would design CityPlace, the giant Southland Corporation headquarters in Dallas.

According to Leonard Stone, before Cossutto came to Dallas for his interview, he had sought permission from Pei to take credit for his role in the design of Dallas City Hall and the East Wing of the National Gallery. Because I. M. Pei was *not* being considered for the Dallas concert hall, Pei had agreed that Cossutto could include his share of those projects among his credentials. Stanley Marcus recalls, "Cossutto was a good contender, but his work was very florid. It wasn't clean, sharp architecture."[11]

5. Arthur Erickson of Arthur Erickson Architects in Toronto, was a native of Toronto whose architecture practice was based in Vancouver. Erickson was in the final stages of Roy Thomson Hall in Toronto. His firm was also involved with the design of the

Museum of Anthropology and Provincial Courthouse Complex in Vancouver and the Bank of Canada Headquarters in Ottawa. After hearing of the plan to construct a new concert hall, the firm had written to the DSO Board of Governors in April 1980, asking to be considered. They were in the midst of work on Toronto's new Massey Hall, scheduled to open in autumn 1982.

Erickson's presentation made a powerful impression on the smaller unit. "He was a stunning architect, and the collection of materials he brought overwhelmed everybody," recalls Leonard Stone. "We talked about colors, fabrics and exterior stone, how it would blend with the skyline."[12] Mary McDermott thought him smooth and polished, almost too sure of himself, although she found persuasive Erickson's argument that his recent concert hall experience might allow him to avoid certain problems.[13]

At the formal interview, Stanley Marcus asked the definitive question that killed Arthur Erickson's chances. "Well, Mr. Erickson, how much time will you personally devote to this project?" Erickson replied, "There will be a design team, and I will visit with the design team a minimum of once a month." Around the table, the expression on people's faces read, "This is our hall, bud, and if you don't pour your heart, life, and soul into it . . ."[14]

6. Philip Johnson and John Burgee of Johnson & Burgee had designed the New York State Theater at Lincoln Center, the Terrace Theater at Washington's Kennedy Center, and the National Center for the Performing Arts in Bombay, India. Johnson also had substantive experience with acousticians, because of his work at Philharmonic Hall (the first redo of what is now known as Avery Fisher Hall, attempting correction of its acoustical deficiencies) and the New York City Opera.

"Philip Johnson's interview was the most intriguing," says Leonard Stone. "Stanley opened up the discussion with each architect with the same question: 'Why would you like to design our concert hall?' Most of them answered, 'I don't want to do another shopping center. I don't want to do another twenty-story building—floor fifteen, floor twelve—they're all the same. I've never done a concert hall. What a challenge it would be to do a statement for the city, a great deal for the arts, etc.' Stanley had a Mont Blanc pen with a little white pad in front of him. He would write questions that he wanted answered, while the architect was talking."[15]

At the start of the meeting with Johnson, Marcus asked, "Well, Philip, why would you like to design our concert hall?"

Marcus remembers Johnson's reply. "You know, Stanley, I don't know that I *do* want to design your concert hall. I'm a wealthy man; I don't have to take anything. I take what I want." Marcus removed the cap from his Mont Blanc, screwed the two pieces together and set the pen down on the table. He looked up, smiled, and said, "OK, Philip, you're off the list. Now we've got an hour and a half or so. What would you like to talk about?" (Marcus later said, "That cooked *him* with the committee!"[16])

The others in the room were breathless with astonishment. Stone recalls, "In other words, what Johnson was really saying was, 'Aren't you honored that I'm here? That you should have to ask me that?' He and his partner, John Burgee, had brought impressive displays and photographs. They gave us a quite wonderful hour of architecture, acoustics, and sight lines. He knew a lot about two of the acousticians, Russell Johnson and Cyril Harris. They were very high on Cyril, but they did say one thing about Cyril that came to haunt him: Cyril was a fundamentalist. His rooms had to be designed in a very static way without anything 'floating.' He didn't want things that would drop in or out—like an overhead canopy."[17]

—⁊⁊—

FOLLOWING each interview, the committee took fifteen minutes to compare notes and discuss the presentation and the candidate. By Saturday afternoon, final deliberations were underway. The committee discussed and argued and reached no decision. They met again the next day to continue the debate. They were split in factions. Mort Meyerson liked Birkerts. Louise Kahn still favored Oglesby. Others wanted Erickson out of Toronto. They could not reach a consensus and finally acknowledged that they were hopelessly deadlocked. Marcus, as chairman of the architectural subcommittee, sent letters to each of the six finalists thanking them for their visit and advising that the committee planned to make a final decision after the interviews with the acousticians in mid-December.

—⁊⁊—

RICHARD Levin was one of a very few who felt, after the initial group had been whittled to six, that they hadn't yet tapped into the cream. Two days after the architect interviews, he drafted a memo to Meyerson and other members of the smaller unit, recommending that they look to a higher level and reopen the candidate list. He wrote: "I believe that our meeting last weekend contained too much subsurface emotion and our 'tentative conclusions' might have been based somewhat on personalities rather than design capabilities. . . . I strongly urge that we invite Richard Rogers in for an interview. I believe his problem-solving capabilities are outstanding. . . . I suggest that someone from the committee, the most logical being Stanley Marcus, call on I. M. Pei and Kevin Roche to discuss their possibilities. . . . I hope I am not out of line or being an obstructionist by making these suggestions but I feel the issue is so important that I would like to put this on the table for consideration."[18]

Levin read his memo to Leonard Stone over the phone and asked his reaction. Stone, a consensus builder, suggested that Levin not send it, but he decided to send it anyway, via messenger, to the other members of the small committee. It resulted in a "second round" over and above the six finalists. Levin later recalled, "Not that we were necessarily rejecting the first six, but we thought we ought to take it up a notch."[19] Requests for three additional proposals went to Kevin Roche/John Dinkeloo Associates in Hamden, Connecticut; to Richard Rogers, who was riding high on the success of the new Pompidou Centre in Paris; and, finally, to I. M. Pei.

Despite the fact that Pei had initially excused himself from consideration, there was an underlying feeling among Meyerson's small group that he was the right architect for the job. Pei knew Dallas and understood the city. He had an established and cordial relationship with many individuals who were key players in the city and would be active participants in the evolution of the hall. Stanley Marcus and Mary McDermott were his personal friends. He had worked hand in glove with Dallas City Manager George Schrader on Dallas City Hall. His firm already had such a strong presence in the city that it maintained a Dallas office—to this day, the firm's only satellite office. Throughout its twenty-year presence in Dallas, the Pei office was managed by Theodore A. (Ted) Amberg, who had moved with his family in 1968 to head up the Dallas City Hall project, Pei's first Dallas building.

—⁖—

MARCUS remembers, "The committee was shocked when Pei initially turned the symphony down. He gave the reason that he was terribly busy and couldn't undertake it. I took his request to be deleted from the list seriously, and frankly, I was wrong. A mutual friend of I. M.'s and mine in New York called me one day. He was familiar with the situation. 'Do you really want Pei to design your symphony hall?' I said, 'It's not a matter of what I want. I think the whole community would feel greatly rewarded if he did.' He said, 'Well, it's very simple. If you want Pei, you ought to call him on the phone personally and tell him so. Come to New York and take him to lunch. I think you can get him to design your building. But don't quote me.' I asked, 'Come on, what's the game?' He said, 'Well, I think Pei feels that since he did the city hall, and since he'd done a couple of other buildings in Dallas, that the vote would be against him because they would want another architect who's fresh. But if *you* really want him—and he has a lot of respect for you—I think you can convince him.'"[20]

Ted Amberg remembers receiving a similar telephone call in December 1980 at the Pei office at One Dallas Centre. Did Amberg think that if I. M. Pei were approached—because Pei had made it very clear that he was not interested and would not participate in this project— but *if* I. M. were approached to be the architect of the Dallas concert hall, would he design the building? "Of course I would have loved to have said yes myself," Amberg recalls, "but I said, 'Clearly, I've got to talk to I. M.' I placed a call immediately to the partners in New York and reached Eason Leonard. We contacted I. M." Amberg could almost see the architect's wide grin at the other end of the phone. Pei replied, "Of course, under those circumstances, of course we're interested."

Amberg relayed this response to the person who prompted the query. (Both he and Stanley Marcus decline to identify their source.) Amberg says, "It was put to me this way: 'Stanley Marcus only wants to make the appointment with I. M. to ask this question if the answer is yes.'" Amberg gave the answer the committee wanted to hear.[21]

Stanley Marcus is nobody's fool, and he knew when a golden opportunity had presented itself. He telephoned Pei to schedule a meeting and flew to New York. They met for a leisurely lunch and caught up. Finally, Pei introduced the topic, asking how the symphony hall project was progressing. Marcus seized his moment. "You know, I. M., we're pretty far into the architect selection process, and maybe we have not communicated well with you, but damn it, you're the person we want! We're about to make a decision in favor of an architect that nobody wants!" Marcus wasn't even sure which of the finalists it would be, but he was certain there was no great enthusiasm among the other committee members for any of the six.

He continued. "I've come up here personally to invite you to design the Dallas Symphony Orchestra hall. We have a competition, a selection process, but I want to assure you that complete unanimity of opinion is shared among us all. We have the right to cancel the competition aspect for cause."[22]

Pei asked, "Do you really want *me* to design this hall?"

"I've given you the honest truth, I. M. Why do you doubt it?"

"Well, you already have four or five buildings I've designed in Dallas. There's City Hall, which a number of people don't particularly like." He enumerated the other structures.

Marcus assured him, "Well, despite and because of those buildings, the building committee is prepared to recommend you as the architect."

Pei was bemused. "You know, I had figured that you wouldn't pick me because I had done so much work in Dallas. That really was the reason I said I wanted to be withdrawn from the competition."

They talked for a while longer about various topics. Marcus was satisfied. He would return to Texas with his mission accomplished: Pei had reconsidered and would meet formally with the selection committee. This was good news for Dallas.[23]

⎯⎯⎯⎯✺⎯⎯⎯⎯

IN mid-December, with Christmas looming, the second round of finalist interviews began.

The dynamics of the interviews were better than the dynamics of the first six. Richard Levin remembers, "None of the three—Kevin Roche, Richard Rogers, and I. M. Pei—had done a symphony hall, which some of the other six had. I remember stating that I thought this was a plus and not a negative. We were looking at the wrong things. You want to pick a consultant and get the best out of him. I felt very strongly that if the architect had *not* done a prize project like a performance hall, this opportunity would bring out the best in him."[24]

Kevin Roche had been Swedish architect Eero Saarinen's partner. His team had finished NorthPark Shopping Center, including the Neiman Marcus store there. Stanley Marcus had been instrumental in adding the Saarinen firm to this second round, but he was personally cool about Roche. "Kevin was a very difficult person for anyone to get excited about," he says today. "He had about as much emotion as a door. His work was adequate, but not exciting. Too much damn starch."[25]

Richard Rogers and his wife were on a visit to the United States, and he was able to work the trip to Dallas into his schedule. "The most incredible personality!" remembers Levin. "He had done the Beaubourg Museum [Pompidou Centre] in Paris, which had only recently opened. He had also been doing some fascinating city planning concepts—the Coyne Street project on the Thames in London. He had great ideas about planning."[26]

Rogers expounded on his ideas about urban development and the arts, presenting a slide show about how arts districts work. "Rogers was flying on the success of Beaubourg," confirms Leonard Stone. "That building was initially designed to receive 5,000 people a day. That was its tourist volume at the time he visited us. The committee was completely taken with his philosophy that systems were going to ultimately decay as a result of use. 'Why bury them into the bowels of the building? Put them on the outside, so that they could be easily replaced: service corridors, plumbing, electrical, escalators, elevators, and the like.' But we knew this was not going to fly for Dallas."[27]

The ideas were intriguing but not appealing. Stanley Marcus says, "I was interested in him until I found out that nobody at all liked his work! He was in the process of building a big office building in London. It was, I thought, crazy—not just contemporary, but a bit crazy, with forms coming out of nowhere—and without charm."[28]

Mary McDermott remembers, "Rogers was a wild man. I think we were all awed by him. He was so hot because of Beaubourg, and he was really gutsy. But we said to ourselves, 'We're *not* that gutsy.' It came down to I. M. and Rogers. We decided that Dallas was not ready for, could not handle Rogers. I. M. was the safe bet."[29]

—⁂—

THE LAST candidate was I. M. Pei. He arrived for his interview dressed in an impeccable grey suit, with a light grey shirt, a wine-colored tie with matching handkerchief in his breast pocket, sporting cufflinks and Corbusier-style glasses. "He was a picture of sartorial splendor, just perfect," Leonard Stone remembers. After introductions, he sat down, and Stanley Marcus opened up with the same question. "Well, I. M., why would you like to design our concert hall?"

The committee heard the answer that it had been waiting for since the beginning of the project. Pei replied, "Stanley, I've never designed a concert hall before. But I've made up my mind that before I die I must do a great concert hall."

"All I heard was 'great,'" Leonard Stone recalled. "If he was going to do it, it was going to be great. There was no question. You thought, clearly, this man would do that."[30]

The committee had many reasons for selecting Pei, but that simple declaration tipped the scales even more heavily in his favor.

As DSA president, Don Stone also sat in on all the architect interviews, including Pei's.

"Two things he said sold the committee on him. One was, 'I am a great fan of symphonic music and symphony halls. I've been in almost every one in the world. I think I understand what makes them work and not work. I'm convinced that one can design a hall that has public space where two people are comfortable, or two hundred people, or two thousand people. I am convinced that that can be done with good architecture.' The second thing he said was, 'I intend to design a symphony hall before I take down my

I.M. Pei (*DSO archives*)

shingle, and I'd love to do this one. If it's not this one it's going to be another one. I want you to understand that I don't assume that I will get two. So whichever hall I get will be I. M. Pei's [symphony] hall; it won't be his assistants'.' Those comments convinced everybody. Pei didn't try to sell anybody anything."[31]

❦

CHARLES Young of I. M. Pei & Partners, who eventually became the principal architect of the concert room interior, remembers the excitement at the Pei firm when they received word from Dallas. "I. M. stepped out of his office during our Christmas party and asked me to come in. He was very excited. 'We've got the Dallas project!' He knew I had wanted to do a theatre for a long time. Since I was a teenager, I have been a great opera and music lover. I spent a year in Europe studying all the great theatres. My undergraduate thesis at Georgia Tech and graduate thesis at Harvard were about opera houses."[32]

———∽———

DSA Board President Don Stone announced Pei's appointment as architect of the new concert hall on December 30, 1980. A key element in the selection had been Pei's pledge to be personally involved in every facet of the hall. Don Stone told the press that the symphony board had "taken precautions" against cost overruns like those the city had encountered on prior projects, notably Dallas City Hall. "We've already made this quite clear," he said. "We've discussed this with Mr. Pei, and he has accepted the responsibility not to have cost overruns."[33] Within a couple of years, that discussion and Pei's pledge were to echo with profound irony, for the phrase "cost overrun" would become closely and painfully associated with the concert hall.

Chapter Seven

SELECTING AN ACOUSTICIAN

I really felt Russell [Johnson] was the only one who had any idea what he was doing. After we concluded our interviews, we discussed it amongst ourselves. It was clear to us that Russell Johnson was the one we felt we could back. The way he answered our questions made sense to us. His answers jibed with what our experiences had been as performers. He was our committee's unanimous selection.[1]

JOHN KITZMAN, DSO PRINCIPAL TROMBONE

THE SMALLER unit of the concert hall committee went about its search for an acoustician in a different fashion. From the beginning, Meyerson realized that there was no point in building a new hall unless it had excellent acoustics. Otherwise, there was little to be said for spending a large sum to replace the splendidly inadequate Music Hall at Fair Park. The committee's plan included visiting representative halls designed by each of its principal candidates, a process that began before the autumn 1980 Europe trip. In addition, the members talked to the architectural finalists about acoustics and what they knew about acousticians. Finally, each acoustician finalist would interview in Dallas.

Meyerson sent out solicitations for proposals to acousticians on EDS letterhead in early October 1980. He specified the following:

The building is to be a single-purpose hall for symphonic and popular music. It is to have approximately 2700 seats with appropriate foyer, public areas and bar/coffee facilities. Also, the structure must include all the necessary space and facilities for the musicians and DSO offices and staff. It is our desire to build a structure that is noteworthy for both its acoustics and its architecture.

This project will be funded by both municipal and private funds, and it is our hope that we can develop a satisfactory plan within the next twelve to eighteen months so that we can go to the public with a bond issue vote. . . . It is our desire to build the outstanding concert hall of the century within the limits of the funds which may be available.

This mandate evolved directly from Eugene Bonelli's work with his acoustics subcommittee. Bonelli says, "The acoustics brief grew out of visits to other halls and studying various materials about acoustics that we obtained. But more important than our reading list were the notes—and I took a *lot* of notes—from the visits to halls and talks with the acousticians."[2]

The pool of acoustical consultants was exceedingly small in comparison to the number of available architects. Three principal individuals and their firms were serious candidates almost from the outset: Cyril Harris, Christopher Jaffe, and, from Artec Consultants, Russell Johnson. The committee also briefly considered Abraham Melzer;[3] the East Coast firm of Bolt, Beranek and Newman; and a German acoustician, Manfred R. Schroeder, who, in 1974, had published a comparative study of European concert halls with some colleagues at University of Göttingen. Melzer was deemed to lack sufficient experience to take on the Dallas project. Eugene Bonelli had run across Schroeder's name during the 1980 European tour, when the committee heard a performance at the Berlin Philharmonie. Bolt, Beranek and Newman had two unsatisfactory halls to its credit: Lincoln Center's Philharmonic Hall (the original 1962 structure) and San Francisco's Davies Hall. Neither building was a strong recommendation for its acoustician. Almost from the beginning it was a three-man competition among Harris, Jaffe, and Johnson.

The committee's initial plan was to visit representative halls by each of the three principal candidates. Jaffe had done the acoustics in the Sala Nezahualcoyotl at the Universidad Nacional Atonoma de Mexico in Mexico City, an architecturally interesting edifice that was one of the early halls in the round, *i.e.,* surrounding the orchestra with audience seating. (The most famous example is the Berlin Philharmonie). The Mexico City hall made a good impression on the committee. Domestically, the group heard Jaffe's Boettcher Hall in Denver, which commanded interest as the first surround concert hall in the United States, but was less satisfying in its sound. Harris had recently opened a new hall in Salt Lake City. His other halls were Avery Fisher at Lincoln Center (the 1976 reconstruction), the Kennedy Center in Washington, and Orchestra Hall in Minneapolis. The Johnson/Artec Consultants halls were El Pomar Great Hall at Pikes Peak Center in Colorado Springs and Hamilton Place in Hamilton, Ontario, which had opened in the early 1970s. Another Canadian hall with Johnson acoustics, Centre-in-the-Square in Kitchener, Ontario, had just opened in September 1980. A fourth Artec hall in Nottingham, England, was nearly complete and looked promising.

According to Leonard Stone, Lloyd Haldeman had favored Harris after his renovation of Lincoln Center into Avery Fisher Hall. Music Director Eduardo Mata wanted Jaffe to get the commission. Shortly after arriving in Dallas, Stone asked Mata, "Who's going to be our acoustician?" Mata replied, "Chris Jaffe," without hesitation, as if the decision had already been made. Mata had worked closely with Jaffe on the Sala Nezahualcoyotl. Stone knew four Johnson halls: those in Hamilton and Kitchener, both in Ontario, Canada; Centennial Concert

Hall in Winnipeg; and the Crouse-Hinds Concert Theater in Syracuse, New York. He was an early proponent of Johnson and Artec Consultants.

Part of what convinced Stone to support Johnson was a comment that Johnson had made: "You must always listen to the conductor, and you must always pay attention to what the conductor tells you, but you must never design a room and a hall to support the particular position of a given conductor, because conductors will come and go. The orchestra will remain, and the hall will remain. So you've got to design a room that will be long-lasting and all-embracing."[4]

AFTER the bond election in November 1979, Stone had received a call from Johnson, asking for an appointment with Stone and Symphony Board Chairman Decherd. Stone was happy to accommodate the request. Their first meeting took place at *The Dallas Morning News* offices. Today, Stone acknowledges, "I did everything I could do to defeat any of the other acoustical candidates, and to engineer Russell into the position of getting the commission. I was so convinced that Russell was 'The One' to do this job that I was willing to go toe-to-toe with my music director, who wanted Chris Jaffe, and toe-to-toe with Mort, the chairman of my committee, who wanted Cyril Harris."[5]

Meyerson denies that he favored Harris, but he did have an uncanny experience early on in his learning process that encouraged him to give Harris every consideration. "Over the course of the two years after I formed the group, members of the committee went to some fifty symphony halls. None of us heard all of them. I went to about twenty-five, including the eight or nine we heard in Europe. The first place I went was Avery Fisher. I was astounded by how long the hall was and how bad the sight lines were. I listened to the first half of the program sitting up in the first balcony. The chairs were at an angle, although the hall was rectangular. I thought that was weird. At the intermission, I turned to the man sitting next to me and asked, 'Excuse me, do you come to the Philharmonic often?' 'Yes, I come to every Philharmonic concert.' 'I'm from out of town; would you mind if I talked to you for a few minutes about this hall?' He said, 'Not at all.'"

Meyerson started by asking about the seats. Could the gentleman explain why they were angled that way? He answered, "Sure. Because we can get sixteen more seats in the hall than if they face toward the center."

Meyerson was fascinated. "Isn't that interesting." Seat count had already come up in committee meetings.

"Oh yes," his concert neighbor agreed and began talking very knowledgeably about Avery Fisher Hall. About ten minutes into this conversation, Meyerson interrupted. "Excuse me, my name is Morton Meyerson, and this is my wife Marlene. I'm from Dallas, and we're thinking about building a new symphony hall, and I'm the chairman of the concert hall committee."

"Hi, my name is Cyril Harris."

Meyerson was stunned. (He later claimed, "I almost passed out!") He managed to recover from his astonishment to reply, "Ah! I've read about you."

Harris replied, "Ah! What have you read about me?"

"I know you're a professor at Columbia. I know that you're an architecture man. I also know that you know acoustics. I also know that you worked on this hall." Meyerson rattled off a few more details about Harris's career.

Cyril Harris commented, "You've been studying me."

Meyerson countered, "No, I've been studying halls." He often wondered if it was fate, or God's will, that had preordained their fortuitous encounter. And Harris did become one of the acoustical candidates.[6]

—⁊—

AT LEONARD Stone's recommendation, Eugene Bonelli and Peter Ryan, then the DSO's concert hall committee liaison, traveled to Hamilton, Ontario, to hear the Boston Symphony on tour. Joseph Silverstein, then concertmaster of the Boston Symphony, had opined that Hamilton was one of the orchestra's favorite halls, a recommendation that came as very high praise.[7]

Bonelli recalls the concert clearly. "They played the Beethoven Fifth Symphony. I was impressed with how the celli and basses sounded. I was overwhelmed with the resonance of the bass, and the way they carried. As I remember, the hall was brick and concrete inside, not wood and warm surfaces. That convinced me that Russell Johnson was right, that bass resonance comes more from the solidity of the surface than it does from specific materials."[8]

During the process of exploring halls, Johnson earned a reputation with the committee for being tenacious. On several occasions, he surfaced without warning during their various visits to both his and others' halls. "Russell had a habit of popping up unannounced everywhere and anywhere," says Leonard Stone. "He would find out where the committee was going next. In London, when we went through Royal Festival Hall, Russell walked in with a horrendous head cold! He was wheezing and sneezing, and looked like he was walking in the rain, had slept in his suit, and it dried on him. He was disheveled and running a fever. He showed up more than once. Finally, it reached the point where Mort said to me, 'You tell Russell that if he shows up at one more place, he's not going to get this job!' Where were we going next? Kitchener, and who appeared? Russell! I tried to convince Mort, 'You know, you ought to be thrilled by having the opportunity to hire an acoustician who continues to go back to his projects to hear how they're doing. He doesn't just design them and leave them.'"[9]

Bonelli took advantage of Johnson's presence to pepper him with questions. "I picked his brain. 'What do you believe are the factors that give a room great acoustics?' I made notes on his answers. Our criteria grew directly out of those kinds of conversations and notes. We had similar conversations with Chris Jaffe and Cyril Harris, but I wasn't nearly as impressed with the way they pinpointed the factors that contribute to room acoustics. Russell showed a better understanding of how to achieve the ideal room acoustics for an orchestra. Chris Jaffe was, in my view, too tied in with the electronic amplification of sound. His experience had been along those lines. Cyril Harris had a formula for a room that he had produced four times—we visited Lincoln Center, Kennedy Center, Minnesota's Orchestra Hall, and Salt Lake City—and I didn't think any of those four halls really worked that successfully. For me, that eliminated him. I didn't want another Cyril Harris hall."[10]

Smaller unit committee member Richard Levin recalls, "We even toyed with the idea of having the acoustician being the main guy. Russell very much lobbied for it. He was a man who appeared to be a genius in his trade. We thought we were going to get the best out of him. He's a fairly idiosyncratic man. We were worried about that, but, you know, that comes with genius."[11]

The selection process culminated in two interviews for each candidate, one with the committee and one with the players. The three candidates made their presentations to the acoustician selection subcommittee on December 12 and 13, 1980, again at EDS, but this time in the office of the president, Mort Meyerson. They would meet separately on the same day with the players' committee in the conference room at Fair Park Music Hall. For the presentation at EDS, each of them was asked to be prepared to outline acoustical objectives he would develop with regard to number of seats and needed flexibility in the use of the hall. More specifically, each was to describe his recommended procedure for acoustical design of the new hall to meet the requirements listed in the solicitation letter inviting proposals. These parameters matched those in the developing program brief.

—☙—

BY THE end of December, Meyerson had announced to the symphony's executive board that Jaffe had been eliminated as a candidate and that the final decision between Harris and Johnson would be made by the end of January 1981.

Bonelli had made up his mind in favor of Johnson at the time that he heard the Boston Symphony play in the Hamilton, Ontario, auditorium. "Russell's Canadian halls swayed me more to him than anything else. These were halls that did not have, in my view, distinguished architects; they weren't great architectural presences. Yet with minimally expensive materials, Russell showed the ability to deliver wonderful acoustics that had that great after-ring and resonance that we wanted but also had clarity. The trip to Canada convinced me."[12]

It remained for Bonelli to persuade the balance of the committee. "I think the experience of hearing music on the European trip demonstrated to the committee members how wonderful sound can be. Russell eventually developed enough credibility. They trusted me, and eventually they developed enough confidence in Russell to believe that [his theories were] not a whim, but rather a recommendation based on substantive evaluation of all the issues.

Russell Johnson (*DSO archives*)

Russell was not personally popular with the committee. In fact, some people thought he was too messy and dressed poorly! My feeling was that those are cosmetic things. If the man knows more about room acoustics than anybody else in the world, then we ought to swallow that in favor of the music."[13]

Perhaps of greatest importance was the reaction of the Dallas Symphony musicians, who accompanied members of the small group on some of the domestic trips to hear other halls. DSO principal percussion Doug Howard, chair of the players' committee, says, "I hoped we would be involved in planning backstage facilities and the amenities for the musicians. It turned out that we were very involved. The first thing our committee did was develop a questionnaire to orchestra members, to get their input." Howard remembers Meyerson's smaller unit bringing in the acoustician candidates and asking the musicians to meet with each one. "We asked a lot of fundamental questions about acoustics in a concert hall, types of materials they would use, hall shapes, basic questions about the parameters that affect the way a hall is ultimately going to sound. We liked some of what we heard, but with some answers, just instinctively, as musicians, we knew that there was something wrong. We weren't buying it."[14]

DSO principal trombone John Kitzman, who served on the players' committee, recalls the process. "We looked at blueprints. We interviewed the acousticians, and we made a recommendation. If the board had decided to go with somebody else, they would have, but we thought that Russell Johnson was the right person. I wasn't interested in anybody else who was considered."[15] Another players' committee member, principal bass Clifford Spohr, was impressed by Johnson's explanations as to what was necessary to achieve good sound in a hall. "He talked in very specific terms: the fact that acoustic clouds that had been placed in a lot of halls over the orchestra did nothing but reflect treble sound, and that to get a good reflection of the full orchestra sound, particularly the bass instruments, you need reflective surface that is massive, thick, and heavy, at least twenty-eight feet in its smallest dimension. Otherwise, the bass sound loops around and doesn't get reflected at all. It was so specific. The other candidates didn't seem to have the specifics of what was needed in their minds. They couldn't describe it to us. Russell seemed very able to address our individual concerns."[16]

The musicians then made their case before the smaller unit, which had concluded its separate interviews with the candidates. As Howard remembers it, "We were called to meet with Gene Bonelli and Mort Meyerson in a classroom at SMU. None of us had ever met Meyerson before. He is a very strong personality. I have to admit that I walked in there and my knees were shaking a little bit, because I had the feeling that Mort didn't like our recommendation. I thought he was leaning toward Cyril Harris. When we told him what we thought, he really grilled us. He wanted to know specifics: 'What is it about Russell that makes you think he's the right one?' I walked out of there with a sense of foreboding that they were going to hire Cyril Harris. I think we would have gotten a much different concert hall had they done that." Howard took the extra step of writing a letter, reiterating the players' feelings.[17] In mid-January, acoustics subcommittee Chairman Bonelli summarized his own thoughts about acoustical goals and the two final candidates' abilities to fulfill those goals. "I found both [Johnson multi-purpose] halls to have better resonance and foundation sound than any of the Harris halls. I would also rank them better from the standpoint of warmth and blend," he wrote.[18] Within two weeks, he reported to the executive board that the orchestra committee fully endorsed Johnson and that Maestro Mata concurred with their choice. While these meetings and deliberations took place, Stone continued to lobby in favor of Johnson, behind the scenes, with anyone who would listen. On February 24, 1981, the Dallas Symphony announced publicly that Russell Johnson and Artec Consultants would be the hall's acoustical consultants.

Bonelli remembers, "We picked Russell because we felt he had a better grasp of room acoustics than any of the others. He had a better sense of the basic principles entailed in producing a great hall. We also felt that he was not so formulaic as Cyril Harris. Since we wanted an aesthetic hall as well, we thought with Russell we could at least get someone who could work cooperatively with I. M. Pei. That may have been folly, but we did think it!"[19]

The Dallas concert hall was a critically important project to Artec, according to Stone, especially because it was going to be designed by I. M. Pei. "Pei is one of the three or four major signature architects of our time," he says. "The world architectural press pays attention to any building that the Pei office produces. If Russell could be associated with it, it was going to bring that much more attention to the facility."[20]

Stone believes that Meyerson's decision to hire Pei and Johnson as equals was brilliant. "That's rarely done. Usually the architect is hired, and quite often the architect hires the acoustician, or the acoustician is made subordinate to the architect. Here's a case where Russell had equal access, equal power, equal weight. Frankly, I don't think I. M. liked that. Certainly he wasn't used to that. But I think that was a good thing, because the role of the acoustician was protected, and it dignified the role of acoustics in that building on an equal plane to architecture. This building's ultimate judgment would come as one of the great acoustical gems and one of the great pieces of architecture of this era. It needed both. Even if architecturally it wasn't glorious, if acoustically it would be great, it would always be referred to as one of the great places to make music."[21]

—⌇—

CITY of Dallas policy mandated that the city must have a contract, approved by city council, prior to making payment on any project. City requirements also included a maximum project cost. No such cost was yet available; furthermore, the city's dollar contribution to the concert hall would not be determined until after the next bond election. The symphony's disbursements to architect, acoustician, and other consultants were all to be credited to its forty percent share of the cost of design and construction of the new hall.

Concurrent with the official announcement of Johnson's selection, Richard Levin, the sole attorney in Meyerson's smaller unit, began drafting contracts between the Dallas Symphony Association and its new architectural and acoustical consultants. By May, Levin had delegated that task to George T. Lee, Jr., one of his partners at the Dallas office of Akin, Gump, Strauss, Hauer & Feld. Because another of the firm's partners was a member of city council, Akin, Gump had determined that all its work on behalf of the symphony would be provided *pro bono,* in order to avoid any conflict of interest. Lee reported to the executive board that the city attorney's office was reviewing the interim contracts. These addressed the preliminary phase of work on the building, and also a rendering and a model.[22]

Pei's draft contract for the preliminary phase was initially projected for $500,000, of which $100,000 was designated for Pei & Partners' professional fees and the balance for the architects' staff and outside consultants. By mid-September, the contract had been renegotiated for a subtotal of $675,000 for I. M. Pei & Partners, comprising $100,000 professional fees, an estimated $525,000 staff time based on actual time worked on the project, and an estimated $50,000 for direct reimbursable expenses such as telephone and travel. Actual billings to the architect, for consulting by outside consultants such as the structural, mechanical, and electrical engineers, were not yet estimated. At the time, the DSO's concert hall fund had $600,000 in it.

The initial contract was to be valid through April 1982 and specified that Pei & Partners would provide a model of the hall. With a bond election projected for calendar 1982, such a model would be necessary for public relations.

Artec's initial arrangement with the symphony was a ten-week consulting agreement intended to cover the initial design development phase. Russell Johnson's firm agreed to work on preliminary budgets and to prepare various reports about different aspects of the hall from the standpoint of acoustics. Four additional letters of agreement would follow before a formal contract was executed.[23] Artec's responsibilities ultimately included theatre consulting, including performance equipment, as well as acoustics.

AFTER the architect selection process, Mort Meyerson had declared that anyone who didn't know anything about acoustics could resign from the smaller unit immediately. Mary McDermott protested, "But Mort, I've learned so much, and it's going to be so much fun! Let me stay!"[24] Meyerson was adamant, going so far as to call McDermott and Louise Kahn at home in an effort to remove them from his small group. "You're ruining my group dynamic," he told each of them. Each woman dug in her heels and refused to capitulate. "You really don't want to do that," they both told him. He backed off.[25]

When the committee had worked together for about a year, he tried again. "At the end of that first year," Meyerson says, "we were preparing to shift from doing the brief and 'make work' work and learning and so on, to really getting with the program. I met with Leonard and said, 'OK, now we need to have the race horses. We can't have plough horses.'" In his view, it was time for Louise Kahn and Mary McDermott to leave. He wanted them off the small group.[26] Once again, two tenacious and committed women stood their ground. Meyerson had met his match.

OVER time, Meyerson's opinion of both women changed. "Mary McDermott was the scion of a very powerful family who had her own problems with her mother and her own position," he recalls. "She brought all that to the committee. She *also* brought energy, enthusiasm, dedication, and other positive qualities. After she made her case the second time, my respect for her grew." By midway through the project, he realized he had come to rely on her opinions and observations and to consider carefully points she drew to his attention. "Mary went from an ornament on the committee to a full-fledged, active member who contributed as much as anyone. That's really quite a tribute to her."[27]

In working with Louise Kahn, Meyerson discovered that she, too, had another side. "It took me several years to see it," he acknowledges. "I stopped listening to the rhetoric of what Louise was telling me, and started listening to content. In the beginning, I thought she was off by a mile in most of what she said. Over time, I noticed that she would have an insight that nobody else had that was absolutely valid. I couldn't hear that before, because she was so irritating and demanding. There was a change in Louise in how she was accepted, not just by me, but by the others on the committee, too. I discovered she wasn't just a society matron who liked power. I actually grew fond of her as I discovered her depth of knowledge about music and her sensitivity, which she never showed in the arena of the committee. I grew to respect her, because she made a very real contribution."[28]

Still, the committee's road was gutted with potholes, and its meetings often crackled as the small group grappled with key decisions about the hall. They were about to face two of the most serious debates of the entire project.

Chapter Eight

A SHORT PRIMER ON ROOM ACOUSTICS

In order that hearing may be good in any auditorium, it is necessary that the sound should be sufficiently loud; that the simultaneous components of a complex sound should maintain their proper relative intensities; and that the successive sounds in rapidly moving articulation, either of speech or music, should be clear and distinct, free from each other and from extraneous noises.[1]

WALLACE CLEMENT SABINE, 1900

THE FATHER of modern acoustical theory is generally acknowledged to be Wallace Clement Sabine, the acoustical consultant for Boston Symphony Hall, which was built in 1900. In an essay published that year, Sabine stated the basic qualities, quoted above, that listeners desire in a space for music: loudness, reverberation, clarity, and the absence of any background noise. Those qualities remain cornerstones of acoustical thought. Sabine's collaboration with the architects McKim, Mead, and White on Boston Symphony Hall gave him practical experience to expand his theories and prescribe how to achieve good acoustics. In 1915, he wrote: "Broadly considered, there are two, and only two, variables in a room—shape [including size] and materials [including furnishings]."[2] The classic rectangular shape of Boston Symphony Hall remains Sabine's greatest legacy to concert hall acoustics, and his identification of materials as a crucial component was prescient. He was a proponent of at least one additional theory that not only influenced his most famous room but also dominated much of twentieth-century concert hall design: the concept of reverberation time, the time it takes reflected sound to decay to inaudibility. Sabine was the first to measure reverberation time in different venues, and he established it as an important criterion for evaluating concert hall acoustics. Size, shape, and materials were the factors that would yield the required loudness, balance, and clarity at the heart of the ideal concert room mandated by the Dallas concert hall committee's brief.

The laws of physics govern the way the sound dissipates. As a person moves farther away from a sound source, its intensity wanes. When an orchestra plays in an open-air environment, the "room" is infinite. Nothing impedes the direct travel of the sound, and the amount of sound each audience member hears is solely a function of the listener's distance from the orchestra. Acoustic shells behind orchestras in outdoor concerts are designed to channel that sound toward the listener, increasing the amount of sound the listener receives. Any enclosed space alters the behavior of sound, because sound waves reflect off of walls and ceilings. For audience members, there are several basic differences between listening to music outside and listening in an enclosed space. The sound reflections in an enclosed space make music seem louder because direct sound from the orchestra is reinforced by the additional sound reflected by the room boundaries. In addition to increasing loudness, reflected sound alters the quality of the music, allowing for warmth, bloom, envelopment, and spaciousness. These are some of the subjective terms most frequently used to describe the acoustic experience of hearing music in a good concert hall. They are qualities lacking when listening to music outdoors. The acoustician's job is to pull together these qualities and achieve the right balance among them.

Another phenomenon that occurs in enclosed space is that music persists longer, apparently "hanging" in the air. The latter effect is particularly noticeable at the conclusion of a loud piece in a concert room or after a significant pause in the music. Sabine's concept of reverberation time is a way to quantify this phenomenon. The combination of direct and reflected sound in a room defines the acoustical personality of the space.

The sound of a musical ensemble such as an orchestra is a finite resource. Even a large orchestra comprising one hundred musicians can produce only a limited amount of sound. Listeners want to perceive that sound with sufficient loudness. The bottom line for a musical acoustician is simple audibility of musical sound: the music must be heard. Reflected sound has farther to travel in a larger room, diluting its strength and making it less loud. Limiting the size of the area in which sound travels is thus the most fundamental component of concert hall design.

—❧—

IN MODERN western civilization, the size of a concert room has been a function of projected audience: How many persons were expected? If a monarch or nobleman chose to include music as a part of an evening's entertainment, the music-making took place in a large palace room, probably the ballroom or throne room, that could accommodate all the invited guests. By modern concert standards, such a room was small, as was the ensemble. A court orchestra in the 1720s, for example, comprised perhaps 18 to 24 players. They might perform for an audience of as few as several dozen listeners and, almost certainly, not more than a couple of hundred. The room served its users' needs.

During the late eighteenth and early nineteenth centuries, as public concert life was established and the experience of hearing live music became more readily available to the middle classes, public auditoriums with greater seating capacity were constructed. Orchestras grew as well. Haydn's orchestra at Eszterháza consisted of 23 players. He wrote his "Paris" Symphonies for the *Concert de la Loge Olympique,* which boasted an ensemble as large as 56 to 65. Salomon's performances of Haydn's "London" Symphonies in the Hanover Square Rooms featured an orchestra of 40 players. Beethoven's Symphony No. 9 was premiered in 1824 by an orchestra of 61, large for its day. Still, new concert halls were built to accommodate such larger ensembles as well as more audience members.

By the last decade of the nineteenth century, the orchestra had grown to monumental size in the works of composers such as Strauss and Mahler. Their compositions call for as many as 100 to 105 players. While large orchestras remained that size through the twentieth century, the expansion of concert halls continued. Sabine's Boston Symphony Hall has a seating capacity of 2,625. Successor halls increased that number to 3,000 and even 4,000, but none of the large halls achieved the acoustical success of Boston or the great European halls.

Only gradually have acousticians and lay listeners learned about the way musical sound behaves in rooms of various sizes and shapes. The area occupied by the audience, rather than the number of seats, determines the absorbing power of a room from clothing, hair, seating upholstery, etc. Modern building codes require more area for the same amount of seating because of fire regulations and other factors governing modern construction. A nineteenth-century hall with a seating capacity of 2,000 persons would only accommodate 1,200 or so today. (The Dallas concert hall would be a large hall in seating area, by historic standards.) Conformance with modern building codes would require "pushing" walls farther apart and increasing the square footage of the audience chamber. That, in turn, would force sound to travel longer, making it less loud. Artec would have to address these issues in designing a new concert hall for Dallas.

ROOM shape is nearly as important as room size in determining the success of a concert hall. Historically, two shapes have dominated, rectangle and fan- or wedge-shape, with the occasional appearance of a third: surround. All of them trace their architectural ancestry to ancient Greece and Rome. They have distinct properties for music. The Greco-Roman arena, although not an enclosed space, is the upper end of the size spectrum. Huge oval arenas such as the Colosseum in Rome are direct predecessors of the modern sports stadium, an unfortunate and ill-advised space for music-making except perhaps for marching bands and heavily amplified rock concerts. Translated to indoor space for music, the idea of the arena becomes a surround hall such as London's Royal Albert Hall, which seats more than 5,000. The surround concept has never gained great currency, probably because surround halls do not respond to the different ways that instrumental sound travels. Although a few good surround halls exist for concert music, notably the Berlin Philharmonie, such a configuration also compromises sight lines for audience members seated behind the players.

The Greco-Roman half-moon amphitheatre is the ancestor of the modern public auditorium with a fan or semi-circular shape, which, by and large, has proven unsuccessful for music. The third shape is the rectangle, which has roots in the ancient Greek *odeion* or music room. It developed into the "shoebox"-shaped concert room, which predominated from the late eighteenth to the early twentieth centuries. Historically, these three principal shapes—the arena-like surround hall, the fan-shaped Greco-Roman amphitheatre, and the rectangle—account for virtually all concert rooms. Early public concert halls were primarily rectangular. The space was easy to build using traditional construction techniques. Rooms remained narrow because of the structural limitations of unsupported transverse timber beams.

—⁓—

ON THE heels of Sabine's pioneering work in room acoustics and the acclaim accorded to Boston Symphony Hall, large multi-purpose halls became popular during the middle decades of the twentieth century. The use of a steel structural frame rather than traditional timber and masonry construction permitted long spans, deep balcony overhangs, and the use of lightweight materials for walls and ceilings. These apparent advances allowed architects to depart from the rectangular form of the traditional concert hall. The new structural designs were validated by scientific calculation of stresses and strains. Architects and acousticians embraced Sabine's scientific work on reverberation time, but not his recommendations on room shape, which were unsupported by scientific data. Instead, they came to favor a shape that fanned out from the stage, thereby increasing seating capacity and providing front-facing sight lines and shorter viewing distances for audience members than the traditional shoebox.

Despite the success of Boston Symphony Hall, fan- or wedge-shaped halls were the design of choice from about 1910 on, becoming particularly common in the United States. In Britain, the influential work of acoustician Hope Bagenal in the 1930s established the purported superiority of this plan. "The best plan is the fan shape with the part of the walls to left and right of platform front turned over to form on section a deep proscenium splay," Bagenal pronounced in *Planning for Good Acoustics*.[3] His authoritative stance held sway for several decades. Relatively few new venues were constructed during the first half of the twentieth century because of the two world wars and the intervening international depression. After the Second World War, new construction boosted reviving economies on both sides of the Atlantic, and large, fan-shaped halls proliferated. In the United States, ringing endorsements perpetuating the reign of the fan-shaped hall came from the theatre and acoustical consultant George C. Izenour, whose massive *Theater Design* remains a bookend of any library on the subject.[4] Only after a substantial number of oversize, fan-shaped halls had been built did it dawn on listeners that the acoustics in those buildings were poor for music. It took rather longer to discover why.

The fledgling profession of acousticians began evaluating halls, comparing reputedly great, good, so-so, and bad halls, in an effort to determine what characteristics separated them into one category or the other. A number of early studies after Sabine emphasized the importance of reverberation time, but none could explain why certain halls with purportedly "ideal" reverberation time still have indifferent acoustics.

In his landmark 1962 study, *Music, Acoustics and Architecture,*[5] Leo Beranek codified acoustical data and subjective descriptions of three dozen major international halls, including some prominent opera houses. It was the first comparative study with extensive architectural and acoustical data for concert halls. Beranek also set forth a glossary for concert hall acoustics, including definitions for terms such as *intimacy, clarity, reverberation, spaciousness, warmth,* and *brilliance,* providing the lay listener with a non-technical vocabulary for use in discussing subjective perception of music.

Beginning in the 1970s, the next generation of acoustics researchers undertook studies that included subjective listener reactions in the evaluative process. Rather than limiting observations to data that could be measured in a concert hall with a single microphone, a group based in Göttingen, Germany, invented a method whereby listeners could compare the acoustical quality of different halls by hearing multiple loudspeaker reproductions of music in a special space called an anechoic chamber (a room with no reflected sound). The researchers simply asked listeners to identify their preference, without requiring them to describe sound.[6]

A key difference in this new approach was the recognition that a pair of human ears can distinguish the direction from which sound emanates. A single microphone cannot. By using listener response instead of microphone response, acoustics researchers established a more direct connection to the way human beings perceive live music. Specifically, they determined that the difference between what the listener's left and right ears receive contributes to a sense of envelopment by the sound. As early as 1966, the German acoustician, Manfred Schroeder, was exploring how sound waves travel in an enclosure with a specific shape and specific materials. In the mid-1980s, he summarized the aspect of his work pertaining to preference studies. "The greater the dissimilarity between the two ear signals (as one would obtain in old-style narrow halls with high ceilings) the greater the consensus preference, *independent of individual tastes.*"[7] Acousticians dubbed this phenomenon interaural (or binaural) dissimilarity. Using the information provided by just one ear, the brain can perceive total sound energy (for example, the loudness of full orchestra), the delay of early sound reflections, and some reverberation. With the input of both ears, binaural hearing—like stereophonic recording—detects the direction from which sounds are arriving, enhancing the listening experience significantly.

The difference is analogous to that of seeing with one eye as opposed to two. The addition of the slightly different picture that the second eye provides allows the viewer to "construct" a third dimension: depth perception. Similarly, the second ear lends the listener the aural "third dimension"—the sense of being surrounded by sound or enveloped by it. Because ears are situated on each side of the human head, the listener receives direct sound simultaneously in both ears. On the other hand, sound arriving from the listener's sides, provided by what acousticians call lateral reflections, reaches each ear at slightly different times. That difference enables the brain to construct the sense of envelopment that acousticians endeavor to achieve for their audience.

This 1970s research yielded an entirely new approach for analyzing concert listening: the concept that lateral sound reflections arriving at the listener's ears from left and right give the greatest amount of difference in what each ear hears. This effect provides a greater sense of being enveloped by the music. Acoustics researchers further determined that narrow rectangular halls provide the intense, early arriving lateral sound that listeners prefer. Fan-shaped halls, on the other hand, do not. After years of conjecture, acousticians were finally determining the reasons that fan-shaped halls were almost certainly destined for acoustical failure. At the same time they were beginning to understand *why* the halls that had achieved legendary status: notably Vienna's Grosser Musikvereinssaal, Amsterdam's Concertgebouw, Boston's Symphony Hall, and Zurich's Tonhalle, had entered that lofty domain. Specifically, their relatively small size, their shape, and comparatively narrow width combined to provide strong, early reflections. What remained was to determine other reasons for those halls' success and also ways in which the known successes could be emulated or improved upon.

—❧—

AFTER size and shape, the next most important component of room acoustics is materials. If one throws a ball against a wall that has a hard, flat surface, the ball will bounce back with less energy than it had when it was thrown but still with quite a lot. If that same wall is covered with spongy material, or a thin material with air pockets between layers, the ball's energy will be absorbed, making its return bounce less lively. Sound waves behave in an analogous fashion. If you place your hand on a thin wall in a room where a double bass or timpani is playing, you can feel the wall vibrate. Any vibration in the wall means that some of the sound energy is lost and the sound reflections off that wall are less strong. The heavier and stiffer the wall, the less vibration one feels. Solid walls, floors, ceilings, and soffits are thus desirable components of a concert room interior. The great European halls have massive walls constructed of load-bearing masonry, as well as high ceilings, which allow for more reverberation.

Russell Johnson had studied nineteenth-century halls and concluded that strong, low-frequency sound (the sound that comes from instruments like double bass and trombone) is a major factor in endowing an orchestra with warmth, a quality defined by Leo Beranek as liveness or fullness of the bass tones, the subjective feeling of strength of bass.[8] Johnson had also noticed that many American halls from the 1950s and 1960s have poor sound because they have thin walls made of furred gypsum board. Use of thin wall materials kept construction costs down, but the acoustics suffered. The best nineteenth-century rooms had solid walls, heavy timber floors, and heavy plaster ceilings, allowing the low frequency sounds to persist. Johnson's colleagues at Bolt, Beranek and Newman, where he launched his career in the 1950s, found his ideas amusing. Their tests showed thin plaster reflecting efficiently to the lowest measurable frequencies. Johnson persisted, however, convinced that either the effects were *below* the lowest frequencies measurable in a test chamber or that the listener is more sensitive to bass sound than scientists surmised. He became a strong proponent of hard surfaces formed by massive materials lining the surfaces of the audience chamber.[9]

The Dallas concert hall committee had issued a simple directive: give us the best concert hall in the world. Johnson was one of the pioneers of variable acoustics devices to adjust the room acoustics in multi-purpose halls. By 1981, he had completed successful halls in Kitchener, Ontario; Hamilton, Ontario; and Syracuse, New York. Variable acoustics devices, including the use of the rear of the stage behind the orchestra to create a reverberation chamber, allowed these multi-purpose halls to be transformed from theatres into successful concert hall venues. Johnson was awarded the Dallas contract, in part, on the basis of his work in these halls.

In 1981, there was a strong case simply to rebuild a nineteenth-century shoebox concert hall for Dallas. Through his work in multi-purpose halls, however, Johnson had developed theories that did not fit with conventional views of acoustics. The new hall would be his opportunity to combine lessons learned from the great nineteenth-century halls with twentieth-century technology to build a modern hall for the next millennium.

Chapter Nine

FINDING A SITE

*Anywhere we locate will be a great improvement over where we are now,
but an arts district will elevate the standing of Dallas as a city which
cares about its quality of life, and with it I think we will tend to capture
other types of audiences for our concerts.*[1]

EDUARDO MATA, SEPTEMBER 1981

DISCUSSIONS about where to put the symphony hall had preceded the City of Dallas' formal plan to develop its Arts District. Even after the Carr, Lynch report was issued in autumn 1977, other areas besides the northeast edge of downtown Dallas remained under consideration. Before Robert Decherd's presidency, board activities concerning the hall were handled through a facilities committee, whose original chair was Philip Jonsson. After the failed 1978 bond election, Bill Hatfield took over as chairman of the facilities committee until Decherd asked Meyerson to assume responsibility for the concert hall project.

Early Site Consideration

By October 1978, Hatfield reported reviewing two proposals from developers for what he described as a "quasi public/private funded facility." One proposal specified downtown Dallas. The other, offered by H. Ross Perot, was on the Electronic Data Systems grounds in North Dallas, where so much of the symphony's patron base resided. City Manager George Schrader and Mayor Folsom met with Perot to discuss his offer. Ultimately, they decided that the proposal was generous, but a new hall should be in a location where the entire community could have ownership. The symphony's executive committee, acutely aware of the need for City of Dallas support, agreed that the facility should remain downtown. One month later, Hatfield had met with real estate developer Trammell Crow to discuss the downtown proposal. The board was leery. Would the new facility be the quality that the orchestra needed? Would the Dallas Symphony have first priority in reserving rehearsal and concert time? Who would bear the maintenance costs? They left the door open, but a consensus was growing that the DSA wanted to be in the driver's seat for planning purposes.

"Through the late 1970s, different people had ideas about how to design a symphony hall with their own property and development ownerships," summarizes Robert Decherd. "None of those sites seemed to be ideal. The one most talked about turned out to be the site of the LTV Tower, now Trammell Crow Center, the so-called 'museum site' because of its proximity to the land designated for the new museum. A lot of anticipatory discussion ran through the bond issue of 1978, which failed. Obviously there was a period of regrouping. People were disappointed. Philip [Jonsson], to his eternal credit, because he had most of the site discussions and negotiations, was already back at it by the fall, talking to people. He continued to make progress, anticipating that some mechanism would be developed for acquiring a site."[2]

Hatfield and Crow met again on December 11, 1978. Now, Crow said he wanted to proceed with the symphony hall, but not on any of his downtown properties. Instead, he recommended an area northwest of downtown, out Stemmons Freeway near Oak Lawn, where the InfoMart was later constructed. Hatfield agreed to check with George Schrader to see if this latest proposal was acceptable to the city.[3] The issue turned out to be moot, because by February 1979, the Stemmons–Oak Lawn site was no longer available.

George Schrader continued to push for the

An aerial view of the Arts District area in 1979 showing the Borden plant. (*Photo by James E. Langford*)

museum site. "That land was formerly owned by some people in the Rio Grande Valley," he recalls. "We identified it before the 1978 bond election. After the election failed, the knowledge surfaced that Trammell Crow had that property under contract to buy. He believed that it was a great office site, and he perceived the failure of the bond election as, in effect, a rejection of the plans for a symphony hall."[4]

Schrader and Mayor Bob Folsom met twice with Crow, trying to convince him to relinquish the Ross Avenue site. Their efforts were in vain. In spring 1979, Folsom finally said, "We might as well give up on this site. We're not going to get it, and we can't afford to condemn it. For my money, I think we ought to just give up." Trammell Crow had told them, "That land is a filet cut of downtown. It's too important as an office building site. Besides, it's the wrong place for the symphony hall." Schrader was astonished. For months, they had been talking about that land as the optimal location. He asked, "Trammell, if you think the hall is in the wrong place, why don't you tell me where you think it ought to go?" Crow replied, "It ought to go on Lucy's property."[5]

Crow's daughter, Lucy Crow Billingsley, had property at the east end of the designated Arts District. Bob Glaze, who had just retired as the chief financial officer of Trammell Crow Company, had been the agent to acquire the Arts District land for her, with the potential that this land might be swapped for other land. Ironically, it was property bounded by Woodall Rodgers Freeway, Central Expressway (a main north-south artery that runs through the east side of downtown Dallas), Ross Avenue, and Routh Street, facing Flora Street! The Arts District vision ultimately called for Flora to serve as a "connecting corridor" to the Dallas Museum of Fine Arts, which had been sited three blocks west.

—❧—

AFTER Mort Meyerson assumed responsibility for the concert hall in November 1979, one of the first subcommittees he appointed was site selection. Mrs. Eugene Jericho, secretary of the board of directors, chaired it; Philip Jonsson was co-chair. Initially, they held weekly meetings to establish criteria for the site and to review candidate land parcels. A minimum of two acres was required. Therefore, site size and configuration were of paramount importance. A relationship to the arts district would be a clear advantage to increase public identification with the evolving concept. Because Dallas is such an automobile-dependent metropolis, ample parking and site accessibility were crucial factors. Ideally, the adjacent land parcels would provide compatible and supportive development: shops, restaurants, and pedestrian-friendly public spaces.

Once I. M. Pei's selection as architect and Russell Johnson's as acoustician were determined, the issue of a site became preeminent. Selling the concept of a downtown Arts District was proving difficult because three potential sites within the designated Arts District had eluded the symphony.[6] Also under discussion through 1980 was a subterranean location across from the Plaza of the Americas Hotel (now Le Meridien Hotel) that was referred to as the "urban site." The site was to be bounded by Bryan, Olive, Pearl, and San Jacinto Streets. Although the land was just one block from the Arts District, it was not actually within it. During the architect interviews, each finalist was asked to assess the feasibility of the "urban site."

By January 1981, the site selection committee had reviewed twenty-five sites and studied eleven in detail. From that group, they recommended primary, secondary, and alternative sites in February, zeroing in on the Arts District–designated land then occupied by the Lone Star Cadillac dealership, Purolator Armored, and the Borden's milk processing plant.[7]

The site plan showed the center courtyard of the museum on an axis with Flora Street. According to Ted Amberg of Pei's Dallas office, I. M. Pei wanted the axis of the symphony

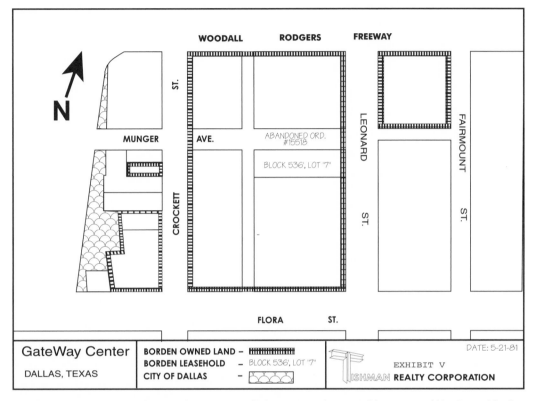

Tishman had an option to purchase Borden property with the provision that part of the space would be donated for the symphony hall site. Note the five small parcels of space in the block at the northwest corner of Crockett and Flora that the City of Dallas acquired through eminent domain proceedings. (*Cook archives*)

hall to be on Flora Street as well. That narrowed the choice to either the Lone Star Cadillac dealership or the Borden site. Amberg remembers, "The Lone Star Cadillac owner [Bill De Sanders] was a wealthy man. He was also terminally ill and had an opportunity to do something really great for the city, by donating part of that land that the Cadillac dealership owned. Leonard Stone and others approached him, meeting at the dealership offices. Months and months of negotiations and cajoling produced absolutely nothing."[8]

Jack Evans, who was elected Dallas mayor in April 1981, continued to meet with De Sanders and developer Trammell Crow about their respective property. According to former City Manager Schrader, Evans did not, at first, recognize the crucial importance of putting the concert hall near the museum in order to ensure the long-range success of the Arts District. Both Evans and his predecessor, Bob Folsom, were reportedly leaning toward a symphony site near Dallas City Hall as more achievable.[9] Schrader, however, was a strong advocate of urban renewal in the downtown area and believed in the concept of the Arts District.

Behind the scenes, Schrader and Mayor Evans reviewed options, quietly negotiating with Leonard Stone and Bill Seay of the symphony board. The key to the site still seemed to be the Borden's plant, occupying five acres on the northeast edge of the central business district. Remarkably enough, in downtown Dallas, a dairy processing plant was still operative in 1981. City Manager Schrader had heard that the Borden company was planning to move its plant out of downtown. He and his staff were trying to determine if the city could acquire the Borden property—strategically situated in the Arts District adjacent to Woodall Rodgers Freeway—at a price that it could afford. The idea was to combine the Borden property with land that the city already owned. Unfortunately, commercial developers had their eye on the same prize. Tishman Realty Corporation devised plans for a development called GateWay Center just south of Woodall Rodgers, bounded by Leonard, Flora, and Pearl Streets. Their proposed site plan included the purchase of 255,783 square feet of land from Borden.[10]

Tishman's GateWay proposal seemed to deal a deathblow to the symphony's hopes for an Arts District site. In May 1981, members of the symphony board were again talking about a plot on the south side of downtown, adjacent to Dallas City Hall and the Dallas Convention Center. The reason was land prices. As the new Woodall Rodgers Freeway on the north side of downtown neared completion, land prices continued to rise on speculation of increased accessibility and commercial activity in the Arts District area. By late spring, Arts District land had skyrocketed to $100 per square foot, as compared with about $70 per square foot elsewhere in downtown Dallas. Analysts speculated that foreign investors, both Canadian and European, had exacerbated the price runups. In fact, local developers, notably Trammell Crow Company, were equally responsible. No matter what site was ultimately determined, once it was obtained, construction could not begin until eighteen to twenty-four months later because of time required to demolish existing structures on the land. With demolition time causing further delay, construction costs could rise more than ten percent per year, making the cost of the hall prohibitive. The symphony's executive board abandoned plans to relocate near the museum site or even elsewhere in the nascent Arts District. It now saw no hope of purchasing the Borden land with the $3 million it had available for land purchase from the 1979 bond election.[11] DSA President Don Stone announced on June 19 that the symphony was looking elsewhere.[12] The following month, the Dallas City Council rejected a proposal to situate the hall on the triangle of land adjacent to city hall.

—❧—

DALLAS has had a city council–city manager government since 1930. Under this system, the mayor is largely an influential figurehead. The day-to-day business of running the city and supervising departments within city hall is the city manager's job. The mayor chairs city council meetings, but the position carries only an honorarium. Consequently, Dallas mayors have historically been prominent business leaders whose personal affluence and business acumen enabled them to lead the city without requiring a significant mayoral salary.

Mayor Evans was president of Cullum Companies, the parent company of Tom Thumb grocery stores, a large chain with market dominance in North Texas. As CEO of Tom Thumb and a major buyer of Borden products, Evans had a lot of leverage and a good business relationship with the head of Borden's.

George Schrader met with the mayor. "You know, Jack, I shop at Tom Thumb, and I buy Borden's milk. Now, I can't think of anybody that's any better situated to talk to the Borden people than Jack Evans."

By July 1981, Mayor Evans was working indirectly on the Borden's idea, leaning on the dairy company to cut a deal with the city for its downtown land. Dick Galland reported to the executive board that Mayor Evans had "breathed new life and ideas into the concert hall site selection."[13] Leonard Stone remembers, "Jack Evans used to phone me every two weeks at home to tell me he was working with Borden's, he was going to get it done, he was committed to getting it done."[14]

Ted Amberg of Pei's Dallas office and Leonard Stone met with Jerome Hackman, director of Borden's corporate real estate department. Borden had reached the point where it was prepared to donate a substantial portion of its property site to the City of Dallas, in return for other considerations on relocation elsewhere in Dallas. Not all the land would be donated. Some cash would exchange hands as well. There were timing questions: When would Borden cease production? When would its downtown facility be demolished?

The week that George Schrader left city hall to return to the private sector, he invited Charles Anderson, his successor as city manager, to join him and Evans for dinner with Eugene J. Sullivan, chairman and president of Borden, who flew in from Ohio for the meeting.[15]

According to a 1986 article in *D Magazine,* that meeting was preceded by a telephone call. The article quoted Evans as saying: "I gave old Eugene a call and told him he had an antiquated plant in our downtown and he needed to rebuild and what did he want to do about it? We talked about a land swap and some other things, and so he finally decided to fly down here. We had breakfast at the Mansion, and I talked to him about the city, how we were dedicated to the city, and how we needed that Arts District, and that if he donated part of that land to the city [and sold the rest], I could get him another place to put his dairy plant. He didn't call a committee meeting or anything. He just looked at me and said, 'How would you like that land donated?'"

The meeting took less than two hours. "I about flipped out of the car when he agreed to do it," says Evans. "Of course, I'd be a fool to tell you that those Borden milk cartons in Tom Thumb didn't have any influence."[16]

Sullivan, who genially told the press, "You have a very persuasive mayor," agreed to donate 25,000 square feet of downtown land, worth $10 million, to the city, and to vacate its milk processing plant. Finally, Borden agreed to sell the balance of the land that Dallas needed to complete the symphony site. In mid-September 1981, Sullivan announced the donation: two and one-half of its five acres at Crockett and Flora Streets.[17] Finally, the symphony hall had a definite location. At the time of the donation, Dick Galland, who was then chairman of the DSA, remembers Sullivan handing him a silver container of dirt and declaring, "This is a gesture of enfeoffment." For Galland, it was the high point of his term as chairman.[18]

Progress on the Arts District

Within a week of the Borden donation, Tishman Realty was reported to be negotiating with Borden to purchase the remaining two and one-half acres of the dairy plant site. *The Dallas Morning News* cited sources to the effect that, if Tishman were successful in purchasing the Borden property, Trizec (another developer) would provide financial backing to develop the land. The announcement had included the information that a developer sought to purchase the Borden property and that the symphony had the option of trading its site for a similar parcel elsewhere in the designated Arts District. Tishman was still considering an office/hotel complex on the site.

Shortly before City Manager George Schrader retired from the public sector, he hired a new assistant city manager, Victor C. Suhm, who had been city manager of a Cincinnati suburb for nine years. Suhm was to have a lengthy relationship with the concert hall. Leonard Stone remembers Suhm as hard working and aggressive. "We were fortunate," he says, "because Vic was determined to see this thing work out."[19]

Schrader and his successor, Charles Anderson, emphasized to Suhm that the resuscitation of the Arts District vision was a priority. With the steep rise in land prices in the district on speculation of commercial development, the original concept of centralized facilities for the visual and performing arts had lost some impetus. Suhm recalls, "Both of them [Schrader and Anderson] felt that the effort to get the Arts District underway was really languishing. The museum was really the only thing that was happening in the Arts District. Basically, they said to me, 'Get it on track, get it going.' We put together a national competition to select a team to make the Arts District real, to put together a plan that could be implemented to define and develop an arts district. That was a major undertaking."[20]

In October 1981, a group of property owners and representatives from the Dallas concert hall committee, the Dallas Museum of Art, and the City of Dallas formed a Dallas Arts District Consortium in an effort to coordinate planning for the proposed district. Each constituent member contributed $20,000 to cover the cost of planning studies. Over the course of the next ten months, they met with various outside consultants engaged by the city: Sasaki Associates of Watertown, Massachusetts, which had won the urban design competition; Halcyon Ltd. of Hartford, Connecticut, a company dealing in commercial concepts attractive to street-level retail users; and Lockwood, Andrews & Newnam, a Dallas civil engineering firm.

Together, the consortium and the consultants developed a list of objectives for the Arts District. They discussed the planning of Flora Street as a main artery through the district and

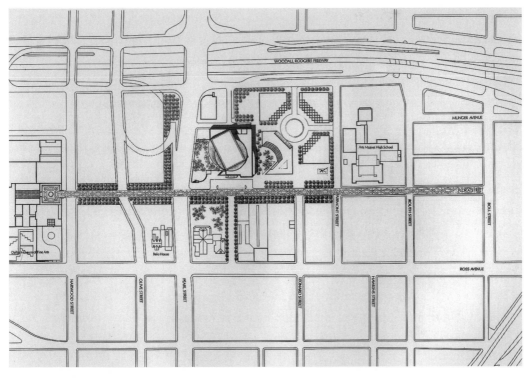

Symphony Hall site plan and Sasaki's Arts District Proposal, May 1982. (*DSO archives*)

ways to handle parking needs. They also agreed to ask Dallas City Council to nominate an impartial person, with no connection to any individual constituent member, who would view the concept objectively as a representative of the Arts District itself. In February 1982, Mayor Jack Evans appointed Dr. Philip O'Bryan Montgomery, Jr., professor of pathology at the University of Texas Health Science Center, to be that impartial person. He agreed to serve as facilitator on a volunteer basis, with staff support provided by the City of Dallas and the Central Business District Association.[21]

The consultants' urban design plan, submitted to the Dallas Arts District Consortium and the City of Dallas in August 1982, reiterated the recommendations that had initially been set forth by Carr, Lynch Associates. Instead of placing museum, symphony hall, and theatre all on the same block, Dallas would establish a mixed-use Arts District with landscaping, offices, restaurants, and shops as well as arts facilities. The consortium felt that it was important to include non-arts activity, because these buildings would otherwise all be "dead"—inactive and unused except during performances or events. If there wasn't an exhibition or a concert, nobody was there. Commercial presence and pedestrian-friendly landscaping would ensure patron activity.

The plan specified a seventeen-block area in the northeast section of downtown Dallas, bounded by Woodall Rodgers Freeway, Ross Avenue, and St. Paul Street. The projections included 10 million square feet of office space, three hotels, and 650 residential units. Sasaki specified "Concert Lights," an outdoor stage adjacent to the concert hall with an electronic signboard for announcements; "Fountain Plaza," a plaza surrounding a fountain modeled after New York's Grand Army Plaza, and a sculpture garden and restaurant as anchors to a "Museum Crossing."[22]

"We were told by people who were applying for the commission to be the designers of the Arts District that, historically, the things that motivate people to gather at places are water [or the sound of water], the ability to sit, drink, eat and watch people moving about, and the ability to purchase cheap trinkets and souvenirs," Leonard Stone says. "The Crow pavilions [in the LTV tower, which was later renamed Trammell Crow Center] started out to be glorious enterprises of exhibition and dance and theatre and noon-hour concerts. Harlan [Crow] actually had two people on staff whose responsibility was programming."[23]

Until November 1981, Pei and Johnson concentrated on planning the hall's interior. The exterior would not be developed until after a site had been confirmed in its entirety. The Pei office could not shift the project into high gear until they had the site. With the concert hall site finally determined, I. M. Pei and his team could move to the next phase of design.

Chapter Ten

HOW MANY SEATS?

We had been charged with building the greatest concert hall in the world, if we could. To me, that meant it had to be the finest acoustical room in the world. I had to tell the board, "You can make this decision for economic reasons, but you will give up fine acoustics." Ultimately, the board made the decision to go with the smaller hall. I think it was the most important decision they made.[1]

EUGENE BONELLI

T HE NEXT major decision for Meyerson's group was seating capacity. At the symphony executive board meeting on December 30, 1980, when Meyerson announced the selection of Pei as architect, he fielded a question about seat count. Meyerson stated that the seating capacity would be in excess of 2,000 but less than 3,000. He was not yet ready to commit himself, his committee, or the design team to a specific number.

No decision regarding seat count had been made in September 1981, at the time of Borden's land donation. At the press conference announcing the gift, Leonard Stone told the *Dallas Times Herald,* "the most successful halls built in the last decade range between 2,000 and 2,400 seats." The same day, Eugene Bonelli recommended to the symphony executive board on behalf of the smaller unit of the concert hall committee that the new hall have a semi-surround look rather than full surround. He reported that the acoustical consultants had recommended 2,000 seats. The executive committee of the symphony board had requested that the consultants deliver an increase in that capacity while maintaining ideal acoustics and the same cubic volume of space within the hall.

The seat count was critically important because it affected not only the size of the building and the income-earning capacity of the DSO, but also the endowment effort. Robert Wolff of Artec Consultants says, "When we first started, the orchestra's brief specified that they wanted a hall with as many as 2,600 seats and the acoustics of the Musikvereinssaal and the Concertgebouw. One of our tasks was to talk them through the mutual exclusivity of those two concepts."[2] Russell Johnson conducted studies, then made a presentation to Meyerson and the smaller unit, explaining how acoustics deteriorate with increases in seat count.

Meyerson and the smaller unit wrestled with economic viability versus forfeiture of acoustical quality. Everyone recognized that higher capacity was practical economically, because it would increase the orchestra's potential to earn income through ticket sales. Meyerson recalls, "Seat count became a hot issue when we compared the economic value of a seat, because you have to calculate what is the value of this seat during a full season considering all performances. It becomes like an airline seat. I was familiar with programs to maximize airline seating. Initially, I said, 'OK, what we want is the most seats that we can get.' We had 3,420, a huge number at Fair Park, yet rarely filled the place. Still, we started by saying, 'Let's get as many seats as we can.'"[3]

According to Martha Blaine, whom Leonard Stone hired as the DSO's orchestra manager in 1981, "Looking at that range from 1,900 to 2,200, the question was always, if the Music Hall seats 3,400 and we're selling most of those seats already, and everybody in the Music Hall and more wants to come to the new concert hall, then how does anybody else ever get in?"[4] The answer was more concerts, but that raised other questions. If the orchestra performed more frequently, what days would remain open for other uses of the building? Who could afford to rent the hall? In fact, interest level was high. Plenty of organizations wanted to use a new facility. Blaine recalls, "We had discussions about high school graduations, celebratory church services, holiday activities at Christmas and New Year's, even whether the seats on the main floor could be removable to allow for a huge New Year's ball like they do in Vienna. The discussions ran the gamut of the kinds of uses. Could other arts organizations that wanted to use the hall find a time? Were the times that the DSO wasn't performing times that anybody wanted? Not until much later did the city begin looking at management for the hall and shaping some of those questions about building use."[5]

The seat count would be driven by acoustics and economics. Meyerson assigned McNeil to research a feasibility study to predict the economic impact of operating an 1,800-seat, 2,000-seat, and 2,200-seat hall for the first year of operation. Her report indicated that low and middle seat counts forecast deficits and the highest count projected net income.[6] Despite that tempting statistic, Meyerson and his smaller unit came to realize that, in this case, economic gain would mean forfeiture of acoustical excellence. Conversely, if the hall had poor acoustics, it would be more difficult to sell the seats and keep them sold to subscribers. According to McNeil, "That would have meant an annual increase in marketing costs to cultivate new audiences."[7] The committee revised its consideration of seat count to a range from 2,000 to 2,600. That range was subsequently narrowed down to a maximum of 2,200.

By mid-1981, within months of the selection of both architect and acoustician, parties close to the project were feeling ping-pong pressures. Stone remembers, "Mort and his smaller unit were on one side, arguing for the best possible hall. Henry Miller and Bob Glaze were on the other side, cautioning us to keep it inexpensive, keep it within budget—it doesn't have to be lavish. No one quite knew yet precisely what we were talking about. What kind of building did we want? What was it going to be?"[8]

The committee learned that it was not possible simply to clone a known success like Carnegie Hall or Boston's Symphony Hall. They studied schematics of those buildings, then reviewed existing fire code regulations, construction and engineering safety requirements, and the need for handicap access. Aisles and exits would have to be wider. Adhering to contemporary construction guidelines, builders could not re-create what was accomplished in halls built a century before. To achieve the excellent acoustics fundamental to the program brief, there would be tradeoffs.

Russell Johnson educated Meyerson and his committee how the number of seats in the room would affect the cubic volume, explaining that an orchestra can produce just so much energy. The larger the volume of the space in which this energy is dispersed, the more difficult it is to preserve the cohesiveness of the sound. Johnson posed a question to the committee. As you sit in a concert hall listening to a performance, and you're looking at an orchestra, where do you think the sound you are hearing is coming from? They replied, "The sound is coming from where we see it being produced, which is right there on the stage." Johnson shook his head and explained.

The committee learned that the sound was actually coming to them from many points in the hall, through reflection and reverberant patterns. The halls around the world with great sound were the smaller halls. Neither the engineering of the time—100, 150, or 200 years ago —nor the needs of performing ensembles during those eras—called for large seating capacity. Smaller halls had been constructed not because builders understood they were acoustically superior, but for practical reasons. Larger halls began to be built as technology advanced, with such innovations as long-span steel trusses, permitting larger structures and a departure from narrow, rectangular rooms. These techniques allowed architects to experiment, resulting in larger, voluminous edifices.

The advent of the public concert auditorium coincided with an increase in concert life on both sides of the Atlantic throughout the nineteenth century and into the twentieth. To arts organizations with a need for earned income, higher seat count was a plus. As urban orchestras started offering their players larger contracts and more weeks of work, they perceived an advantage to larger seating capacity. The downside was proportionally larger buildings—and a decline in the quality of sound.

MORT Meyerson conferred at length with DSO Music Director Eduardo Mata. One of the first things that Mata told him was, "The difference between a live performance and a recording is intimacy."

Meyerson queried, "What do you mean?"

Mata said, "I can reproduce for you the sound of a symphony orchestra, given enough equipment, so that you can't tell the difference between whether you're sitting in a symphony hall or you're listening on a sound system. Now if that's true, as electronics get better, you can even enhance it so that it's better than live performance. So what's the thing that separates a live performance of the music from the recording? Intimacy."

"Well, what do you mean, 'intimacy'?" Meyerson persisted.

"It's the emotional bond that's built between the players, the music, and the audience," Mata explained. "You can feel it. Sometimes orchestras are on and sometimes they're off. Sometimes audiences are on and sometimes they're off. When things work, the orchestra is on and the audience is on. Then, it's magic." He added, "The thing that we need, Mort, is we must have an intimate environment."

Meyerson's curiosity was piqued. "Eduardo, what are the characteristics of it?"

"You start with [this]: The farthest seat in the back of the hall should be no more than ninety feet from the conductor's podium."[9]

Meyerson pondered this statistic, trying to visualize that distance in his mind's eye. "The committee's program brief specified intimacy," he said later. "We want the audience to feel each other, yet not be on top of each other. We want them to have comfort, but not be so comfortable that they go to sleep. We want to use the right materials, acoustically speaking, for chairs, and yet we want to balance that and have it still be comfortable. But most important, audience members must be able to see the conductor and the orchestra. We want there to be a feeling that each listener is part of the playing of the music. If you're too far away, you can't do that."

Mata's intimacy parameter provided Meyerson with a frame of reference. He wanted to know what was the maximum number of seats possible without forfeiting acoustical excellence and favorable sight lines. Meyerson asked Johnson for a hockey stick chart. Flummoxed, Johnson asked, "What's a hockey stick chart?" Meyerson explained, "Up to a point, we can add seats and not have an impact on acoustics. At a certain point, we start affecting acoustics as we add seats. At another point, you will probably find that the addition of a few more seats materially degrades the sound. That's a typical logarithm chart; that's where the hockey stick curves. I want to know where that elbow is."

In response to Meyerson's request, Johnson conducted some studies. He reported to Meyerson, "If you want to have absolute top rate acoustics, the right seat count is about 1,400 to 1,500." Exasperated, Meyerson told him, "We *can't* have that; that's chamber music size."[10]

Johnson gathered some cubic cardboard boxes and started adding and subtracting boxes to show cubic feet. As Meyerson describes it, "He used cubic feet as the equivalent of where you got this hockey stick negative effect in acoustics and then, how many seats can you put in a hall under what kind of configuration with perfect sight lines at that hockey stick. The answer was 2,069."

—❧—

MEYERSON relayed this information to his board president, Don Stone. "Don, I've got a major problem here."

"What's that?"

"I've just spent several years learning something about acoustics. Where they start deteriorating substantially is somewhere a little over 2,000 seats. Now, economically, we should have a hall that accommodates 2,300, 2,400, 2,500 people. We're going to have to make a decision here, and this means compromising. Every decision you make, you make choices, there's a consequence. If you choose for great economic gain, then the consequence is going to be you'll degrade the acoustics."[11]

Within the smaller unit, they argued among themselves. Bonelli remembers, "Stanley Marcus argued for the larger hall, based on economic grounds. We needed more seats to sell to be economically viable. I argued, on the other hand, that with the growing quality of home sound systems and the quality people were going to be able to experience acoustically in their home, the thing that would draw people out in the twenty-first century would be room acoustics that were superior to anything you could get from any home sound system. That would keep our audience strong. We would be better off presenting the concert more times than having more seats to sell at an individual concert. To me, it was clearly an economic versus artistic dispute. I don't think anyone disagreed that the smaller the hall, the better the acoustics. Russell kept saying that much above 2,000, you could not achieve 'ideal' room acoustics. Good acoustics depend on the skill of the acoustician, but once you exceed a certain cubic volume, no one has yet found a way to achieve the success we have in the Meyerson or that you have in the Musikvereinssaal, which is smaller than the Meyerson. I believe Russell was right, and all of my experience confirmed that."[12]

The decision in favor of a smaller hall took place at a meeting of the building committee at Meyerson's house when Johnson presented his findings. Johnson had brought his series of sets of cubes showing rough cubic footage for a hall, for 1,000 seats, 1,500 seats, 2,000 seats, and up to 2,800. Johnson explained that acoustics is nothing but filling cubic space with sound. He reiterated what he had told Meyerson: "If you give me a small hall, a very small hall, under 1,000 seats, I can guarantee you perfect acoustics. With 2,000 seats it gets more dicey. Above 2,000 seats, it's impossible." For emphasis, Johnson added, "I really cannot control what the sound is going to do with any degree of certainty if you give me a large hall."[13]

Meyerson says, "Don [Stone] and I had agreed before that he and I would push the board for the 2,069." Don Stone recalls the meeting at Meyerson's house. "Mort played with all those cubes. He finally said to us that night, 'Tell you what: If you don't agree with me, I'm going to go public with the fact that we're not going to be building a hall that has the opportunity to be a world-class hall, in which case we ought to stay in Fair Park and not spend everybody's money.'"[14]

Meyerson posed his last argument as a series of rhetorical questions. He asked the members of the smaller unit, "What is the purpose of this hall? Are we here to build a circus? A football stadium? A basketball arena? Are we private homeowners? Are we trying to generate a return on capital? No. All that we have to do is produce enough revenue that we're economically viable, because we can't go out of business like the symphony did before. But that's the only consideration. Now, if we're going to build a new hall, and we're going to compromise the acoustics so that you have average acoustics in a beautiful hall, I *won't* build a new hall. The whole purpose of the symphony is not to look good; it's to hear. So why don't we get rid of all the marble and glass and limestone and let's put all the money into acoustics— because that's what you listen to. *Then*, we'll just be like Boston. Nobody will care once they hear the beauty of the music. But if we want beautiful acoustics and we build bigger than 2,069 seats, we're making a mistake." They voted, and he won.

Nancy Penson's recollection is that she, Louise Kahn, and Mary McDermott sided with Mort in favor of a smaller, acoustically superior hall. According to Don Stone, then DSA president, "The rest of the group caved. It was very difficult for me, as a person who spent his life as a merchant selling things, to have to have a hall that was smaller than we were currently selling, and have it for the rest of our life, the rest of my life, the rest of the symphony's life! We would never have more than 1,800, 2,000 seats available to sell. Of course Mort was able to intimidate all of us! Correctly so. That's why the hall is the size it is, and that's one of the reasons that it's such a good hall."[15]

By October 1981, the smaller unit had settled on a room with the cubic footage of a 2,000-seat hall, with the proviso that the consultants should be directed to find a way to provide seating for at least an additional 200 seats.[16] Following the established procedure, Meyerson took the matter to the large committee, then to the symphony's board of governors. The same argument resurfaced: how to build an economically viable center. "The symphony board was cooperative," recalls Meyerson, "but the board is dominated by its leadership, so it depends on who is the president. The most powerful of the presidents as an advocate for doing something as significant as this was Don Stone. He was president when most of the stuff hit the fan. How many seats? What's the volume of the room? Those were the real bone-crusher decisions we had to make. The seat count was a monumental decision. If it hadn't been for Don Stone's leadership, we wouldn't have gotten that decision. Don was the leader. He's one of my idols. He knows music, he loves music, he loves theatre. He likes the arts. I think his broad breadth of viewpoint, and [his wife] Norma's, allowed him to make what I consider to be the right decision. I could have had somebody else as the president of the symphony at that time. I could have been arguing quality and sound and they wouldn't have known what I was talking about. So we were lucky."[17] The committee had weathered its first major crisis in the evolution of the hall.

—⁊—

JOE Walker, the CEO of J. W. Bateson Company during the construction phase, later calculated that if one divided the final seat count—2,062, including the choral terrace—into the total construction cost of the building, each seat in the hall cost $40,000. "We built Texas Stadium, too," Walker says. "There are 65,000 seats out there. Those seats average $265 per seat. When you sit in the Meyerson, it cost $40,000 for each of those seats. That's just construction; that doesn't include land or design. It's an astonishing amount."[18]

Chapter Eleven

A SKETCH IN THE SAND:
EARLY DESIGN

U PON hiring the acoustician and architect, Meyerson and his committee charged I. M. Pei with preparing a schematic theory of what the place would look like. The architects worked in general terms. The site had not yet been determined, no budget had been proposed, and Pei had other projects that would preclude his active involvement for some months. By April 1981, Meyerson was able to present a revised program brief to the symphony's executive board, the acoustician, and the architect. The brief listed all external and internal spaces that had been identified as needs by the orchestra players, symphony staff, and Meyerson's committee, in consultation with the acoustician and architect. After recommending modifications to the symphony's space list, I. M. Pei & Partners and Artec were to assign square footage for each area. Cost estimates would follow.

Superior acoustics had been established as a primary goal for the concert room. Artec Consultants' parameters for the size and shape of the audience chamber would necessarily influence, if not determine, what I. M. Pei & Partners did with the balance of the structure. During the first few months after Artec was selected as acoustician, Johnson and his staff concentrated on assisting Melissa McNeil in the refinement of the program brief and educating Meyerson and the members of his committee about the characteristics of other concert rooms. Johnson and Pei visited several concert halls in the Netherlands in May, and the Artec group conducted interviews with DSO staff members and musicians.[1] Johnson submitted a preliminary report in mid-August 1981, reflecting the initial phase of Artec's services. The report included illustrations in plan and section of numerous halls, plus general information about space and equipment requirements, noise and vibration control, and room acoustics.[2] Artec had released little pertaining to the new design, just some schematic "bubble diagrams" intended to indicate relationship of spaces within the building. Artec suggested allocating of 20,000 square feet for the audience chamber with 1,800 square feet for the performance platform and an audience capacity of 1,800 plus 200.[3]

—◦—

WHEN Artec was awarded the Dallas contract, Russell Johnson's firm had only five consultants: Johnson himself; Robert Wolff, a theatre planning specialist; Carol Allen, a draftsperson; and two other acousticians, Nicholas Edwards and Robert Essert. Edwards, who is English, joined Artec in 1979, shortly after completing his second degree in architecture at University of Nottingham. His curriculum comprised environmental science, including room acoustics, a topic in which he had become interested. A Nottingham professor recommended him to Johnson, who offered Edwards a job in New York designing concert rooms. With the British economy slumping and employment prospects grim, Edwards thought quickly and accepted. He brought his girlfriend, Janet Burman (they subsequently married at New York City Hall), who became Johnson's bookkeeper and personal assistant. The business was operating out of Johnson's and Wolff's apartments on Manhattan's upper west side. Edwards started at $9,000 per year.

During the next two years, the firm's fortunes began to change. New projects came in, notably a multi-purpose hall in Nottingham, England, and a concert hall in Calgary, Alberta. The staff expanded by two and moved to a real office (though still not an air-conditioned one). They were on the verge of becoming a major player in the room acoustics business. Landing the Dallas project could effect that change. Major American cities don't decide every day to build concert halls. Everyone at Artec knew that the Dallas hall had the potential to provide an enormous boost to the firm's reputation. And they were elated when they got the good news in February 1981. They celebrated with inexpensive champagne in plastic cups.

—◦—

EDWARDS was headed to Southern California for two weeks of vacation at the end of July 1981. On his way out the door, he remembers, Johnson turned to him and said, "Well, while you're away, design me a concert hall for Dallas."

Edwards responded in the same light vein. "Sure, no problem."[4]

In fact, he'd been thinking a great deal about the Dallas room, as had they all. Packed into his suitcase for the holiday were three theses by researchers active in room acoustics and

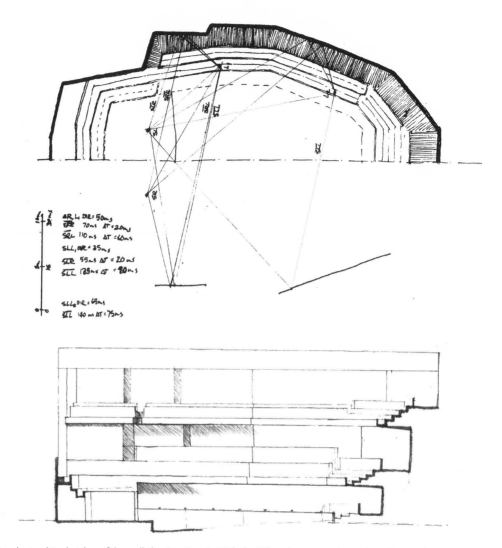

Developing his sketches of the wall shaping, Artec's Nicholas Edwards proposed complete plans and sections for the concert hall. (*Courtesy Nicholas Edwards*)

theory: Michael Barron, Dieter Gottlob, and Yoichi Ando.[5] Edwards remembers the next two weeks in vivid detail. "By that time, I'd been at Artec long enough to understand Russell's concepts of concert hall design through our work in Nottingham, Northampton, Colorado Springs, and Calgary. We'd gone through the design process in depth and completed some difficult projects. What Russell was saying about room acoustics was completely at odds with what I had been taught at university on the subject, or anything I could find in a textbook. And yet I was *sure* he was right and that the textbooks were wrong. But I'm a scientist by background. I was convinced that the problem was the lack of scientific knowledge. If Russell was right, we ought to be able to show why scientifically. All three researchers—Barron, Gottlob, and Ando—were recognizing the importance of lateral sound and writing about it for the first time."[6]

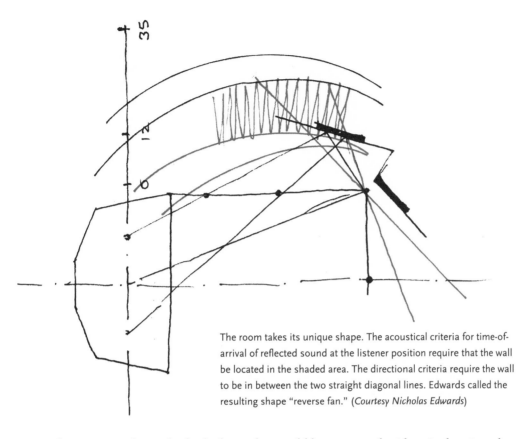

The room takes its unique shape. The acoustical criteria for time-of-arrival of reflected sound at the listener position require that the wall be located in the shaded area. The directional criteria require the wall to be in between the two straight diagonal lines. Edwards called the resulting shape "reverse fan." (*Courtesy Nicholas Edwards*)

Earlier acoustic theory had relied on what could be measured with a single microphone. "The difference between lateral sound and what you can measure with a microphone is direction," Edwards explains. "Direction is important because we have two ears on the sides of our head, facing left and right. Minute differences between signals in each ear create a sense of envelopment by the sound. These researchers were discovering that. If one accepts as a basic premise that direction is important, it raises new questions about designing concert halls. You want a hall with strong lateral sound. What shape is a concert hall with strong lateral sound? In 1981, no one knew."[7]

During the next two weeks, while he and his wife relaxed at his uncle's home in Tarzana, California, Edwards made it his business to find out. With the acoustics theses and a stack of blank paper at hand, he began jotting down ideas and drawings as he studied the recent research and compared it with Russell Johnson's theories. "For many years, Russell had argued against fan-shaped halls, but he couldn't say why," he recalls. "He'd reply, 'Because that [rectangular concert rooms] is what was done in the nineteenth century and it works!'—which wasn't convincing in a brave new 1950s or 1960s world. Russell decided there must be more to acoustics than what the scientists were measuring. He knew that rectangular 'shoebox' halls worked very well compared to the horrible fan-shaped things being built in America. I picked up on things he wrote in his early papers about the importance of room shape. He was clearly

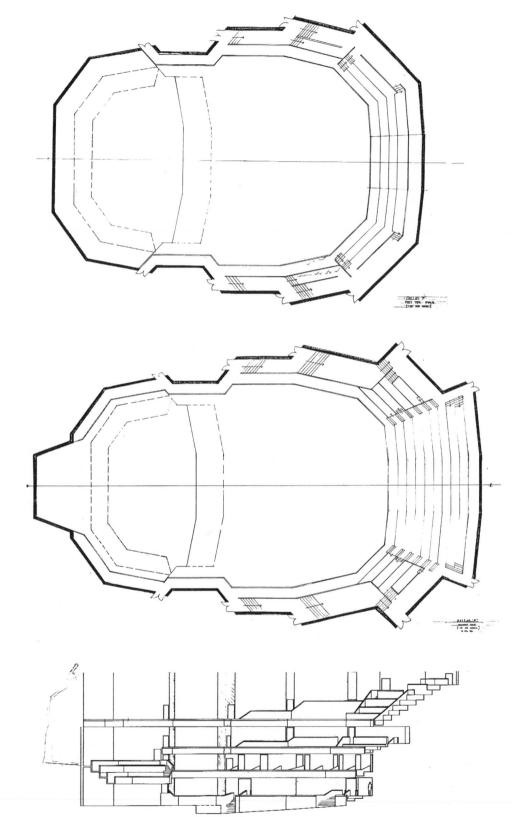

Artec's Jeremie Franks completed the first formal in-house drawings on December 18, 1981, adhering to the parameters of Edwards's reverse-fan design. (*Courtesy Nicholas Edwards*)

on to something related to the directionality of sound. The theses I took with me on holiday reinforced that. I decided I was going to combine Russell's experience, led in a particular direction, with this new research, and take some revolutionary steps."[8]

Edwards began sketching and jotting down concepts on July 28. By the end of the first week in August he had filled 113 pages with ideas and drawings, including the first draft of what later became a computer program to simulate the three-dimensional behavior of sound waves in a concert room. Systematically working through each area of the hall on each level, he generated sketches that indicated the best placement for walls in order to optimize the all-important lateral reflections. The early sketches were labeled "surround study" and "shoebox study." As his ideas crystallized, the terminology shifted, and he began calling the evolving room shape "reverse fan." By the time he finished, he had a full set of drawings in plan and section for each level of the proposed hall, along with a detailed narrative explaining the theories he had used to arrive at the design.[9]

In proposing a shape for the concert room, Edwards divided the audience into a number of separate areas within each level and positioned the walls of the hall so that each of these areas was provided with early lateral reflections, those reflected by the walls of the room and arriving from the listener's left and right. This design approach, essentially an architectural interpretation of the scientific criteria he derived from the theses he had studied, was unprecedented. Through sketches that tested his proposals, he was able to show that the great concert halls of the past conformed closely, but not precisely, to his newly determined parameters for early lateral reflections. It was an extended exercise in validating instincts. He later said, "I was convinced not only that here lay an explanation for the acoustical superiority of the shoebox hall over the fan-shaped hall, but also that science had now led concert hall design into the uncharted waters of 'reverse-fan' shaping."[10] When he returned to New York, Edwards presented Johnson with the stack of 113 pages and asked him to review it. A week passed, then another. Finally, Edwards couldn't stand it any more and mustered the courage to ask Johnson, "What did you think of my memo?"

First, a pause. Then, "Nick, I'm speechless."

Edwards wasn't certain what Johnson meant. "I couldn't tell whether he was speechless at the effrontery of someone just two years out of college going away and thinking he could design a concert hall, or speechless because he could suddenly see everything he had worked toward suddenly being validated and pushed forward with a strong scientific background. I just didn't dare believe that he meant he was going to pick up this design and run with it. Did I think I had a chance at that? Come on, I was only twenty-seven. I'd watched Russell Johnson design a few halls. I'd just designed my first ever concert hall on a major project of international importance. You don't expect to get it built. You expect to have someone come back and say, 'Yes, OK, very good first attempt, you're a student, and I can show you six areas where you're wrong in this one.'"[11]

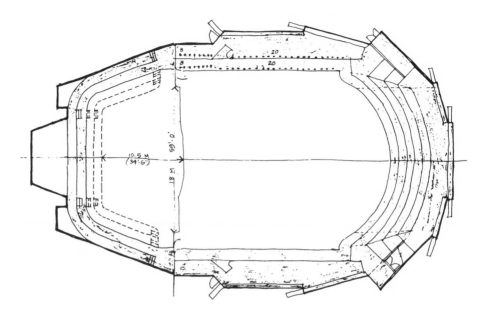

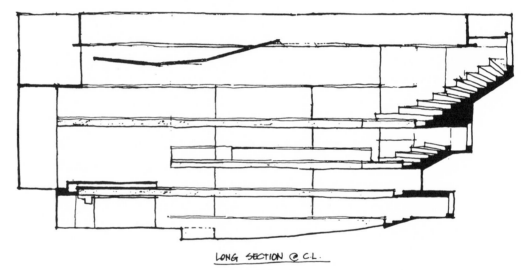

LONG SECTION @ C.L.

Artec draftsperson Carol Allen prepared practical room layouts with seats, aisles, exits, and sight lines in February, 1982, retaining Edwards's reverse-fan design. (*Courtesy Nicholas Edwards*)

But that didn't happen. When Artec's Jeremie Franks completed the first formal in-house drawings on December 18, 1981, they adhered to the parameters of Edwards's reverse-fan design. A more refined set followed on February 19, 1982, by which time Artec draftsperson Carol Allen had taken his rough sketches and prepared practical room layouts with seats, aisles, exits, and sight lines. Allen requested a meeting directed toward finalizing details of sight lines, size of performance platform, what to prepare for the Pei group and in what scale.[12] In the interim, Johnson provided I. M. Pei with the initial concept for the hall interior.[13] By mid-March, Artec had forwarded specifications to I. M. Pei & Partners on the exact size and shape of the concert room, and the Pei group had determined that it could accommodate approximately ninety-five percent of Artec's design.[14]

―◦◦―

UPTOWN at the offices of I. M. Pei & Partners, business was booming. At the time Pei accepted the Dallas commission, he was working on the Texas Commerce Bank Towers in Houston, the Raffles City Complex in Singapore, the Fragrant Hills Hotel near Peking, and an addition to the Museum of Fine Arts in Boston. He would not be free to devote substantial time to the Dallas project for approximately nine months. In the New York office, Eason Leonard handled contractual arrangements and Werner Wandelmaier oversaw the administrative management of specific assignments within the contract. To establish the groundwork for a Dallas design team, Pei consulted with Ralph Heisel, a senior associate with whom he had worked since the early 1960s. Pei wanted to involve Charles Young in the concert room because of his strong interest in theatre and opera. Heisel, in his capacity as project architect

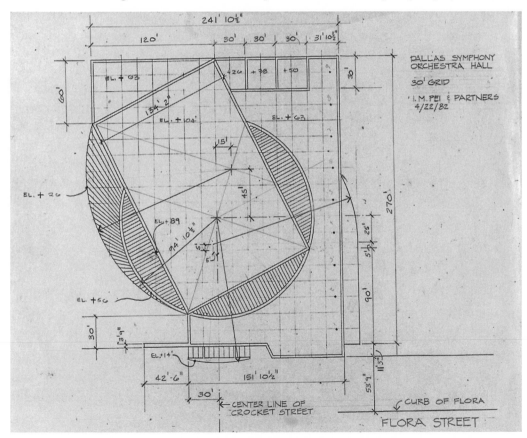

James Langford's drawing illustrates the building on a 30-foot grid. The shoebox is rotated within the grid. The circular lenses center over the audience chamber. That center point also aligns with the center of Crockett Street. (*Courtesy James E. Langford*)

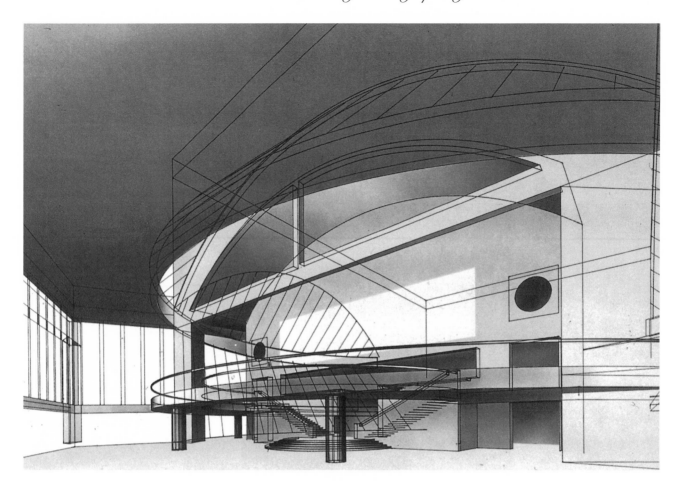

Above and facing page
Early interior views of the hall's public space were computer-generated by Paul Stevenson Oles and air-brushed by Ian Bader. (*Courtesy James E. Langford*)

for the building, pulled Ian Bader, a young and gifted project designer from South Africa, from another project to assist with the Dallas concert hall. Subsequently, after the initial design concept was developed, Heisel added George Miller to the team as project manager. "I wanted someone who could handle himself well with the client," Heisel remembers. "In a project manager, you also need someone who is sensitive to design. I had worked with George on two other projects and admired his professionalism and integrity. He's thorough and efficient in his pursuits, and I knew he would be efficient in handling the management aspects of the project."[15]

The design group focused initially on studying the symphony's needs and wish list as set forth in the program brief. Pei and his staff began consideration of their design with the acoustical model of the concert room that Artec had prepared. According to Eugene Bonelli, "What we got from Artec was a basic plan of the room: its basic shape, the configuration of the stage, the configuration of the balconies hugging the walls."[16] The acoustical and architectural teams referred to this plan as the "geometry" of the room.

Robert Wolff of Artec Consultants recalls, "We set out the geometry of the room and got the orchestra to approve our approach, then provided the model and single line drawings of

that geometry to Mr. Pei. One month later, he came back and said he could make architecture out of it. Over a longer period, Pei studied our drawings. It was a good nine months before he really started work. That allowed us to work with the Dallas Symphony Orchestra members, which was very useful time."[17]

By spring 1982, I. M. Pei & Partners had Artec's drawings for the acoustical design of the concert room. Artec's design consisted essentially of the walls of the hall, the shaping of the space on each level, the placement of audience and performers, and the reverberation chamber. Charles Young and his assistant, Gordon Wallace, were responsible for developing the interior of the concert room, which meant they interacted most closely with the Artec team. The balance of the architectural group, headed by Ralph Heisel, at one point numbered thirty-five people. They worked on everything else, from design concept to building the models in the model shop. Pei himself was the fulcrum between the two teams working on the design of the building. Although Pei's personal focus was primarily on the building's exterior and lobby spaces, nothing was decided for the concert room without his approval.

Within a couple of months after the Borden donation, in January 1982, I. M. Pei called Ralph Heisel into his New York office to discuss the building. They knew the site was shallow and that a 2.5 million square foot office development was planned east of the site. (The development was not built.) Pei's early thoughts were to recognize the skyscrapers as well as the Arts District.

Ian Bader, who worked with Heisel's group and directly with Pei, recalls moving quite quickly in the initial design stages. "I found I. M.'s ability to visualize space without the use of drawings very exciting," he says. "We would have conversations in his office about the building without any drawings at all. He's an incredibly effective communicator, and interesting ideas came out of those conversations. Initially, there was the notion of inner and outer structures and, although their interrelationship was not clearly defined early on, ultimately they would be mediated by a series of crystals which would, in the final design, become the skylights."[18]

The I. M. Pei & Partners model shop, on the east side of Manhattan in the thirties, produced a series of block models, each consisting of a kit of parts that the design team used to render the basic building diagram in three dimensions. According to Bader, building the models with different interchangeable parts was one way to advance the design rapidly. "We also did distilled diagrams: simple inkline drawings on Mylar, to deal with alternate possibilities for exploring geometric relationships between the parts of the building."[19]

The architectural concept of geometry governed the building design from its earliest stages. Bader explains: "There are two geometries in this building: an orthogonal geometry, which is basically a grid of squares, and a rotated geometry, which is a 2:1 rotation relative to the orthogonal squares. The rotated geometry is also rectangular. The game of the building is really about the interplay between these propositions, and specifically generates the spatial interest of the lobby spaces. That's what gives it energy. The distortion of the offset circles provides the visual interest, the sense of engagement, because it's forever unfolding as you move through the space. The building is unprecedented in its use of these geometries."[20]

The skylights were two types: upper glass enclosures, called lenses, and another shaped like a portion of the surface of a cone with a non-vertical axis. It became known by its proper geometric name: a "conoid." For Bader, the invention of the conoid was the most fascinating moment in the project. "For the longest time," he says, "we had the idea of two tangential circles in the plan, but it wasn't clear at all what the relationship between the inner and outer circles would be. I. M.'s idea for the most simple and effective solution was to join the two circles with a series of straight lines. Because the conoid is a portion of an offset cone, geometrically it could be made of flat pieces of glass, meeting each other in standard aluminum window frames. No two of the glass panels in this curving and progressively sloping wall are the same."[21]

Once the basic geometry had been established, Pei and his architects addressed the relationship between the exterior of the building and the concert room. Bader remembers, "It became apparent relatively quickly that the most effective solution would be to render the outer envelope translucent, or transparent, and the inner chamber opaque. The transparency

of the outer envelope made the presence and movement of the public an essential component of the architecture. The visibility of this life is part of the celebration of the space. The
architecture is designed to emphasize this transparency. Sunlight streams in and bounces off
interior walls, so that when you look at the building from the outside, it's transparent,
because you're seeing an illuminated surface within. At night, the building inverts itself and
becomes a lantern."[22]

The geometric rotation meant that the concert hall portion of the building would sit at an
angle on its site. Project architect George Miller explains: "The site was difficult, because its
dimensions were such that it didn't really provide adequate square footage in the foreground
for appropriate lobby space. The first thing that I. M. did was to rotate the rectangular volume
of the acoustical box to allow greater space for the lobby and the support spaces. He also did
that as a gesture to downtown Dallas and the new art museum, so that the conoid
faced the center of town. Another design feature that I. M. was interested in
achieving was the look of the building glowing like a lantern at night. After
all, attending the symphony is a nocturnal event for the most part. I. M. felt
that the building should beckon people."[23] That wish translated to the
transparency in the lobby areas.

The design team believed that it was important for everyone
to enjoy the procession and eventfulness of entry into the building.
"I. M. has very strong urban convictions," observes James Langford,
who was only one year out of college when he joined Pei's staff late in
1980. He remained on the team until 1985, and now has his own practice in
Dallas. "I. M. wants a building to respond to the city. He knows Dallas; he understands what Dallas is about: going around and being seen. The lobby spaces are
designed to be seen in. The public spaces put people on display. It was important to
I. M. that the building open up, so that you could see people moving around at night when
the lobbies were lit up. All the glass makes the hall interior visible at night from downtown
Dallas office buildings."[24]

Axonometric drawing of
the hall. (*DSO archives*)

Cigar Box Unveiling

Early in 1982, Heisel called Leonard Stone to schedule a meeting at the Pei office in New York.
He was greeted in conference room number two by Pei, Heisel, Ian Bader, Charles Young,
Russell Johnson, and Nicholas Edwards. Pei announced, "We want to reveal the building to
you." "Terrific!" came Stone's reply. He remembers, "I expected huge models and oversize
drawings to be brought in. I. M. looked over to his colleagues and smiled. They had a small
white box like a traditional cigar humidor. They pushed it toward me. 'Where is it?' I asked.
They indicated, 'In there,' nodding toward the box. It looked like a trick. I opened it. Inside

was a series of clear Lucite and opaque white, alabaster-like shapes. Ian Bader started to put the shapes together. It was like a piece of Tiffany jewelry: no more than three inches by three inches. Once the assembly had been completed, I. M. lifted it up to present to me. I was like Gulliver, and this was Lilliputian. They placed it in my hand. I could look through and see the transparencies, the glass lenses, the shape. I fell in love with it. I envisioned this miniature model a thousand times larger, on the site. It made total sense. The cube, the music chamber, the block surrounded by the public spaces, and light to get in and people to look out. I thought, 'Absolutely everything that I. M. and I had talked about, here it was, sitting in this little thing in my palm.' I wanted it as a personal treasure and memento!

"They looked at me as if they were waiting for me to say 'yea' or 'nay.' I have no idea if I had said, 'God, this is horrible!' what they would have done. But I just gushed about it. It was just sensational. If that first model still exists, it's got to be photographed in somebody's hand. It's a stunning photographic concept.

"I asked, 'May I take this back to Dallas?' I wanted to give it to Henry Miller as a fund-raising aid, not realizing at that time that the Pei group was going to come up with the most stunning series of models imaginable. This was just a little toy! That's how I first saw the design in three dimensions. If anybody had attempted to describe it to me on the phone—'It's a box surrounded by a lens . . .'—I couldn't have imagined it. One simply had to see it."[25]

The basic form of the building resembled its appearance today, with the significant difference that it then included an entire additional level of public space. Street level, the ground floor, was conceived of as comprising the arrival and entrance vestibule, coat check, box office, telephone zones, pocket galleries, sales shops, restaurant, and exhibition space. The mezzanine level, which Pei & Partners called *piano nobile,* was to be orchestra level and the actual entry to the music chamber. The size, shape, and general appearance of the building were beginning to pull together.

Chapter Twelve

PRACTICAL CONSIDERATIONS

T HE DSO concert hall staff was meeting regularly with the musicians' committee, the design team, and the concert hall committee small group to monitor progress and refine details of the interior space and performance equipment. Everyone's list of questions was detailed and long. The musicians wanted to know how larger instruments such as percussion, double basses, and harps would negotiate the backstage area. What storage locker facilities would be available to them? Would they have warmup areas separate from a lounge? What about dressing rooms? Could the stage accommodate an acoustic riser system to improve sound and sight lines? Would the choral warmup room be soundproofed? How much space was allocated to the orchestra library?

Orchestra manager Martha Blaine and director of concert hall planning Melissa McNeil sought out the musicians repeatedly for their input as to how all the pieces might fit together. As orchestra manager for the DSO, Blaine was in charge of all the production, artists, the pops series (which was in its infancy), the summer Starfest concerts, and any touring the orchestra might undertake. She and McNeil worked on the technical and practical aspects of ingress and egress from the musicians' and the stagehands' points of view. Blaine's prior experience as an orchestra musician was an asset, because she understood what it was like to play on many different stages. "We asked them, if you could have your wish list of everything you wanted, what would it be like? Once we had that wish list in hand, it was made into an architectural program that would tell you, for instance, adjacencies. Who needs to be near whom?

Should the soloist's dressing room be next to the conductor's? Should the men's dressing room for the orchestra be next to the men's chorus dressing room? Or should all the chorus rooms be together and the orchestra together? Where is the Green Room in relation to the musicians and the soloist and public access? Of course the wish list is always longer than what you finally get. But we also asked them to rank each item as we went through the process, so that the things that absolutely had to be there were the ones that we hung on to tenaciously."[1]

Blaine understood the nuts and bolts of hauling in music stands, chairs, and large instruments for "runout" concerts to outlying communities such as Greenville, Texas. She had sympathy for the players' practical needs. "We tried to anticipate. We did a lot of work with architectural programming, which is where you decide what you're going to do, what you need to have happening in order for that to come to pass, who's going to go where when, what's the path the musicians will walk from the time they park their car until the moment they move onto the stage."[2]

Blaine talked to all the members of the players' committee and other musicians in the orchestra. "Do you prefer to go this way or that way?" she asked. "If we put shelves backstage for your instruments, do you feel the instruments are safe there? Are they too high? Too low? Would you rather have something else?"

She also made it a point to involve the stagehands. The DSO's stage manager, Johnny Gutierrez, had been involved in building Starfest, the summer pops concert series, for several years. Blaine says, "Johnny gained expertise about how to construct, how to put things together, not in the sense of building a finely tuned concert hall, but in the sense of what was necessary to make it work. He was responsible for the light cables ending up in the right place. He had to make sure the steps were placed where the musicians could get onto the stage. He had to make sure that, if you backed the truck up, you could offload without being in a ditch or in the dirt, or dropping something."[3] She brought Gutierrez in as a visitor to the team when they discussed what the stagehands would require to move all the orchestra equipment. They asked him what he and his crew needed, technically, to carry out their job on the stage, to ensure that the maestro was taken care of. The questions came thick and fast. Can you see when and where to get the maestro on stage? What about getting a soloist, or soloists, on stage? If a piano concerto is programmed during the first half of the concert, what do we have to do to move that piano on and off?

A great deal of discussion took place concerning the acoustic riser system that was an important component of Artec's performance equipment. The unit was to be a steep, stair-step, one-piece platform that would fit on the stage with a screwed hardwood support system. The performance platform was to be a lift that would move the entire riser unit (with chairs, music stands, etc.) to a lower level, where it could be shifted to a storage location. It would allow for use of the stage level as a flat performance platform for dance, popular music and other events not associated with pure concert halls. Artec argued that the riser system would improve sight lines and acoustics for audience members seated on the orchestra floor. Risers would also improve the strength of the cello and double bass sound. As a further fringe benefit, Artec contended, the riser system would allow for low-cost changeover from a morning DSO rehearsal to an afternoon function or booking that was non-DSO-related.[4]

They debated whether the risers should be built in, automated, or portable. Where would the piano go if they were built in? How would the acoustics be affected if the piano were on the risers, because of some reverberation factor? Blaine says, "We had endless conversations. Johnny was part of that, because it was his job to get that piano to that perfect place. We had lots of funny things: 'The piano won't go through the door! Got to change the door a little bit!'"[5]

Victor Marshall, the symphony's artistic administrator, conferred with the design team regarding guest artist areas and dressing rooms, such as the size of rooms and their distance from the stage. He had been listening to suggestions and complaints from visiting artists at Fair Park. "I knew the soloists should be acoustically isolated if they wanted to practice in the dressing room while the concert was going on," Marshall comments. "Guest artists couldn't do that at Fair Park. Once they arrived at the hall, if the concerto was programmed on the second half, they couldn't practice or warm up the first half of the concert; they just had to sit there."[6] Comfort and privacy were factors as well.

Members of the smaller unit endeavored to put to practical use their own observations from visits to other halls in formulating their challenges to the design team. How would handicapped patrons be accommodated in terms of seating within the hall and access to rest rooms? Were there sufficient men's and women's rest rooms at each level? Did the lobbies require portable bars on the upper levels as well as permanent ones at street level? How would the food service staff transport food from the subterranean kitchen to the lobby-level restaurant? Should the front elevators be electric or hydraulic? Would the noise of freight elevators in the rear disrupt a concert if they were used during performances?

The design team wrestled with these and other queries. They met with the Dallas Fire Department to ensure that the building would meet and exceed existing fire code safety regulations, and with representatives of Dallas Power & Light to determine how electric power would be provided to the building. Pei's office was the clearinghouse for addressing space needs. The architects wrestled with the practical options specified by musicians, symphony staff, stagehands, and committee members.

Interlude: Building the Symphony Team

The Dallas Symphony's marketing director position opened up in early 1981 when Steven Adler accepted an offer to work for a major theatrical promotion company in New York. Leonard Stone asked Martha Blaine if she had any recommendations based on her years in orchestra management. She suggested Douglas Kinzey, marketing director of the Louisville Orchestra, where Blaine had been orchestra manager before Stone recruited her to come to Dallas.

"The manager of the Louisville Orchestra and I hired Doug when he had graduated from Indiana," Blaine remembers. "We brought him in initially as an intern. When I arrived in Dallas in March 1981, I learned that the marketing guy had just left. Leonard said, 'Let's start looking for people. Do you know anybody?' I said, 'I do know a young man. You should probably talk to him.' I called Doug and asked if he'd be willing to move to Dallas from Louisville. He said, 'Yes, I guess so.'"[7]

Kinzey came down for a weekend including concerts and a series of interviews. The final segment took place in Stone's home in the Lake Highlands section of Dallas. Leonard Stone had realized quickly that he had a very strong candidate on the hook. "We had a deli luncheon. We had run him around the night before, which was a Saturday, introducing him to board members and staff. People asked me, 'You're not going to hire him, are you?' They thought he was a meek and quiet individual."

Stone perceived strengths in Kinzey that others missed. "Marketing people almost always have one of two essentials. They either know how to go for the jugular, or they are highly organized. Rarely do you get somebody who's got both. Doug laid out his portfolio. He described his campaigns. He told me what he was willing to do to make them work. I turned to my wife after he'd gone out to get some fresh air—it was a very hot Sunday—and said, 'This is a very special commodity. This is very rare. He and I will get along famously.' Still, Doug wasn't sure he wanted to move to Dallas. The best thing I did when I made the offer was give him about a five-minute time limit to make his decision."[8]

Kinzey accepted. When Leonard Stone came to the DSO, it had just over four thousand subscribers. Melissa McNeil, her successor, Steven Adler, and Stone had raised it to six thousand by the time Kinzey took over the marketing department. Between Kinzey's arrival and the late 1990s, subscriptions soared to the low thirty thousands. Stone says, "It's one of the great marketing successes in the cultural arts, for which Doug Kinzey must get massive credit. We gave him every piece of ammunition he needed. As the executive director, I understood the importance of marketing. Many people who run arts organizations feel it's almost sinful to have to sell. It's as if they think: 'Our art form is so wonderful. Shouldn't people just be knocking at the door?' They were victims of the 'if you build it, they will come' syndrome, the *Field of Dreams*."[9] Kinzey's marketing initiatives were to propel the Dallas Symphony into one of the healthiest orchestras in the United States.

Interlude: Bill Seay Becomes President

Well before Don Stone's term as DSA president was supposed to end, the Lazarus family in Cincinnati, owner of Sanger-Harris's parent company, informed him that he was going up the corporate ladder. "I was promoted to be vice chairman of Federated Department Stores," Stone recalls. "I made a deal with Fred Lazarus that I would commute out of Dallas using the

Federated planes. For about a year and a half I was able to do that, then it became impossible. At that point, in March 1982, we decided we had to move to Cincinnati." The term of his presidency was not scheduled to expire until May. He met with Leonard Stone and said, "I'm going to have to leave as president. I'm sorry to do this because it's the second time in a row. Robert [Decherd] did it, and now I'm doing it."

Leonard Stone and Director of Development Al Milano discussed possible successors, individuals with strong leadership and fund-raising skills. Milano suggested, "You know, Bill Seay has raised money for us from time to time." Seay, who was chairman of the board and CEO of Southwestern Life Insurance, had chaired the DSO's 1978 Challenge to Greatness fund-raising campaign. Stone did a little bit of research. He remembers, "I found out all these wonderful things about Bill: dedicated, committed. Everybody loved this guy, and he was not far from retirement. Now we had to recruit him."[10]

William H. Seay became president of the DSA in 1982. (*DSO archives*)

Unbeknownst to the symphony, Mayor Jack Evans was thinking about recruiting Seay to become chairman of the City of Dallas sesquicentennial celebration. "We discovered we were in a bit of a competition with the city," says Leonard Stone. He convened a Saturday luncheon at Dallas Country Club with Seay, Henry Miller, Dick Galland, Don Stone, and Jack Evans. The purpose of that luncheon was to convince Seay to accept the DSA presidency.

Seay listened to their pitch, then expressed two concerns. He looked across the table at Miller and said, "You know, Henry, somebody is going to have to raise a lot of money to do this thing. I'm not worried about the symphony, but I'm worried about this concert hall project that you're talking about. If Jack is OK about me doing this and chairing his sesquicentennial committee at the same time . . ." He glanced across at the mayor.

Evans said, "I think we can accommodate that."

Seay continued, "I'll take on this responsibility succeeding you, Don—remember, I haven't been on the board; you're going to have to bring me right up to speed—provided, Henry, that you take on the fund-raising chairmanship." Seay knew that Miller, with his experience, contacts, and love of music, would be the perfect chair of the fund-raising campaign.

Miller replied, "Well, Bill, you know, I have done it for the opera, and I've done it for the summer musicals, and I did it in 1974 with Dick [Galland] for the orchestra. I really need to think about this."

"Take all the time you need."

DURING the next couple of weeks, Leonard Stone called Seay almost daily to ask, "Bill, are you in?" He would answer, "I haven't heard from Henry." Every call from Stone would trigger a call from Seay to Miller's office, to ask if he had made a decision. Each time, Miller would demur. "I haven't decided yet." After several days of this pattern, Stone was getting anxious, and a little impatient. There was so much work to do. As diplomatically as possible, he told Seay that they really had to have an answer. That evening, Seay called Miller at home. Miller equivocated again. "No, Bill, I haven't made a decision. I still need some more time." When he hung up the phone, Juanita Miller was curious. She had heard only her husband's part of the conversation. "Who was that?"

"Bill Seay."

"What was it all about? What did he want?"

"He wants me to do the fund-raising for the symphony if he takes on the presidency."

She said, "Henry, you need to do this, for the city and for the symphony!" Henry and Juanita Miller talked about it for fifteen minutes, then Miller phoned Seay back. "Bill, I've finally found the time to think about it, and I'll do it."[11]

—⁊⁊—

DON Stone officially resigned as board president effective February 19, 1982. Seay assumed the presidency. Within months after he took office, Leonard Stone received a call from Annette Strauss, who was a member of the symphony board and the Dallas Park Board. She asked if Stone knew Liener Temerlin. Stone had met him a few times. She said, "I think he would be a wonderful person to have on your board. If you have him invited to the board—"

Stone interrupted, "Annette, I can't do that. I can make recommendations, but I'm not the decision maker there."

She said, "Leonard, you will thank me and the Dallas Symphony will thank me for the rest of your life if you get Liener Temerlin involved and active." Stone carried that message to Seay, who also had Temerlin in mind to join the board. Temerlin, the head of the Dallas office of advertising giant Bozell & Jacobs, remembers Seay calling him to have lunch. "He told me at lunch that he wanted me to join the symphony board, assuming that the board would approve the invitation. He said he wanted to visit with me at greater length to discuss the possibility of my following him as president."[12] With two incomplete presidencies preceding his own, Seay was taking steps to ensure a smooth transition during the critical years that lay ahead.

Part Three

1982–1985

Art work used for the 1982 bond election campaign, at which time
the hall was referred to as The Dallas Concert Hall. (*DSO archives*)

Chapter Thirteen

1982 BOND ELECTION

Vote Yes: A Great Concert Hall for a Great City.

SLOGAN FOR THE 1982 BOND CAMPAIGN

T HE 1979 bond election had provided funds for land acquisition. Constructing the edifice would cost considerably more. The terms of the 1979 city policy for cultural arts facilities dictated that another bond initiative would take place. Almost on the heels of the 1979 victory, long-range plans were on the drawing board for the larger, later program. By spring 1980, DSA Board President Robert Decherd and the symphony's Leonard Stone had identified Philip O'B. Montgomery III to chair a symphony hall committee that would plan and run the bond campaign. (His father, Dr. Philip O'B. Montgomery, Jr., was subsequently selected by Mayor Jack Evans to coordinate the Arts District.)

As early as summer of 1980, the younger Montgomery enlisted the aid of a political consulting firm, Seib, Starling & Associates, to develop planning strategy. "This series of bond elections was part of a shift in Dallas' image of itself," Montgomery says today. "It's a tradition that extends back to Erik Jonsson's mayoralty and the decision to build the airport and the public library system. Going into the 1982 election, that process was mid-course. Dallas/Fort Worth International Airport, then less than ten years old, was having a major impact on corporate relocations. Throughout the twentieth century, accomplishments such as landing the regional Federal Reserve Bank to Dallas was one of a series of major projects that developed Dallas ahead of its peer group of cities. All these things were part of Dallas' shift from a regional to a major national corporate center."[1]

To evaluate the effect that a symphony hall would have on the city's economy,

Montgomery's committee commissioned an economic impact study from the LWFW Group in December 1981. Its purpose was to examine the market and assess potential economic impact through diversified use of the concert hall, including food and beverage services.

That same month, Assistant City Manager Vic Suhm wrote to DSA President Don Stone, encouraging him to secure advance commitment of private sector support if the symphony wished to be supported for the August 1982 capital improvements program. He suggested that the DSO emulate the museum program from 1979. As it happened, the symphony was several steps ahead of them. Because Phil Montgomery had started early, he had already assembled a broad-based bond election steering committee made up of civic leaders representing all segments of the city's population. By early 1981, he was reporting the steering committee's monthly progress to the symphony's executive board. Sydney Reid-Hedge, director of volunteer services, had enlisted hundreds of DSO volunteers from the Dallas Symphony Orchestra League—members of the Innovators, the DSO Guild, the Junior Group—to help with the 1979 campaign. Her volunteer "machine" was well oiled, well staffed, and well organized, but the momentum for this new initiative still surprised her. "The league volunteers worked with dedicated resolve in both 1979 and 1982," she later said.[2]

Public awareness and approval were key to achieving the symphony's goals. To that end, Montgomery's group, with the symphony's blessing, hired Weekley, Amps & Gray to devise and implement the campaign strategy. John Weekley, Judy Bonner Amps, and Enid Gray had helped the museum achieve its goals in the 1979 bond election. In the early 1980s, they were the top political consulting firm in Dallas. Montgomery also persuaded the Richards Group, on a quasi *pro bono* basis—"They did it for practically nothing," he acknowledges—to develop and produce the campaign advertising materials.

With the campaign strategy and theme set by early autumn 1981, the groundwork for the election was laid. Virtually overnight, the slogan "A Great Concert Hall for a Great City," coined for the campaign, was omnipresent throughout Dallas. Passage of the bond issue would ensure major public funding for construction. The symphony planned to approach city council in June 1982 to request placement on an August ballot.

How Much Will the City Spring For?

The land was substantially in place, and the design had evolved from concept to two-dimensional schematic drawings. Artec had produced the first interior drawings of the concert room. The symphony could now present to the community a concrete image of the projected building. *This could actually happen.*

The symphony had yet to determine the dollar amount it would ask the electorate to approve as the public contribution. The formula for capital cost construction was sixty percent city/forty percent Dallas Symphony Association. But how much *was* sixty percent? Cost projections for the building varied, but there was no question in anyone's mind that I. M. Pei's fee would be very high and that the hall would be more expensive by the time it was complete than initial estimates forecast. Pei had run nearly one hundred percent over budget on Dallas City Hall, and he did not have a reputation for thrift. Assistant City Manager Vic Suhm later commented, "Pei is a great architect: creative and a good designer. But controlling costs with Pei is a contradiction in terms. It doesn't happen. The level of fees you pay a Pei is not normal. The city didn't have a choice, because the symphony association was totally committed to Pei."[3] Prompted by local media coverage, public perception could easily shift against the project because of a sense that costs were not under control.

Director of Development Al Milano and Leonard Stone made an appointment to visit with Mayor Jack Evans in late 1981 to discuss the forthcoming bond election. They asked, politely, if he intended to support the DSO's being on the bond election ballot.

Evans shot back, "Yes, I couldn't very well have been the chairman of the campaign that saw you there for the land and now be mayor and *not* support you for the building!"

Relieved, Stone and Milano got down to business, "OK, let's talk about the dollars," Stone invited.

Evans considered his reply. He appeared to have already given the matter some thought. "Leonard, you can't be on this ballot for more than $30 million, because if you do, the city would think that you were out of control. As a matter of fact, you ought to be on for less than $30 million. I'd recommend somewhere between $28 and $29 million." It was not what Stone and Milano had hoped to hear.

Late that evening, Stone's telephone rang at home. Evans didn't bother identifying himself. "Leonard, your face looked kind of pained when I said it couldn't be over $30 million," he said. "Do you understand that in order to win you've got to get the citizens' support? Thirty million dollars is a lot of money. You have to just trust me that I really do know what I'm talking about."

Stone replied, "Mr. Mayor, I accept that."[4]

Milano and Stone had already calculated their total, adhering to the sixty/forty formula devised by George Schrader. If the public sector's share of slightly under $30 million equaled sixty percent, then the remaining forty percent would be about $20 million to be raised by the symphony. According to Stone, "That's how we arrived at the initial $49.5 million budget figure for the building. That figure was formula-driven. It lacked any concrete relationship to a structure, a site, materials, size, scale, or scope. From that meeting in Jack Evans's office in April 1982, four months prior to the bond election, the foundation for the tension among the city, the media, and some of the board was laid."[5]

IN APRIL 1982, Harlan Crow, whose company was one of six private developers owning land in the Arts District, told *D Magazine:* "Our city has the chance to build something that will give us character, a world character of fine quality. Most major cities have something special that's desirable. Dallas really lacks that, and here's our chance to make something."[6] Mort Meyerson also perceived that long-term possibility, but he knew that, short term, passing the bond issue was essential if the hall were to become reality. He told the executive board so on April 30, 1982, stressing the importance of the first public viewing of the model, scheduled for unveiling on May 12.

With strategic timing, the symphony held two key press conferences, both geared toward maximizing positive associations with the prospect of the hall. First, on April 22, 1982, the symphony revealed results of the economic impact study prepared by LWFW Associates. The consultants had taken into consideration that the City of Dallas already owned three performance venues: Fair Park Music Hall, the Majestic Theatre, and the Dallas Convention Center Theatre, adjacent to Dallas City Hall. They forecast new tax revenues, additional earned income to the DSO (because of an expanded season) and to Fair Park Music Hall (which

A 1982 model of hall built in the I.M. Pei & Partners model shop. (*DSO archives*)

would have additional nights available for alternative performances), and hundreds of jobs for the construction phase. Dozens of local companies would benefit from the construction. Most important, the city would benefit from immediate and recurrent annual local expenditures associated with the hall and its attendant activity. Finally, LWFW predicted that a new symphony hall would provide a significant attraction to companies seeking to relocate their headquarters. Joseph F. McCann, a spokesman for snack food giant Frito (now Frito-Lay), told *The Dallas Morning News:* "If we have a world class opera and a premier symphony, that's a part of the mix that can make the community attractive so that we can get the guys we need to run our business. As a company working in a community, to get top people, we have to offer a good place to live."[7] The LWFW study argued that, as more high-level business professionals came to the Dallas area, they would seek quality environment in the broadest sense. That meant cultural amenities. The climate for building was optimal.

The second press conference on May 12, 1982, took place at downtown Dallas' historic Union Station. I. M. Pei unveiled the model of his firm's design for the proposed concert hall: a shoebox rectangle, wrapped in a square, which in its turn was encircled by curving glass walls soaring from ground to roof on three sides. The hall was to sit diagonally on its site, both to maximize use of the land and to communicate with the Dallas Museum of Art three blocks west, and with the rest of downtown Dallas. The music chamber—the room at the heart of the structure—would seat 2,200. Pei described his design as one for people. "Since music is such an important part of a city's life, its citizens should feel a part of the building that houses its major musical organization," Pei explained. "This is the feeling we have strived to create."[8] Prior to the press conference, Meyerson convened a breakfast meeting of the concert hall committee in the fifth-floor presentation room at EDS so that Pei could present the model privately to them. After the Union Station press conference, the displays and model were completely disassembled and rushed to the Hilton on Mockingbird and Central, where they were then reassembled for the DSA's annual board of trustees meeting.

Press and television coverage of the unveiling was favorable. A few days after the public unveiling, *The Dallas Morning News* architecture critic David Dillon published a thoughtful assessment of the design, noting some changes in Pei's style. "The overall design of the hall, a complex integration of a square, circle and rectangle that produces an unconventional symmetry, leaves no doubt that abstract geometry as the Modernists understood it is still the driving force in [Pei's] work. But the prodigal use of glass, ordinarily a minor element in Pei's material vocabulary, together with the abundance of public space within and around the hall suggests that the design also has strong populist roots."[9] Pei acknowledged a debt to the Pompidou Centre's transparency and look of continuous animation. Shortly after the design was unveiled, Stanley Marcus told *D Magazine,* "I think that this will be one of the most photographed buildings in America." He was right.

—❧—

MONTGOMERY discovered there was a lot to running a campaign: "You've got the whole volunteer organization, the paid media, the tactical issues of writing and designing, timing, mailing, conceiving all the literature and paraphernalia that goes behind it. Somebody's got to make all this gel and happen. You've got the whole political environment and the media to deal with. It's a multi-faceted effort which all occurs simultaneously. That compounds, builds in a huge crescendo, then reaches its climax and stops on one day."

With such a huge task before him, Montgomery selected a few chiefs to commandeer his army of volunteers. By mid-May 1982, he was able to complete his permanent staff and infrastructure for the Dallas concert hall bond election committee. He chose Buck J. Wynne III, then a law student at Southern Methodist University, as campaign director. Amanda Dealey was vice chairman of the campaign, and Pat McBride was volunteer chairman. Mary McDermott was phone bank chair, assisted by Jeanne Johnson Phillips. Montgomery secured donated office space in the Quadrangle, a commercial development less than a mile outside downtown. The office was a center for organization, mailings, and volunteer coordination.

Melissa McNeil and John Adams were the only paid symphony staff whose responsibilities revolved specifically around organization of the concert hall project. That included bond elections. Montgomery relied on McNeil extensively during the campaign. "She's a fabulous administrator and manager," he declares. "I just couldn't have begun to have undertaken this effort without her help. She was more than a liaison; it was a managerial role. Her job was concert hall planning, but that was enlarged to include the planning and administrative support of the campaign from the symphony organization's perspective. The people power was focused in Sydney [Reid-Hedge]'s whole volunteer organization; the phone bank was staffed by volunteers."[10]

With assistance from McNeil, Montgomery hired Nela Wells as a paid campaign coordinator. "They were looking for someone to run the headquarters operation," Nela Wells (now Moore) recalls. "They needed support for the volunteer function and a liaison with the political consultant. We established a system for the phoners. One stack of cards became four: 'yes,' 'no,' 'undecided' and 'no contact.' I kept things in order so that we were able to track results efficiently. When the [political] consultants walked in the office, they could take one glance at the cards and know how things were going."[11]

Montgomery reported to the DSA Board in mid-May that he had recruited five hundred confirmed volunteers. The target volunteer total was one thousand.[12] Political consultant Enid Gray credits Nela Wells's organizational skills and, especially, Montgomery's recruiting gifts. "Philip had this incredible capacity to pull together wonderful groups of people," she says. "He created a new volunteer slot every day, every week. A lot of these people were young and eager, either unmarried or recently married and without too many responsibilities. Volunteering for this campaign became the thing to do, a social thing, and fun. You have to have that camaraderie or it doesn't work. Of course you have your ongoing internal squabbles, which is normal, and unavoidable. You get on with it—and we did."[13]

According to Nela Wells Moore, the volunteer group was not restricted to symphony subscribers. "This younger, professional group of volunteers was motivated by the vision of a downtown with a life after dark, where people would want to go," she says. "It was a civic thing that started with the DMA, the whole concept of an arts district. But with the symphony campaign, it began to take on a life, because with the addition of the concert hall the possibility of having this special place in Dallas became reality. It was a rare time in Dallas."[14]

The symphony's leadership raised about $300,000 to support the bond campaign. "At the time," says Montgomery, "$300,000 was a good, healthy budget for a referendum like that. Our budget did not include television, but it did include some radio ads, plus the LWFW study, support for extensive phone bank operations, speaking engagements throughout the community, and direct mail. Our efforts were geared toward educating voters, ideally through the phone bank, with call-backs to undecided voters to try to firm them up, then a massive get-out-the-vote effort for three days leading up to election day. It was a classic 1980s campaign. Phone banks were working because people would still answer their phones. It was an effective tool. We did a little door-to-door campaigning, but that was a lower priority simply because it's not as efficient as getting on the phone and calling people. We had hundreds of people calling from separate facilities. Louise Kahn was a stalwart on those phone banks! Nancy Penson and Mary McDermott, too—they were all in here regularly, working hard."[15]

—⁓—

FOLLOWING Mayor Evans's advice, Leonard Stone presented his board with a bond election figure of $29,700,000, just under the $30 million cap Evans had counseled. (That figure was subsequently reduced to $28.6 million, resulting in a revised total projected budget figure of $47.7 million.) On behalf of the orchestra, Bill Seay made a presentation in late May to the city's park and recreation board, then the governing body of the city's cultural activities. Park Board President Starke Taylor and Betty Marcus (Stanley Marcus's sister-in-law) demanded a commitment from the Dallas Symphony to guarantee the concert hall's operations costs: security, maintenance, utilities, etc. In their arguments, they cited the museum's commitment to increase its endowment by $5 million in order to ensure that such operational costs would be available to them in perpetuity, rather than the museum's relying on the city to pick up those costs.

DSA Board President Seay was taken aback. They had not foreseen this development, and the design budget was already tight. Mort Meyerson and Stanley Marcus had both called him to express concern as to whether the symphony could afford the additional expense. The memory of financial collapse only eight years before was all too vivid in their minds. During the following weeks, a series of meetings took place in an attempt to reach a compromise. City council remained adamant, reiterating its insistence on the symphony's commitment. Backed into a corner, the symphony board executive committee adopted a resolution on June 14 to assume responsibility for operations and maintenance costs, provided that the city continue to treat the symphony on the same basis as its other major cultural facilities and institutions.[16]

Two days later, Dallas City Council heard the concert hall proposal and voted for its inclusion on the August 3 ballot. They announced the complete bond election slate one week later. Proposition 4 was a $28.6 million item representing the city's sixty percent contribution to the projected $47.7 million cost of the hall.[17]

—❧—

THE ELECTION was seven weeks out. This time, proponents were taking no chances. The official campaign shifted into high gear between mid-June and early August, capitalizing on the extensive groundwork laid during the previous two years. Montgomery oversaw an elaborate strategy of building broad-based, non-partisan public support for the issue throughout the city. "It was very simple," he observes. "Organize early, have a large volunteer force, have a very specific, clear plan along the lines of the sixty/forty arts funding policy."[18] His plan for the final, intense weeks leading to election day included four key events, beginning with a campaign kickoff at the Quadrangle headquarters scheduled for June 27, and the deadline to register to vote for the bond election, July 2. Absentee balloting began on July 14 and concluded on July 30. D-day, of course, was August 3: election day.

In late June, the Dallas County Appraisal District began mailing tax increase notices to homeowners. For most of them, the rise was a staggering fifty percent. Bond backers cringed, fearing a reaction similar to the one that had caused the 1978 bond initiative to crater.[19] Working with the symphony, the concert hall committee mailed a flyer to Dallas voters urging approval of the $28.6 million proposal. All told, they would spend more than $220,000 of their $300,000 budget on mailings, data processing, newsletters, yard signs, bumper stickers, transportation of the hall model, and radio and newspaper ads to supplement the volunteers.

The oversize model of the symphony hall, produced by the I. M. Pei & Partners in-house model shop, included artificial trees and miniature cars in the parking lot and on the street. Initially, all the automobiles were luxury imports like Mercedes and Jaguars. When it arrived from New York, DSO public relations staff winced at the potential gaffe, recognizing that the high-priced cars were bad politics. The directive came forthwith to replace them with less exclusive vehicles representing a broader cross-section of the community. Locating American cars and yellow school buses to the right scale presented a challenge, but Ted Amberg's secretary managed to find some that satisfied both the DSO and Pei. The model made appearances throughout the city. Amberg's office coordinated its transport, and he or his secretary accompanied the model on its travels around Dallas in a specially equipped truck complete with custom lighting for various installations, public relations and fund-raising events. Over a period of several months, after the unveiling at Union Station, it stayed at NorthPark Mall a while and went to two private homes for receptions.[20]

Over at the Fair Park offices, symphony staff knew how much was riding on this campaign. Music Director Eduardo Mata had signed a three-year extension to his contract in the spring, making it clear that the dream of a hall was essential to his ambition for the orchestra. "A lot of wishful thinking went into the signing of this contract," he told *The Dallas Morning News,* "for everything I hope to accomplish here will be set back at least 10 years if Proposition 4 fails to pass. . . . The hall is the next logical step in the orchestra's life, and I feel its development is tied practically and psychologically to the passing of the bond issue."[21] Supporters of all the arts recognized that, if the hall failed in its funding bid on August 3, the entire concept of a Dallas Arts District would likely collapse.

The corps of volunteers was key to delivering the symphony's message. Between June and the first of August, orchestra members and DSO staff joined Phil Montgomery's army, calling on residents throughout Dallas to secure votes and make certain that people voted. Victor Marshall, artistic administrator of the DSO, and Montgomery alternated days making speeches prior to every DSO Starfest summer concert. Hundreds of others enlisted by Montgomery and his team coordinated direct mail and phone bank efforts. Everybody was nervous about the August timing. Much of the community could be out of town, on vacation with children, especially in affluent North Dallas where the symphony had a strong base of support.

Weekley, Amps & Gray, the DSO's political consultants, were on secure turf. They understood the market. "We're just putting proven political techniques to work for the arts," consultant Judy Bonner Amps told *The Dallas Morning News.* "The idea is to identify your 'yes' votes, stay with them and be sure they get to the polls. Nothing very innovative about that."[22] Her partner, Enid Gray, recalls, "Targeting is what I did, mostly. You identify your potential supporters, figure out where they are and go after them. It doesn't happen accidentally that people go out and vote. You obtain your lists, put them together, and call and call and call."[23]

And call they did. Coordinated by Mandy Dealey and Pat McBride, the volunteers plowed through Weekley, Amps & Gray's telephone lists with a vengeance. In spite of *The Dallas Morning News'* assessment that the economy was shakier than it had been in 1979, the volunteers' tenacity and sheer numbers began to have an impact.

By late July, Montgomery had conducted three sequential polls indicating that voter response to Proposition 4 was becoming more positive. He and his committee had fulfilled 150 speaking engagements promoting the hall. The corps of volunteers, whose ranks had swelled to 1,200, had mailed 200,000 flyers and contacted 40,000 households. Intensive telephone bank efforts were scheduled for the two days prior to election day, and election day itself.[24]

On July 26, one week before balloting, the symphony announced that it had received more than $11 million in gifts and signed pledges from private sources for construction of the new concert hall. The donations were contingent upon passage of Proposition 4. "If the voters say 'yes' on Proposition 4, we are confident that we can complete our fund-raising successfully and that the concert hall will become a reality," Board President Seay told the press.

—❧—

DOUG Howard, chair of the players' concert hall committee, opines that the 1982 bond election was the point that the orchestra finally got involved, realizing that the hall might really happen. "We all knew that the building was our future," he says. "Without it, we had dreary prospects as an orchestra."[25] Backers were committed to swaying East Dallas, where they seemed to feel the election might hinge. The North Dallas vote was also essential to victory. Orchestra members worked very hard in both areas, playing outdoor concerts and calling on voters door-to-door to distribute leaflets. Everyone expected that this would be the closest vote among the various propositions on the ballot. "The polling data generally showed that if we could turn out the vote we could win," Montgomery said later. "I was always confident we could win, but it never really hit me until the week before, when I sensed we had it. We had the numbers. We just had to drive it home."[26]

It worked. On August 3, Dallas voters approved $28.6 million as the city's contribution to fund DSO construction costs. At Union Station in downtown Dallas, supporters had set up a poll-watching party that turned into a jubilant celebration as the results were tabulated.

Celebrating the 1982 Bond election victory were, from left, Mandy Dealey, Pat McBride, Carole Ferguson, Phil Montgomery, Mary McDermott, Enid Gray, Buck Wynne, Judy Bonner Amps, Nela Wells, George Truitt, Melissa McNeil. (*Courtesy Melissa McNeil*)

The *Dallas Times Herald* reported that, with all 235 precincts reporting, the concert hall *had* been the closest issue, passing with a 57.5 percent majority.[27] Firefighting facilities, police sub-stations, and municipal service centers had carried the vote—but the symphony hall had passed. After four years of navigating local politics and a wayward economy, the idea of an arts district with a symphony hall had finally taken hold.

Montgomery and his team had promoted the ballot initiative not as a concert hall but as a civic institution. From his perspective, it sold on civic pride. "We did not try to sell it as world-class music. We sold it as a world-class facility that would make Dallas arts stand out. We always talked about how the hall would be measured acoustically against the greatest halls in the world. We highlighted the public benefits, such as the fact that so many Dallas school-children would attend concerts in the hall. We talked about the enlargement of the audience, what the symphony's and the hall's stature would do for the city as a whole. Those were the reasons we argued for the hall as public investment. Knowing that Dallas would have one of the best halls in the world really made a difference to people. That attitude is what won the bond election."[28]

The bond issue had been the largest to pass in the city's history: a $247 million package including $18.4 million for expansion and rebuilding of the Dallas Zoo and $18 million for renovation of Fair Park in preparation for the state sesquicentennial, as well as more mundane items such as street improvements. George Schrader withdrew the first bond issued and presented it to Leonard Stone as a memento. Stamped "Specimen," it now hangs framed in Stone's Tampa, Florida, office.

Chapter Fourteen

THE TAB STARTS
TO RISE

I'll never forget that frightening moment when Stewart Donnell told Melissa McNeil and me, 'This building is going to cost you guys $84 million.' It turned out that Stewart predicted almost exactly what happened. The Meyerson ended up costing $81 million plus, without the land. Stewart was so on, and this was years before.[1]

LEONARD DAVID STONE, 1997

GOING into the 1982 bond election, the projected cost of the building was officially publicized at $47.7 million. That figure was computed arbitrarily by plugging in the sixty/forty formula dictated by the City of Dallas policy. The symphony was on the bond issue for $28.6 million, representing the public's sixty percent share. The complementary forty percent figure for the symphony's private sector commitment yielded the total. All costs over this amount were to be funded entirely through the symphony's resources.

Cost and the Economy

Once Pei's design began to take shape and Artec had stipulated the parameters for the music chamber, Meyerson and his committee realized that they required a more elaborate and detailed budget forecast. The numbers required adjustment each time some aspect of the design changed or was refined. Early in 1981, Stone asked Johnson, "Do you know anyone who could take a set of schematics and then talk in terms of high-end material, average material, or low-end material? This or that number of seats, then project what this would cost?" Johnson replied, "Yes, there's only one person I know who could do that and come within a fraction of a percentage of accuracy: Stewart Donnell."[2]

Donnell, a Scot who had settled in Canada, was at the time affiliated with a Toronto-based firm, Hanscomb Roy Associates.[3] Early in his career, he had done cost projections for university buildings, hospitals, parking garages, and office buildings. Then, in 1969, Donnell collaborated with Johnson on Hamilton Place, a hall in Hamilton, Ontario. That was his first dealing with a music performance/theatre facility. "That experience, incidentally, changed my professional life's direction," he later observed. "I knew that this was what I wanted to devote my energies to. Within the practice, I developed cultural venues: museums, art galleries, and performing arts centers."[4]

At Johnson's suggestion, Donnell telephoned Leonard Stone, who invited him to Dallas and arranged a meeting with Meyerson. "We had a good discussion for about two hours one morning at EDS," Donnell recalls. As Donnell was leaving, Meyerson asked, "Look, Mr. Donnell, can you have a proposal in here in four days' time?" Donnell sent the proposal, and a few days later Meyerson called to say he was hired. The DSA had soon added Hanscomb Roy Associates to its list of outside consultants.[5]

Customarily, cost consultants receive a program brief articulating each space in the intended facility. Donnell says, "From that, our first step is to translate those areas into net areas. Rooms require partitions on each side; all require a corridor for access. We then translate those spaces into gross building area. The program brief often overlooks or excludes items such as public circulation, mechanical space, electrical space, duct shafts, and staircases. We bring that together from the program to develop a building size in gross square footage to accommodate the net functional areas. We then ask questions of the owner which are easy to ask but difficult to answer. What architectural quality is expected: externally, internally, and within the performance room? We've got to know who the acoustician is, and his acoustic criteria, and what equipment he and the theatre consultant want to respond to programming requirements. We price the building and equipment on those terms to come up with the basic construction cost and a capital budget incorporating professional fees and other owner costs."[6]

The Dallas project was unusual in that the architect and acoustician had already been selected by the time Hanscomb Roy Associates was brought in. In most performance hall projects, the program brief is developed by the theatre planner, in conjunction with the owner and the users. In the case of the Dallas concert hall, the reverse had taken place: Melissa McNeil began drafting the initial draft program brief before Artec was engaged as the consultant for acoustics, theatre planning, and performance equipment. She developed the brief primarily based on input from Meyerson's smaller unit and Doug Howard's players' committee. The DSO had used prototypes of the brief as a basis for soliciting proposals from architects and acousticians and, eventually, to select the principal consultants, including the cost consultant.[7]

Before Donnell's formal engagement by the DSA in autumn 1981, he had already provided some preliminary figures for the smaller unit and the executive board. Based on the program brief, he calculated the initial cost of the building program in July 1981 at $65 million, based on the original project's scope, seat count, and quality, but reduced that figure almost immediately to $55 million to reflect the removal of 43,000 square feet.[8] Donnell soon squeezed the lower figure even tighter, first in September, to demonstrate what could be built for $50 million, then again in October, when the DSA Executive Committee voted to place a $45 million cap on the building cost. That figure left them, they reasoned, with a $4 to $5 million cushion that would absorb inflation or unforeseen delays. A pattern of shifting cost estimates was thus established early.

Periodically, Hanscomb Roy revised its cost estimates to reflect the most recent design decisions. Each of its interim reports between November 1981 and September 1984 evaluated what must be sacrificed in order to maintain the budget. Every time the design was modified to add one detail, another detail was forfeited. In theory, the bond issue figure of $49.5 million was immutable. "I think it's important to know that there was a political reason to be at $49.5 million," says Stewart Donnell. "That meant, in colloquial terms, a 'bare bones' building in terms of areas, finishes and materials. I think it was well known in the committee that this figure was going to be enhanced as the project developed and the funds became available. It *had* to be. Otherwise, the project would never have been built."[9]

By early 1982, the building was in a period of transition from the program brief to early sketches. "In small group committee meetings and design team meetings I attended, we were going over the design as it was evolving, reviewing the basic building budget and, on the other side of the table, talking about possible enhancements," Donnell remembers. "Those fell into two principal categories: building construction and performance equipment." Performance-related equipment included acoustic canopies, acoustic adjustment curtains, piano lift, reverberation chambers, performance lighting systems, projection equipment, loudspeaker treatment, banners, chorus risers, audience chairs, and other items.[10]

In the first year of scaled-back budget projections, less than $2 million had been allocated for those items. The $45 million cap meant that available funds for special performance equipment were stripped down to only $1,328,000. One of Donnell's periodic project budget summaries advised the smaller unit, "This is an unrealistic amount to provide for any meaningful level of equipment and as such imposes severe restraints on the range of uses of the hall if not rendering it virtually inoperable."[11] Donnell and his colleagues met repeatedly with Artec and the Pei group to develop a list of options that accompanied each cost estimate as an addendum. The list included upgrades in certain performance equipment and materials that the acousticians and architects would particularly like to have restored to the design, if the money to pay for them could be found. Both design teams asked the Dallas Symphony to consider these items in order to fulfill their stated goals.

The process of estimating the additional cost took six months. A project budget summary from Hanscomb to the DSO in mid-May 1982 came in at $68,470,000, including the preferred options. Hanscomb wrote: "The Smaller Unit of the Concert Hall Committee instructed the project team to produce a building design for classical music within a $45 million project cost limit. . . . the result is a severely stripped-down building and an insufficient contingency. To supplement this base building design, the team has generated a list of options that they counsel the client to consider to fulfill the Dallas objective of achieving a world class facility, should sufficient funds become available."[12]

Meyerson remembers, "We knew right away that we had a problem. At that point, we were no longer conceptualizing. We hadn't broken ground for the building, but we had the plan and estimated costs, and we knew that we were between a rock and a hard place. We had to modify the plan. We did it with surgical knives. The small committee, under my leadership, made most of the decisions. Then we would get advice and consent from the large committee or from the board."[13]

In lengthy, sometimes heated, discussions, Meyerson's core group evaluated each item that comprised the total price tag. Supplemental funding was not available. Furthermore, until the bond election passed, they did not yet have a sixty percent commitment from the city. Their top priority, the sacred touchstone against which all compromises must be weighed, was the quality of the sound. Subsidiary priorities were maintenance of the limited seat count, backstage usage, and lobby area. Amenities that were not essential to the preservation of the acoustics were easier to cut. Pei's original renderings for the building showed an extra lobby level above street level. It was axed, and the entire building dropped by one level. A rehearsal hall, originally planned to double as a small recital hall, was also cut. A piano lift, to speed stage changes on programs with a piano soloist, was eliminated. (Mort Meyerson later said that decision was his greatest regret, and that had he been able to do anything differently, he would have retained the piano lift.) Corporate entertainment suites were deferred indefinitely; they would not be completed until 1998. Escalators between levels also dropped from the plans, along with the stage extension lift, a listening system for the hearing-impaired, the sound system for pops concerts and a single-piece orchestra riser unit that was a central part of the acoustical plan.

In mid-July, Meyerson wrote to Pei and Johnson, confirming the cost restrictions he had imposed during a June meeting.

Dear I. M. and Russell:

I would like to reiterate in writing the position I took in my conference room meeting before last in Dallas.

The architect and acoustician must resolve their differences and jointly come up with an approach that will allow us to build an architecturally beautiful, acoustically superior concert hall for less than $50 million.

It is absolutely clear in my mind that I will be unable to, in good faith, support a plan when I know that our capability for money-raising from all sources won't yield us more than $50 million.

There must be architectural treatment that allows us to have appropriate lobbies, finishes, and construction within the budget. In addition, there must be acoustical approaches that will give us the sight lines and quality of sound we want, and still remain within our budget.

I am aware of the importance of making a statement with this building for I. M. In addition, I believe you have been laboring mightily with a sincere interest in what is best for the City of Dallas.

I am further sure that Russell has been making recommendations to the committee with the same thought that it is in the best interest of the city. You are trying to protect us from making mistakes and short-changing ourselves in areas where we will be paying a price in the future.

On the other hand, the financial realities indicate that we cannot have grandness beyond our means, nor can we have multi uses beyond our budget.

In our last meeting I was told there are deferred items and items that need decisions made in August. I am calling a meeting of the large committee and executive board in mid-August[14] at which time we will hash these things out and come to a final conclusion.

I must have a defensible, make-sense plan for a $50 million concert hall, and, in addition, a list of items that will be left out with a price tag for each that is reasonable.

I am not carping or complaining about your services. I am merely stating the objective and the facts we will have to live with.

I look forward to seeing the product of your joint creativity.

Sincerely,
Mort[15]

The letter was hand-delivered to all parties attending a July 12, 1982, meeting among I. M. Pei, Russell Johnson, Nicholas Edwards, Leonard Stone, Melissa McNeil, and Stewart Donnell of Hanscomb Consultants. Stone's reaction was elation: "Bravo!" he wrote on his copy, which he forwarded to Mort Meyerson with this follow-up report.

At the outset, I. M. Pei affirmed that we were now looking at a structure without limestone or travertine floors. I agreed. I. M. Pei and Russell Johnson clearly understand that no performance systems shall be created below street level, thereby avoiding substantial and currently unaffordable construction costs within the proposed garage area.

Advising all consultants that the best we could envision doing was a building range of between $48 and $50 million, I placed before them the challenge of bringing the construction cost down to $31 million, maintaining the non-performance furnishings at $1.1 million, site preparation and owner's co-related costs to $¾ million and performance systems of $3.6 million.

The message was powerfully, tactfully and clearly delivered.

Given the budget of $3.6 million for performance systems, Artec said it would come up with the best recipe for spending that amount that would provide a movable acoustic riser system that could and would work without having to be moved and stored into space below grade level.

I know when we left New York, the I. M. Pei group felt, all at the same time, challenged, depressed, re-directed and possibly even frustrated, but clearly determined to meet the objectives. With respect to the Artec group, it is my personal feeling they felt relieved to finally receive a direction to which they could respond now that the rehearsal room and systems below grade were out of the question.

I gave the team until July 31, 1982, to provide Stewart Donnell a shopping list and the construction resolutions so that Donnell would be in shape for a mid-August presentation of a revised budget conforming to the objectives. . . . [16]

Shortly after the bond election passed in August 1982, a campaign steering committee meeting took place for Cornerstone, the fund-raising program that was slated to shift into high gear within a few months. Mary McDermott reported that the concert hall committee had approved a budget of $49,570,00 for the building, a figure that represented a savings of nearly $2.5 million from the $52 million working budget that had included the second-floor level. Other consequences of the cut were the relegation of the kitchen facility to the building basement, a reduction by half of seating area in the restaurant, removal of the entertainment suites and the symphony shop, and some circulation space. The pluses—in addition to a lower price tag—were a less costly building from the standpoint of maintenance. Plus, Pei asserted that the building's proportions were improved, because the structure was not so vertical. The minuses were a bit more daunting. A budget pared down to $49.57 million meant no limestone exterior or travertine floors, no acoustical riser system, no organ.[17]

Hanscomb submitted a tightened, pared-to-within-an-inch-of-its-life budget—Project Budget #8—in November 1982, coincident with the completion of Pei's schematic drawings and the commencement of design development. The introductory remarks to the budget numbers had a grim tone.

> At this stage, HCI [Hanscomb] reports that the project is within the budget limit set by the Client. However, it should be noted that in order to keep within the $49.5 million budget limit, certain cuts in specification, equipment, and space have been necessary to keep the accepted design viable in financial terms. . . .
>
> The building is brick clad with carpeted lobby areas; 29,000 sf basement area and 6,700 sf of administration area are unfinished. The audience chamber wall and ceiling finishes are paint on plaster; the floors are coloured concrete. Finished to remaining areas are utility. The basic requirements for acoustic isolation and performance integrity are, however, still intact. . . .
>
> In summary, it must be emphasized that, although the building still maintains exciting architectural expression, sound structural, mechanical and electrical systems, and high acoustical quality provisions, it cannot, in HCI's and the design team's opinion, absorb further cuts in budget and still adequately respond to the Client's original brief.[18]

Behind closed doors, the committee acknowledged that $50 million was rapidly becoming unrealistic as a target figure. One enhancement at a time, the symphony would have to raise the funds privately.

The delays in land acquisition inevitably resulted in higher costs. Still clinging to the lower figure, Donnell advised the smaller unit in December 1982 that cost escalations were projected to be 0.75 percent per month over the fifteen-month period from November 1982 to March 1984, the projected bid date. Meyerson listened grimly, ran his own calculations, then reported to the DSA Board Executive Committee the next day that the estimated cost had already increased by $2 million because of delays. He estimated that each three-month delay would cost another $1 million.[19] The arithmetic was all too easy. Four million dollars a year meant a whopping 8 percent annual increase, and both the board and Meyerson's committee already knew that the project had been pared back to a functional, basic hall. Sobered, they approved Pei's October 1982 schematics and, in December, his subsequent plans and revisions. The price tag remained, at least for the moment, at $49.5 million. The façade was brick; the public areas were to be carpeted. Only the seat count, now projected at 2,179, remained uncompromised by economics.[20]

How much of this stern stance was for the public record? In retrospect, most of the participants acknowledge that everyone knew all along that the hall would cost substantially more. Ted Amberg, then head of Pei's Dallas office, says, "We knew the cost was up in the $60-plus million range, back then, but they couldn't publish it. Frankly, as the design progressed, they didn't ignore it, but they agreed to deal with it later. The deal was, the city's share was going to be sixty percent, the same percentage as the museum. That would have meant that the cost would have to be held to $50-some-odd million dollars. Realistically, it was more in the $60–$70 million range. This higher figure was already known, but they couldn't make it public because then there would have been a public outcry. The city would have said, 'Look, we're giving you sixty percent, and sixty percent has a cap on it.' The symphony boards all realized that they would have to raise the difference privately, which is precisely what they did, to their everlasting credit."[21]

Louise Reuben Elam, a City of Dallas staff architect from the public works department who was assigned to the project shortly after the 1982 bond election, says, "The Symphony Board and the consultants had a vision of the building that included marble travertine floors, limestone walls, wood paneling, moveable acoustic canopies, reverberation doors, and other performance equipment; however, the original budget was not sufficient to accommodate all of these elements. A reduced scope building could have been constructed, but it would not have been the building that you see today. At the beginning, the vision didn't match the budget!"[22]

"Certainly the public was not cheated," declares Amberg. "When the city finally found out about the real cost, people like Louise Reuben [Elam] and Cliff Keheley at city hall felt they'd been left out. But the city got a magnificent building. The overrun was funded privately. I guess some people had their noses out of joint because they weren't kept totally informed. But had they been totally informed, there was a concern that somehow they would squelch it and force the building to be built less grandly than it needed to be done."[23]

Cost consultant Donnell agrees. "The point is this: they got wonderful quality. With the exception of any additional costs incurred because of delays, value-for-money was certainly achieved in the enhancements. There is no value-for-money in contractor claims for delays and redoing something that wasn't done properly in the first place. There's no value-for-money in certain aspects of change orders, because these tend to be overpriced by everyone involved. But for the large majority of the enhancements—the stone and travertine, that beautiful wood in the concert room, the high quality railings, the wonderful public lobby areas—Dallas did get value-for-money."[24]

Design Changes

In any building program, elements of design change as a project evolves. For the four years of its design phase, the Meyerson design underwent an almost constant series of modifications. Some were driven by an ongoing clarification of needs. This was, after all, virgin territory for all parties concerned. Pei had never designed a concert hall. Single-purpose performance halls were still a rarity. Even Russell Johnson had only designed one, Jack Singer Hall in Calgary, Alberta, and was implementing some theories for the first time. Donnell had not previously done cost consulting for a single-purpose concert room, only for multi-purpose halls. As for the Dallas participants, they had been conceptualizing since the late 1970s, articulating a series of needs on the basis of inadequacies at Fair Park and the collective experience of musicians and staff in other venues.

The most significant design change to date was surely Pei's forfeiture of the entire upper lobby level in August 1982. City council also approved an Arts District ordinance in February 1983, which, among other provisions, mandated that all parking in the Arts District must be underground or otherwise concealed from view.[25] That meant another redesign to the symphony hall building, which in turn increased design fees and inevitably caused delays. The ordinance excepted the Dallas Museum of Art parking, some of which was already under construction at the time and thus was grandfathered in before the new policy took effect. Pei's design team returned to the drawing board, because much of the audience would now enter the building at subterranean levels.

Most large cities have bustling activity on their streets. In most urban performing arts facilities, people enter at street level, and on foot. Dallas is different. It is a city of drivers, not pedestrians. Because the climate is so unforgiving in the summer, residents will drive short distances of a block or two rather than walk. For four to six months of the year, people move from one air-conditioned space to another. In reassessing public access to the symphony hall, the design team concluded that most patrons would enter from the lower level rather than street level. The building would require two entrance lobbies: one to serve patrons entering from Flora Street, and one to welcome those who parked underground. Parking for the public and for orchestra and staff would somehow require segregation to ensure ease of access for the players. The entire bottom one-third of the complex would have to be re-thought—after the city completed its plans for a multi-level Arts District garage.

Pei wanted to preserve a sense of occasion and provide a wonderful first impression to all who entered the hall. If most of the audience were to come in via the parking garage, that meant the lower lobby level would have to be redesigned. Few buildings in the world have such an elegant entry off two parking garages as the lower level that Pei conceived for the Meyerson. Visitors coming in both from the valet parking area or the main Arts District garage are greeted by open space, high ceilings, the beautiful box office arc, and the graceful curved staircase sweeping around to the upper lobby.

SHORTLY after the city announced its plans to finance and build a public parking garage in the Arts District, Pei announced that the projected site for the hall was too small to accommodate his design. He had originally projected a need for two and one-half acres. Now, he asserted, five acres was essential for the building. Could adjacent parcels of land be acquired to increase the acreage? Assistant City Manager Suhm began to explore the possibility of buying or swapping land adjacent to the Borden's site. As the design of the hall shifted, the total price tag threatened constantly to break through its artificial ceiling. Pei's redesign shifted some of the programmed space, such as coat check and box office, into the lower lobby. It also meant reducing the size of the restaurant by half, because Pei believed that the entry level to the concert room's orchestra level should be devoted to lobby space.

Charles Young, the Pei & Partners architect primarily responsible for the concert room, believes that the building design improved as a result. "It was tighter as a composition, because the proportions became more horizontal," he later said. With the second level gone, the loading dock at the rear of the building would be underground, improving the appearance of the exterior. The main lobby areas were lowered to street level, making them visible from the outside, rather than one flight up. Overall, the structure was smaller, with a total reduction in size of approximately 30,000 square feet, from 210,000 to 180,000 square feet. That meant it would be less expensive.

Members of the smaller unit of the concert hall committee were relieved to learn that Pei's redesign would reduce basic building construction costs from over $33 million to just over $31 million. Stewart Donnell reported to them that the total net savings of the lowered building concept would be approximately $3.5 million. The $49.5 million total tab still seemed feasible. Future operation and maintenance costs would be proportionally lower as well.

But, that ceiling figure was promptly threatened by discussion of upgrades in building materials that I. M. Pei envisioned. He was careful to remind the committee that the finishes he recommended for the interior of the concert room and exterior of the structure were not covered by the existing budget. Not to be outdone, Artec's Russell Johnson stubbornly defended the indispensability of performance equipment Artec had specified.

Shackled by the apparent immutability of a $50 million ceiling, Hanscomb could allow for only a five percent contingency fund. Pei pointed out the inadequacy of that percentage for the high costs entailed in his vision of the building. He reiterated to Donnell and the smaller unit that the curved glass lenses of the conoid surfaces had no two pieces of glass the same size and enumerated several other engineering challenges that could compromise the budget: the difficulty of building the circular beam around the building; the high air-conditioning tonnage of the facility because of the large quantity of glass; the possible need for an electrical heating element to reduce condensation on the windows in light of elevated humidity in the hall; and the likely high cost of the double truss system for sound isolation around the interior of the hall.[26]

Hanscomb's contract extended over a period of approximately two and one-half years, between 1981 and 1984. Cost consultants generally work for the duration of construction documentation. "In other words," Donnell says, "we were gone once there was a contractor on board. HCI had finished its job."[27] The City of Dallas and the concert hall committee selected J. W. Bateson Company (now Centex Construction Company) as first-phase construction manager for the Dallas job in June 1984. Bateson reviewed Pei's architectural drawings during the summer, then in September studied various components of the drawings in order to develop a guaranteed maximum price for the building.[28]

Chapter Fifteen

TESTY PARTNERSHIP: DESIGN ISSUES

Everybody on that committee knew that this hall would be a flop if the acoustics did not work. No matter how beautiful a structure you build, if the acoustics are not good, it is a failure.[1]

RICHARD LEVIN

In the final analysis, the acoustical requirements were so immutable that, from an architectural point of view, the challenge was to optimize a predetermined spatial volume. The behavior of sound in the room was the essential value. The architecture of its surfaces had to follow.[2]

IAN BADER

BEFORE the 1982 bond election, contracts with the Pei and Artec offices were negotiated by the Dallas Symphony Association. The Pei office was under contract directly with the DSA through the end of schematic design. The City of Dallas could not sign contracts for a project that had not been approved. The bond election provided that approval. Clifford Keheley, City of Dallas director of public works for the duration of the Meyerson construction, recalled, "We had to modify the Pei & Partners contract to some extent to make it a public contract, because it was turned over to the city."[3]

The symphony continued to negotiate with Artec through August 1984, when Leonard Stone reported to the board that contracts with Artec were nearing finalization.[4] According to Keheley, the city's subsequent dealings with Russell Johnson and Artec were somewhat different from those with I. M. Pei & Partners because Artec had had letter agreements instead of a formal contract with the symphony association. Theirs was from the outset a city contract. Keheley believes it was advantageous for the city to negotiate directly with Artec. "Russell handled everything. The symphony association gave us the scope of the services that they wanted from the acoustician. Leonard Stone was a great fan of Russell Johnson. When nobody else believed in Russell, Leonard did. Leonard basically said to the city, 'Here are the things we want Russell to do.' Obviously the symphony knew a whole lot more about those things than I do! We took the scope of services that the symphony outlined, and negotiated the contract accordingly. There were no loose ends."[5]

By awarding separate contracts to I. M. Pei & Partners and Artec Consultants, the symphony association had structured its design team as equal partners. Without either firm having control over the other, long discussions ensued as to the balance between acoustic and visual/aesthetic solutions.

The City Gets Involved

The recently completed Erik Jonsson Central Library had officially opened, and the Dallas Museum of Art was in its final year of construction. In his capacity as director of public works, Keheley was involved in both projects. "Having gone through the experience of the museum, I had some idea of what we were going to be confronted with at the symphony

hall," he says. Almost immediately, he remembers, the concert hall manifested major differences from the museum project. "Principally, that happened because the symphony, rightfully, separated the architect and the acoustician, which meant that you actually had two different egos, philosophies, and concepts competing with each other over the same territory." As he remembers it, the division was not only between the architectural and acoustical camps, but also in proponents of each of those camps on the symphony board. "It wasn't a large canyon, more of a small divide, but there were people who clearly expressed their interest in the architecture, the comfort, the patron amenities, and others who were more inclined toward purity of acoustics and the importance of the acoustics to the reputation of the hall."[6]

Artec determined the volume and dimensions of the room. Pei was charged with making it beautiful. The Artec team initiated design work with consideration of sight lines and acoustical theory. According to Meyerson, "Russell came up with a design that clearly was more than an acoustical design for the room. I felt that Russell was going too far into aesthetics and that there would be an immediate clash, because I. M. would push back. Like all architects, naturally, I. M. had originally wanted to have

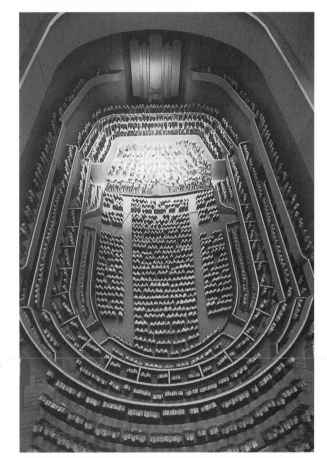

In Artec's first model of the interior, the places where the walls step in near the concert platform at terrace level eventually became the bases of the grand columns. (*DSO archives*)

James E. Langford's drawing is one of the first interior perspectives of the architectural interventions on Artec's design of the concert room. Note the large columns added at left and right to visually "support" the reverberation chambers. (*Courtesy James E. Langford*)

the acoustician work for him. Within a short period of time, there was a clash about what was needed for aesthetics versus what was needed for acoustics."[7]

The disagreements that arose were inevitable, and are inherent in the basic relationship between architect and acoustician on any building for music. Nicholas Edwards, who is both an architect and an acoustician, explains: "The essence of concert hall design is that musicians and audience share one common space. That's something the architecture ought to reinforce. But concert hall acoustics is primarily about reflected sound. What reflects it? Walls, soffits [the horizontal underside of a balcony or cornice], balcony fronts, ceilings, and floors: the surfaces that define a room. This is the fundamental problem between the acoustician and the architect. They're both playing with exactly the same elements. If you place the audience on several tiers, in a particular position to hear strong lateral sound, you've started defining architecture for the room. You cannot do acoustics without doing architecture. Conversely, if the architect—with no acoustical knowledge perhaps—starts to define where the walls, ceilings, and audience will go, he or she is also going to define the acoustics in the process. These elements all pertain to room shape, which is the next most important thing after room size."[8]

Not surprisingly, the disagreements between Artec and the Pei office were virtually all related to the interior design of the music chamber. Artec's design parameters called for placement of walls, ceiling, balcony fronts, audience and chorus seating, concert platform, canopy, soffits, reverberation chamber, a stage extension lift, piano lift, and control rooms. "We produced an acoustical sketch placing the walls in the right positions from an acoustics

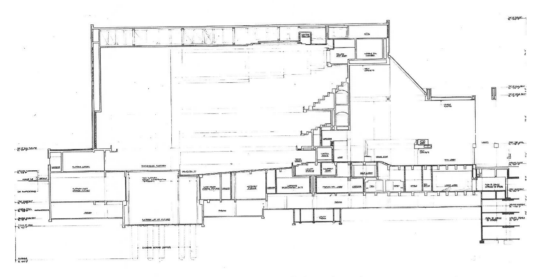

Plan and section of the hall. The longitudinal view, from 1984, still shows the orchestra riser wagon and its storage area. Both were eventually eliminated from the building design. (I.M. Pei & Partners drawings, *DSO archives*)

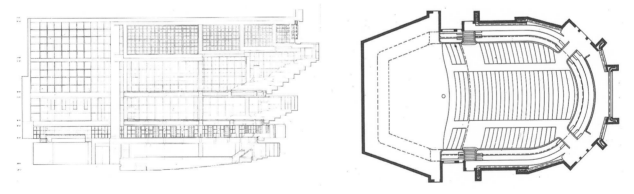

point of view," says Edwards. "We then went to the Pei group, and after a bit of a battle over this very subject of who's going to put the walls in place, the Pei team ran with our sketches, then imposed on them an order, an architecture, a grid, a geometry that was a rationalization of the acoustical sketch into a work of architecture."[9] This area of design could have been the source of the most contentious disagreements between the architect and the acoustician; however, Charles Young's proposals resulted only in minor changes to the alignment of some of the wall panels. He maintained almost all the acoustical shaping of the hall, including the reverse-fan walls at the rear.

The first significant argument arose about two columns that Pei wanted in the audience chamber. "I. M. wanted a visual means of support for the portions of the reverberation chambers that are visible above the grand tier boxes," says architect James Langford. "It also 'stopped' the chambers. The columns terminated the overhead reverberation chambers and carried them to the ground. The large front columns provided a structural logic that was repeated throughout the interior design with columns that terminated the splayed walls further to the rear of the hall."[10] Artec did not want a proscenium, which would separate the performers from the audience. According to architect Charles Young, "Russell originally had the reverberation chamber running around the stage end of the room, over the top of the organ, so it completely encircled the room. We felt that that made the room look too much like a hemicycle, with both ends of the room the same. With the big canopy and the organ, the stage end of the room was so different that you really needed elements of comparable scale to balance them, to set the composition and also to provide additional support for this big volume of the reverberation chamber. So we put in the columns, and Russell was at first concerned about the sound. Then he thought about it some more and agreed that that would probably be OK."[11]

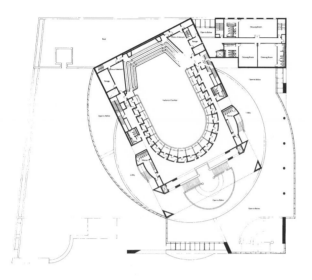

I. M. Pei & Partners dropped a rectangular box into the rest of its plan for the concert hall. (*DSO archives*)

Leonard Stone recalls, "Artec's stance was that there was a danger that sound would be compromised by the imposition of those pillars. Those of us who listen to music in that room now aren't aware of anything negative happening. The pillars are huge, but they're not structural elements; they're design elements. It was Charles [Young] and I. M.'s attempt to frame what I would call the music-sending end of the room."[12]

When it was suggested that the symphony add or remove something from the room, Eugene Bonelli often took the lead in asking Johnson to quantify the impact of such removal. "What percentage of the sound would be lost or changed?" "Russell, will that hurt the sound two percent? Three percent? Ten percent?" Members of the smaller unit remember his perpetual answer: "Everything and anything you're going to do in that room will affect the sound to some degree."

"We didn't unequivocally agree with Russell on everything, because I. M. made some very good points on aesthetics," says Bonelli. "If Russell couldn't quantify and convince us that there was an acoustical problem, we would automatically go with I. M. Whenever we *were* convinced, we decided in Russell's favor. For example, when we discussed the size of the hall and the resulting seat count, I was absolutely convinced that if we went beyond a certain cubic volume and number of seats, we would compromise the acoustics."[13]

Another major dispute erupted over latticework in front of the scrim concealing the reverberation chambers. Bonelli remembers, "Russell wanted nothing in front of the concrete doors that open and close the reverberation chambers. I. M. felt they were hideous and would look awful. One time he said, 'When people look up and say how ugly it is, you can tell them they're seeing acoustics!' He wanted grilles. Russell insisted there was potential for sound distortion. I pressed him repeatedly to quantify what that meant and how bad it would be. We were never satisfied that he was able to do that."[14]

In collaboration with John Walsh, a Vancouver-based researcher, Artec's Nick Edwards and Bob Essert conducted a series of tests with mini-microphones, picking up music in the larger interior models. "For the tests concerning the grilles in front of the reverberation chamber doors, we produced a tape in which the distortion of string sound could be heard," Edwards explains.[15] Leonard Stone adds, "Russell was very worried that, because of the sameness of the grille latticework, notes could hit those and bounce repetitively. We looked at all kinds of solutions, like images of churches, up in the domes, the illusion of structure: *trompe l'oeil.*"[16]

Walter van Greene's early drawing (April/May 1982) of the hall interior shows the side elevation of the audience chamber. This precedes I. M. Pei's imposition of a grid to conceal the reverberation chamber doors, and is an early example of the architect's interior finishes, such as the back-lighting of the onyx.
(Courtesy James E. Langford)

Pei maintained that the area needed concealment, arguing that his design included the grilles. Johnson insisted that it would interfere with the acoustics. Disagreement over the latticework extended over a period of about four years. Again, the issue of quantifying arose. Schrader demanded that Johnson state how much would be sacrificed acoustically by the inclusion of the grilles. "Would it be fifty percent or one percent? we wanted to know. He wouldn't quantify." Meyerson, with Bonelli's concurrence, finally decided that, to make Pei happy, scrims would be built and installed at the front of the room in front of the reverberation chamber doors. If there were an acoustical problem, the grille would be removed. "We have never been able to determine any acoustical distortion because of it," says Bonelli. "I always felt it was a case of Russell's overcompensation. This was his first real opportunity to build a truly great hall."[17] Schrader adds, "We told him, 'If you can't tell us, and it looks awful, for the opening night, let's design a temporary one. What will a temporary one cost?' Bateson figured they could design a wooden one that would look like travertine, and paint it, for about

$65,000. We said OK, we'd put up a temporary one and see how it works, how much of a sac-
rifice in acoustics there is. It's still there! And it didn't cost a million dollars!"[18]

—❧—

THE ACOUSTIC canopy system suspended above the stage was a source of ongoing annoyance to the Pei office.[19]Artec's design concept allowed for the large canopy to be raised, lowered, or tilted according to the optimal acoustic settings for various types of music. Leonard
Stone recalls, "Behind the large canopy was a huge soffit that extended about eighteen feet up
to the ceiling at the back of the building. I. M. Pei thought it was an aggressive, offensive,
heavy hulk of material hanging there. 'I have to deal with this acoustic girdle,' he would complain. Russell needed this extended soffit to reflect sound back down to the stage. There was
no moving I. M. and there was no moving Russell." Charles Young later said, "If we were
designing the hall only from a visual point of view, then we wouldn't have had the canopy. If
we had known that canopy was going to be as low as it is, we could have designed the pipe
organ a little bit lower, and we would also have made the canopy a more neutral surface. As it
comes out, that patterning on the canopy becomes too aggressive."[20] Young struggled to give
the canopies personality and an attractive design.

Meyerson and his smaller unit grew exasperated with the continuing disagreements
between the Pei and Johnson camps. Beginning in spring 1983, Meyerson charged Leonard
Stone with mediating the disputes. When the canopy design remained unresolved, Meyerson
sent him to New York with a mission: "You've got to help bring these guys to some kind of
resolution on the canopy." After a lengthy meeting on April 20 with Johnson and Wolff of
Artec, Stone filed his first report to Meyerson.

> I obtained reaffirmation of the basic grinding areas of contention between architect and
> acoustician. They are:
>
> 1. The large vertical pillars on either side of the hall near the stage.
> 2. The placement of the soffits for the audible sound chamber that wraps around the
>   hall from the front of the stage toward the back near the top balcony.
> 3. The shape of and construction materials for the acoustic canopy.
> 4. The soffit ledges of the audible sound chamber behind and above the organ.[21]

Stone summarized each party's position and proposed possible solutions.

By autumn 1983 both parties were still at an impasse over the canopy. Each was holding
true to the principles that governed a lifetime of work. In this case it boiled down to acoustics
vs. aesthetics. Meyerson had reached the limits of his patience. He called a meeting of the
smaller unit. "We had what appeared to be an irreconcilable difference between I. M. and

Russell," he later said. "The smaller unit met, and we reviewed the options. We can fire one, we can fire the other, we can fire both, or we can put 'em in a room, turn up the heat real high and let 'em both faint, and make them figure out what to do. We chose the last."[22]

Meyerson met with Pei and Johnson in October 1983 to present his ultimatum. The problems had reached the conflagration point over the design of the upper one-third of the music chamber. Reporting to the smaller unit, Meyerson related the results of his mediation.

> As you know, Russell Johnson and I. M. Pei have been at loggerheads over the handling of the soffit at the stage end of the hall. We have been patiently trying to get them to agree since June. As of last week not only had they not agreed, but each one had independently announced that if they did not come to an agreement, each would resign. . . .
> I met with Pei and Johnson and set forth four alternatives:
>
> 1. Fire both consultants;
> 2. Get the small committee to make a decision in favor of one or the other;
> 3. Redesign the stage end of the room to remove the soffit and canopy arrangement;
> 4. Redesign the entire upper third of the hall.
>
> . . . I asked both parties if the third and fourth alternatives were possible, with a minimum of delay to the entire project.
> We had a pleasant conclusion of the meeting. Russell Johnson stated we had broken new ground and he would see if the changes were possible. He felt they were, but at that time did not feel it was appropriate to make a commitment. I told him that I wanted a fast "no" or a slow "yes," but not a slow "no."
> I. M. Pei said that he had never considered this approach as a possible solution but was greatly encouraged to be able to work with Russell Johnson to solve what he considered to be the most stringent of the straightjackets—the upper third of the room.[23]

The compromise solution was to change the soffit to a large, adjustable, four-piece canopy system suspended over the stage. Charles Young explains, "One of the reasons that Artec wanted to run the reverberation chamber around was it provided a big horizontal ledge for reflection of sound. We came up with the alternative of the three flanking canopies that would provide the same horizontal surface that the ledge would have."[24] This was the breakthrough in resolving the dispute. The three subsidiary canopies to the side and rear of the large one were painted sky blue, to blend with the ceiling of the audience chamber. Consequently, the audience is largely oblivious to the presence of anything other than the main canopy that extends over the stage. (Pei's people often referred to it as "the spaceship" or "the Starship Enterprise.")

Another concern was the acoustic impact of people walking up and down the aisles at concerts between movements, particularly women in high heels, because the sound of footfalls could interfere with the music. The Pei team proposed a carpet runner, but Artec argued that any carpet would provide too much absorption in the room. Pei's group abandoned the carpet suggestion.

Symphony staff and board could not help but be aware of the tension between the consultants. According to Dolores Barzune, "They were really unhappy with one another. It's not only different personalities. It behooved Russell to want the acoustics to be better, and it behooved I. M. to want the architecture to be best. It's analogous to the role of the symphony association to hold the rein financially, and the role of the conductor to want more artistically. I think we were very, very lucky, and I don't for a second discount the luck, but I also think we were very, very smart to select the two that we selected, in spite of the fact that they generated sparks off each other. I think that factor might have made the building even better. If they'd gotten along, you'd think somebody wasn't doing his job. It was hard for them to be in the room together. Of course, none of us really had first-hand knowledge of that; you just kept hearing about it from everyone, how badly they were not getting along."[25] According to Artec's Edwards, the rumors were exaggerated. "I never heard I. M. even raise his voice once," he declares. "He and Russell were always courteous to each other. They disagreed about design, but not with one another. That's part of the reason that the relationship ultimately worked."[26]

Paul Stevenson Oles did day (above) and night (below) renderings of the hall for the I. M. Pei & Partners office. These drawings were used by the Dallas Symphony for publicity and promotion through the grand opening in 1989, despite the fact that both drawings include the extra level that was eliminated in the redesign of summer 1982. (*DSO archives*)

Don Stone believes that his board's wisest decision was having Pei and Johnson report to the symphony board, and eventually the city, separately. "Pei didn't like that arrangement, and he fought it," Stone says. "Everybody insisted that's the way it was going to be, so that Pei didn't have the last word on anything that had to do with acoustics. The music chamber was Russell Johnson's, and everything else was I. M. Pei's. They fought like cats and dogs. They gave the board a tremendous amount of aggravation, but I'm sure that's why the music room is as good as it is. If Pei had had total control, as he would normally have in construction or design process, then the materials that went into the music room would have been Pei's decision. In this case they were not. Johnson had the final word on upholstery, chairs, floor covering, many of the things that the architect would normally determine."[27]

"Of all the things that Mort did, this was probably the best: having the acoustician be his own man and having the architect be his own man," summarizes Dolores Barzune. "The tension between those two gave us a better hall."[28]

Chapter Sixteen

MAJOR GIFTS I: THE HALL ACQUIRES TWO NAMES

The Dallas Symphony Association, Inc., is convinced that music is an integral element of civilized existence; that music, in its finer forms, provides pleasure, peace, inspiration, and intellectual stimulation; that by listening to music discerningly, one can gain knowledge, understanding, and self-discipline to expand the scope of life; and that music, as a basic form of communications, can transcend boundaries of culture, differences in economic and educational backgrounds, and barriers between nations.

CORNERSTONE CAMPAIGN LITERATURE, DECEMBER 1982

DSO Development Director Al Milano initiated a series of visits with people the symphony hoped would be major donors, to get a sense of their commitment to a new hall, as early as 1979. The list included many of Dallas' most prominent and wealthy citizens, among them Trammell Crow, Bob Glaze, Eddie and Louise Kahn, Margaret McDermott, Cecil and Ida Green, J. Erik Jonsson, Philip Jonsson, Irvin Levy, and John & Nancy Penson. Leonard Stone recalls, "When we unveiled the model in spring 1982, Cecil and Ida [Green] were invited. I heard Ida turn to Cecil and say, 'This is going to cost us money!' They were, of course, aware of the fact that they were going to have to be involved." Their gift ultimately was indeed very generous: $1 million.

The Cornerstone Campaign

As the 1982 bond election drew nigh, the symphony hired an outside auditor, Mercantile Bank, to conduct a forensic analysis of the monies the symphony had raised and the monies that had been pledged toward the new hall. Well aware that it had a responsibility to Dallas voters to raise at least its forty percent share under the sixty/forty split, the DSO development department was preparing to roll out a major campaign to be called Cornerstone, chaired by

Henry S. Miller, Jr., with Erik Jonsson as honorary chair. In the most general sense, Cornerstone's objectives were public service and financial soundness. Its four key goals were capital funding for the concert hall, operating funds for the orchestra for the duration of the campaign, debt elimination to ensure future debt-free operations, and endowment. Cornerstone's goal was $39.8 million over a three-year period, during which it would displace the symphony's annual fund drive. The dollar goals broke down to $20.9 million for the concert hall in private funds to supplement the $28.6 municipal bond issue approved August 3;

The logo for the Cornerstone campaign.

additional endowment of $10 million; annual operations in the amount of $7.1 million to balance budgets for fiscal years ending 1983, 1984, and 1985; $1.4 million to cover accumulated budget shortfalls for fiscal years through 1981; and, finally, a contingency fund of $400,000. At the time, this was the largest comprehensive development program any symphony orchestra had ever undertaken.

Miller retired as CEO of his company when he accepted the assignment, in order to devote his energies full time to Cornerstone. He knew that it would be easier to get brick and mortar money than endowment funds. The seeds for the Cornerstone campaign were planted during the planning for the 1982 bond election. Shortly before the election, Miller had received eight letters of intent pledging a total of $10 million in contributions for the hall, contingent on successful passage of the bond issue. There was also a substantial pledge from Jack and Nancy Penson, plus a major contribution from an anonymous foundation. Between gifts and pledges from the private sector, the symphony already had forty-two percent of its campaign goal in hand before officially kicking off the formal campaign.[1] Willem Brans, who became development director in August 1981, later said, "We felt that the moment was right to go public with the campaign, the architectural model of the hall, and then move to the major gifts level, because we had essentially received all the leadership commitments at that time."[2] The additional major gifts they sought would provide the named components of the hall. The Cornerstone literature proudly announced: "Opportunities: To Perpetuate Honored Names By Donations of Endowment to the Dallas Symphony Association, Inc., in the context of The Cornerstone Campaign, 1982–1985."

The kickoff luncheon was to take place at Dallas' Fairmont Hotel on January 14, 1983. Miller had persuaded Isaac Stern to deliver the keynote address, coinciding with Stern's appearance with the symphony that weekend for subscription performances of the Sibelius

Violin Concerto. Performances were Thursday and Saturday evenings. The luncheon was scheduled for Friday. Brans was dispatched that Wednesday to pick up Stern at D/FW airport, driving Stone's Cadillac because it was comfortable and had a huge trunk. He took with him Edison B. Allen, vice chairman of the C. W. Shaver Company, the DSO's fund-raising consultant for Cornerstone.

The Dallas appearance was Stern's last domestic engagement preceding a three-week international tour of the Far East. He would be flying directly to Tokyo from Dallas. Brans says, "He had more luggage than you see in cartoon people on the QEII. It was an *immense* amount of luggage. He came to the baggage area with a big cigar in his mouth. He was in an easygoing mood. While we waited for his luggage, I explained who we were and that Ed and I had worked out a script for him, with bullet points, to talk about the hall. 'Do you want to know more about it?' He stood there with the cigar, looking through the script. 'Well, I'm not going to say any of this.' I suggested, 'Perhaps these are things you could refer to.' 'No, I'm not interested in any of that. I'm not going to say that.'"[3]

Brans thought, "This is going to go downhill from here." His big star, who was the major drawing card for this event, had just told him that he was not going to follow the script. Brans felt as if his own job were in jeopardy. Were they going to embarrass themselves with a headstrong artist calling his own shots at the most important event in the fund-raising campaign?[4] He and Allen still had to transport that artist to his hotel and get him to rehearsal. They walked to the car, popped open Stone's trunk, and stared in disbelief. The trunk was enormous, all right—and full. A complete set of empty stereo component boxes left virtually no room for luggage. "We jammed one or two small pieces of Stern's luggage into the trunk," says Brans. "The rest of it had to be wedged into the back seat, where Stern preferred to sit. He was *not* a happy camper."

During the half-hour drive from the airport into downtown Dallas, Brans and Allen briefed Stern as to the plan for the luncheon. They dropped him off at the Fairmont Hotel, where Allen, who was based in Atlanta, was also staying. According to Brans, "Ed and I went up to his room. We killed a six-pack of Heineken trying to figure out how we could deal with this! We were laughing, because it was such a crazy thought: Isaac Stern was going to do exactly what he wanted to do, without any prompting from us."[5]

That Friday, luncheon guests had been invited for 11:30. There was an open bar, which was rare in Dallas at that time, at least for fund-raising events. It was a glittery and well-heeled crowd, comprising the high and mighty of Dallas: Mayor Evans plus the DSO's entire prospect list for significant gifts. Four hundred potential donors were there, mostly couples and representatives of the corporate community. As Brans remembered, "It was very good attendance. Basically, many people felt, 'It's a nice day; we're going to not go back to work.' As president of the symphony board, Bill Seay chaired the luncheon. Henry Miller was introduced as head of the Cornerstone campaign. I. M. and Eileen Pei, Eduardo and Carmen Mata, Russell Johnson, and arts district coordinator Dr. Philip Montgomery were presented to the assembly.

The program was thoroughly scripted and carefully timed. According to Brans, "We had prepared a video. We were doing things in 1983 nobody was really doing for campaigns yet. They hadn't seen this kind of stuff." As the videotape played, one empty seat remained at the head table between Henry Miller and Eduardo Mata: Isaac Stern's place. Brans's palms were very sweaty, because the keynote speaker hadn't yet appeared. Stern was presumably still upstairs in his room. Brans quietly asked Sydney Reid-Hedge, the DSO's director of volunteer services, to find a house phone and call him. "Sydney, of course, is the soul of graciousness," said Brans. "She said, 'Mr. Stern, we are all gathered downstairs, and we would love to have you join us.' He made some kind of grousing remark, but I think he was pleased that a woman called him from downstairs to ask if he'd come down! The whole room was listening to speeches. The video was to be shown just moments before Stern was scheduled to speak."

Finally, through the main door, Isaac Stern entered the ballroom where the luncheon was under way. Brans remembers, "He was wearing house slippers, bedroom slippers. He shambled through the room. Of course, all eyes went to the soloist. He was the star of the afternoon. He took his place. He was sleepy-looking." Following the video, Seay introduced Leonard Stone and Mayor Evans, each of whom made brief remarks about Cornerstone's stimulus for the city's artistic development and the beneficial impact of the new concert hall and the Arts District. Bill Seay introduced Stern, who rose to speak with his glasses on top of his head.

"He had no notes. He talked a little bit about his experience at Carnegie," Brans remembers. "Then he launched into a lyrical rhapsody about the art of music. He spun an extended metaphor of a beautiful tree which is full of fruit that's always available, and that anyone who wants to reach for it can just reach up and pluck off the tree to taste and experience. It was a perfectly worked-out set of remarks. I suppose that he had given it a hundred times before, for Carnegie Hall's board, for other facilities."[6]

If that was the case, no sense of repetition colored his remarks. Stern began by complimenting his audience. "I want to congratulate this city on the enormous change in atmosphere that I sense. You've come a long way." His allusion to the orchestra's low point in 1974 and the city's improved perception of itself instilled pride in his listeners. He concluded by saying, "The eventual winners of all this are you, the people. That you see it so clearly is a moment I think you should congratulate yourselves. . . . The combination of the efforts of both the city and the private sector are of massive importance so that neither one nor the other has political priority in the future of the hall. . . . Music is probably the most important of the arts because it is the least concerned with words and therefore does not give easily to being misinterpreted for political or private reasons. It is up to us to reach out and take as much of this glorious fruit as we can absorb. I am delighted to be here at the inauguration of this exemplary effort, this clear sign of vitality in a city that believes in itself and has pride in its future. God bless you."[7]

His listeners were entranced. Brans says, "None of us could have written it. Isaac Stern is a poet. He's a poet on the violin; he's a poet with words. I don't think most poets would be able to come up with the kind of lyricism that he did. They loved it! People were in tears. They were floored. Standing ovation! We had a press conference scheduled right afterward, in a room set aside where Bill Seay and Henry Miller would talk with the press. Bill Seay—there's a guy who ran an insurance company for forty years—he said, 'Oh, Oh! This is the greatest day of my life! I can't believe what I've just heard!' People were just raving about this thing. A model of the hall was set off to the side. Most of the people there had seen it already, but now it had been given this metaphysical validation. This was the launch of launches. I've never been involved with a launch as euphoric as this. It reached everybody who was in the room."[8] Leonard Stone remembers Stern's talk with equal enthusiasm. "Isaac's speech was nothing less than brilliant. He described the building and its architectural components as if they were a piece of music. The audience was enraptured."[9]

Stern's address had a profound impact on Margaret McDermott, a Dallas arts patron, a major force on the board of the Dallas Museum of Art, and the widow of Eugene McDermott, a Texas Instruments co-founder who had died in 1973. Initially, when then–Development Director Al Milano had approached her about a gift for the concert hall, she had pledged $1 million. "The need for a concert hall was well known," she later recalled. "We all wanted a concert hall as an integral part of the cultural life of the city. At the inaugural luncheon for the Cornerstone campaign, I was so impressed with the spirit of wanting to do things right, particularly two speakers: Henry Miller, who had accepted the terrible task of raising money for the symphony, and Isaac Stern, that great violinist, who took time from his busy schedule to come to Dallas to make a real plea for a concert hall. In later years, I've told Isaac Stern how I was motivated by the luncheon and how his presence was a major factor in our gift."[10]

Each guest at the luncheon had received literature about Cornerstone, including a list that detailed which parts of the hall could be named for major donors. Margaret McDermott studied the list carefully. After the kickoff luncheon, she went to her ranch north of Dallas, as was her custom on weekends. Working with her Texas Instruments calculator, she determined that her family could afford $5 million to make the first major gift for the concert hall. She later said, "If I could afford it, I would have given more. I'm so glad that I gave what I did."[11]

After the weekend, she called her daughter Mary, who had accompanied her to the luncheon. "Come over, I have something I need to talk to you about." Mary McDermott (now Cook) remembers her saying, 'I thought that was so wonderful on Friday. I think we need to do something important. I wish I had enough money to name the building. I can't, but if the [McDermott] Foundation could do $2 million, I could manage $3 million."

Mary McDermott was thrilled and suggested they telephone DSA Board President Bill Seay at his office. "Bill, this is Mary. Listen, you need to come over to Mom's this afternoon. It's *really important.*"

Seay did not hesitate. "What time do you want me? I can be right over." While waiting for him, Margaret McDermott jotted down the conditions of her gift on a little scrap of paper. When he arrived, Mary escorted him in. Margaret McDermott joined them, and announced her intent to name the concert hall for $5 million. The timing was right, she stated, and the Cornerstone luncheon had inspired her.

Stunned, Seay tried to digest what he had just heard. Then he collected himself, and suggested they get it written down. Coincidentally, the McDermotts' personal attorney was also the symphony's counsel. They agreed that Seay would call him to arrange for the papers to be drawn up.

—·—

SEAY took McDermott's little slip of paper home with him. He had it in his hand when he walked into his house. He said to his wife, Margie, "You'll never guess that happened to me today!" and absently handed her the slip of paper, still a bit dazed by this extraordinary gift.

"No, where have you been?" she asked, taking it in her hand. Seay had responded to Mary McDermott's summons so promptly that he hadn't had time to telephone home.

"I've been to Margaret McDermott's because Mary called and said they wanted to visit, that her mother had something really exciting to tell me. Margaret just gave us $5 million."

Margie Seay was as amazed as her husband had been, and listened, thrilled, as he related the afternoon's events. When he got to the part about Margaret's conditions, he described her paper. "It looked like an old grocery list," he told his wife. "She had turned it over and written on the back. She said, 'These are my conditions,' then went through them. Say, where *is* that paper? Where's that piece of paper I brought in?"

They looked around anxiously. "He knew he had handed it to me," Margie Seay remembers, "but he didn't have it, and I didn't seem to have it in my hand. Sure enough, I thought it was just a scrap he'd picked up outside!"[12]

They found it in the trash.

—·—

A RESOLUTION approved by the Dallas Park and Recreation Board on April 14, 1983, officially named the concert room the Eugene McDermott Concert Hall. The McDermott gift was a magnificent boost to a very successful campaign. At that point, the symphony established that there would be two major names associated with the building. One would be the concert room proper; the other would be the entire symphony center. The hall had its first major named component. The symphony continued its quest for the second naming donation, the one that would name the entire edifice.

Margaret McDermott made her gift in the form of a Texas Instruments stock certificate. Because the proceeds of the donation would not be used until construction began, the money would grow. She stipulated that all interest earned on the lump sum be set aside and used to acquire art for the building. McDermott served as chair of the art committee until the building opened, when she relinquished the role to Linda Marcus.[13]

—⟨⟩—

FOR economic reasons, the smaller unit had assumed in its early discussions that the building exterior would be masonry. Brick is a widely used building material in Dallas, and it is both sturdy and affordable. Leonard Stone recalls, "Pei's first drawings were stunning, but the artist's renderings looked like a granite or limestone exterior. We knew we couldn't afford that in a $49.9 million building, much less marble travertine floors inside. We'd have to use brick. Pei hated the idea that this building would be brick. The difference in cost was nearly $2 million to trade up to limestone. Where were we going to get that money?"[14]

Isaac Stern delivered the keynote address at the Cornerstone kickoff luncheon. (Photo by Holly Kuper, *DSO archives*)

The symphony had developed a remarkable relationship with a wealthy Dallas family that also administered a private, charitable foundation. Both the family and the foundation made most gifts anonymously. The foundation had already pledged cash and mineral interests for the hall calculated to be worth $5 million. Shortly after the formal rollout of the Cornerstone campaign, the foundation trustees asked Meyerson for a list of components for the concert hall that would not be possible within the framework of the $49.5 million budget. Meyerson cited the limestone exterior, estimated at $1.8 million, and marble travertine flooring in the public spaces, for an additional $1.4 million.

Board President Seay, Leonard Stone, and Development Director Brans, along with Cornerstone Chairman Miller, met with the foundation trustees and attorneys in late October 1983, arranging for a tour of the Arts District and a conference call to Pei's New York office to discuss particulars. The symphony representatives described what the museum and other Arts District buildings would look like. Their message was, "The concert hall really needs limestone, in order to communicate aesthetically with the museum across the way."

In a meeting with the foundation's trustees and DSA representatives, the family matriarch, a woman in her late seventies and the foundation's chairman, said very graciously, "I understand everything you've said. But I am getting on in years. When I walk into that building, what am I going to be walking on?" Stone told her, bluntly, "Carpet." "Oh no, no. If that building is going to have limestone on the outside, it has to have marble floors on the inside." The trustees then indicated their willingness to give the money for the limestone exterior if the symphony would commit to raising the additional money for the marble floors inside. The foundation confirmed its offer and conditions within a week.[15] The pledge of $1.8 million was in addition to the previous $5 million pledge, making the foundation's donation the most substantial yet for the hall. As far as fund-raising was concerned, Stone and Miller were out of the frying pan and into the fire. But at least they had the financial commitment to underwrite the limestone.

—☙—

HENRY Miller's Cornerstone campaign continued to do exceptionally well. Shortly after Margaret McDermott's splendid gift for the concert room, the symphony's development office was able to announce a series of major gifts for named components in the symphony center. Louise Kahn donated $1 million for the orchestra's music library and archives room. Cecil and Ida Green endowed the grand stairway in the main lobby with $1 million. The first-tier foyer at box-seat level was underwritten by a $1 million gift from the Dallas Clearing House Association. Nancy and John G. Penson elected to fund the music director's Green Room, where conductors and guest soloists could greet audience members after performances.[16] Nancy Penson's mother, Elizabeth Hudson Penn, underwrote the music director's dressing room. (Toward the end of her life, Elizabeth Penn had started making annual contributions for a new concert hall. These monies helped to underwrite expenses for the committee's tour of European halls, but at the time of her death in 1981, fell short of the million dollars needed to fund the music director's dressing room. Her grandchildren contributed the balance in her memory.)[17] Henry and Juanita Miller chose to name the board and conference room. The Diamond Shamrock Corporation chose to sponsor the box office; the Rosewood Corporation opted for the observation room. All of these were major catalysts for the additional monies that began to flow in from other individual and corporate donors in response to Isaac Stern's speech and the kickoff luncheon.

Everything was on track, with one significant exception: The hall still lacked a signature donor. Members of the executive board had been courting several wealthy Dallasites who might be in a position to foot the $10 million price tag for naming the hall, including real estate developer Trammell Crow, NorthPark Shopping Center developer and sculpture collector Raymond D. Nasher, and EDS founder H. Ross Perot.

Leonard Stone remembers receiving a phone call just a few months after his arrival in Dallas. "It was shortly before the November 1979 bond election. Ray Nasher called to ask Robert Decherd and me to lunch. His father, Israel M. Nasher, had died recently. Ray told us, 'I believe the bond election will fail. I have a piece of property adjacent to NorthPark, and I'm seeking a way to honor my father. If the bond election fails, as I believe it will, I want you to know you can come back to me and talk to me about that facility. I want to do something to honor my father's memory.'"[18]

At the time, the Dallas Symphony's subscriber base was heavily concentrated in the area surrounding NorthPark Shopping Center, which had been developed by Nasher. "In 1979, if you stuck a compass in the epicenter of where our audience was, it would have been NorthPark," says Stone.

"Well, the 1979 bond election did not fail. Ray subsequently came forward with a very generous offer.[19] In a different time and for different reasons, it would have been magnificent. But given what we needed to accomplish, it didn't fit. We had already published the Cornerstone brochure, stating, 'If you want to name the building, it will be $10 million.' Ray approached us and offered to obtain the right to name the building in return for a $10 million gift that would come in ten consecutive annual $1 million contributions. By now, we were working diligently with the Carl Shaver company. Our account executive was Ed Allen, out of Atlanta. Ed said, 'Leonard, you need to understand what the real value is of that $10 million. Discounted, it's probably closer to $6 million, because of inflation.'"[20]

If the symphony received the $10 million in one lump sum, the funds would earn interest, and the amount would increase, just as the McDermott gift was already accruing substantial interest toward the art fund. According to Leonard Stone, "Ray's first offer went through his close friend, Bill Seay. They were part owners of the Texas Rangers baseball club together, and of course, Bill was then president. Bill's successor was Liener Temerlin, who was also good friends with Ray. Along with me, they were the two board members who continued in dialogue with Ray. Over about a year-and-a-half to two-year period, Liener Temerlin and I deliberated."[21]

Nasher's proposed gift had certain terms and conditions attached. He wanted his family to have representation on the symphony board in perpetuity, and he wanted the right to discuss artistic decisions such as selection of the music director and guest conductors. The artistic demand was not a privilege nor a power that the symphony was prepared to grant to a board member, not even one who was a signature donor. According to Stone, "The breaking point came when Liener and I pushed Ray to step up in that first year with more than $1 million. There was correspondence; the file grew. We couldn't move him. A group of us had dinner in January 1983, on the Saturday evening following Isaac's performance of the Sibelius concerto. Isaac had done the keynote speech at the Friday lunch. We dined in a private room at the Mansion: [my wife] Tamara and I, Liener and Karla Temerlin, Isaac Stern, Ted Amberg, I. M. Pei, Patsy and Ray Nasher, and Eduardo and Carmen Mata. One of the models of the hall was there. Isaac, who was committed to Israel, was talking with Ray about Israeli artists who could do some art work for the building. If you could have been a bird, eavesdropping, you would have thought we were dining with a couple who were going to ultimately claim the name of this building, although Ray told me it was going to be the Israel M. Nasher Concert Hall."[22]

The process went on without coming to a conclusion. The Nasher prospect cratered in late spring 1984. Not long after it disintegrated, Miller called Stone to report a discussion he'd had with Harlan Crow. The Crow children wanted to honor their parents, and they were anxious to consummate a deal quickly. The children understood that the real dollar value of the Nasher gift would have been $5.6 million. They were prepared to give that amount up front to consummate the deal. Miller and Stone both knew that that amount was far more advantageous than the increments Nasher had proposed. Stone said excitedly, "Henry, I think this is terrific." It was also all they had. That was about to change.

———

IN ORDER to name the building for a major donor, the symphony had to obtain clearance from the City of Dallas. In closed session at the end of May 1984, the park and recreation board deliberated whether a $10 million donation to the symphony could secure the naming of the building. Park Board President Betty Marcus, also a prominent arts activist, allowed that her agency had no objection in principle but would withhold final approval until orchestra officials submitted a name to the city. "The question was asked that, if someone gave $10 million to the city for the building, would we object to naming the building for the donor?" she told *The Dallas Morning News.* "Provided that there's not too many strings, I don't think anyone would want to turn a gift like that down." In June 1984, Ray and Patsy Nasher's names were still being widely bruited as the most likely naming donors.[23]

———

WHEN Mort Meyerson took the job of building committee chairman, he told Robert Decherd that he could not do fund-raising at the same time. "I was more or less a tangential player from the fund-raising standpoint. People would discuss it with me, they would ask me questions, but nobody really pressed on me to do much work on that part. There was always a conversation going on about who would be the naming gift. There was discussion with Nasher, to name it for his father. There were discussions with the Crow family, for the kids to name it for the parents. There were several other conversations."[24]

H. Ross Perot had been on the prospect list. Henry S. Miller, Liener Temerlin, and Richard Freling, a tax attorney who had joined the board at Temerlin's invitation, were all active during the fund-raising process. Miller asked Meyerson for advice on how to approach Perot. They discussed tactics with Temerlin, who was friendly with Perot, and with Freling. Finally, Meyerson told them, "Look, you tell me what you want to do. You need to go and formally ask him. The better thing to do is to let me just go talk to him by myself, because he's more likely to pay attention to what I'm saying." As chairman of the concert hall committee and the small group, and as president of EDS, Meyerson had kept Perot informed about the status of the concert hall project. "I had an obligation to keep him briefed about what I was doing. As we experienced troubles or made breakthroughs, I would tell him about it. He was fairly knowledgeable about what was happening."[25]

Negotiations for General Motors' acquisition of EDS began in earnest in February 1984, with a signed contract by September of 1984. Meyerson remembers, "I was up to my eyebrows in General Motors stuff at that time. One day in July, I went to see Ross in his office and said that the symphony needed one donation that would be the pacesetting donation, which would allow for the possibility that the hall would be actually built. The donation would be $10 million, and I was there to ask if he would consider donating the $10 million and naming it for his mother, who had recently passed away, or for the Perot family. That took me about five minutes.

"He looked at me and said, 'Yes, I will make that contribution,' which just floored me. Then he added, 'That would be upon only one condition.'

"I asked, 'What's that?'

"He said, 'That we name it for you, because you've put so much of yourself into this. I think it would be a wonderful honor.'

"I thought about that for a few minutes. I said, 'Ross, I now am embarrassed about this because you could—you might think that I've come here to ask you to do something, maybe with the hope that you would do that [name it for me]. I must tell you that I don't want to do that, that I think it's inappropriate, and I think it would best be named for Margot, your mother, or for the family.'

"He looked at me with his fierce eyes and said, 'You're not listening to me, Meyerson. You can have the money, or you can not have the money. But you won't tell me upon what conditions I'll give it.'

"I said, 'I think I've heard you. . . . We'll do it.' I mean, how could you—what would you do? Say no to $10 million? The entire meeting took less than ten minutes."[26]

—❦—

DSA Board President Temerlin was in Chicago for an agency meeting. His wife called him at his hotel. "Liener, Ross Perot wants you to call him." It was about 10:30 or 11:00 P.M. Temerlin said, "It's too late; I'll call Ross in the morning." He knew Perot, and talked with him often, but had no idea what he wanted. The next morning he returned the call. After chatting briefly, Perot remarked, "Liener, you're very cavalier with $10 million!"

Temerlin was taken aback. "What are you talking about, Ross?"

"Well, the symphony had sent a brochure [stating] that they would name the hall after anyone who would give a gift of $10 million. I'll tell you what. I will give you the $10 million, with a couple of provisions."

Temerlin collected himself and broke in. "First of all, Ross, I want to express my appreciation."

"Let me tell you what the conditions are," Perot continued without pausing. "One is that you follow the designs of I. M. Pei and make sure you deliver the world-class hall that we all want."

"We have no intention of doing anything *but* that, Ross."

"Two is that you don't name the hall after me [or my family]. I want you to name it after Mort. I want it to be called the Morton H. Meyerson, not the H. Ross Perot, because I know how long and hard Mort has worked on the hall. Also, Mort is the person who helped get EDS to the position it enjoys today. I don't want you to name it the Meyerson, but the Morton H. Meyerson; there are a lot of Meyersons around. Let the focus be on Mort."

Temerlin was as amazed by Perot's second condition as he was by the enormity of the pledge. "Ross, the argument could be made that that's as generous as the $10 million!"

Perot went right on. "And three is that you put a portrait of Margaret McDermott somewhere in the hall. Margaret and her family have taught this town how to give. Margaret laid the groundwork to get this hall done, like she's laid the groundwork for so many other things. Without Margaret's gift, we wouldn't be where we are today. She's a remarkable woman, and you just don't see Margaret['s picture] anywhere, and I'll pay for the portrait."

Temerlin replied, "Well, I can certainly promise point one, and I'm sure there will be no problem [with the others]."

Upon his return to Dallas he placed a call to Margaret McDermott. "Let me come out to see you." He recited the provisions of Ross Perot's gift. McDermott said decisively, "There will be no portrait of Margaret McDermott."

Temerlin remembers the interview vividly. "I said, 'Margaret!'—I knew in my heart of hearts that her refusal was not going to stop Ross's gift, but I still protested—'Ross says that's a condition of his $10 million donation!' She said, 'It's high time someone in this town said "no" to Ross Perot!' I called Ross to tell him that. He loved it! He said, 'You tell Margaret for me'—not that he couldn't pick up the phone—'that I'm going to go ahead and get it done.' He named a very bad portrait artist, whom he insisted he would commission to paint it. Margaret, of course, is a great connoisseur of art. She thought that was very funny. I had Ross's letter of commitment the afternoon [of the telephone conversation]."[27]

—∽—

THAT same morning, Perot called Bill Seay to announce, "I understand that a $10 million gift up front will secure the right to name the hall. I would like to do that, and I'd like to name it after Mort." As soon has Seay got off the phone with Perot, he dialed Leonard Stone at the symphony. Stone said, "I think I should call Henry, because he's been talking with the Crows." Miller was in Japan.

—∽—

MILLER remembers, "Mort Meyerson, Bill Seay, Bob Glaze, and I had already been to see Ross Perot several times. Ross seemed to be interested, but we couldn't get him to act. Right after we had gotten this oral commitment from Harlan Crow, Juanita and I were in Tokyo with a group from the Dallas Museum of Art. Leonard Stone called Tokyo, saying that Mort Meyerson advised him that Ross Perot had agreed to give $10 million, all in cash. He asked if the Crows could pay theirs in cash. If so, then the naming of the hall would go to the Crows. I said, 'Well, I don't know.'"[28] In discussions with Crow, Miller, Seay, and Glaze had secured a verbal commitment that the family would contribute $10 million, consisting of $5 million up front, $2.5 million at the end of the first year, and the final $2.5 million at the end of the second year. According to Miller, this was not at all unusual, and his committee felt that they had an agreement on both sides.[29]

In Miller's absence, it fell to Seay to call Harlan Crow officially and say, "We've just had an offer of $10 million cash up front. If you can match that, it's yours." The symphony did not want to get into a "bidding war" between Harlan Crow and Ross Perot. Crow told Seay, "No, this is a lot of money that I'm offering, this is what I can do now. We cannot do more now. We have great respect for the Perot family. If you can get something better than what we're proposing, take it."[30]

After Miller returned to Dallas, he talked to Crow, who told him, "Mr. Miller, you know in this business we don't have much cash. I thought $5 million *was* a lot of cash up front. I can't commit $10 million all in cash now. If Mr. Perot can do it, let him do it."[31]

Perot confirmed his pledge in writing on September 25, 1984, contingent upon naming the hall for Meyerson. When the commitment letter arrived at Temerlin's Bozell & Jacobs office, Temerlin called an afternoon meeting of the executive board in his home. "I told them the provisions of the gift. Everyone roared about the Margaret McDermott story, but they also wanted to applaud this extraordinary gesture. That became the weathervane and the high water mark to finish getting the rest of the money. Everyone was delighted, and we [prepared to make] the announcement."[32]

One week later, the Dallas Symphony announced that the new hall would be called the Morton H. Meyerson Symphony Center. A press conference took place at Dallas City Hall in late October, in conjunction with the city council meeting at which the naming donation was approved. Temerlin proudly declared, "This is one of the most significant events in the eighty-four-year history of our orchestra. Mr. Perot's action is a signal to the entire community about the generosity of sharing. It is meant not only to honor Mr. Meyerson, but symbolically all of the employees of Electronic Data Systems." The funds, the largest gift the Dallas Symphony had ever received, would be paid in January 1985 and were to be used for construction of the symphony center.

The media descended on Perot even more than on Meyerson. Such a magnanimous gesture was unprecedented in Dallas philanthropy. Meyerson himself did not get a lot of interviews. "There was more interest in the press on the subject of one man making that big a contribution in the name of another man who was not part of the family. That was more newsworthy than I am. But the point is that I was born in Fort Worth. I had immigrant grandparents. We didn't have much money. We were Jewish. We were kind of aliens in society in Fort Worth. The very idea that I could be the CEO of a big company was strange enough for me to absorb. There's a precedent for that, however. There are people who come from immigrant backgrounds who go on to become leaders in industry one way or another. I don't know of any who also have their name on a symphony hall."[33]

The toughest condition to meet would be adhering to the original design parameters. Perot continued to insist that everything must be "world class." "That was Ross's way of saying 'the best,'" says Leonard Stone. "He would ask, 'Are you sure these materials are world class?' Of course he wanted it to be the best, for all kinds of reasons. Mort wanted that; everybody did. But this orchestra also aspired to be world class. If the building proved to be an acoustical gem, it would not only amplify the strengths of the orchestra, it would also amplify the weaknesses."[34]

———❦———

LATE in 1984, weeks after the donation was officially announced, the DSA Board presented Meyerson with a plaque containing the pen that had been used to sign the document naming the hall: The Morton H. Meyerson Symphony Center.[35]

Chapter Seventeen

JUGGLING THE
BUDGET

EARLY in 1983, Mort Meyerson formally recommended to the DSA Executive Board that it hire a construction coordinator to act as liaison between the still-unidentified contractor and the architect.[1] The first candidate the smaller unit discussed was Vince Carrozza, the developer who had built Edward Larrabee Barnes's Dallas Museum of Art, and come in on budget. Carrozza declined, and the idea of a liaison languished for some months. The committee then took a serious look at former City Manager George Schrader, who remained a member of the DSO's board of governors.

During his years as city manager, Schrader had engineered the city's policy for funding land acquisition, capital construction costs, and maintenance of civic cultural structures—including sports stadiums, libraries, and arts facilities—and operations support of cultural arts facilities. Schrader had brought Reunion Arena in on budget and had worked with I. M. Pei on Dallas City Hall. He already had a good relationship with Pei, as well as encyclopedic knowledge as to how the city operated. Since his resignation as city manager, Schrader had worked in the private sector. The symphony board realized what an asset he could be.

Seay called Schrader for an appointment in spring 1984. He showed up in Schrader's office with Henry Miller. "We're very worried about the symphony hall," they told Schrader. "The DSO is going to be a major financial supporter. We're making a major investment in this project. We believe we ought to have a representative, and we'd like to know if you'd be willing to take on the job." Schrader asked what it would entail. The reply was a familiar litany. "We believe that it's over budget, that it's got problems. We need somebody to take care of it. We'd like you to take charge, represent our interests, as our agent."

Schrader asked more questions. The symphony had a building committee chaired by Meyerson, he learned. The symphony was paying the architect, with the right to assign his contract to the city. The architect was preparing plans. They had an acoustician and a cost consultant. They did not yet have a builder.

Schrader suggested, "Let me talk to the DSO staff and the city staff to find out what's the current status." His first visit was to Stone at the symphony's Fair Park offices. "Leonard, I've been told that the symphony hall that's being planned is over budget." "Oh yes! I don't know why somebody at the city doesn't do something about it! I'm not managing the budget; the city is." Schrader went to see friends at city hall and posed much the same question. "Do you have any sense of how great the cost of this thing is?" They told him, "Oh, it's way over budget. We don't know why the symphony hasn't done something about it. We [the city] don't have any exposure beyond $28.6 million. Everything else is the symphony's cost. They're the ones who are making it go over. They want to pay the money, fine. I think what we need to do is just go ahead and get it out for bids and start over again."[2]

Clearly there was no connection between the two camps. Each made assumptions without real knowledge of what the other party was doing. Initially, Schrader thought he didn't want to get in the middle of what appeared to be a no-win situation. Much later, he chuckled, "I thought it was interesting that each party believed that it was the other's responsibility." Shortly before the hall opened in 1989, he told a *Dallas Morning News* reporter, "I said no three times, and finally I ran out of excuses."[3] Upon further reflection, he decided that the hall was such an interesting project, and so important for the city, that maybe he could help. He accepted the job, resigned from the DSA Board (to avoid any conflict of interest) and, in March 1984, began to work on the hall.[4] His initial title was chairman of the physical facilities committee. That title rapidly gave way to project manager.

In that capacity, Schrader kept communication lines open not only between the city and the symphony, but also among the various other major players: acoustician, architect, contractor, press. He began attending meetings of Meyerson's smaller unit and the design team. He attended DSA Executive Board meetings and reported to its members on his activities and the hall's progress. On a daily basis, he also interacted with city hall personnel involved with the Meyerson Symphony Center and, of course, with symphony staff. Meyerson himself relied on Schrader increasingly. "He became my right-hand person to get things done," Meyerson remembers. "I'd say, 'Look, George, you need to make decisions on this stuff, and I can't go through the symphony board and city council getting this stuff sold. Do it. Then, if necessary, I'll try to figure out how to raise the money later.'"[5]

WITH great fanfare, the new Dallas Museum of Art opened at the western end of the Arts District in January 1984. The Dallas Theatre Center, whose Frank Lloyd Wright–designed campus in Turtle Creek was the city's most distinguished architectural landmark, opened a second location downtown. Called the Arts District Theatre, it occupied the 2400 block of Flora Street, four blocks east of the museum and just one block away from the symphony site. Even though the new concert hall lagged behind schedule, the concept of the Arts District was starting to take shape. City council voted to approve the Arts District parking garage that month.

———— ❧ ————

SCHRADER'S first activities as project manager were to assess the overall status of the project and get a better handle on costs. He remembers Pei telling him that the architectural plans were ninety percent complete, but that I. M. Pei & Partners was not responsible for cost, and that the DSA had a cost consultant.[6] Schrader suggested that the DSO have a contractor sit down with Pei's people to do its own estimate for construction, according to I. M. Pei & Partners' plans. "They got a contractor to take the plans and estimate the cost. It was a firm whose cost estimation of the concrete structure was very dependable. They quit figuring the cost of the building when the total reached between $90 and $100 million. They just announced, 'We don't think we need to go any further.'"[7]

Bill Seay and Henry Miller were alarmed and exasperated when Schrader relayed this unfortunate news. They decided to stop things where they were and assess options. They could throw the plans out and start over, then redesign to a figure that was less. But the symphony and the city had already paid more than $10 million in architectural fees to Pei's firm. That meant if they decided to get rid of Pei and the total budget was $50 million, they would have to lower the budget to $40 million right off the bat before engaging another architect— who would levy his own fees. They decided to keep Pei, but the budget clearly needed major reevaluation. The new figure they arrived at was $75 million.[8]

Schrader knew that Cliff Keheley and Louise Reuben Elam at city hall and Melissa McNeil at the symphony had a meticulously detailed acquaintanceship with all the pieces of the building. "Louise and Melissa crawled through those plans inch by inch," Schrader said afterward. Neither the size nor the shape of the building could be altered. They *could* substitute less expensive materials. Instead of terrazzo flooring [small chips of marble set in cement, then polished] in the music chamber, for example, they could use concrete. They made similar substitutions here and there with an eye toward reducing cost.

The difference between this process in 1984 and what had taken place in earlier cost reductions had to do with timing. Now, the question was: What could be left unfinished until a later date? The smaller unit had answered that question the year before, in evaluating what additional funds would be needed for desirable enhancements. They concluded that the basement spaces (meeting rooms, a founders room, and practice rooms) and administration spaces were not essential to the opening of the building, and could therefore be eliminated at that point.[9]

McNeil describes Schrader's style as a combination of doggedness and soft sell. She believes he lent balance and restraint in an atmosphere that had become increasingly charged. "George is a visionary. He urged us not to make decisions by a certain date if, in fact, they could be deferred for some length of time, because circumstances might change and allow us to get more rather than less. It was a very good lesson for me to work with someone like George, because I work around schedules and current information. He counseled, 'Don't make the decision until you have to make it, because situations change.' And indeed they did. We had some very generous people who came forward as the building progressed."[10]

So, in mid-1984, more than a year before the real groundbreaking, cost projections were clearly far higher than the purported $50 million ceiling. Resolution of the parking garage and the attendant challenges of a second, lower lobby area were compounding the problem. Some estimates edged toward the $90 million range. Hanscomb Consultants furnished Schrader with an estimate for about $50 million but made it clear that the building was very likely to exceed that amount substantially, probably up to the $64–65 million range. As Hanscomb's Donnell remembered, "The basic building budget was for a brick building, plaster interiors, carpet on the floors, perhaps not so much glass or lobby area, and with less equipment. All of that changed."[11]

Before a construction manager could be hired and undertake solicitation of subcontractor bids, one last hurdle had to be cleared: the operating agreement between the city and the symphony. Assistant City Manager Vic Suhm negotiated on behalf of the city. Under the terms of the sixty/forty financing partnership, the symphony was to be designated principal tenant in the building for a period of ninety-nine years with guaranteed preferential scheduling. The building would be owned and operated by the City of Dallas. After considerable debate, the city agreed to absorb the new hall's operating costs for at least five years, including maintenance, minor modifications, ordinary security, janitorial services, utilities exclusive of telephone, and fire and casualty liability indemnification.[12]

—⁊—

SCHRADER'S recruitment was one of the last actions of Seay's presidency. As the May 1984 annual meeting approached, Leonard Stone met with Seay to discuss a successor. "At that time, the way the board was structured, there was no specific chair-elect, or somebody standing in the wings," says Stone. "I went over to Bill's office to talk about it. I said, 'I have somebody in mind.' He said, 'I have somebody in mind, too.' I suggested, 'Why don't we write down on pieces of paper who we think and then we'll exchange it? I handed him a piece of paper that said, 'Liener Temerlin,' and he gave me 'Liener Temerlin'! We asked Liener. He was thrilled. He said, 'Leonard, I don't know anything about orchestras. You're going to have to be there and coach me when it comes to talking about composers and music. But I'm going to be there for you to help you with style, with packaging, with marketing.'"[13]

Temerlin, then chairman of the board of Bozell, Jacobs, Kenyon & Eckhardt, turned out to be an excellent choice, not only from the standpoint of marketing and advertising, but also for fund-raising and handling political issues. He was a strong personality who was accustomed to leadership. Shortly after Temerlin took office, Leonard Stone got a sense of what to expect from his new board president.

"One of the first conversations I had with him in his capacity as president, his secretary, Dovie, called. 'Leonard, Liener wants you over here right away.' '*What?*' 'Immediately.' I protested, 'Dovie, I'm in Fair Park, and you guys are about eight miles of heavy traffic away, clear out in Las Colinas!' She insisted, 'No, he wants you here right away.' I hung up and said to my assistant, Julia George, 'What do you think this is? Gosh. Right away!' Anyhow, I went to my car and rushed over there. When I arrived, he said, 'Hi, Leonard, how are you?' Anxiously, I asked, 'Liener, what is it?' He asked, 'Do I have pops season tickets or classical season tickets?' I said, 'Liener, is this the way we're going to work together?' Dovie piped up, 'This is the way he operates!' We worked it out. I didn't have to do that too often. But, he was fabulous. Every time I went out on a fund-raising call with Liener, I got an education: in vocabulary, phrasing, disarming people, developing the case statement. He did it all, with logic and with charm. He ingratiated himself."[14]

Temerlin would need every ounce of that charm and savvy over the next few years. He became president at a very difficult time in the hall's development. Costs were rising, media coverage was increasingly negative, and tension between Pei and Johnson was ever more heated. The economy was about to head south. Although no one knew it yet, Meyerson was about to resign from the concert hall committee because of business commitments associated with General Motors' purchase of EDS.

Temerlin had just assumed the presidency when the city's public works department contracted with J. W. Bateson Company as construction manager, which meant that construction was about to begin. The Bateson firm had the advantage of having worked with Pei on previous projects. "We understood I. M. Pei," says Joe Walker, retired CEO of J. W. Bateson (the firm changed its name to Centex in July 1996). "We felt that we could work with him, and we knew that he was going to design from the very first day to the very last day. He would never quit designing, never quit changing things."[15] Walker's forecast was accurate, but even he did not foresee the extent to which the hall would metamorphose.

Most building contracts are awarded to a general contractor for a fixed amount after a competitive bidding process. In this case, Bateson was named general contractor at cost plus a negotiated fee and was authorized to bid out subcontracts. The City of Dallas had recent experience working with Bateson on the Dallas Museum of Art and thus presumably favored the company. The reasoning behind the initial arrangement with Bateson was that a construction manager, as opposed to a "lump sum" contractor, would help to ensure quality and cost control.[16]

Cost consultant Stewart Donnell believes the form of contract affected the cost discrepancy. "This was a negotiated contract with Bateson. They were a wonderful firm but, had the building been built another way, it would have cost, I think, perhaps as much as $3 million less, if you figure five percent of the $67.5 million construction cost as the premium for this method of contracting."[17] Bateson's Joe Walker defends his former company's contract as probably the least expensive method of construction delivery, in part because of the project's complexity and the large number of changes. "The cost reductions in the early stages and the addition of many finishes at the end would have carried the competitively bid lump sum contractor markup," he points out. "Bateson's fee was only 2.97 percent—far less than the lump sum fee would have been." Most important, from Walker's perspective, was that the City of Dallas and the symphony board needed a partner and team member, rather than an adversary, which the lump sum contract could have produced.[18]

Louise Reuben Elam, the City of Dallas architect assigned to the project, oversaw the process of bidding out to numerous subcontractors, including firms to handle concrete, glazing, wood paneling, flooring materials, masonry, steel, miscellaneous metals, roofing, electrical, and mechanical systems. "Louise was my counterpart at the city," remembers Melissa McNeil. "She is a superb architect who understood overall design and detailed technical issues related to the hall. Together we reviewed every page of blueprints and specifications—and there were hundreds of them—including such mundane but critical items as stairway design, isolation of air-handling units, and placement of electrical outlets. Louise also dealt with all paperwork related to running a city construction project, as well as [handling the] interface with other city departments. She was invaluable to the success of this project, and invaluable to me."[19]

When the City of Dallas calls for bids on a building with the intent of awarding a contract, in order to begin construction, the city must identify project funding. The only funding that they knew they had for the symphony hall was the bond money, because much of the private sector money was pledged but not yet received. The symphony had to provide the city with proof that it had raised its forty percent or that it was in the process of doing so. Warren Gould, a fund-raising consultant with the Carl Shaver Company who later joined the DSO as development director, remembers, "The Perot gift was channeled through the Communities Foundation of Texas, where it accrued interest for several years. By the time those funds were paid over to the symphony and the city, they had increased dramatically. That also was the case with the 1982 bond election proceeds, which gained interest."[20]

City architect Louise Reuben Elam remembers, "The budget problem became very apparent when the construction manager was hired. Before that, the architect had been preparing construction documents that were to be bid by general contractors. During the development of the plans, we had an outside cost consultant [Stewart Donnell of Hanscomb Consultants, Inc.] on the project. Based on his estimates, we were in budget, other than some of the performance equipment and upgraded finishes. We knew all along that more performance equipment was required than what was budgeted. But, we believed the basic building components, such as the concrete structure and glazing system, were *within* the budget. Toward the end of the construction document phase, the symphony board determined it was their preference that the city hire a construction manager to oversee construction of the building. J. W. Bateson Company was selected. Their first task was to provide a GMP [guaranteed maximum price], based on the plans the architect had produced. When Bateson provided the GMP, we found that even the basic building was over budget."[21]

Walker knew as soon as his company began internal estimates for the job that the $49.5 million figure was seriously under. "The symphony board had hired an estimating company [Hanscomb Consultants] that never had any financial risk in the job. They came up with the $49.5. The company was an estimating service without responsibility for final costs. They didn't have to back up their calculations by signing a contract guaranteeing the cost estimate. We argued about the differences in our figures. The estimator insisted, 'My estimates are accurate.' We countered, 'You're *not* right; our figures reflect the market.'" In order to reconcile with Hanscomb, Walker and his staff broke down the job into each specialty contract or trade listing: mechanical, electrical, structural steel, glass and glazing, concrete work, limestone, etc., and compared its breakdown item for item with Hanscomb's. Walker recalls, "We found that he was below the marketplace on every item, and we never agreed. We were talking with Cliff Keheley and Louise Reuben [Elam] at the city, and agreed among ourselves that the best way to determine the accuracy of the estimates was to advertise for competitive bids on each trade. We went to the marketplace and received five mechanical and five electrical bids. Both came in at or close to what we [Bateson] had predicted."[22]

The validation of their stance was a Pyrrhic victory, because Bateson still had a problem: an $88 million job, for which its client wanted to spend $49 million. According to Walker, "Because Pei's design was nearly complete, it was very difficult to make structural changes or delete finishes without compromising the design integrity of the building. Our team made every effort to reduce the cost but preserve the outstanding design. We feel that we made good, sound decisions based on the best cost." Walker remembers telling Cliff Keheley in November 1984, after an initial review, that the concert hall as designed would cost the better part of $100 million. "This was not a pleasant chore! We checked, and we double-checked our first total estimate, which was $88 million. I knew it was going to be a real problem when Cliff reported to the symphony that we had revised our estimates up to $100 million. At that point, there was no alternative; we knew we had to make this job go. All we could do was report the cost we had calculated."[23] Meyerson convened a meeting of the smaller unit at EDS on November 28, 1984, to review the situation. "It was a very deliberate and somber meeting," Leonard Stone later told *The Dallas Morning News.* "The reality of the numbers finally sank in."[24]

Bateson started working to reduce the cost, an exercise they rapidly realized already had a lengthy history. Throughout the remainder of 1984 and through summer 1985, they studied aspects of Pei's design that were expensive because of their complexity. The operative philosophy was to simplify the details and reduce the cost where possible but preserve the design. For example, in certain areas Bateson changed cast-in-place architectural concrete to portland cement, plaster and limestone to pre-cast concrete. Both changes were less costly. The large columns in the audience chamber were conceived as poured concrete columns. They became structural steel and plaster. Walker comments, "That was a good decision no matter whether you were going to save money or not, because we could not have poured concrete precisely to Pei's specifications. We finally reduced the cost to $65.9 million and clearly described everything that had been changed or deleted. The political atmosphere was rough and the public sector was, in general, very critical. The newspapers were always ready to report something negative about the concert hall. Every time someone complained to us about the building cost, we reminded them that the City of Dallas taxpayers were only obligated for the $28.6 million approved in the 1982 bond election. The private sector would fund the remainder. The citizens of Dallas got one heck of a deal, because of the desire and generosity of private sector, which funded the completion of the building."[25]

After Bateson came up with its $88 million guaranteed maximum, the design team, the cost consultants and the symphony staff went back to work with them to pare the overall budget back to $75 million. The priority remained to open up a building that would be usable from the outset for its primary purpose: the presentation of symphonic music. Any items that could be reinstated after the opening were eligible for deferral now. According to Schrader, "We took out plaster. We left the ceilings open. We took all the finishes out, and we got the budget back within $75 million. Then we sat down with the full symphony board of governors. We said, 'We have a building here. Here's what we took out. Here's what we left in.' I had a secret hope that by substituting finishes in the plans and by leaving some spaces unfinished, we could salvage the opportunity in the future if we really wanted it. We could have the building that we wanted."[26] When the $75 million price tag became public through a memo from City Manager Charles Anderson to council members in January 1985, everything hit the fan. Because the intermediate figures had not been publicized, the official price tag had hovered artificially around $50 million since late 1982. In the eyes of the media, the cost of the newly named Meyerson Symphony Center had just skyrocketed by a whopping fifty-one percent.

Pointing out that most of the enhancements were in the original plans for the hall prior to the 1982 bond election, City Manager Charles Anderson recommended that the council issue

$32 million in certificates of obligation to provide for interim financing of the hall to cover the symphony's share.[27] Such certificates did not require approval from the electorate and thus would not necessitate another bond issue. Some council members were skeptical of the DSO's ability to raise sufficient funds from the private sector to repay the certificates and demanded guarantees from the symphony. Obliged to defend its credibility, the symphony engaged MBank Dallas as independent assessor to ascertain the reliability of its donors and pledges. By the end of January 1985, MBank had reported that, as trustee for hall contributions, it had reviewed donor pledges and could vouch that all donors should be able to honor their commitments.[28] Two weeks later, city council approved the certificates of obligation.[29]

It took considerably longer than two weeks for the recriminations to die down about the major hike in the price tag. *Texas Monthly* magazine published a blistering condemnation in March 1985. ". . . Dallas' hall is vastly more expensive than any other built in North America in the last five years—twice what Toronto's cost, three times the price of Baltimore's and San Francisco's. . . . this 50 percent increase in cost is so flabbergasting that it takes only the slightest touch of cynicism to believe the cost will be higher still by the time the building is completed in 1988. . . . Today, with the new budget figure before us, it is clear that the symphony had a secret agenda all along and always regarded that $49 million as nothing more than a pacifier to stick in the mouth of the inquiring voters. . . . Once the bonds were passed, the symphony simply, privately, let its aspirations soar another $26 million."[30]

Assistant City Manager Suhm and DSA Board President Temerlin appeared before city council to brief its members on the explanation for the hike. Suhm later said, "Just picture a city council which has a constituency to answer to. We were talking about increasing the cost of a public building by *fifty percent!* It was such a huge increase over what had been anticipated, that it appeared to the city council that things were out of control. You've got to do a lot of explaining to get that kind of approval." He and Temerlin prepared a carefully orchestrated briefing, enlisting the assistance of Public Works Director Cliff Keheley to assemble and organize the information.[31]

Temerlin's recollection: "I had to give the address to the city council about getting their cooperation. We had no choice but to be very up front with respect to all aspects of what was going on, [accounting for each facet of the cost increase]. I told Leonard [Stone], there's a phrase I use around my agency. Any time you're communicating with anyone, it must be MLEK: Moral, Legal, Ethical, and Kosher. It's not enough just to be legal. You must tell everybody all the facts, all aspects. That was true in all our dealings with the city. I think we won their minds and hearts, with a few exceptions."[32]

The vote was not unanimous—but it passed. Ross Perot's 1984 gift of $10 million, in trust and earning interest at the Communities Foundation of Texas, helped to mollify the critics. The city's announcement that the 1982 bond funds had accrued nearly $7.5 million in interest that was also available for the hall was another public relations palliative. Those two windfalls amounted to $17.5 million of the estimated $25 million increase. With oil priced at $30 per barrel, the DSO's development staff hoped that it would only have to raise another $7.5 million to reach its goals for the hall. The DSO Board and Dallas City Council each approved the revised budget of $75 million in January 1985. J. W. Bateson's fee was set at 2.97 percent of a guaranteed maximum price (GMP) of $65,875,555. Canterbury Excavating Company was recommended for the site preparation contract, valued at $1,048,943.[33]

—❧—

DALLAS City Council awarded its initial contract to Bateson in mid-August 1984 for the symphony center's concrete foundation and basement. The city budgeted $9.7 million for this phase of construction. That figure was rapidly revised upward. In the first round of bidding, the city received no bids for concrete. A second round yielded two concrete bids in June 1985: one at $26 million, the other at $44 million. At the end of July, city council voted to pay Bateson to do the concrete work if a third series of bids was rejected.[34] For the more specialized architectural concrete that would be visible above ground, they would solicit further bids at a later date.

According to city architect Louise Reuben Elam, "We had already been through one series of cost-cutting exercises. We reached a point where the guaranteed maximum price was finalized and we were ready to bid the project. We bid several of the subcontracts: concrete, the structural system, glazing, which included the lenses and conoid system, and the mechanical system. When the bids came in, we found that these subcontracts were substantially over budget, particularly concrete."[35]

Some of the increase was covered by $7.5 million in interest earned on the $28.6 million in bond funds that Dallas voters had allocated in August 1982. The balance was to be absorbed by the private sector. At the time of the Perot donation, DSA Board President Temerlin had carefully stated that the original estimated cost of the facility was "expected to rise, not only because of delays in the construction schedule related to land acquisition, but also because of plan changes to enhance the functional capabilities and aesthetics of the Center." Temerlin foresaw, correctly, that the symphony's donors would absorb most of the additional costs.

Schrader instructed Pei's staff to set up a schedule to identify the last date they could substitute limestone for plaster, the last date they could make a decision as to terrazzo versus concrete on the floor. His hunch continued to be that, as the building emerged from the ground and became visible to Dallas' citizenry, people would rally in their determination to have the hall built with the finest materials available.

The hall was now two and a half years behind schedule—and groundbreaking had yet to take place.

Chapter Eighteen

LAND PROBLEMS: ROUND TWO

Ross Perot's $10 million commitment boosted the Cornerstone funds to $41 million, exceeding the original goal of $39.8 million. Under Henry S. Miller, Jr.'s leadership, the Cornerstone campaign eventually exceeded that goal by $6 million. That was the good news. The bad news was that construction could not yet begin, because the land issue had once again become a political football. Before construction got under way, the Borden site had to be vacated and razed. Furthermore, Pei had announced to George Schrader, "We need more space for the building." The site was too small, he explained, for the building he envisioned. He also cited traffic problems around the donated land.[1] Borden's original donation was land on the west side of Crockett Street. Pei, Ralph Heisel, and Ian Bader had developed the first concept sketches based on that portion of the Borden site. Pei requested an additional two acres of land that Borden still owned east of Crockett.

Tishman Realty had options on the balance of the Borden land, which had increased in value as the Arts District began to take shape. Mayor Evans and his staff at city hall negotiated with Tishman for several months, but talks bogged down in December 1981. Pei's needs appeared to have been met when, in January 1982, Tishman Realty agreed to trade 40,000 square feet of land adjacent to the symphony hall site to the City of Dallas for city-owned land to the west that was intended for an exit ramp off Woodall Rodgers Freeway. The land exchange would result in 88,000 square feet of land for the concert hall.[2]

At a meeting of the smaller unit on March 10, 1982, the committee learned that, as a condition of Tishman Realty's exchange of property for the hall, Tishman required a commitment from the city to provide two thousand parking spaces beneath the concert hall, a need that had been identified as far back as the Carr, Lynch study, but not yet addressed. Construction costs for the hall foundation were certain to rise as a result. Furthermore, the schedule for completion of the hall would also be affected. Construction of the new hall could not begin until the underground garage was completed to street level, providing a platform on which to build. Garage completion meant demolition and removal of part of the Borden's plant, which was contingent on the consummation of the Tishman/Borden transaction. That transaction, in its turn, depended on the land exchange between Tishman and the City of Dallas and on the purchase of the Purolator site. No date was set for any of these events.[3]

To finish the site, the city needed to firm up several important details concerning land acquisition and use. For the next year, city officials worked furiously to resolve this flurry of deals pertaining to the concert hall site and its immediate vicinity. They needed additional land for the plaza and parking. The size and location of the underground parking facility remained unresolved, and proposals went back and forth regarding a mega-garage that could serve the needs of all the business towers that were on various developers' drawing boards.

Outgoing Mayor Jack Evans was honored at a symbolic groundbreaking in April 1983. (*DSO archives*)

Until its new facility in South Dallas was complete, Borden required a temporary location before it could vacate the plant on the land donated for the symphony hall.

The Arts District plat still resembled a free-form patchwork quilt, with minuscule parcels of land abutting the larger holdings of development groups that smelled good business potential. Five small, privately owned parcels of land were sandwiched into the irregular edges of the donated Borden land. The owners of those five small tracts were not selling, prompting the mayor and Arts District supporters to ask city council in March 1982 to authorize the city attorney's office to begin eminent domain proceedings. It would take ten months to negotiate and settle with them all, at twice the cost of what had originally been estimated.[4]

The next issue was to locate sites for additional surface parking and the plaza. The city arranged a number of land swaps with Tishman, which held options on additional Borden land contiguous with the symphony hall site, and with Triland Development, which had acquired the Purolator Armored site east of the Borden/Tishman land. The Tishman land would provide the plaza; the Triland property would provide a temporary space for Borden.

The situation following the August 1982 bond election resembled a Catch-22. By

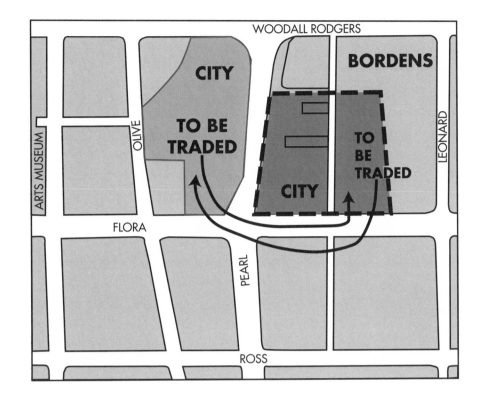

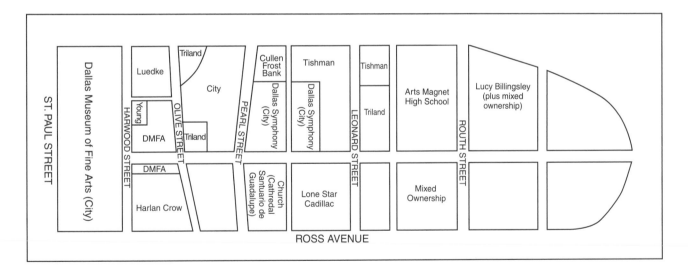

Top The proposed land swap between City of Dallas and Tishman Realty for an additional 40,000 square feet of land for the symphony hall site, January 1982. (Adapted from map by Jean Gowan in *The Dallas Morning News*, redrawn by Nicholas Arnold)   **Bottom** Ownership of various plots within the Arts District in spring 1982. The City of Dallas eventually bought or swapped for Tishman land on both sides of Leonard Street and Triland property at Leonard and Flora. The latter site served as a temporary location for the Borden plant until the South Dallas location was completed. The Lone Star Cadillac property eventually became the site for the 1,650-space underground parking garage. (Adapted from map by Elmo Stokes in *D Magazine*, redrawn by Nicholas Arnold)

September 1982, the operating agreement between the city and the symphony was not yet in place. The land exchange between Tishman Realty and the city was unresolved. City council was to be briefed in early October, with a vote in mid-October. If the council failed to approve the swap, the hall would once again be delayed. One month later, on October 13, 1982, the city finally approved a memorandum of agreement for the sharing of concert hall costs, but the land exchange among Tishman, Borden, and the city had still not come before the council. Obstacles pertaining to land acquisition seemed destined to derail the schedule one more time. If Borden did not grant approval to Tishman Realty and the city to demolish part of the milk processing plant by March 1, 1983, excavation for construction of the parking garage and building foundation could not commence by the end of March.⁵

In November 1982, the city announced it would finance a 1,200-space parking garage beneath the new hall, at a projected cost of $16.5 million. City Manager Charles Anderson noted that the cost could be as high as $40 million.⁶ In terms of infrastructure and long-range Arts District planning, the garage was a major step forward.

Then the other shoe dropped. Confounding all expectations, and complicating the already Byzantine series of swaps, purchases and sales, Tishman allowed its option on the Borden land to expire in December 1982.⁷ Several factors contributed to the breakdown in negotiations between the city and Tishman, including a soft market for office space, Tishman's failure to identify a lead tenant, and the city's requirement that Tishman provide access to the property by April 1, 1983. Also, early removal of a portion of the Borden facility to free space for the concert hall would be quite costly.⁸ (Tishman did renew its option in January 1983.)⁹

Arts District coordinator Dr. Philip Montgomery told the press in early January 1983 that the first priority was to get the parking lot started. "It's costing a lot of money to delay the construction, and it's hurting the symphony's fundraising. The mayor has taken a very determined stand that he's going to make this work while he's still in office. This is his baby, and he is not going to go out with a turkey around his neck."¹⁰

During the final months of Jack Evans's mayoralty, city land acquisition people were sorting out these intricate land deals that were a roadblock to getting hall construction under way. At this early stage in the history of the concert hall, securing land for the underground parking garage was a higher priority than property for the building proper. Debate continued over the relative size of the garage under the hall and another one planned under adjacent property. Pei's plaza surrounding the hall would have to be deferred until the garage plans were settled. Tishman had taken out another option for the Borden land on which the symphony had set its sights.

City council was expected to approve the land exchange between Borden and the city, which would allow Borden to relocate. On a temporary basis, until its South Dallas location was ready, Borden planned to relocate to the old Purolator Armored site, now owned by Triland, so that excavation for the concert hall could begin. The Borden move would, in turn, free a similar adjacent parcel for the concert hall. Excavation for the city-owned parking garage required negotiation with Harbord, another Canadian developer that had purchased the Lone Star Cadillac property. And the city was looking into the possibility of purchasing the Cathedral school at Cathedral Santuario de Guadalupe, so that Flora Street, the "spine" of the Arts District, could be suitably widened.[11] The bartering continued to be extremely complex. Final details went to city council for approval in early March 1983. Among them were the

A model by I. M. Pei & Partners shows the planners' vision with the projected large office towers that were never built. The only one of the projected high-rise buildings to be built was the LTV Tower, now called Trammell Crow Center. (*DSO archives*)

last eminent domain settlement, transference of ownership to Borden for its temporary site, and the sale of thirty acres in South Dallas for Borden's permanent new facility.[12]

As the ink was drying on the final agreements, Assistant City Manager Vic Suhm was served with a lawsuit by Texas Attorney General Jim Mattox on behalf of the Texas Department of Highways and Public Transportation,[13] charging that the City of Dallas did not own the exit ramp land it had sold to Triland in December. Triland intended to build a hotel and office complex there.[14] At the heart of the dispute were the air rights to the exit ramp off Woodall Rodgers Freeway onto Pearl Street. Resolution of the disagreement took nearly fifteen months, forcing additional delay before hall construction could proceed.

As Suhm remembers it, "We didn't want that Arts District ramp there anyway. It's noisy, and it's ugly. We envisioned pedestrian traffic for Flora Street. Cars exiting Woodall Rodgers at thirty or forty miles per hour didn't sound like a good proposition. The city had acquired the land before the Arts District plan was done, and before we knew where the concert hall was going to be. But we'd never given up the actual title to it to the state. So, I traded it to Triland for the last piece that we needed to site the hall. I tried to get the state to agree to it, but they wouldn't, so I just did it. They sued me and the city!"[15]

The case, which hinged on right-of-way and federal highway funding, fueled a briskly burning fire in the local press, which was scrambling to keep track of almost daily changes in the intricate land saga. Despite the scheduling of a court proceeding on April 4, 1983, between the State of Texas and the City of Dallas to clarify ownership of the disputed land, the DSO tentatively planned for a groundbreaking.

The symphony and the city were able to stage a symbolic groundbreaking in honor of outgoing Mayor Evans on April 29, 1983, knowing that construction could not proceed until the lawsuit was resolved. Alluding only obliquely to the dispute, Mayor-elect Starke Taylor told the press, "We have some problems, but we're going to settle them."[16] Planners still expected, optimistically, that the concert hall would be complete early in 1987. The State of Texas–City of Dallas suit settled in August 1983.[17] Another two years would elapse before construction could proceed.

By June, Pei's staff was working on redesigning the parking garage. Under the revised plan, the DSO garage beneath the concert hall would include only two levels instead of four, which would mean that construction could proceed on the structure more rapidly. One hundred forty spaces were now to be allocated to DSO musicians, staff, press, and VIPs. The adjacent Arts District parking garage, to be sited beneath the former Lone Star Cadillac property, would be multi-level and have far greater capacity to accommodate the public. Plans for the garage altered in January 1984, when city council approved an additional $5.5 million to the earlier amount. The garage would increase to 1,651 spaces and be situated beneath a proposed office building on the existing Lone Star Cadillac site and adjacent to the Cathedral Santuario de Guadalupe.[18]

The Central Dallas Association, an association of downtown businesses, had created a nonprofit corporation in October 1982 called Dallas CBD Enterprises. The organization's purpose was to provide an entity that would make good on the land swaps and deals negotiated in 1982 and 1983, because the city had yet to obtain voter approval for bond funds to acquire the properties. The new organization's principal order of business in June 1983 was to consider purchase of additional Borden property located in the Arts District adjacent to the site already designated for the symphony hall. It prevailed upon a consortium of three banks, RepublicBank Dallas, N.A., InterFirst Bank Dallas, N.A., and Mercantile National Bank, to make a loan of $28.2 million that would fully finance purchase of the property. An important aspect of the deal was a property exchange that would ensure the availability of additional land for the symphony hall and make it possible for the City of Dallas to acquire additional right-of-way needed in the Arts District.[19] The transaction was completed on September 1, 1983, at which time Dallas CBD Enterprises leased back the property to Borden for eighteen months.[20]

Essentially, the $28.1 million loan that Dallas CBD Enterprises had taken in order to secure the Arts District land served as a financing bridge until the City of Dallas could secure voter approval to use taxpayer funds. Reporting to the Cornerstone steering committee on concert hall progress in early September, Leonard Stone apprised the committee of the CBD Enterprises/Borden transaction.[21] The $3 million available from the 1979 bond election was believed to be sufficient to acquire the five small parcels of land that had been the subject of the eminent domain hearings. Now the designated Arts District would be complete.

The symphony's executive board adopted a resolution in January 1985 that, among other things, authorized the Dallas Symphony Association to contribute the Borden tract to the City of Dallas as a portion of the site, and for the association, on behalf of the symphony, to pay a total of $39 million for site acquisition and construction of the symphony center.[22]

In early April 1985, the city was negotiating with Dallas CBD Enterprises for a land swap that would exchange the former Purolator Armored tract for a tract that would enlarge the symphony site.[23] The final piece of the land puzzle fell into place during the next two months, when CBD Enterprises purchased the necessary Borden's land with the intent that it be used for development of the Arts District. First, city council agreed to pay Dallas CBD Enterprises about $3.6 million for half an acre of Arts District land. Then the city swapped more than an acre at the northeast corner of Flora and Leonard for an equivalent piece at the northeast corner of Flora and Crockett.[24]

By early August 1985, City Manager Chuck Anderson had requested that CBD extend its loan for six months to allow time for passage of a bond program.[25] Dallas City Council authorized an agreement with Dallas CBD Enterprises in early September that provided for the city's demolition of the old Borden plant buildings, construction staging and storage on the symphony hall site, and the temporary lease of adjacent city-owned property for parking.[26] On November 5, 1985, Dallas voters approved a proposition authorizing city council to issue $28 million in General Obligation Bonds for the acquisition of 206,905 square feet of cultural facilities sites within the downtown Arts District.[27] CBD Enterprises was now able to prepay its promissory note to Borden, Inc. The closing took place on December 23, 1985.[28]

—⁊—

CBD Enterprises accomplished its mission. Borden was able to move to its temporary location, the land parcels were swapped and, if necessary, paid for, and final plans for Arts District parking were approved.

The downturn in the economy put the brakes on development of the Arts District as it had originally been conceived. According to Assistant City Manager Vic Suhm, "Had the development momentum continued, had the economy not crashed, it would have led to a lot of buildings the caliber of Trammell Crow Center along Flora Street, but with inviting, pedestrian-friendly activity and businesses at street level. We would have achieved a high concentration of uses in that area, with street-level glass and an invitation to pedestrians to come into retail spaces, coffee shops, bookstores, things that would have given the district street life. Halcyon, whose forte was commercial and retail spaces, had the design criteria and plans that would do that, and Sasaki [the Arts District consultants for landscape architecture] was a big part of that, too. The building of the Dallas Museum of Art and the Trammell Crow Center [then called the LTV Center, a fifty-story office tower designed by Skidmore, Owings & Merrill] was consistent with what we wanted to achieve, but at that time, because of an experience of six or seven years of overbuilding in the downtown area, there was this sense of optimism that it was going to continue. Of course, it didn't. When the economy turned sour, there was far greater supply than demand for space, so nobody else could afford to build."[29]

Part Four

1985–1989

Chapter Nineteen

TROUBLE IN
RIVER CITY

ROM 1985 forward, the story of the Meyerson Symphony Center is a saga of struggle
and stubbornness. After several rounds of budget cuts, the smaller unit was bloodied
but not beaten. They had come this far and found themselves left with plans for a building substantially less elaborate than what they had originally envisioned, but with its critical
acoustical and architectural components intact. And the orchestra was clearly on the
upswing. Emanuel Borok, a splendid new concertmaster, arrived in April 1985, and the sound
of the strings improved immediately. A European tour was planned for May; its prospect
boosted morale.

Martha Blaine, the DSO's orchestra manager, visited Europe several times in preparation
for the tour, doing advance work in the venues where the orchestra would perform. "We
were working with two agencies, Harold Holt out of London and [Hans Ulrich] Schmid out
of Germany, for the German portion of the trip. Press people and representatives of other
halls were contacting us. Everywhere we went, people were saying, 'We hear you're building
a concert hall that's going to be the best hall in the world.' People had that expectation. The
early parts of our planning for the tour to Europe, all they knew about Dallas was J. R.,
Southfork, and 'you killed your president in Dallas.' We had a big job to do on behalf of the
city when we promoted that first European tour."[1]

Blaine and Marketing Director Doug Kinzey entrusted public relations for the tour to
Dvora Lewis, a London-based agent who had collaborated with artist manager Harold Holt

for many years. Lewis remembers talk of the new hall while planning for the tour. "Doug told me it was scheduled to be opened within three to four years, and that I. M. Pei was involved. This would obviously be a major moment for the orchestra. He stressed that it was important that the hall opening be put on the map internationally."[2]

DSA Board President Temerlin placed great significance on the long-range impact of the tour. "I thought it was very important to raise money, almost first and foremost, to send the orchestra to Europe on a tour. We knew it was a big gamble. Some of the reviews we were getting in the Dallas papers were not all that great. In my heart of hearts, I felt that if the world, and the European press, gave the symphony high marks, it would be a lot easier to raise money here. It's the out-of-town briefcase syndrome."[3]

Temerlin's gamble paid off. Mata and the DSO received excellent reviews in cities renowned for their own superlative orchestras. Shortly after their return, three of the symphony's volunteer organizations—the Dallas Symphony League, Junior Group, and Innovators—announced a contractual commitment to endow a principal keyboard chair in perpetuity, within four years. Other than cost controversies and delays associated with the Meyerson, the orchestra's affairs seemed to be in hand. The symphony and the committee were determined to bring the building to fruition.

———❧———

CIRCUMSTANCES were not making their task any easier. The political climate was heating up, particularly with city-wide racial issues and the attendant accusation that the symphony center would only serve the needs of an elite, wealthy segment of the population. Even more critical, the Dallas economy, which had been brazenly healthy for a number of years, began to falter. Matters were about to worsen.

On September 18, 1985, Dallas City Council gave final approval to the operating agreement between the city and the symphony. The DSA's lease stipulated that the city would pay the Meyerson's operating costs for ten years. Annual cost was expected to be $1.3 million.[4] The next day, a last-minute amendment was tacked on, through which city council mandated that the DSA would be required to pay ten percent of the utility costs after ten years and possibly as much as twenty-five percent after twenty years.[5]

With that long-standing debate finally resolved, a groundbreaking ceremony could finally take place. The participants, each with his or her own shovel, were Board President Temerlin and his wife, Karla, Leonard and Tamara Stone, Mort and Marlene Meyerson, Margaret McDermott, Nancy Perot, Mary McDermott Cook (who had recently married), Henry and Juanita Miller, Doug Howard as representative of the DSO musicians, Mayor Pro Tem Annette Strauss, and Billy Allen of the City of Dallas Park Board. Also in attendance were Richard Levin of the smaller unit, Fred Hoster, Doug Kinzey, Mark Melson, Melissa McNeil, and other symphony staff.

Participating in groundbreaking, September 1985, were, from left: Leonard and Tamara Stone, Margaret McDermott, Mary McDermott Cook, Doug Howard, Nancy Perot, Liener and Karla Temerlin, Billy Allen, Annette Strauss, Marlene and Mort Meyerson. Victor Marshall is in the background. (*DSO archives*)

The event was carefully orchestrated, with balloons, fireworks, cannon, and a full complement of media representatives to cover the event. Proceedings began at the marketing center in the LTV Center with a catered celebration and multimedia presentation to the press. A brass quintet from the DSO's ranks provided live music. The shovel-wielding dignitaries then gathered at the Belo Mansion, one block east on Ross Avenue. At 9:25 A.M., construction halted, and live broadcast of the ceremony began. Annette Strauss, Mary McDermott Cook, Mort Meyerson, and Liener Temerlin all made brief remarks. They dug in their shovels simultaneously as the site sign was formally unveiled, and the cannons and fireworks went off. A model of the hall was on view after the ceremony at the DSO's marketing center in the LTV tower, where the chief participants adjourned to field press questions.

———∽———

THE city's economic decline became more noticeable. "People could see the handwriting on the wall," says attorney Richard Freling. "The oil and gas industry was changing. Real estate was beginning to depreciate, and the banking industry was starting to get into trouble. There were a lot of tell-tale signs that the economy was due for a downturn."[6] And down it turned. By 1986, the recession was serious, and office vacancies in downtown Dallas were soaring. Unemployment was up, and the price of oil was down. Large fortunes were suddenly not so large.

In a front-page article about a proposed site for the open-air Starfest concerts at North Lake Park near D/FW airport, *The Dallas Morning News* architecture critic David Dillon reported on January 15, 1986, that "the opening of the Morton H. Meyerson Symphony Center [was] scheduled for late 1989." DSO Public Relations Manager Mark Melson called Dillon to inquire where he had obtained his information, because the late 1989 date was months later than any date the symphony had released. Dillon claimed that the Pei office and the city's public works department had told him the project would take twenty-three to forty-four months from groundbreaking, which put completion in spring 1989. He had added a few

Victor Marshall and Leonard Stone at groundbreaking. (*DSO archives*)

months "for safe margin" to come up with his late 1989 figure. Dillon added that the symphony had been providing dates that were so inaccurate and so consistently optimistic that he simply ignored its time estimates these days.[7]

Frostily, Melson asked Dillon to at least attribute his completion estimates so it would not appear that the symphony was providing the late 1989 date. Dillon acknowledged Melson's request as fair and agreed to try to do so in the future. His parting shot was that the three-year completion date the symphony had publicly forecast was "ridiculous." The symphony was furious. With all the negative press that had been bandied about in 1985 when the $75 million figure became public, this incident was doubly injurious. The DSO was becoming very sensitive to slight changes in the wind of public opinion, and local press did not appear to be helping. Telephone inquiries from Leonard Stone to city hall did not yield any source for the comment Dillon had reported.[8]

In March 1986, Mort Meyerson's involvement in EDS's sale to General Motors forced him to scale back his activities with the hall. "I will remain a strong financial and moral supporter," he wrote to members of the smaller unit, "but at this stage of the game it is better for someone new to take over the leadership." He chose to turn things over to Eugene Bonelli. Meyerson says,

"Because Gene was far and away the most knowledgeable, I asked him if he would assume the chairmanship, which he did. He kept me abreast of things by telephone, but I stopped going to the meetings. All the work in these things is the planning, the conceptualizing, the costing. Once you've left the bids and you start construction, then it's just a matter of making sure that you can execute what's there. The city had a very large role in that. They had people who knew how to do that. We had a contractor who had responsibility. The requirements for what the committee did became much smaller."[9]

Those requirements may have appeared less stringent to Meyerson, but Bonelli took his new role seriously. "Mort was so busy with EDS. He asked me, and I agreed. Once we got into construction, we didn't have so many small group meetings. But the construction process involved almost weekly meetings with the city attorney, city staff, and the contracting people. We often met in a satellite city office on Jefferson in East Oak Cliff, south of downtown Dallas. Mort simply didn't have time for all that."[10]

Pei's contract was scheduled to expire in September 1986. In March, six months before its expiration, the smaller unit voted to increase the architect's contract amount in order to defray the cost of additional professional services and to ensure continuity and accountability on the project. They recognized that, in order to increase Pei's compensation and remain within the $75 million budget cap, it would once again be necessary to find other areas to cut back. Wearing his DSO construction administrator hat, George Schrader requested that the city proceed with modifications to the Pei contract "to ensure uninterrupted construction administration by the architect." In April 1986, when city council reviewed a supplemental agreement with Pei that called for a $3 million increase in his fees, *The Dallas Morning News* pounced. Its article detailing the increase,[11] and a subsequent editorial, so incensed Cliff Keheley that he wrote a letter to the editor demanding clarification and correction.

Firstly, it has been clearly stated by both the City of Dallas and the Dallas Symphony Association that the project cost, which has been established at $75M, is to be maintained. The increase in professional fees will be funded by savings in other areas of the budget and will not result in an increase to the $75M project cost.

Secondly, the $12.1M that you have stated as being I. M. Pei's fee, is the total for all professional fees for the project. This amount includes I. M. Pei's electrical, mechanical, structural, security and lighting subconsultants. Additionally, it includes the fees for all other consultants under contract with the City of Dallas for the project, including the Acoustical and Performance Equipment Consultant, the Organ Designer, and the Cost Control Consultant. The total project fees do amount to more than the fees for an office building, but this is to be expected for a building which is as complex, highly specialized and unique as this one.

Thirdly, the project budget was increased on one occasion only. At that time functional and aesthetic enhancements were incorporated into the project. This increase is being funded through private donations to give generations of Dallas citizens an outstanding public facility.[12]

In April 1986, Dallas City Council voted, after considerable debate, to approve the increase in Pei's fee by $3 million to a total of $8.7 million, forcing deletion of some planned enhancements to the hall, such as possible replacement of wood trim with plaster in the concert room. The smaller unit responded by preparing a presentation emphasizing the importance of those enhancements and pledging that the private sector would come up with the funds to underwrite them. The city's $28.6 million contribution to the project would remain inviolable, they promised. These additions would not cost the taxpayers any more than they had voted in 1982. They were persuasive. Less than four weeks after the approval of Pei's fee hike, city council approved an additional $2.5 million in city funds for lighting and sound equipment.

The damage had been done, however, and a mantra was taking hold: *The project is over budget; it's costing the citizens of Dallas more than they bargained for; Pei and his group are out of control.*

DESPITE the faltering economy, pledges that donors had made to the symphony center continued to arrive on schedule. In June 1987, Leonard Stone told *The Dallas Morning News* that only one gift, originally committed to three annual installments, had failed to fulfill its third payment. Fortunately, the total donation was not enormous; Stone described it as "less than six figures."[13] Considering the large number of individual gifts upon which the DSO was relying, its percentage of donations pledged and received was remarkable.

Political support continued unwavering from the mayor's office, if not from city council. The council problem was exacerbated by Dallas' governmental system. Every two years, city council personnel changed, and the process of education began anew. Each new council member had a different background and different level of experience with public projects. Whereas Dallas' mayors had historically been plutocrats, its councilpersons were a wild mix of constituencies and interests.

To counter the negative publicity and a sense of latent mistrust of the project, the symphony tried to focus on the positive aspects of the Meyerson Symphony Center. The construction industry had slowed down with the slump in the economy; work on the Meyerson had helped to fill the employment gap. Statistics indicated that interest in, and attendance at, cultural events was on the rise, despite the dip in the economy. Still, much of the rhetoric rested on faith: that the hall would be beautiful, and an acoustical masterpiece, and the generator of economic well-being that had been foreseen a decade before when city fathers conceived the Arts District.

Chapter Twenty

CONSTRUCTION

*What made building the Meyerson special was the level of quality required.
Hardly anything in the whole building is standard. Everything is custom.
We were always emphasizing pride, quality of workmanship, and ownership of everything we did, all the way down to the workers, building form-
work and millwork. To this day, it's still my favorite building.*[1]

BOB LEMKE

FOLLOWING demolition of the Borden's milk plant, huge amounts of dirt were being
hauled out as excavation began for the parking garage. The dirt truck drivers, communicating in CB radio parlance, could be heard referring to the giant hole in the ground
as "the bandstand."

Power cranes were to arrive in January 1986 for installation at the construction site, where
a "staging area" was now possible because of adjacent land acquired by the city. The Bateson

Left Demolition of the Borden Plant. (*DSO archives*)   **Right** After the Borden plant was demolished and excavation
began, truck drivers referred to the symphony hall site on their CB radios as "the bandstand." (*DSO archives*)

crew and George Schrader hoped that excavation would be complete by the end of January, allowing work on the lower level to proceed so as to bring it up to grade (*i.e.,* street level) by September 1986.[2]

For a while, everything sailed along on schedule. Concrete footings for the crane towers were poured. The city continued its acquisition of land for a proposed opera and ballet the-

By late 1986, the foundation work had been completed. The floor had been poured for the basement level and a uniform column pattern was visible in the lower lobby. (*Photo by Miguel Casanova, courtesy City of Dallas*)

atre, and the Dallas Area Rapid Transit (known locally as DART) commenced a review of rail lines with an eye toward future location of an Arts District station. Bateson sent construction documents—the architect's completed plans and specifications—out to bid.

Sasaki's preliminary plans for Betty Marcus Park, the plaza to the west of the hall's main entrance, had arrived from the city by late summer. The budget for the hall included $250,000 for this amenity. Plans called for cedar, elm, bald cypress, and red oak trees, as well as ground cover around granite walkways.

In September, Schrader reported that construction was running approximately thirty days behind, but he and Bateson still forecast a December 1988 completion date. A contingency fund of $1 million remained intact. Four weeks later, after a spate of bad weather, parts of the

Miguel Casanova

Top An early I. M. Pei & Partners exterior model includes the extra *piano nobile* level, which was eliminated in 1982. (*DSO archives*)
Bottom This I. M. Pei & Partners model is much later, after the Pei group and Artec Consultants had agreed upon the final design of the concert room. (*DSO archives*)

Top The concert room has been built up to the grand tier level, and to the left are the mechanical areas beneath the future Betty Marcus Park. (*Photo by Miguel Casanova, courtesy City of Dallas*) **Bottom** Form work is in place for the concrete walls, which would support the limestone exterior. (*Photo by Miguel Casanova, courtesy City of Dallas*)

Above Shortly before the grand opening, the limestone and marble travertine for the Grand Staircase are substantially complete. (*Photo by Miguel Casanova, courtesy City of Dallas*) **Facing page** The steps leading up from the lower level lobby are still raw concrete, but marble has been installed on the sides of the low wall adjacent to the stairway. (*Photo by Miguel Casanova, courtesy City of Dallas*)

Limestone work is finished on the Wall of Honor shortly before the opening, but the east lobby flooring is incomplete.
(*Photo by Miguel Casanova, courtesy City of Dallas*)

Top Landscaping continued after the exterior of the hall assumed its shape. *(Photo by Miguel Casanova, courtesy City of Dallas)* **Bottom** South and west of the hall, postmodern skyscrapers define the Arts District as the business center of downtown Dallas. *(Photo by Miguel Casanova, courtesy City of Dallas)*

Facing page The main lobby. (*Photo by Greg Hursley, courtesy Centex Construction Company*)
Above A play of circles draws the eye around the lobby in a constantly shifting panorama.
(*Photo by Richard DeWeese, courtesy Meyerson Symphony Center*)

Abby Suckle's roses added color to the Fogelson Pavilion and made I. M. Pei happy.
(*Photo by Nathaniel Liebermann, courtesy Mary McDermott Cook*)

Greg Hursley, courtesy Centex Construction Company

I. M. Pei designed onyx lamps to add sparkle to the lobby. (*DSO archives*)

Miguel Casanova

Facing page Artec Consultants' large canopy and the Lay Family Concert Organ dominate the Eugene McDermott Concert Hall. (Photo by Donald Fuller, courtesy Meyerson Symphony Center) **Above** C. B. Fisk, Inc.'s Opus 100: the Herman W. and Amelia H. Lay Family Concert Organ. (*Courtesy Meyerson Symphony Center*).

Ellsworth Kelly's *Dallas Panels: Blue Green Black Red.* (*DSO archives*)

Miguel Casanova

I. M. Pei's conoid, viewed from Betty Marcus Park. (*Photo by James Langford*)

Top A view from the corner of Pearl and Flora streets. (*Photo by Miguel Casanova, courtesy City of Dallas*)
Bottom The Emery Reves Arch of Peace. (*Photo by Greg Hursley, courtesy Centex Construction Company*)

Eduardo Chillida's *De Musica* provides dramatic counterpoint in the plaza at the front entrance. (*Courtesy Meyerson Symphony Center*)

The main public entrance on Flora Street. (*Photo by Greg Hursley, courtesy Centex Construction Company*)

Eduardo Chillida's *De Musica* complements both the Meyerson and the downtown business district. (*Courtesy Frank Ribelin*)

Audiences love the warm ambiance of the Eugene McDermott Concert Hall.
(*Photo by Miguel Casanova, courtesy City of Dallas*)

Miguel Casanova

building were visible above ground; however, the project was now fifty-seven days behind schedule. That time was never made up.

Oceans of concrete poured into the area. One percentage point at a time, in increments that seemed microscopic, Schrader reported progress on the parking garage beneath the hall, the nearby Arts District garage under the old Lone Star Cadillac property and, finally, the

A forest of scaffolding supported the grand tier, which was still under construction. (*DSO archives*)

foundation. He had plenty of other tasks to keep himself busy, such as overseeing the ongoing bid process. Numerous contracts remained unawarded, including the important mechanical engineering contract. Schrader also monitored negotiations between the city and Artec for renewal of the acoustical and theatre consulting contract. In January 1987, work began on components that distinguished the hall as a space for the arts: the stage platform, backstage areas, and supporting wall for the box-seat tier. It was still concrete, but it was far more exciting than parking spaces.

Concurrent with work on the garage, Bateson was working with the Pei group to plan for construction phases that lay a year or two out. For much of its first year under contract as the construction manager, the Bateson team—Vice President for Business Development Bill

Austin, Construction Manager Coy Porter, his assistant Laurie Dale, Project Engineer Bob Lemke, and Quality Control Manager Paul Lyons—solicited costing information from contractors it thought might be the winning bidders, in order to assemble its guaranteed maximum price. Now they began to put together and advertise bid packages for all the subcontractors: mechanical, electrical, plumbing, concrete, mill work, flooring materials, masonry, steel, roofing, paint, and others, for a total of more than thirty.

When Bateson landed the symphony hall contract, it had recently finished Edward Larrabee Barnes's Dallas Museum of Art. The on-site architect for that project was Paul Lyons, who was responsible for overall construction administration, including quality assurance. Bateson's construction manager, Coy Porter, was impressed with Lyons's work at the museum. He knew that Lyons had established a good working relationship with Barnes and felt that Lyons could do the same with Pei. Porter asked Joe Walker to recruit Lyons for quality control of the symphony hall. Walker delegated the task to Mike Wagner, Bateson's executive vice president for operations. At first, Lyons was unenthusiastic about working for a contractor. "The attitude and enthusiasm of Mike Wagner and Joe Walker got me going," he says today. "Bateson really wanted to do that project, and not just as a profit center. They knew it was a going to be a big civic event and one of the premier buildings of this century. I realized that I had the chance to do a once-in-a-lifetime project at the age of forty-two."[3] One of his conditions was that Bateson budget a generous travel allowance for him. "There's only one way to do quality work with the I. M. Pei office," he told them bluntly. "You take the Pei architects to the various [suppliers'] plants and manufacturing facilities, you build them project-specific mockups, and you have them approved. That way, when each item gets to the job site, it is in fact what they want, what's been signed off, and work doesn't have to be torn out."[4] Wagner agreed.

In his capacity as quality control manager, Lyons would be responsible for taking the architects' drawings and specifications and ensuring that the execution of their directives met the highest standards. Soon he was flying to New York regularly for design team meetings and accompanying Pei's architects all over the United States and Canada to visit materials suppliers and subcontractors. He spent most of his time dealing with architectural concrete, limestone, the glass conoid and lenses, and the interior finishes of the concert room, because these were the areas of greatest personal interest to Pei.

A new player added to the local team was Glenn Redmond, who was hired as the architects' on-site representative. An architect and a musician, Redmond had worked with Pei's group on the Arco Tower, contracting through Hidell Architects, the Dallas firm of a former Pei project manager. Pei's Dallas office subcontracted construction administration for several projects, including the symphony hall, to Hidell Architects. As the architects' representative, overseeing day-to-day construction of the building, Redmond joined a growing group of persons who would be on-site full time for four years.

Paul Lyons made half a dozen trips with Pei architects to Bedford, Indiana, about a hundred miles south of Indianapolis, to visit Hardings & Cogswell, the limestone producer. Its Bedford quarry was the source of limestone for the Dallas Museum of Art, and had furnished

Left Excavation for the Arts District garage began shortly after demolition of the Borden plant. (*DSO archives*)
Right Long before the orchestra level floor contained rows of fixed seats, it served as a staging area for the construction crew. The equipment on the floor includes a compressor, steel reinforcement bars, and lumber. (*DSO archives*)

stone to Pei for several other projects. Those prior collaborations had established a good working relationship and mutual understanding. On the first trip, they discussed general parameters and needs for the symphony hall. The second trip included a tour of various quarries. For each subsequent step, including pulling the blocks, ascertaining the homogeneity of the stone, storage time to leach out water within the stone, cutting, and polishing, Lyons and a Pei architect returned to Indiana to oversee quality, production, and consistency of appearance.

They selected limestone from a special part of the Hardings & Cogswell quarry that had not been opened in nearly fifty years. "Those guys are old country boys," chuckles Lyons. "If you tell them what limestone color they're looking for, they know where to find it, but they hold you up until they negotiate the price they want. Once they get that price, it's amazing how they can produce those limestone blocks!"[5]

Stone is a natural product that, in some respects, behaves like hardwood. Pei favored Indiana limestone because he liked its character. On an ordinary office building, the stone would have been simply quarried, cut and shipped. The Meyerson limestone required a lengthy approval process to meet Pei's standards. Bateson's Bob Lemke recalls, "We went through multiple sample submissions to get approval for color, texture, and grain."[6] Perry Chin, a Pei architect who also worked extensively on the conoid and lenses, remembers Pei's suggestion that the stone be cut against the grain. "He wanted it to have a weathered look," Chin explains. "Limestone is composed of calcium, sand, and mineral deposits. Sometimes it contains shells and fossils. The softer portion will be eroded by wind and rain, resulting in a coarse, sandpaper

Main entry into Eugene McDermott Concert Hall, showing Bateson's form work for the first tier lobby (loge level) and the grand staircase leading up. (*DSO archives*)

texture. We worked with Harding & Cogswell to develop machinery that would achieve the rough-textured finish."[7] The company designed a stiff-bristled steel brush system mounted on a roller, to be used under running water at the end of the polishing line. The process gouged out the softer part of the limestone, yielding the texture and striations that Pei sought.

All the hard work and attention to detail paid off. One year after construction began, when the first limestone began to arrive in Dallas, the quality and consistency were superb. Lyons remembers with satisfaction, "Very few pieces were rejected. Minimal. The trucks came in with the stone masonry, did their work, put the cladding on the outside of the building. We had some field fitting, but actually that was minimal, too."[8]

—⁓—

THE CITY'S Cliff Keheley remembers, "A good bit of the early construction during '85 and early '86 was the underground portion of it, partly because the design was still being refined. By late 1986, the fundamental shape of the building was becoming visible to everybody. We were starting to make decisions then for events that were going to come along well down the line. We even had to make a couple of trips to New York [to meet with] Pei and his group. We had to go on to Boston to talk to Sasaki Associates about the street that we were building in front of the symphony hall. All of this was tied together: the garage, the street, the utilities, and the building. We were trying to manage all of that coherently. As the building reached the point where it was becoming visible, we started getting into making money decisions that would have an impact on us later."[9]

Concrete remained the largest item in the budget, exceeding even I. M. Pei & Partners' fees. It wasn't simply a matter of there being a lot of concrete—parking garage, foundation, support beams, columns, roof components, reverberation chamber doors, and the like. Some of the concrete was exposed, which meant that its function was aesthetic as well as structural. Like the limestone, it also had to meet Pei's discriminating standards for color and texture and be free of surface flaws. Not surprisingly, a number of the early columns had to be redone, particularly during summer 1986, when the first exposed concrete was being poured.[10]

James Langford, who was a junior member of the Pei team from 1981 to 1985, later explained why Bateson encountered such problems with the exposed concrete. "Architectural concrete is more expensive than regular concrete used for pavement and sidewalks. The aggregate is much finer and the mixture includes special ingredients, ultimately yielding a product with a smoother finish and tight corners. The form work into which architectural concrete is poured is very expensive—almost furniture grade, because any imperfection in the form work will show up as an imperfection in the concrete once the form work is removed and the architectural concrete exposed to view. The precise timing of the removal of the form

Left View from rear orchestra level, looking toward the stage. The concrete for the shear wall behind the organ has been placed and stripped. The reverberation chambers above the stage on either side are starting to take shape, as is the choral terrace. The proscenium columns to each side of the stage are also visible. (*DSO archives*) **Right** View of loge level lobby, looking south toward downtown and the Plaza of the Americas (now Le Meridien), the west façade above what would become the Fogelson Pavilion. Behind the scaffolding, where the diagonal supports are, is the top of the stairway leading from loge level to dress circle level. The conoidal columns are to the right. (*DSO archives*)

work is also critical. If it is left too long, the concrete can discolor. The form work also creates a burden for the general contractor because generally he cannot proceed with other work until the form work is removed.

"At the Meyerson, the exposed concrete was poured in place before the limestone subcontractor began work setting the stone," Langford continues. "It had to integrate with the limestone joints, which left no room for error on the part of the architectural concrete subcontractor. The cost of this precision work was a major reason that the concrete costs were so high."[11]

Ted Amberg (middle) and I.M. Pei guide an unidentified visitor through the site. (*Photo by Miguel Casanova, courtesy City of Dallas*)

Architects' representative Redmond was also struck by the demands presented by the specialized concrete work in Pei's design. "I. M. Pei is known for using architectural concrete as a design element, exposing the structure of the building in places. The average contractor forgets how difficult it is to do architectural concrete, because it's not a conventional way to do it. Bateson had experience in architectural concrete. They faced a challenging technical problem in all the exposed concrete, but particularly the columns. We went through a lot of different types of forms, including some fiberglass forms specially made for the job. My recollection is that there were thirteen columns poured that were taken down. Some of them were on the building; others were mockups that were off the building. The problems varied: The columns leaked or had a lot of bugholes, air pockets in the surface, and it was absolutely essential that the surface be smooth and look as close to the limestone as possible. It takes a higher quality of concrete placement and form construction. We went to great lengths to deal with that.

Ultimately, Bateson hired Robert Kirk, AIA, a local architect who was an architectural concrete consultant, to assist. He adjusted the mix design to get the components just right and instructed Bateson about the placement procedure. When he came on the project, the first column he tried was an improvement, but still a little off. With the second column, he got it right. From then on, the columns were good."[12]

By midsummer 1987, the garage at second basement level was nearly complete. Crews were working overtime to finish the concrete work underneath the building and at the ground floor. The exterior concrete was up to three levels above ground, and the first limestone and granite slabs had been placed on the Pearl Street wall on the west side of the structure.[13]

—⌘—

THE NUTS and bolts of a construction project fell into a rhythm. Job meetings took place every week. Ted Amberg represented Pei's Dallas office on a daily basis. He was sometimes joined by George Miller or another key member of the New York architectural team at these weekly construction meetings. Melissa McNeil, John Adams, George Schrader, and, frequently, Leonard Stone participated on behalf of the symphony. Bateson's key people were always

George Miller (left), I.M. Pei and Glenn Redmond discuss a problem on site. (*Photo by Miguel Casanova, courtesy City of Dallas*)

there: Coy Porter, Laurie Dale, Bob Lemke, and Paul Lyons. Representing the City of Dallas were Cliff Keheley, director of public works, and architect Louise Reuben Elam, who kept their eyes on things. Glenn Redmond attended in his capacity as architect's on-site representative.

Bateson's crew was pumping concrete up to the reverberation chamber by the end of August 1987.[14] Once they reached the roof level, another concrete problem came under discussion. A major principle underlying Artec's acoustical theories is silence, which translates in practical terms to sound isolation. Artec had specified roof concrete approximately 13 inches thick in order to isolate fully the concert room from extraneous noises, particularly those of commercial aircraft headed into and out of nearby Love Field Airport. As had occurred in so many other phases of the building, the astronomical concrete bids forced a reevaluation of how costs might be reduced in this area. The concrete roof issue heated up to the point that it drew city council attention.

Russell Johnson was adamant that the concrete must be as Artec had prescribed in its original plans. Once again, Meyerson's committee asked him to quantify what reduction in acoustical quality might occur if the roofing concrete, for example, were completed at a lesser thickness than Artec had mandated. According to Eugene Bonelli, the committee was never successful in getting him to do that and overrode him. The smaller unit finally took the position that if Johnson could not convince *them* that the thicker concrete was needed, they would make the decision as to what they thought was right. The concrete was reduced in thickness, which resulted in savings in structural roof truss design. City architect Louise Reuben Elam recalls, "We went through another set of cost-cutting exercises to try to reduce the cost of the concrete and other items. The original plans showed a total of 22 inches of concrete slabs for the roof and attic, to buffer the concert hall from aircraft noise. The two were reduced to a total of 11 inches."[15] (The concert room ceiling concrete was 5½ inches thick; the roof concrete thickness varies in order to create slopes so that rain water runs to the roof drains. It ranged from a minimum of 5¼ inches to a maximum of 9¾ inches.)[16]

"I'm convinced that Russell saw this as the chance to crown his career with a good committee and adequate funding, the chance to build maybe the finest hall he would build in his lifetime," says Bonelli. "He was determined to have every flexibility and every assistance in doing it. The thickness of the concrete in the roof is an example. When we cut that back, we knew we were taking a risk, but we've never heard an airplane in the room, so obviously we didn't need [the thicker concrete]. He was giving himself a cushion. That's why we always needed to challenge him. We had to cut back what we couldn't afford. We had to try to find out what really was essential and what was not."[17]

THE GLASS portions of the exterior presented a particular challenge. They consisted of two different types: the upper glass enclosures, or lenses, and the lower enclosure on the west side flanking the limestone "shoebox" exterior, called a conoid.

Perry Chin was responsible for most of the related drawings. Early in the design phase, he was presented with the design and a volumetric study model with intersections of circles, a large one at the base of the conoid, a smaller one thirty feet above. "Basically we had a volume of voids, represented by glass, and solid, represented by the limestone portion of the building," explains Chin. "We began the task of defining this geometry, so that we could document it and present it to the contractor and *he* could construct it from those documents. Each lens is a portion of an asymmetrical cylinder. At the ends, where it leans against the wall, or on the roof side, we had an almost perfect arc. This is very important to maintain a pure circular geometry."[18] Looking up from the hall lobby, one sees the continuity of the circle touching the outside corner of the hall. Thirty feet below, the conoid is tangential in one corner to the lenses, then fans out toward the rear of the hall. Pei's group found that the cone shape was the most appropriate geometry to satisfy the design requirement. The interesting thing, says Chin, is that the cone is asymmetrical, unlike an ice cream cone. With the asymmetrical cone, the center of the circle shifts toward the outside near the entrance of the building, culminating in a tip ninety feet above street level.[19]

The glass for the cone and lenses requires subdivision and support from aluminum mullions which, in their turn, rely on steel support. Such a complex structure was fraught with the risk of error when the three elements of glass, aluminum, and steel came together. The company awarded the contract was Zimcor, in Montreal. Chin's architectural drawings were all done by hand with the aid of a calculator. Once Zimcor took over, the plans were computerized. Its bid indicated that all aluminum, steel, and glazing work would emanate from one manufacturer and location, rather than three. (Zimcor did subcontract the steel to Dominion Bridge, then the largest steel manufacturer in Canada.)

Lyons remembers more than a dozen trips to Montreal with George Miller, Perry Chin, and sometimes Dan Cecil, one of the structural engineers. "The conoid undoubtedly was the most complicated facet of the project, because no two pieces of glass were alike," declares Lyons. "No structural truss was the same length and configuration; none of the cross-bracing is the same. If we had not had CAD software in those days, I don't know how we would have done the engineering for the conoid. We did a lot of shop drawing review with Perry [Chin], the lead architect on that, and Dan Cecil. To have done it without a computer would probably have been impossible."[20]

Once again, careful planning and scrupulous attention to detail were mandatory because there was no tolerance for error. "Everything about the conoid and the lenses had to be precise and exact," recalls Bob Lemke. "Having the glass, mullions, and steel work all coming from Zimcor helped some. Also, it keeps a clear line of

Late in 1987, the building still lacked a roof, and Bateson had not yet erected the conoid ring beams. The shadow of the LTV Tower falls across Cathedral Santuario de Guadalupe. In the background is the Crescent hotel and office complex. (*Photo by Miguel Casanova, courtesy City of Dallas*)

responsibility and accountability. Whenever you do that, you can also achieve higher quality."[21]

The logistics of transporting and hoisting the concrete doors for the reverberation chambers into the building was another challenge Bateson had to resolve. The door frames—high and in several sizes—were made in Waco. According to architect Glenn Redmond, because the doors, once assembled with concrete and frame together, were so heavy, Bateson knew they would require installation with a crane before the roof went on. "They had to be placed on the reverberation chamber floor in approximately the location where they would stay.

Afterward, they cast the concrete in place in the framework. When it came time to install the doors, they used a chain hoist to lift them into place and put them on the hinges."[22]

— ❧ —

FIRST violinist Mary Reynolds would drive over from Fair Park Music Hall after rehearsals to watch the construction as the structure began to rise out of the ground. "I'd park where the Cullen-Frost Bank used to be and try to imagine from the models how everything would look. I just couldn't wait for it to be done."[23] She finally got a look at the interior when the orchestra took its first hard-hat tour in October 1987. "We came down the main staircase, which was all just concrete, wood and scaffolding—kind of dangerous, actually," she remembers. "We were careful with our footing! The orchestra walked out onto the stage. It was concrete. There was no roof yet. That's where we had our photograph taken."[24] (The photograph, which shows the players standing in full concert dress and hard hats, most with their instruments, was used for the DSO's 1988–89 season brochure, along with several other photographs of the construction.) Principal timpanist Kalman Cherry recalls, "We were very optimistic that first hard-hat tour. We knew right away that it had to be one hundred percent better than anything we'd ever had, because we walked as far away from the stage as we could get, and we were still relatively close to it, compared to Fair Park."[25] Associate principal viola Barbara Hustis concurs: "The orchestra was pretty excited as a group. People could finally see that the hall was happening, even though, at the time, it seemed a big mass of concrete."[26]

The "topping out" ceremony—capping the building with a roof—took place on June 10, 1988. Director of Public Works Cliff Keheley took advantage of the timing to request that city council allocate an additional $2.5 million of accrued interest for further enhancements to the hall.[27] The list of amenities included $1 million for loudspeakers, circuits, dimmer switches, and microphones; $500,000 for custom seating in certain areas to improve acoustics; and about $1 million, grouping together miscellaneous additional charges for more signage, patron furniture in public and office spaces, kitchen equipment, site work, materials testing, and engineering fees. Keheley argued that rentals of the completed facility would be more profitable with the lighting and sound equipment enhancements, but city council was leery. Even the knowledge that sale of the 1982 bonds would continue to generate interest that could cover the city's increased share did not persuade them. They forestalled any decision on further funding, requesting a formal plan from the symphony for its concert hall costs.

— ❧ —

BATESON'S Joe Walker describes the concert hall interior as having been constructed from the top down. "The scaffolding was a forest of metal all over the auditorium, because we had to build the ceiling, which was ornate, with painting and prep work out of the normal sequence. Normally you build up from the bottom. In this auditorium, we had to start from the top and come down. We couldn't install the terrazzo floor because it would have been damaged. We couldn't finish any of the auditorium until we finished the ceiling."[28] The plan was to take down one tier of scaffolding at a time and complete work on the side walls and balconies.

Then I. M. Pei stopped the job. He wanted to make some changes in the ceiling. "We were stopped dead," says Walker. "We couldn't do anything in the concert hall. We had to let the men proceed with plasterwork, painting, and acoustical work, and whatever else had to be

About one year before completion, the Meyerson had been "topped out" The ring beam supporting the conoid was up, and foundation work was complete on Betty Marcus Park except for its concrete base and surface landscaping. To the center and right, utility trenches are visible on Flora Street. (*Photo by Miguel Casanova, courtesy City of Dallas*)

done up there, because once the scaffolding came down, they weren't going to get up there again! It had to be done then. But I already knew that Pei wanted to give the owner the best he could, so he never quit designing. We were always getting changes that would absolutely tear up our schedule. He would change the shop drawings after we had drawn them up and gotten them ready to construct."[29]

As quality control manager, Paul Lyons enjoyed the highest respect from his colleagues. According to Bob Lemke, "Paul was very intuitive with regard to what I. M. wanted. He spent a lot of time with George Miller, Ted Amberg, and sometimes I. M. himself, filling in some of the grey areas, taking in what's in the specs and on the plans and determining the level and degree of quality to get the building done right. Paul then had to communicate that to the workers through constant reminders in our weekly meetings with subcontractors. We always spent time at those meetings dealing with quality control issues, not only on the quality of the workmanship, but also building in the right order. If you don't do certain things in the right order, the end result can be a mess. You end up tearing out more trying to do your job than you actually get done! We had to redo a lot of things that Paul would not initially accept."[30]

"Paul was a character," architect's representative Redmond adds. "He was large, and he sometimes cussed like a sailor. He had a very commanding presence. As a result, he had a lot

No two pieces of glass in the conoid are alike. (*Photo by James E. Langford*)

to say about everything. I think the project owes a lot to Paul's oversight. If the Bateson people didn't know the answer, he made them find out, slow down, and pay a lot of attention to detail. He made my job a lot easier, because he headed off things that would have been my responsibility had he not been there. There's no way, in a building that complex, I could have caught everything he caught. He took a lot of the heat, throwing sparks off people, arguing with the Bateson people."[31]

According to Bateson's Coy Porter, Lyons's input to the construction management team ensured that each subcontractor would approach the project more from the architect's viewpoint, and less as a contractor would.[32] Redmond believes that at a deeper level, Lyons probably knew more about all aspects of the job than anybody at Bateson. "His personality was such that he thrust himself into the middle of everything that went on. He exerted a lot of power, and it was all to the benefit of the project. The force of his personality got things done right, especially finishing the job, when it was so hectic. It didn't look like it was going to get finished by September 6 [1989]. Paul basically told the subcontractors, 'Do whatever it takes to finish. We'll sort it out later. We have no choice but to finish. The symphony has committed to that date. It's past the point of making any kind of change in the program.' That was a very hazardous position for a contractor to take, because he was not giving them any financial guarantee that they were even going to be paid for the actual time it took to finish. I think ultimately Bateson had to negotiate the final payments with a lot of the subs. I suspect that a lot of people broke even, rather than making a profit on the job. I really commend the subs for doing it. They did what it took. Bateson pushed them hard to make it happen. Again, Paul Lyons had a lot to do with it. At that point, Paul was the pusher, even though that was not really his job. The project manager was Coy Porter, who has a real level head. In the midst of all the confusion, Coy remained calm. He and Paul worked together well, because Paul was the heavy, and Coy remained even-tempered."[33]

Joe Walker reiterates the importance of Porter's role. "Coy sweated bullets all the time trying to get that job through. I could have put somebody down there who got mad every time someone made a change. He was the ideal guy, because he got along with everybody: with Pei, with Perot, with Schrader, with Cliff [Keheley], with the contractors. Coy kept us in the team mode."[34]

FOR Cliff Keheley, the toughest period occurred in spring 1989. "We were really working hard, pushing the schedule. The president of Centex, Bateson's parent company, brought up a guy from Houston for a meeting with us. The president said they were committed to doing whatever it took to get the job done, and that he was bringing this guy in to help Joe [Walker] out. I wondered, what could Joe possibly need? We needed less help at that point, not more! The guy from Houston stated, 'The City of Dallas has not been committed to this project. You're not helping us get this hall done on time.' By that time, I had very little patience left. I looked him in the eye and said, 'Well, I don't know who you are or where you came from, but you just got here, and the rest of us have been here a good long while on this project. We're going to finish this job, and we don't need your help. I'm going to ask your boss to get you off this job.' I did, and he got kicked out. That's the stage we were at. Those were really tough times because everybody was at his emotional limit."[35] As the opening drew closer, those limits would be stretched again and again.

Chapter Twenty-One

ONGOING POLITICAL AND PRESS CHALLENGES

It is the only major arts facility and the only important public building under construction in Dallas. And it's three years behind schedule and more than $30 million over projections.[1]

THE DALLAS MORNING NEWS, APRIL 30, 1989

BILL Schilling succeeded Liener Temerlin as president of the Dallas Symphony Association Board in May 1986. Saddled with a legacy of delays and cost problems, Schilling did his best to move the project forward and, of course, to propel the fundraising juggernaut. He says, "In my capacity as president, it was my responsibility to see that the volunteer support for the symphony continued to expand. That would include fundraising and board development, a collective effort to get leaders of the business community involved. Actually, the president at that time was involved in most aspects of the operation. A lot of our work was done through committees. Lots and lots of committees!"[2]

Political tensions surrounding the concert hall increased as the city began to process Bateson's change orders. Cliff Keheley says, "At the outset, it had all the appearances of a perfect marriage. The city wanted to build a symphony hall and felt that it had a good partner in the Dallas Symphony Association, which was actively raising funds. Everything was going along splendidly. The political problems arose as the project got into construction and we started having to handle change orders. Each one had to be approved by the city council, because these were public contracts. No city council I've ever worked for clearly understood what a change order is. In this case, they were always suspicious that the project would run out of budget in spite of our assurances that the symphony association was funding these changes. They'd ask, 'How do we *know* that we're going to get the money?' Remember that the city fronted the money for the symphony, which meant that we had put up the money and were anticipating return from the association. Some council members became very anxious about the ability of the association to fulfill its obligation with these escalating costs. The council members viewed their role as overseeing the project on behalf of their constituents. They didn't want to have to go back to their constituents and explain a disaster. Keeping up with expenditures and attributing them to this side or that side was a complex management problem."[3]

The city's $28.6 million contribution was theoretically an immutable figure, excepting specific items approved subsequently by city council. Throughout the design phase, in order to adhere to the budget, Meyerson and his committee had cut virtually everything that did not pertain to the essential acoustical integrity of the design. In 1986 and 1987, as the building began to take shape, some of those things started to get added in again. As the structure emerged above ground, it was visible to passing traffic and those working in neighboring office towers. The Meyerson became much more real to Dallas citizens. Selling is easier, of course, when you can see the product. Leonard Stone, Liener Temerlin, and the members of the concert hall committee all wanted to enhance the music chamber with the addition of wood paneling and terrazzo floors rather than acoustically undesirable carpet. They hoped to add other visible materials that would enhance the building's architectural luster and overall ambience.

The symphony was in a quandary. Its plans had originated during a time of prosperity and optimism. Many of the financial commitments individuals had made to the orchestra for the hall were based on the expectation of business profits. Now those profits were less certain, complicating an already challenging fund-raising program. The economy remained in a tailspin, and appeared to have no silver lining around its large cloud. Eugene Bonelli remembers, "So many people who had money to give no longer gave, which meant that we had a smaller pool from which to try to get people to donate. One of the main reasons we were successful is that we were given such priority in the city among its donors because of the excitement of opening the building and the distinction and international reputation the Meyerson was already developing. It was a very popular, exciting thing to give to, but raising money was still very difficult."[4]

Downstate in Houston, a new opera house was preparing to open for David Gockley's Houston Grand Opera, a troupe that was drawing increasing national attention and acclaim. The inherent rivalry between Houston and Dallas was an undercurrent that helped to stabilize the brouhaha about purported cost overruns and encourage ongoing financial support of the Meyerson. Oil-dependent Houston was facing the same economic problems as Dallas, and Dallas was not to be outdone by its neighbor to the south!

Former DSO General Manager Fred Hoster describes the political environment at the time as chaotic. "It was like being in the middle of a Waring blender. We had a hundred different bosses. Leonard [Stone] said to me many times, if this had been a private sector project, people just would have walked away from it, because it wasn't worth the effort and mental aggravation. Several members of city council were adamant. This was a guaranteed-maximum building: $75 million, which meant that any expenditure that was made had to be either approved or the cash had to be there guaranteed before you could move forward. These councilpersons kept saying, 'This is an $85 million, this is a $100 million building.' They didn't know what they were talking about, but it caused a lot of grief to be shed on us as a result of that, because we spent a lot of time defending the fact that we were still under the guaranteed maximum."[5]

Matters had reached one crisis point in January 1985 when the press learned that the building itself would cost $75 million. Each incremental increase after that prompted an analogous response of protest and outcry from city council opponents, who found willing reporters to write down and publish their remarks. "As the project wore on, the council was taking extensive heat from its constituents about the cost," remembers Cliff Keheley. "The media were taking shots at the symphony association. The changes in design costs were frustrating to the construction manager and to me, because we were trying to keep track of all these changes, and also trying to get the hall built."[6]

——— ❧ ———

Public relations pertaining to the hall remained strained. The local press had found a whipping boy in the cost increases, which had become all-too-frequent announcements. *The Dallas Morning News* architecture critic David Dillon, who covered the hall's progress from 1982 on, believes that DSO personnel created their own problem. "The symphony had some people who were giving out misleading or incomplete information on a regular basis," he says. "They ran up against some reporters who were more vigorous [in pursuing the story]. They were always doing a shuffle. They weren't playing it particularly straight. I remember they were always getting caught up in their own red tape in finances. There was always a crisis about being over budget. They'd give funny numbers."[7]

It became apparent that the DSO's operating requirements would exceed what normal sources could provide. The symphony's development department quietly geared up special efforts to secure major gifts that, over a payment period of several years, could be applied to operating costs. They called it "program fund giving." According to Warren Gould, at the time an outside consultant with the Carl Shaver Company, "It was a euphemism for seeking major gifts that could be expended."[8]

Nearly as much of a problem as the cost issues were the repeated delays, which had been exacerbated by the convoluted process of securing the land. Cost consultant Stewart Donnell believes that those delays affected construction costs. "Sometimes—very rarely—costs go down," he says, "but in this case the right window for bidding the project was lost in the early

1980s through no fault of anyone; it just happened. The building took approximately two and one-half to three years to evolve. Costs were rising. That was when the economy was still strong. It was during construction that the bottom fell out of the marketplace. That made it difficult to swallow."⁹

Leonard Stone and Doug Kinzey were forced to revamp their marketing strategy for several consecutive seasons as the opening date stretched farther out on the calendar. Stone says, "The Meyerson was supposed to open up in '86, '87, then it finally opened in '89. I drove Doug crazy when I came to him and said, 'Doug, guess what? You're going to have to keep that audience in Fair Park another year!' He'd have brochures floating in his mind about the glories of moving in. He was foaming at the mouth to introduce the move-over brochure! Because Doug was facing something that he probably wouldn't admit to himself, nor would any other people admit: that the fabulous, in-Dallas marketing effort we were doing—and he was the man whom I charged with the responsibility—to counteract the negative media, simply didn't work. We had building models in the [Fair Park] music hall lobby and took those models all over the city. We had a speakers bureau. We had all these public parks concerts. We had dog and pony shows coming out of the gazoo. Doug did it all, and he did it brilliantly. The media *still* hammered us."¹⁰

Chapter Twenty-Two

HOT TICKET:
THE STRADIVARIUS
PATRON PROGRAM

A T T H E Dallas Symphony offices, various fund-raising activities were simultaneously in high gear. Henry Miller's Cornerstone campaign, initiated in 1982, had concluded in 1985, having exceeded its goals. Cornerstone had been crucial to the symphony's long-range financial planning, but it also presented a development conundrum, because it had become the sole repository of all fund-raising during those years. "Cornerstone was the 'basket,' and we put everything into the Cornerstone basket," explains former DSA President Dolores Barzune. "When you put all the income in a big pot, you really don't know what goes to annual fund, capital campaign, or endowment. There's no demarcation, and it can be very dangerous, if someone plays fast and loose with the monies. We learned not to put our eggs in one basket."[1]

With Cornerstone completed, the development department undertook the process of re-educating the public about annual fund giving. Additionally, smaller unit members Louise Kahn, Mary McDermott Cook, and Leonard Stone concocted a high-end patron plan that would provide special privileges to donors at a certain level, then $1,500 annually. Modeled after the Dallas Museum of Art's major donor program, the new symphony program was christened "Stradivarius Patrons" toward the end of 1983. Stone needed four things to make the Stradivarius program work. "First was the program, which had to be well thought out. Second, we needed funding. Third, I needed a staff operative who would get the program going, and do it well, and that was JoLynne Jensen. Finally, I needed that volunteer board leadership, which I identified in Dolores Barzune. Initially, Dolores didn't want to do it. [Development Director] Domenick Ietto and I had to really talk hard to get her to do it. She was fabulous. I think what probably convinced her as much as anything else, beyond her understanding of the need, was she had a wonderful affinity with JoLynne. They were just like ham and eggs."[2]

Dolores Barzune was a former music teacher with a long history as a symphony volunteer. She had been the president of the symphony's Junior Group in the late 1970s and later of the Dallas Symphony League. The wife of a prominent Dallas physician, she was energetic, enthusiastic, and altogether committed to the Dallas Symphony. She was willing to do anything to make the hall happen. "I kept saying I didn't want to chair the Strad program," Barzune reflected in 1996, "but actually I'm very proud of the work we did, because we had never had a program for recruiting people."[3] Barzune and Jensen did hit it off famously, and they proved to be an effective team working with Stradivarius patron prospects.

According to Domenick Ietto, who became development director in September 1985, "Dolores made an incredible difference in the organization by stepping forward when she did. She was excited about the Strad program and its potential to attract leadership to the symphony. But she also had quite a bit of concern about the amount of her time it would require, because we had planned a slew of events for the Strad group throughout the year, and she wanted to be an active participant. We had to guarantee her that she would have all the staff support that we could bring to bear, and assure her that we wouldn't have unrealistic expectations. We needed somebody like Dolores to do the job."[4]

The program required funding to promote it and to underwrite the initial benefits until it became self-supporting. Inasmuch as the projected cost of the hall had escalated, and new enhancements to the structure were under discussion on a regular basis, it was clear that additional funds from an independent, untapped source would be not only welcome, but also necessary. The solution came from a new corporate underwriter: Merrill Lynch.

Ietto remembers, "The Stradivarius program was in place, but the corporate funding through Merrill Lynch that shifted the program into high gear did not come about until 1986." Merrill Lynch had hired Sports Etc., a New York–based firm specializing in matching large corporate sponsors with sporting events to coordinate some of its sponsorship activities. "They suggested that Sports Etc. take a look at the demographics in the arts to determine whether they could apply some of the deals on sporting events into high-profile arts organizations," says Ietto. "Initially, they considered conventional sponsorships of performance series, but the DSO already had many sponsored performances and series. Merrill Lynch was focused on the need to stand out in the crowd. We couldn't identify exclusivity for them in terms of sponsoring concerts."[5]

The Stradivarius program was a good fit. Ietto, Barzune, and Jensen needed funding to distinguish the "Strads," as they came to be known, from other patron programs. "We assembled a 'dream scenario,' a series of exclusive special events and benefits for the Stradivarius patrons that no one else would receive as part of the symphony-going experience," explains Ietto. "Then we put the Merrill Lynch stamp in as many places as we could envision in order to identify that their funding was making these benefits possible. It worked magnificently."[6] Merrill Lynch provided $225,000 to sponsor the Stradivarius program for three years, the first time a fund-raising program had secured corporate underwriting. "This was a *very* big thing in the orchestra world," says Jensen. "People were talking about this all over the United States. Beforehand, it was unheard of to obtain sponsorship for fund-raising."[7] Once the contract with Merrill Lynch was formalized, Jensen and Barzune had a budget that permitted them to make the perquisites of the Stradivarius patron program very attractive. They structured the donor program by tying tiered benefits to certain levels of giving, with the idea that membership would help to promote a feeling of involvement between donors and the symphony. Patrons received preferred parking passes at Fair Park Music Hall and invitations to small post-concert receptions and encore performances with guest artists.

The Strad program was an important development in the evolution of the Meyerson. As Ietto points out, "The desire to be a part of the program and the profiles of individuals identified with the program were paralleling many hall-related activities, identifying that this would be a world-class concert hall, with a focus on intimacy and a certain degree of exclusivity. Of course that was a double-edged sword, because of accusations of elitism. That was a fine line we had to walk very carefully."[8] He often countered that challenge using the analogy of persons traveling by air. Just as passengers in first class don't reach the destination any faster, the experience of listeners in a symphony hall is available to everyone present, regardless of ticket price or location.

The symphony offices had no room for the development team at Fair Park, so Jensen set up shop with Ietto and the rest of his staff in the old United Fidelity building on Dallas' Main Street. They soon moved again, the nomads of the symphony staff. "Someone had donated space at the Praetorian Building, an old, raggedy office," Jensen recalls. "We *never* had donors visit there! Previously, it had been an office with a lot of desks lined up in four rows. You could tell because there were holes drilled through the floor for telephone lines. We'd be walking and all of a sudden a heel would get caught in one of those holes, or in the ragged threads on worn green carpeting. It was an OSHA nightmare!"[9]

Substandard office conditions did not interfere with Jensen's energy. "Two things intrigued me about the opportunity. One was the new concert hall and the excitement that was beginning to build. The other was the opportunity to create a new program. That's what I do best."[10] When she started work, the program had a name, a logo, and a verbal commitment from Merrill Lynch. Jensen worked with an outside public relations firm to design brochures, letterhead, membership cards. The development office had no computer system; this was an era of IBM DisplayWriters. Barzune provided her with a stack of directories so

For the first hard hat party in October 1987, JoLynne Jensen and Warren Gould climbed the scaffolding and tied up large red-and-white banners. Louise Kahn (center) and Margaret Jonsson Charlton were among the Stradivarius Patrons who got a first look at the hall that day. (*DSO archives*)

On a hard hat tour, from left: Leonard Stone, Patsy Donosky, Bill Schilling, Liener Temerlin, Dolores Barzune, Eugene Bonelli, Nancy Penson, unidentified, and Mary McDermott Cook. (*DSO archives*)

that Jensen could enter names of club members and socially prominent Dallasites into the system. Barzune remembers, "At the beginning, I'd take my pen and pencil and the symphony subscriber computer printouts from Ticketmaster, go to the music hall to see who had good seats, then take their names down. Certainly, if they had good seats, they were eligible to be Stradivarius patrons!"[11]

The concept was an immediate success. A kickoff reception and dinner took place in September 1986 at Fair Park Music Hall, in conjunction with the Thursday evening opening performance of the symphony's fall season. Over four hundred people attended, and Stradivarius-level contributions began to roll in. In retrospect, Jensen believes that the program took off in large part because of the prospect of the concert hall. "If we had introduced that Strad program at some other time in the life of the DSO, it would not have been as successful. One of the benefits we offered was priority for tickets in the new Meyerson. Our first year goal was $500,000. We exceeded it; we raised $565,000 that first year. Our second year goal was $650,000, which included a ninety percent renewal rate plus an increase through new Strad patrons.

"People loved the program, and they brought in their friends. They liked the parking pass, which brought them closer in to the entrance at Fair Park. They loved the small post-concert receptions and encore performances in the Crescent ballroom with guest artists. They'd leave Music Hall, and the Crescent was pretty much on their way home, whether they were going up Central Expressway or the [Dallas North] Tollway. They'd come in for dessert and coffee and an encore performance with Lynn Harrell. People felt as if they had just had an evening with Lynn Harrell in their living room."[12]

JoLynne Jensen arranged the first hard-hat tour of the Meyerson for the Stradivarius patrons in October 1987. "We had Bateson clean up the concrete floor, which had been poured by then, but there was no stage nor ceiling, just floor and walls, and lots of scaffolding. The Bateson crew made a pathway for us to lead the group. The Saturday before, we spent all day bringing in tables and chairs for three hundred Strad patrons who had made reservations. The event was catered, with all kinds of food, beer, and wine. [Fund-raising consultant] Warren Gould and I climbed up the scaffolding that day to tie up large, red-and-white banners labeled 'organ,' 'loge level,' 'grand tier,' 'choral terrace,' so that people could get a sense of the building.

"I had asked the Bateson people to paint a line where the stage would be. The day before the event, I was at the top of the Texas Commerce Bank Building in the Sky Lobby [one block south of the construction site]. I looked down, because it's a great view of the Meyerson from there. All I could see was a fluorescent orange, six-inch-wide line that the guys had painted on concrete to indicate the stage! The construction workers were so excited about this first tour that they built a platform and a stick person to indicate where the conductor would stand."[13]

As the building rose out of the ground, hard-hat tours became more frequent. Tour participants convened at the Bateson trailer, donned hard hats, and tromped over to the site, accompanied by a DSO staff member. "This is what you're doing for the orchestra, the association, the City of Dallas," they would hear. "It was a wonderful way to thank many of our donors," recalled Sydney Reid-Hedge. "The building belongs to the city; it's not just the symphony's. We felt that people who have been generous to us should be the first to see the hall in whatever state it was."[14] That included city officials and representatives as well as symphony supporters. Hard-hat tours quickly became a hot ticket, as donors and subscribers grew more interested in monitoring progress on the building. A dream was on its way to reality.

Chapter Twenty-Three

MARKETING CENTER AND BOX SEATS PROGRAM

Leonard Stone had said to me, "Dan, this is the Mercedes Benz of the symphony that you're selling. This is high-end stuff!" I agreed, and I conducted the program at that level: "This is a marvelous opportunity that will come only once. This is what the Dallas Symphony is doing for the city, and here's how people can participate in this venture."[1]

DAN ELLINOR

LIFE, in the form of the press, had handed the Dallas Symphony lemons. They decided to make lemonade. Meyerson, Stone, and Temerlin met with each other and with their various colleagues to discuss options. A marketing and public relations campaign to increase community awareness of the hall and enhance the development department's efforts was clearly in order.

As early as 1982, when the cost-cutting measures first reached a point that Stone and Meyerson were becoming uneasy about maintaining the quality goals for the facility, I. M. Pei came up with the idea of designating certain desirable seats in the music chamber along the same lines as luxury suites at sports stadia. Stone recalls, "In a moment of frustration when I said to I. M., 'We're going to have to cut, cut, cut, cut, cut, because it's getting too expensive and we don't have the money,' he thought of using the boxes as a vehicle to make money. He made an analogy with the sky boxes in sports stadia. I loved the idea, and I said, 'Why not?' Basically we did time shares. You couldn't sell the boxes, but you could sell long-term leases." Stone had seen a building model in the marketing center for the Crescent, a recently completed high-rise office tower, hotel, and upscale shopping plaza just north of downtown and within view of the symphony hall site. He had also looked at the marketing models in North

Dallas for the Galleria enclosed shopping center. "The Crescent model was on a mechanized tabletop, and the building model rose out of the table," Stone remembers. "The Galleria gave you this fantastic dog and pony show in their marketing center. At the end of the presentation, they pressed a button and the curtains separated, revealing windows overlooking the construction site. I said, 'I have *got* to do both of those for the Meyerson.'"[2]

While the DSO was still talking with Ray Nasher about the naming donation, Stone approached him about the idea of placing a model in NorthPark Shopping Center, a Nasher development. Stone also asked Henry Miller to talk with Harlan Crow, Trammell Crow's son, because the LTV Center (now Trammell Crow Center) was a Trammell Crow project. Would the Crow Company provide the Dallas Symphony with a small space, *gratis,* on the east side of that building, overlooking the construction site?

The LTV Center was nearly complete and scheduled to open in November 1984. It would be the first commercial project in the Arts District. Its location on Ross Avenue, in the block just east of the Dallas Museum of Art, was prime real estate in the renewing area. Moreover, the office tower overlooked the concert hall construction site. In June 1984, five months before the LTV Center opening, DSA President Temerlin reported to his executive board that a feasibility study was underway for the establishment of a marketing center to be located in space donated by the Trammell Crow family in the LTV Center.[3]

Trammell Crow Company accommodated the request, confirming fifteen hundred square feet of donated space.[4] On February 4, 1985, Concert Hall Planning Coordinator Melissa McNeil and her assistant, John Adams, relocated from the symphony's Fair Park offices and set up shop for a symphony marketing center in their new digs. The symphony held a press conference with I. M. Pei, using the occasion to unveil the interior model of the hall.

The design developed by Artec Consultants in conjunction with Charles Young of the Pei firm called for a tier of boxes at the mezzanine level of the hall, ringed in a horseshoe with optimal acoustics, advantageous views of the stage, and—very important for Dallas—maximum visibility to the rest of the audience. In 1985, at the conclusion of the Cornerstone campaign, Leonard Stone brought in Warren Gould to assist with fund-raising. Stone assigned Gould responsibility for conducting the initial feasibility study on the box seat sales.

The marketing center's triumph was a multimedia show that transported the viewer into a scale model of the projected hall. "The Pei & Partners model shop had built a ¾-inch: 1-foot scale model of the music chamber, at the time one of the largest interior scale models ever constructed," says Leonard Stone. "Peter Wexler came up with the idea of putting a scissor-lift under it to raise the visitor up into it. It was my idea to do the dog and pony show, which Peter designed for us. It was a gem."[5]

Wexler, the New York–based designer who had consulted for the symphony's summer series since 1979, explains. "They wanted to know how to 'climb into' Russell and I. M.'s model of the room. I came up with the idea of bolting it to the ceiling, building a tall black box around it, and entering via a black elevator platform at floor level. You'd say, 'Please step in here.' 'What is this?' 'You'll find out. Just step in here.' Once people got on the elevator, it rose. We had an excerpt playing from Strauss's *Don Juan*. Lights then came on above the visitor, who automatically turned his head upwards as he 'entered the hall.'"[6]

Exiting the elevator, visitors stepped into a full-scale model of a Meyerson box, complete with eight chairs identical to those in the hall today. Before them, in a darkened space, was a multi-screen slide show that Wexler had assembled. It opened with a view across the hall of boxes like the one the visitor was occupying. A tape recording of the orchestra tuning and the voices of audience members chatting "pre-concert" enhanced the illusion. Stone recalls, "The soundtrack included a voice exclaiming, 'Oh, look, there's the mayor!' and another 'Isn't that Stanley Marcus?' above the sound of the orchestra. After the lights dimmed, you saw a show. No arts organization had ever done anything like that. It was virtual reality ahead of its time, trying to give the visitor as close an experience as possible to what the live concert hall would be."[7]

ⅆⅆ

LIENER Temerlin appointed Craig Hall to chair a committee that would establish the value and terms and conditions of box seat use. The committee consisted of Richard Galland, Henry Miller, Ray Nasher, Temerlin, Bob Glaze, Warren Gould, and Leonard Stone. Another board member, Richard Freling, worked on the tax considerations and legal aspects of the box seat program.

Freling, who was then a partner in the Dallas headquarters of Johnson & Gibbs (and now with the Dallas office of Jones, Day, Reavis & Pogue) had joined the DSO Board at Temerlin's invitation in June 1984. Temerlin put him to work right away as one of the architects of the box seat program, an area where Freling's knowledge and experience as a tax lawyer and a businessman could greatly benefit the symphony. "We wanted the cost of the box seat options to qualify as a charitable contribution to the symphony," Freling explains. "In order to accomplish that, one must determine whether there is value received for what you pay. Every season ticket holder, in effect, has the opportunity to renew his or her season tickets in the seats assigned to them. The cost of a box seat option represents a charitable contribution only to the extent that the cost exceeds the value of what is received."[8]

The box seats were not necessarily the best seats in the house acoustically; however, there were to be *no* bad seats in the Meyerson for listening. These box seats had excellent sight lines, the highest level of comfort and elegance available in the hall, private vestibules, and incalculable prestige. Freling notes, "If you want a pure acoustical experience, the dress circle seats, right above the box seats in the center, are probably the best place. Therefore, we concluded that there was no special value to the boxes; you just have a right to buy the tickets in the box.

Thus, the value received was minimal, and most of the cost represented a charitable contribution. We also had to stipulate that whatever right one obtained was non-transferable, except within a family or a corporate structure. It couldn't be sold, because if it could be sold, then it had a value in the marketplace and the amount of the charitable contribution would be significantly reduced or eliminated entirely. It would be more like boxes that are sold in sports stadia."[9]

—∞—

THE DALLAS Symphony formally launched its box seat program in March 1986. Depending upon the payment schedule, box holders held renewal options for either twenty-five years or ninety-nine years. The seats went for $10,000 for the minimum unit of seven concerts in a classical series. Fourteen concerts was $20,000, and the full subscription series of twenty-one concerts was $30,000. The pops concerts pricing structure was different but generated additional income. "Nobody walked in off the street to acquire these box seats," observes Leonard Stone dryly.

Sales for the box seat program were initially entrusted to a team of volunteers pitching the boxes through telemarketing. The effort lacked direction, and in June 1986, Leonard Stone hired Dan Ellinor, a Dallasite with extensive real estate sales experience, as special gifts representative. Ellinor observed five volunteers for a few days, then scheduled a meeting with Stone. "Your prospects are hearing too many different stories," he told the executive director. "Send them all to me and let me make the presentation, so that they hear one story, and that's the *only* story." Stone recognized the wisdom in Ellinor's request, and they worked together to refine his sales pitch.[10]

Stone and DSO General Manager Fred Hoster presented Ellinor a list of six hundred persons who had donated generously to the Cornerstone campaign. It appeared to be a great list, but Ellinor immediately ran into problems. First, he discovered that summer was a bad time to seek money on behalf of the symphony. "I had no idea of the seasonal nature of the product," says Ellinor. "When the season ends, that's it for the orchestra until the fall. Patrons don't give money; they don't purchase seats. We had to learn to accept that down time." He also learned a few lessons about the economy. The savings and loan crisis was imminent, and oil prices had begun to tumble. One prospect asked him, in mixed irritation and amazement, "Do you read the paper? Do you know what the price of oil is? And you're calling *me?*" After three weeks, Ellinor put the list away and regrouped. "I had to pick a target market," he remembers. "Bankers were out; oil people were out. I had met Dolores Barzune and liked her a lot. She was moving very fast with the Stradivarius program. I knew I needed its members on my side, not as a staff member, but as one of them, so I joined. Next, I called everyone I knew of any prominence, many of whom had nothing to do with the symphony. All my friends had great contacts. I made the presentation as if I were selling to them, except I altered it to say, 'This is what the symphony is doing for the city; this is how people can participate in this venture.' They were excited. I could feel momentum building, and my phone started ringing."[11]

Ellinor also pondered the faltering economy and zeroed in on the one profession that was clearly profiting from the demise of the city's financial structure: law firms specializing in bankruptcy. He discovered that this sector of the legal profession was a growth industry. In a city that was otherwise nearly paralyzed by layoffs, bankruptcy lawyers were hiring staff as fast as they could. The second group he selected was doctors, primarily obstetricians-gynecologists. "They seemed to have more camaraderie with each other; I don't know why," Ellinor allows. "I started with a group at Presbyterian [Hospital of Dallas]. One of the physicians there purchased box seats. Once you get into that medical fraternity, there's a grapevine. Dozens of doctors belonged to that practice. They became a mainstay."

By January 1987, seven months after he began, Ellinor's commissions had exceeded his draw and the program was rolling along well. Ross Perot bought hundreds of thousands of dollars worth of seats for the Perot family. In the large central box of twelve seats, he took eight and Mort Meyerson took four. That netted $240,000 for the box seat program. Perot also opted for the same seats for pops concerts.

What amazed the symphony development staff was Ellinor's success in closing sales with so many individuals outside the DSO's traditional donor base. In fact, the box seat program held particular appeal for a number of Dallas corporations, which purchased a substantial percentage of the options. The unexpected bonus, however, came from individuals Ellinor brought in who had not previously contributed to the symphony. He sold more than 900 of 1,969 available box seat options by mid-August 1987. One month later, the symphony had received pledges on sixty percent of its box seats. The orchestra's demographic statistics indicated that seventy percent of its buyers were first-time contributors, with physicians and law firms accounting for a substantial percentage of the sales. The polished sales presentation was clearly effective, but Ellinor acknowledged that, more often than not, taking prospects over to the site for a hard-hat tour to look at the actual boxes was the most effective ploy, the one that closed the deal.[12] Tours became a customary extension of visits to the marketing center at LTV, instilling a sense of involvement and ownership in those who viewed the scaffolding supporting the hall's interior.

The influx of cash gave rise to a debate within the symphony board as to whether the proceeds from box seat sales would be used for endowment or transition funds to operate the orchestra. "There were two sides to the debate," explains Freling. "One group was very conservative about the use of these funds; another group was more flexible in its approach. The conservative group wanted the funds dedicated entirely to endowment. The other group thought that it made sense, for a variety of reasons, to be able to use these funds, when necessary, to subsidize operations during this transition period. I had started out relatively in the middle and drafted a compromise resolution. Ultimately, I swung around to the view that, with the kickoff of an endowment fund campaign, and with the creation of a new endowment fund called the Fund for Excellence and the establishment of transition funding that was intended to supplement operations, it was important to be able to use these funds to maintain the orchestra in a stable environment."[13]

The DSO had completed its 1986 fiscal year with a $411,000 deficit, a figure that struck queasiness into the stomachs of long-time board members, to whom the memory of 1974 was all too vivid. 1987 was a better year for the orchestra, remarkably so in light of the economy, but still the final tally in May, at the end of the fiscal year, showed a deficit of $160,000. By the time the board convened its annual meeting in May, box seats had sold $7.4 million of an available $19 million. Leonard Stone assured the trustees and governors that, although it had been a very tough year, with many major orchestras in extreme difficulty, the Dallas Symphony Association did not have to use its extended credit line.[14]

Executive board meetings in spring and early summer 1987 included ongoing discussion of how to apply the box seat revenue. Liener Temerlin opposed using the funds to reduce the orchestra's deficit from operations. He pointed out that if the association had used the box seat money to defray its outstanding $7 million obligation toward completing the Meyerson, the association would now be able to go to city council and say that its portion had been raised.[15]

Fueled by a sense of anticipation because of the hall and high morale in the wake of the 1985 European tour, the perception was that the orchestra was in a growth mode. As Freling remembers, "We were presenting a greater number of concerts. The whole cost structure of the orchestra was certain to escalate once we moved into the Meyerson. The debate had been about whether we were kidding ourselves, using smoke and mirrors, by using the box seat revenues to fund operations during this time, and there's some legitimacy to that. On the other hand, one could say that the box seat campaign was just another form of marketing that enhanced our annual operating revenue. Therefore, it was probably legitimate to use those funds for everyday operations. Had the box seat revenues not been used to subsidize operations during this transition period, the orchestra would have operated at a significant deficit, and that would have undermined our Fund for Excellence and other fund-raising initiatives. Whereas, through the combination of annual fund-raising, distributions from the existing endowment fund, and revenues from operations, added to the box seat revenues, we went through this whole period effectively without a deficit. I know of few orchestras in America that are able to say that."[16]

The discussion continued throughout 1987. Freling formally introduced his draft box seat option funds distribution resolution in January 1988. It placed a cap on the amount that could be used for operations. The balance was to be reserved for the endowment fund. The board approved the resolution.

Subsequently, the symphony reinstated an endowment campaign and obtained transition funding. According to Leonard Stone, "One of the most important things that Richard Freling did was to engineer these new resolutions. The board stopped its bickering and agreed to continue funding operations with the box seat money until such time as the endowment was sufficiently large so that it could spin off enough to narrow the gap between income and expense."[17]

Freling later said, "We actually reversed the resolution that established a 'cap' on the use of box seat revenues and continued to use those revenues to fund operations. This process took place over about three to four years. We were at a crucial time where, if we had not been able to use these funds, and we had not had bridge funding, we might have been forced to curtail, or scale back some of our operations or not pursue the vision of excellence that we wanted. We were working studiously to reduce our operating costs and raise our revenues, so that a greater percentage of the total budget was funded through operations. It was our plan that, by increasing the net contribution from operations to our budget, we would buy the time to build the endowment in the new Fund for Excellence, and the enhanced endowment would generate enough distributable income that we wouldn't be faced with the tremendous annual pressure to raise money.

"So, the use of the transition funds as a segment of the endowment campaign, as well as our ability to allocate the revenues from the box seat options to operations, played a vital role in giving financial stability during this transition period. These two factors played a very important role in where we are today, which is a very financially sound symphony orchestra, although substantially under-endowed."[18]

THE Marketing Center at LTV, as it came to be known, served several functions in addition to being headquarters for box seat sales. Symphony staff and board brought in prospective donors and subscribers to educate them about the hall. They held parties and receptions there. Former DSO Marketing Director Doug Kinzey later said, "We just booked that marketing center and booked it some more: appointments, receptions. It was not only for leasing boxes, but also for anticipation. It accomplished the hardest thing to do on paper: the feeling of being there. The $350,000 investment returned nearly $20 million, but that's only in leases. The investment in the public's anticipation of the hall was worth a great deal. We had the feel, touch, and taste of what Dallas was about to achieve."[19]

Most important in the short term, however, was that the program generated cash. According to Leonard Stone, "Until that box seat money emerged, there was no guaranteed predictable way that we could narrow the gap between income and expense and keep an orchestra of ninety players functioning for fifty-two weeks—and build the building! It was just not possible. I always envisioned, when we created the box seat program, that this would be money up my sleeve to be used for rainy day situations. Those rainy day situations became the need to balance the annual budget for a period of several years, and we did."[20]

Leonard Stone was so fixated on marketing the box seats that he convinced Don Stone to buy the rights to two of them when he still lived in Cincinnati. Both men still chuckle at the memory. Leonard Stone says, "I was one hell of a salesman. The idea of these seats was that, since you could obtain them for ninety-nine years or twenty-five years and have the right of renewal, once they were spoken for, there was a real possibility they may never come on the market again. I remember talking to Don, and saying, 'Don, two of your three children live in Dallas. You don't want your kids standing over your grave cursing you because you weren't smart enough to get these seats, when they want to sit in the best seats in the house and Dad and Mom weren't swift enough to do something about it while they had a chance.' 'OK, Leonard, sign me up.' I have to believe he did it for three reasons: (1) I was doing a persuasive song and dance on him. (2) He wanted to support the Dallas Symphony. (3) He knew that, when his days in Cincinnati were over, he was going to come back to Dallas to retire."[21]

Stone and his wife, Norma, did eventually return to Dallas. And they are still regular loge patrons of the Dallas Symphony at the Meyerson Symphony Center.

Chapter Twenty-Four

MONEY, MANIPULATION, AND POLITICS

Never was the axiom "time is money" more true than in our case.
Murphy's Law was also at work—with a vengeance.[1]

JOHN L. ADAMS, OCTOBER 1988

B Y 1987, two years after groundbreaking, the push was on to reinstate some of the enhancements that had been cut out in 1982 and 1984. "We looked for opportunities to put them back in," says George Schrader. Miraculously, money to finance the embellishments was trickling in. Schrader asked the architect and acoustician how much it would cost to reinsert the terrazzo floor, as designed, and other materials that had been taken out. The answer was $4 million. Their shopping list came back itemized at $1.5 million for wood paneling in the concert room, $750,000 for wood veneer finish on the acoustical canopy planned for above the stage, and $150,000 for a stone or terrazzo floor in the concert room. The balance of the $4 million was to be allocated toward marble travertine, rather than carpet, in the public lobby spaces.[2]

The financing was byzantine. Under the terms of a budget increase, if approved, the DSA would receive $2.45 million from the city. It fell to the orchestra to borrow the additional $1.55 million. Stone remembers, "George Schrader, Bill Schilling, and I went out to EDS and brought Mort that information. The four of us went down to the EDS cafeteria. Mort told us to wait there and said, 'I'll be back.' He went upstairs and talked with Ross. When he returned, he had that unique Mort smile on his face, where you never knew what the heck he was thinking. He said, 'The man says he'll give you two, but you gotta raise two.' If Ross Perot said he'd give you $2 million, you'd trust him. I would, anyway. We told the city to go ahead and to reincorporate all that into the building, and they did. We only raised about a half a million of our two. Ross had pledged the $2 million, but he hadn't given it to us yet. We were prepared to take his word. Now, we were at the time where the city had to let out the bids for these particular enhancements and go through the minority contracting process. Bids had to be out for a certain number of days, then recalls, discussions, and pre-bid conference. It's not a one-day process. It takes weeks and weeks and months. If this was all to be in place and complete by the time the building opened, it had to be bid by a certain date and accepted by the council so that the contracts could be offered. We were a million and a half dollars short, and the city had to have verification on the money."[3]

At the August 1987 executive board meeting, Liener Temerlin announced the $2 million challenge grant which, if met, would provide the $4 million needed to fund what was now called Phase II enhancements: wood finish on the music chamber walls, revision of the canopy design, limestone in place of plaster on the front wall of the grand terrace in the music chamber, terrazzo flooring within the music chamber, marble travertine flooring throughout the public spaces and onyx fixtures in the ceiling and canopy.[4]

All these items, he pointed out, had been in the original plans for the building but deleted at various stages in order to reduce cost. All of them would be difficult to install after construction was completed. Retrofitting would be prohibitively expensive. With $400,000 in hand toward the challenge grant, the executive board passed a resolution to raise the remaining $1.6 million within thirty days. Simultaneously, they amended the January 1985 resolution that had placed a $75 million cap on the building.[5]

The DSO remained short of its goal by the end of August. Stone talked to Perot regularly to give him status reports. Perot repeatedly demanded, "Why aren't you fulfilling your end of the bargain?" Stone assured him, "We will; we're just slow. We haven't done it yet, but we will." The first Sunday in September, Temerlin, Schilling, and Stone met with Meyerson to discuss their options. Meyerson offered to meet with Perot to suggest that they co-sign a note guaranteeing a $1.55 million loan to the symphony, to be cleared by funds that the DSA would raise by the end of calendar 1987.[6]

After meeting with Meyerson, Perot scheduled another meeting with George Schrader, Ted Amberg of the Pei & Partners Dallas office, and Cliff Keheley of the city's department of public works. He then called Stone and announced, "I want to talk to the symphony board." According to Stone, it was the only time that Perot ever made a formal appearance at a symphony board or committee meeting. The executive board convened a special 7:00 A.M. meeting on September 10 at the Sheraton Hotel to accommodate Perot's request.[7]

Stone revealed to the executive committee that Meyerson and Perot had offered the association their challenge grant nine months before, in December 1986, contingent upon the association's raising a like amount in order to fund the enhancements. The City of Dallas had a final deadline of September 15 as the last date it could accept favorable bids for such enhancements. The city refused to increase the construction cap from $75 million to $79 million unless it had the cash in its bank account by that date.[8]

Ross Perot expressed his and his family's pride in the donation that they had made and their satisfaction that the building would be so appropriately named for Mort. But, he stressed, *the building must be world class.* He chastised the board for its failure to meet the challenge grant in order to ensure that all design enhancements specified by Pei in his original plan would be installed. He expressed displeasure that no single individual appeared to be in charge of construction on behalf of the association. He wanted a quality control and supervisory representative in place. "He kept asking, 'Who's the czar in charge of this project?'" recalls George Schrader. "Cliff Keheley was the administrative head in charge of construction. Louise Reuben [Elam] was the staff field contact on top of the details. That wasn't good enough. Ross wanted someone who could make a decision, and he wanted it to be Mort. So Mort became the czar."[9]

After Perot's exhortation, the executive committee unanimously adopted a resolution accepting the short-term bank loan from Perot and Meyerson for $1.55 million, with the understanding that the DSA would raise the funds by the end of the year. Any unpaid balance as of December 31, 1987, would be retired out of 1988 box seat option revenues. With the agreement in place, Perot gave the symphony a green light to call its banker, First Republic.[10] The DSA contact there was Harvey Mitchell, a member of the board of governors.

Dallas City Council meetings take place on Wednesdays. The symphony called a special breakfast meeting on Tuesday, September 15, at the Plaza of the Americas Hotel. Stone said to Mitchell, "Harvey, we're going to write a check for $2 million. Half a million is in our account, and the other million and a half will come from Ross and Mort, but it's not there yet. Will you just cover us?" As Stone recalls, Mitchell replied, "Leonard, the federal bank inspectors are in the bank now. This is not the good old days. Ross is going to have to sign a note." According to Stone, "Perot was offended that the banks wouldn't take his word and that he would have to sign a note, but he agreed to do so."[11]

With the note still unsigned, Stone went to city hall the following day for the council meeting. He first placed a telephone call to the DSA's legal counsel, Mike McCullough at Thompson & Knight. "Mike, I'm going to give the City of Dallas a check for $2 million. I have to do that at 1:30 today. I know I don't have the money in the bank, because Ross hasn't yet signed the note. Am I liable for anything?"

McCullough told him, "Well, you know you're not supposed to write a check if you know you don't have money in the account!"

Stone said, "Mike, I know that."

"But you have every expectation that the money will be in the account?" McCullough asked.

"Yes," Stone replied. "Well, I am *told* that they deposit nightly. I can't get the city to delay."

McCullough replied, "I think you'll be OK. If not, we'll send you newspaper clippings in jail."

Stone ran over to city hall with the check after obtaining a second signature from one of the DSA Board's other signing officers. Before city council opened its session, he talked with Mayor Annette Strauss, who had succeeded Starke Taylor as mayor in April 1987, to brief her on the week's developments and present her with the check.

The agenda item came up: the DSO was requesting that council increase the $75 million construction ceiling to $79 million. With private money covering the tab in its entirety, city council was hard pressed to deny the request. The vote to increase the overall budget by $4 million passed. Waving the $2 million check in the air, Mayor Strauss announced exultantly, "The private sector comes through again!"

With his heart in his throat, Stone thought to himself, *We don't have the money in the bank!* Mayor Strauss presented the check to Cliff Keheley, the head of public works, and moved on to the next agenda item.

Stone walked up to Keheley and asked, *sotto voce,* "Cliff, can you make this check disappear for twenty-four hours?"

He said, "Absolutely not. We have to put it through."

The following morning, first thing, Stone picked up the signed note from Perot's office and rushed over to the bank to be there when it opened.[12] Wood paneling, terrazzo floors in the concert room, and other materials and performance equipment additions were back in the master plan.

—❧—

A DSO fact sheet about the hall, issued by Doug Kinzey and Warren Gould in October 1987, listed the estimated project budget at $79 million. That figure included basic building construction, performance equipment, and fees. It did not include the parking garage. The estimated date of opening was listed as mid-1989.

Then came the inevitable round of dealing with media reactions to the latest increase. Reporters were having a field day each time a cost increase was announced. City council members inimical to the project generated vivid and copious publicity every time they commented on a new development. Most of the coverage was negative, and considerable bad blood flowed between city hall and the symphony's offices at Fair Park. Matters weren't helped when a crane collapsed at the site in February 1988, injuring two workers.[13]

—❧—

SYMPHONY hall topics were now a standard agenda item at weekly city council meetings. In the midst of minority unrest and African-American council members such as Diane Ragsdale demanding that the council pass legislation removing the City of Dallas' employees pension fund from any investments in South Africa because of apartheid, and other tensions, symphony representatives periodically returned to council meetings to report progress and make their case when changes were requested.

In May 1988, eyebrows were raised at city hall when council members learned of a proposal to spend $2.5 million on another round of enhancements for interior design improvements and performance equipment. An $18,000 appropriation for motorized window shades drew particular fire. (These were for the glass lenses and the conoid, to help control air-conditioning bills.) Council members Craig Holcomb and Lori Palmer queried the justification for $1 million in acoustics and performance lighting systems intended to make the Meyerson a better recording venue, removable seats for handicap access, signage, kitchen equipment, additional engineering fees, even some infrastructure items such as street paving and landscaping. With these items, the total, official cost would inch up to $81.5 million. Palmer and Holcomb questioned the DSA's ability to raise sufficient funds to cover its share: everything over the public sector commitment. Other council members demanded to know what the impact of the hall's cost would be on funding for other city-supported arts organizations.[14]

In late June 1988, a flap over what seats would be installed incited city council's ire. Stanley Marcus, Meyerson, and other members of the smaller unit were concerned about audience seating. Bids from chair companies began to come in early in 1988. The City of Dallas opted for the low bidder, JG Furniture. When the prototype arrived, Russell Johnson rejected it for acoustic reasons. Bateson requested a prototype from S&H Chairs, a German company. When it arrived in November, Pei rejected it for aesthetic reasons.

Meyerson remembers the discussions. "There was some talk that we should buy them from a U.S. company, yet the best seats were German, period. We had them do mockups, and we sat in them. It became very clear that the best quality seats were the German seats. They got the contract, but then there was difficulty getting the finished product out and in time and delivered." "The German seats were ugly, and hard," remembers George Schrader. "There was almost no upholstery on them. Russell insisted on them. The doubts about delivery finally preempted the German seats."[15]

Keheley appeared before the park board to argue in favor of an increase of half a million dollars to $829,000 for custom-made seats constructed with more wood and less padding. He explained that the acoustical properties of the seats would allow for more sound reflection and less sound absorption. His audience at city hall was unimpressed with anything other than the price tag. "I don't have a problem if the $2.5 million [in additional enhancements] gives more diversity to the hall," said park board member René Martinez, "but I do have a problem if we're going from a Cadillac to a Rolls Royce."[16]

Considering the shape the economy was in, such questions were justified. After taking over from Bill Schilling as DSA president in May 1988, Dolores Barzune made numerous appearances before city council. "Sometimes I went before the arts, education, and libraries committee. Other times I appeared in front of the entire council, to give them assurance that the fund-raising was progressing. As president, I was putting myself on the line to say that we *would* get this money raised. They questioned every solitary thing we added. 'How's the fund-raising coming, Dolores?' 'What are you doing to raise the money?' 'What are you projecting you're going to make on the opening?' It was their job to make sure we stayed in line."

The heat was on in more ways than one that summer. With $9.7 million outstanding toward the private sector's contribution to hall costs, city council demanded a plan from Barzune as to how she would raise the remaining funds by 1991, when most of the debt payments would fall due. She did her best to reassure them, but certain council members remained skeptical. "I'm not hall- or symphony-bashing, and it's wonderful that you don't anticipate any problems," Councilman Craig Holcomb told Barzune, "but if the symphony is not able to raise that money, then the city is going to have to step in and pay for it, which will create a bad taste in people's mouths."[17] In retrospect, Barzune feels that Holcomb and other council members such as Max Wells and Jerry Bartos, although sometimes critical, remained champions of the symphony hall project and the efforts of symphony leaders.

Howard Hallam, then a DSA Board member and later board president, recalls, "The press kept referring to cost overruns, stating that the cost of the Meyerson was out of control. It *wasn't* out of control. We were deliberately adding enhancements to the Meyerson, and saying we could raise the money for it, and it was worth doing. That's exactly what we did. The smaller unit would decide to add enhancements. They would make an announcement to that effect through the executive board, and the press would pick up on it and say, 'Oh! The cost of the Meyerson just went up again!' I do remember going to one meeting out at Liener's home, at which we discussed the final batch of enhancements that raised the cost of the building from $78 million to $81 or $82 million. We discussed this for two hours. Finally the board voted unanimously to do it. It was a once-in-a-lifetime contract and, by golly, we were committing ourselves to raising the money to make it, to pay for it. And that's what happened. In the press, however, it was portrayed as a project out of control."[18]

As part of an attempt to monitor and correct the situation, Mayor Strauss commissioned an update on the LWFW economic impact study that had been released to assist in voter persuasion for the 1982 bond campaign. In June 1988, LWFW presented its report of the task force on arts and culture, as part of the mayor's commission on international development. The LWFW research and analysis resulted in a rosy forecast: a potential $40 million annual economic impact for Dallas, including $600,000 in local tax revenue, and approaching eight hundred jobs created, primarily in the service industries. To a city bludgeoned by a worsening economy, these words were balm. The employment impact was immediate, because nearly a thousand jobs were associated with actual construction of the building. Long-range estimates, over five years, predicted $400 million would be pumped into the Dallas economy.[19]

The report also pinpointed problems that needed to be addressed, specifically in the area of international tourism. "Dallas is not likely to be a global center for commerce if it is not also a center for culture," LWFW quoted the mayor's commission on international development as saying. Completion of the Meyerson would add substantially to the city's international prestige as a cultural center.

July's media crisis revolved around another $2 million appropriation by city council. Estimates for the cost of operating the Meyerson now stood at about $2 million *per annum*. Revenues were projected at $900,000, including food and beverage concessions, rental fees, and miscellaneous income. While that income figure represented a significant improvement over earlier estimates, the figures still foretold an annual deficit exceeding $1 million. City Councilwoman Diane Ragsdale, a vehement opponent of the Meyerson, fumed, "I am constantly amazed that we're willing to throw out good money for extremely elite art."[20]

Another brouhaha arose in late summer 1988, when a rumor circulated that drugs were present on the construction site. As Bateson's Joe Walker remembers it, "One of our employees came to us and said, 'We think there are drugs being used on the job site.' I didn't know what kind of drugs. We didn't know how we might be affecting civil rights in our efforts to control drugs. The whole industry was developing guidelines on how to control drugs on construction sites. So we began to lay out a strategic plan to take care of it. In the meantime, Marty Griffin, a local TV broadcaster came to the site. All of a sudden, one Wednesday, we were on TV. The announcer stated, 'Drugs are at the Meyerson.' The public drama continued the next day with the front-page headlines: 'Drug sniffing dogs cause suit by unions.' 'Workers sue city over drug search.'

"The first order of business was safety. Any drug problem compromises safety. The first thing that came to our mind after Marty Griffin's news report was that if somebody gets hurt tomorrow on the job site, because of drugs, we were responsible. We had to act immediately. I called Cliff Keheley and told him we were going to have to respond to this TV broadcast right away. We did not have time to develop a fail-safe approach. We delegated responsibility to a narcotics consulting group in Corpus Christi and asked them to come up to Dallas to eliminate drugs and ensure that we had a safe project."[21]

Unbeknownst to Walker, Narcotics Consultants of Spicewood, Texas, brought six Labrador retrievers with them to search for drugs the next day. Bateson closed the project to all personnel to allow the dogs to search the building. The dogs found nothing. The next step was to have the dogs circle each worker. "Our alternatives would have been to frisk the men, search them by hand," Walker explains. "The best alternative was *not* to touch the workers and allow the dogs to do the work." Unfortunately, the workers had to kneel, and they voiced heated objections. The next day, Griffin reappeared on television with a report claiming that inhumane treatment had stripped the workers of their dignity. Now the union planned to sue both Bateson and the city.[22]

As the press coverage intensified, Bateson's senior vice president, Bruce Lady, acknowledged that he had known about the drug search in advance. Cliff Keheley authorized Narcotics Consultants of Spicewood to conduct the search the day before it took place. He told the *Dallas Times Herald* that he did not consult other city officials beforehand; however, Bateson's Walker remembers the two of them discussing the options. "I would have seen a bigger problem of not doing it," Keheley told the press. "If there's any suspicion at all of illegal activity on that site, we don't want it." Don Brainerd, the president of Narcotics Consultants, told the workers they could either be searched or quit their jobs.[23]

Bateson's Walker had a major crisis on his hands. He called Keheley to announce his intent to deal with the union directly, an unusual tactic. Walker told the union representatives that Bateson shared its objectives: to build a great building *and* build it safely. "Our intent was not to demean anyone; we just want a safe job," he told union representatives. The representatives agreed to arrange for Walker to talk to union leadership at the union hall. "They brought their lawyers, and I had to bring mine," Walker remembers. "I didn't let our lawyer talk. I explained our position. We did not know exactly what to do, but we had to act swiftly to control any drug problem if it existed. Finally, I asked them, 'What can we do to make the workers happy?' One of the union leaders offered, 'You could apologize to the men.' I said, 'I'll be happy to.'"

The next day, he went to the construction site and gathered all the men together. He stood on the concrete in the area that is now the orchestra floor and apologized, telling them, "We are very sorry that the testing happened the way it did." They accepted his apology, dropped the threat of a lawsuit, and work resumed. As it turned out, Narcotics Consultants found no drugs anywhere on the job site, or on any person. Another negative story about the Meyerson had still dominated local press for an intense few days.

The press attacks did not let up. Next came a flap about who would run the symphony center: the city parks department or outside bidders: Leisure Management International of Houston, Ogden Allied International of New York, or Theatre Operating Company, which was already running Fair Park Music Hall and the Majestic Theater in downtown Dallas. The parks department, which held authority to make the decision, estimated that it would cost the city $600,000 to manage the center for six months. They projected revenues at less than 10 percent of that, $53,730,[24] a precipitous drop from the $900,000 that had been forecast just two months prior. The park board opted to retain control. When they hired a manager in November 1988, the *Dallas Times Herald* reported that "the center is facing cost overruns of more than 60 percent and other financial problems."[25]

Chapter Twenty-Five

PLANNING THE GRAND OPENING FORTNIGHT

P OSITIVE public perception was essential to the success of the hall. In February 1987, the symphony announced that Liener and Karla Temerlin would chair opening festivities for the Morton H. Meyerson Symphony Center. Temerlin had relinquished the presidency of the Dallas Symphony Board in May 1986. He remained chairman of the board, however, and as chairman of the fortnight committee continued to be closely involved with all facets of planning for the hall.

Temerlin formed his committee promptly, initially calling monthly meetings. It was clear he expected commitment and a high degree of involvement from everyone. He advised all his committee members that, beginning in early 1989, meetings would become more frequent. Temerlin says, "I had committee meetings at my house with great regularity. We almost always had one hundred percent turnout. These people worked incredibly hard. All of them were unbelievably involved. We ended up with the concept of a gala fortnight of concerts and celebrations."[1]

The fortnight was loosely patterned after a marketing ploy of Dallas retailing giant Neiman Marcus. The store had presented a series of themed fortnight-long special presentations over the years, linking merchandising and special events through a connection with a particular country. The Dallas Symphony fortnight concept would introduce the new hall in all its aspects: symphony, choral work, chamber music, solo recital. The focal point was to be four major concerts, for which patrons would purchase special ticket packages.

Temerlin's plans were expansive and ambitious, setting fund-raising goals of $2.5 million gross and $2 million net for the fortnight. In addition to careful and thorough budgeting, his program included a comprehensive press plan, glamorous dinners for fortnight patrons in exclusive private homes, recognition for orchestra members, construction crew, and City of Dallas staff and officials, and an extensive array of free community events. Temerlin also appointed a press entertainment subcommittee to focus on air and ground transportation, meals, social events, and tourist opportunities for the extensive complement of international press representatives expected to descend upon Dallas.[2]

Liener Temerlin (*DSO archives*)

The symphony still did not know when that fortnight would take place because of all the changes that continued. Each time an aspect of the interior design changed, the possibilities for delay extended. J. W. Bateson, the construction company, was cagey about committing to an opening date. Finally, Leonard Stone told Cliff Keheley, "We're planning our 1989–1990 season; we have to know where it's going to take place, at Fair Park or the Meyerson." Keheley was direct and honest. "At this stage of the game, we're not going to be complete by then." He told Stone that the projected completion date was somewhere between December 1989 and early 1990. "We've got to know," Stone insisted. "We don't want a split season, starting in Fair Park and finishing at the Meyerson. We want a full season in the new hall." Keheley said, "I'll see what I can do."

He took up the issue with Joe Walker of Bateson, reminding him that the contract called for Bateson to finish the building in September 1989. Walker replied, "But the project is well behind schedule, and we both know the reason!" Keheley said, "Of course I know: because of all the changes and the lack of decisions." He rattled of a list of sticking points. I. M. Pei and Russell Johnson had still not resolved matters such as the acoustical canopy system over the stage and the risers in the choral terrace. Then he asked, "If we get decisions made timely for you, can you finish in September?" Walker answered, "We'll do our best." Keheley told the symphony association it could inaugurate the orchestra's 1989–90 season in the Meyerson. At this time, Walker called a meeting of the presidents of all the companies working under contract on the Meyerson. He told them, "We've made this commitment; were asking you to match it, because we can't do it without every one of you. We must have your best effort to finish the job by the agreed-upon time."[3] He secured all their commitments to the same goal. With a target date in hand, all parties now had the same focus. "The paramount mission was to stay within budget to deliver what the people funding the project expected," says Keheley. "But now we had a commitment to have the building finished in September."[4]

Leonard Stone did not announce the opening immediately. He had planning to put in place. At the recommendation of long-time DSO supporter Louise Kahn, a member of Meyerson's smaller unit, Stone and Temerlin initiated a search for a concert hall opening coordinator. A detail-oriented person, Kahn was increasingly concerned that too many little things were being overlooked because of larger issues related to completing the construction and financing of the hall. She wanted to ensure that community activities attending the opening of the hall would not be neglected and suggested that Temerlin and Stone consider adding a staff person.

They hired Jane Holahan in March 1988. Kahn had worked with Holahan at the East Dallas Community School and at the Dallas Public Library, where Holahan had headed the fine arts division for several years. Holahan remembers, "Louise thought she needed one more pair of eyes. She wanted an office out of Bozell [& Jacobs, Temerlin's advertising and public relations firm] that she could call that wasn't straight to Liener [Temerlin]. She always wanted to know what was going on. I'd say she was directly involved in more aspects than anyone else!"[5]

Holahan was to work directly with Fred Hoster, the DSO's general manager, and with Wolford McCue, head of the public relations division of Bozell. By May 1988, when the DSA officially announced that the opening would take place on September 6, 1989, plans for the grand opening fortnight had been expanded and refined. McCue, who had nonprofit experience with Dallas' United Way prior to joining Bozell & Jacobs, was responsible for tactical development of the press plan for the opening. The overall strategy was to focus on national and international press and sell them on the Meyerson. "It's not that local press wasn't important, but the local press had history with this hall," McCue later explained. "They were tied up in negatives that kept resurfacing: squabbles in city council, the charges of elitism, the escalating cost of the project. We gauged that the national press would focus on bigger issues."[6] These included the business side, which the "big guns"—*The Wall Street Journal, The New York Times, Time, Newsweek,* and the like—were certain to zero in on. As for the international coverage of the music side, McCue foresaw that positive press coverage, nationally and internationally, would influence readers in Dallas.

"We chose, too, to focus on the quality of life story, the idea that a thriving community depends on the arts," he later said. "Unfortunately that message was conflicting locally with the reality of kids needing day care, or teachers needing raises. We knew that we were not going to win people over prior to the opening just with the music angle. We had to focus on the larger context. We knew that, historically, a building could have this kind of impact. We realized that a physical entity can drive people's emotions. So we tried to focus on the importance of the building not just as a concert hall but as a place that people would acknowledge as a special part of the city."[7]

Internally, promotion was handled by the symphony's marketing and public relations department, headed by Doug Kinzey. Temerlin's agency worked closely with Kinzey to focus on local and state-wide press. The national contact was publicist Connie Shuman in New York. Coordination of international press was entrusted to Dvora Lewis in London, who had been so helpful with public relations for the orchestra's European tour in 1985.

Early in 1989, Lewis traveled to Dallas to meet with Stone and members of the fortnight committee. "I was immensely impressed by Leonard's vision," she recalls, "because what he said to me was, 'Bring us the world. This hall has to make an international statement. Unless we put the word out to the world, it will be a parochial event.' He understood that, if the Meyerson was to become a major international venue, the message had to be given to the world. One does that through journalists coming overseas from Europe and beyond." European journalists are able to accept hospitality, as well as the cost of accommodation and transportation costs, and would expect those matters to be arranged and covered. Lewis asked Stone, "Do you have a budget to bring the world?" He replied, "Whatever you want, you have the budget, within reason." Given that green light, Lewis began to map out her strategy.[8]

Domestically, the press relations plan extended beyond music and architecture critics. At Bozell & Jacobs, McCue developed a comprehensive list that included art press, general music magazines, acoustics press, society writers, and general news on a national and international level. The newly formed press entertainment subcommittee sought out information on other new and recently renovated halls such as those in Indianapolis, Tampa, Calgary, Houston, Sydney, and New York's Carnegie Hall, including both press relations plans and reviews after the openings.[9]

The marketing and sales efforts developed accordingly, with help from DSO staff and board members and the additional leadership and staffing power that Temerlin, through Bozell & Jacobs, brought to the overall plan. "I had an agency of four hundred people to [call on in order to] get the job done," McCue explains. "Liener was absolutely committed to having the job done properly, frequently depending on the Bozell staff for execution of various tasks. He knew that if the staff here was assigned to the project, it was going to get done. Liener frequently skirted the traditional method of doing things. He's definitely a micro-manager. He's interested in the details. We must have redone the letterhead for the fortnight fifteen times before he was satisfied," he cites as an example. "You have to understand that Liener was a better copywriter than anyone else at Bozell. He could add figures faster, think things through faster, come up with the best solution better than anyone else in the building.

"In a way, my work also meant 'managing' Liener," McCue continues. "Liener *needed* managing. He's the kind of person who has a hundred ideas an hour, not all of them necessarily good! Yet a person of Liener's creativity, sense and vision has more big breakthrough ideas than any CEO with whom I have worked. As often as not, my intervention was on behalf of volunteers or symphony staff. On the other hand, we didn't always see the vision of a great idea that Liener would have, for example, the marketing center and the sale of rights to the box seats, which became a significant revenue stream to the DSO. It seems dimwitted of me, looking back."[10]

Former Development Director Domenick Ietto offers a different perspective on Temerlin's obsession with the Meyerson, once the project garnered his attention. "Liener was instrumental in creating the kind of excitement surrounding the hall that could only come from somebody who had made a career of packaging and presenting products in a way that made them almost irresistible," he says. "Liener was masterful in that way, particularly with respect to the box seat program. I remember him express the idea about the box seats, 'Once they're gone, they're gone forever.' They would no longer be available. That struck a chord with a lot of people, creating a sense of urgency to sign up and write that check."[11]

Temerlin had excellent, widespread contacts in the Dallas business community. He and Leonard Stone began to approach major Dallas area corporations for signature underwriting. Headline sponsors were American Express and American Airlines, each of which eventually donated half a million dollars toward fortnight activities.

"The train just kept going," says McCue. "The corporate community wanted to get involved in its success, and the social aspect added to its appeal."[12] The symphony staged a huge society-oriented press conference at the elegant Crescent Court Hotel to announce the signature donations from American Express and American Airlines and garner additional publicity for the grand opening fortnight. In addition to the media, they invited current and potential symphony patrons.

"From that point on, we were selling tickets for the fortnight," says Jane Holahan. "It was separate from any other fund-raiser the symphony had done. People who had already purchased box seats were re-approached to buy tickets for the opening. Because of the generosity of American Airlines, we were able to put together a fortnight patron package. For $5,000 per ticket, you were seated in one of the box seats for each of the six performances in the first two weeks. The ticket included invitations to major parties. And American Airlines threw in a first class round trip ticket to any of its destinations except Tokyo."[13]

Cyndy Hudgins, a member of Temerlin's fortnight committee who had served as president of the DSO League, assumed responsibility for ticket selling. Box seat money for the fortnight package rolled in. The symphony not only sold *all* the box seat packages, but also created a "Golden Circle" in the front section of the orchestra to accommodate demand.

"The ticket structure for the fortnight was geared to raising money," recalls Jane Holahan, "but there was also a larger concern. Because so much city money was involved and the Meyerson was a city facility, they wanted it to be a democratic opening." Early discussions included a street fair and events specifically geared toward Dallas' Hispanic and African-American communities. "Another event they determined would be very important was a free concert to inaugurate the hall," says Holahan. "Admission would be by invitation and by ticket, of course, but it would definitely be free. The concert would include a wide swath of

Liener Temerlin (left) succeeded Bill Seay as DSA president in May 1984. Leonard Stone is at right. (*DSO archives*)

citizens. Structuring the list of invitees was a labor of love. We included everybody from George Schrader to the smallest community arts groups to representatives of the city."[14]

Excitement about the hall was building steadily within the concert-going community. Marketing Director Kinzey placed subscription tickets on sale for the first season in the Morton H. Meyerson Symphony Center in February 1988. For the first ten days, the calls flooded in, and the box office filled 1,000 orders per day. Kinzey hired six temporary workers to absorb the extra work load. Within two months he was well on his way to the first sellout in the Dallas Symphony's eighty-nine-year history. By the end of May, requests for the orchestra's Saturday night series were at 153 percent of capacity, and 22,000 subscriptions had been sold of a possible 24,000 to 25,000.[15]

As the professional staff, Leonard Stone and Warren Gould had responsibility for negotiating the working conditions and terms of each major gift. Stone in particular had to be flexible and keep his eye on many simultaneous activities. Over a period of eighteen months, his staff shifted among numerous locations. They started in the basement of Fair Park Music Hall, where the DSO had maintained administrative offices for many years. One department at a time, symphony personnel relocated. The development office moved from the old Praetorian Building into the office towers of the Crescent. The marketing department expanded its LTV Center space with the elevator model and the box seat program. Bateson and the Pei Dallas office operated out of adjacent trailers on the construction site. Those trailers became daily convening points for hard-hat tours and meetings, both scheduled and impromptu.

Chapter Twenty-Six

HALL MANAGEMENT AND
A DOCENT PROGRAM

NINETEEN EIGHTY-EIGHT was the worst year yet in the Dallas recession. Oil was at its lowest point. Persons unaffected by the prolonged slump in oil prices had suffered as a result of the October 1987 stock market crash. "The economy was awful," recalls JoLynne Jensen, head of the DSO's Stradivarius patron program and now associate director of development. "Real estate was dropping as quickly as it ever had. People were going bankrupt. *Companies* were going bankrupt! We were wondering, 'Omigosh! How are we going to achieve all our goals?' The amazing thing is, we did. I guess by that time, as people saw the building drawing closer to completion, they were inspired. It's that Dallas 'can-do' attitude. There was no way they were going to leave this building unfinished."[1]

Dolores Barzune assumed the presidency of the DSA in May 1988. She identified several strategic goals to accomplish during her tenure. "One was the annual fund," she says, "which had been rolled into the general fund, the capital campaign. That was a big mistake. It needed to stand alone. Then, when I came in, our endowment was at $18 million. We knew we had to make endowment a line item and make it a priority for this institution. I feel this was my biggest contribution to the long-range plan for the Dallas Symphony. We had to repay Ross Perot and Mort Meyerson for the $1.5 million note that they signed at the bank to help the Symphony go forward. Our last challenge was the $9.6 million that we still owed the City of Dallas. I had four different task forces at work on these goals. At first I thought we were going to have to raise about $11 million. That number kept getting bigger. By the time I left office, it was right at $14 million. The only way we could do it was through a team effort, or it wasn't going to get done."[2]

She drove past the hall regularly. "The year before the opening, I'd either be down [in the dumps] because we hadn't done as much as I wanted, or I'd take one long look at the hall and think, 'That's what it's all about; that's why it's going to be so important.' It was almost like a talisman that you'd touch and think, this is something real I'm working for. I'm going to leave this as part of a legacy. I don't mean me especially, but whoever was looking at it. Many times I would use a trip to the building as a way to rev 'em up and remind our Board why we were working so hard. We'd get so bogged down. I went through there with a hard hat on practically every day."[3]

December 1988

With the structure drawing steadily closer to completion, the city embarked on a search for a facility manager to coordinate security, maintenance, and scheduling. If the hall were to be used by other arts organizations, as the city intended, someone would have to establish a system for leasing the space at times when the Dallas Symphony did not require it.

Ted DeDee, then director of concerts at the Eastman School of Music, got the job. "I knew quite a bit about the Meyerson before I moved to Dallas," says DeDee. "I had been following its progress for about five or six years, through a number of sources."[4] He knew that the Meyerson had all the earmarks of a superb facility and was attracted by the opportunity. Because the position would be funded by the City of Dallas, DeDee interviewed with Phil Jones and Jerry Allen, city employees who directed the office of cultural affairs. Leonard Stone and John Graham, executive director of the arts management program at SMU's Meadows School of the Arts, also participated in the interview process.

DeDee was only peripherally involved in the construction aspect of the hall, which at this late date, more than three years after groundbreaking, was in its home stretch. He describes his position as "detail and function police" in the nine months before the hall opened. His experience at Eastman and in prior jobs had taught him not to expect that the architects would catch all the practical details in a new building. "It's important to have another set of eyes that looks at the functionality and the financial side of operating the building," he points out.[5] Even though his involvement came at the tail end of the construction phase, DeDee still had an opportunity to correct some oversights before they evolved into problems.

Especially because he came in so late, DeDee's experience was invaluable. The city's estimates of what it would cost to operate the hall vacillated wildly during the construction period. So did its guesses as to what revenues the Meyerson might generate to offset the operating cost. During summer 1988, the city's cultural affairs director, Jerry Allen, claimed it would cost the park and recreation department about $2 million *per annum* to run the hall.[6]

In August 1989, just before the hall opened, the estimate had settled down to $1.3 million.[7]

Shortly after DeDee's arrival, Jane Holahan approached him to inquire if he would be interested in coordinating a docent program after the building was officially opened. DeDee was indeed interested, and Holahan brought him up to speed on what plans were already under way. During her years at the Dallas Public Library, Holahan had developed a docent program for public tours. When the J. Erik Jonsson Central Library opened downtown in 1982, she conducted and coordinated library tours with Sharan Goldstein of the National Council of Jewish Women, Dallas chapter. A similar program at the Meyerson seemed like a good idea, because the hall was a city-owned building. Holahan and Goldstein presented a proposal to city council in autumn 1988. The reaction was enthusiastic, but council members encouraged them to coordinate with other volunteer groups in the city as well as the symphony's volunteer groups.

Goldstein remembers, "When the hall was under construction, we knew it was going to be necessary to train a group of volunteers to show the hall off to the citizens of Dallas. Because of the economic climate at the time, people were very angry about opening what they perceived as an expensive, elitist hall. We were very sensitive to the fact that the hall did indeed belong to the people of Dallas. We wanted to make them feel a part of it, that they had true ownership of the building." She and Holahan assembled a core group in September 1988, one year before the hall's opening, comprising representatives from all corners of the city. "We were going to have students as our docents, retired people, individuals deeply involved with music, and people to whom this was going to be a brand-new experience. We were very concerned that we draw everybody in to the building."[8]

The docents-in-training began their education process in late 1988 with printed materials provided by Artec Consultants and I. M. Pei & Partners, supplementing their reading with occasional hard-hat tours of the building. Working with Miriam Jaffee, Barbara Rabin, and Sondra Hollander, three of Goldstein's colleagues at the Dallas chapter of the National Council of Jewish Women, Holahan and Goldstein sorted through the literature, selecting items that they wanted the docents to emphasize and developing a general outline for a tour. Ted DeDee took those documents and consolidated them into a formal docent manual, a reference primer with background on design, major donors, materials, and various architectural terms as well as practical considerations such as logistics of layout and itinerary for prospective tours.[9] He assumed responsibility for training the docents.

—❦—

ANOTHER of DeDee's initial contacts at the Meyerson was Louise Reuben Elam, the city's architect. After his first review of plans for the main lobby, he asked her, "Where are the electrical outlets in the lobby?"

She indicated some discreetly placed outlets for floor-cleaning machines, acknowledging that their remote placement would necessitate the use of extension cords to reach throughout the spacious public areas. "Do you need more outlets?" she inquired.

"Yes," DeDee assented promptly. "If the symphony wants to present a reception or a private dinner in the lobby, and the caterer wants to have a carving station with a roast beef, or an ice sculpture lit from below, where do we plug in the lights? Where do we plug in the warming equipment?"[10]

Louise Reuben Elam got the picture. The floor was not yet installed in the lobby. She and DeDee called a quick meeting with representatives from Pei & Partners and from Bateson. They agreed to add a few more circuits and install additional wiring underneath the flooring in the main lobby to accommodate the needs DeDee had cited. He also made recommendations about overhead lighting and kitchen design. He began interviewing subcontractors that the city would engage for custodial, security, and restaurant services, and he hired permanent staff to operate the hall.

In retrospect, Elam commented, "Ted was hired very late in the project. It was unfortunate that he was not on board earlier. Ordinarily, the building manager is involved during the development of the plans, to ensure that the building's functional and operational issues are addressed. Manager/operators have valuable knowledge about building use and the many details that require accommodation, since they live with this building type on a day to day basis."[11] Apparently, even though DeDee identified the need for additional outlets, somehow they were not installed as planned. JoLynne Jensen of the DSO development department remembers working on plans for a cocktail reception to be held in the lobby one week before opening night in conjunction with an open rehearsal. Two weeks before the hall opened, while flooring, banisters, wood, water fountains, and other components were being installed, she did a walk-through of the lobby areas with Meyerson Assistant Manager Bruce MacPherson and the caterer, Kathy McDaniel from City Market. McDaniel was assessing the space, and suggested, "I think we'll set the coffee on a table in front of the window. Let's see where there's a plug over here for it." The three of them looked, and then looked some more. In the entire main lobby, they located two plugs: one behind each bar, for a blender.

For the reception, McDaniel's catering staff used Sterno to keep the coffee hot. After that, Jensen remembers the construction crew cut down through marble and up through concrete to run electricity. "I don't think I. M. Pei ever envisioned this lobby being used for anything but ingress, egress, and intermission," she later observed. "He never foresaw lunches, dinners, and all the other things we use this building for now. He designed it to be a concert hall for symphonic music. People walk in to attend the concert. They get a drink during intermission. Then they leave. That was his vision for it. It does all those things beautifully, but it does so much more."[12] DeDee brought a new ingredient to the Meyerson mix. He represented neither the city proper, nor the symphony, but the building itself. "The fact that the Meyerson is a public/

private partnership meant that it was very much in the public eye," DeDee says. "The taxpayers felt that their money was going into a public building to support symphony music. That created a lot of controversy. All this was occurring at a time when the general makeup of the Dallas population was changing, and there was greater pressure for a different representation. Projects funded in the future would be pushed by different interests from those that would support the Meyerson Symphony Center. Within the political arena, those interests were becoming much more vocal about so much money going into this building. Their stance was, what a shame that it wasn't going toward something that would serve a wider public base in a better way.

"One of the reasons I was hired was that I had worked closely with minority communities in presenting events at Eastman. That successful experience helped me in marketing the Meyerson. When I arrived in Dallas and listened to people screaming, 'This is only a building for the rich white folks of Dallas,' it made me stand up and say, 'No, it's more than that! This is a public building, meant to be used and appreciated and shared by the *entire* public.' That led me to work not only with other arts organizations who thought they could perhaps use the Meyerson as a place to perform, but also other organizations who hadn't thought they'd even walk in the door, let alone use the building for an event."[13]

By late spring, he had hired several staff members, including Bruce C. MacPherson, who had been a protégé of DeDee's in Buffalo some years before. MacPherson was looking for a new job at the same time that DeDee was forming a team. He joined the Meyerson staff in April 1989, as assistant manager of administration. All his prior experience had been with existing, often historic theatres. "The Meyerson was my first experience with a facility that had no history. I was part of the history. It was very much a learning experience. That was one of my reasons for coming to Dallas. Not many people in arts management get the opportunity to open a new facility. It's not something that comes along every day. To have that opportunity was fabulous."[14] Working with his old friend Ted DeDee made the job especially attractive. "It was a suitable 'marriage,'" he says. "We started in an office at the Majestic Theatre, then we moved to a trailer in the old Bateson lot."[15] MacPherson quickly grasped what DeDee had known since December: It was very late to be hiring people for facility management.

MacPherson's primary responsibility was to develop a budget for the annual operation of the building. That meant salaries, utilities, maintenance: all the expense lines as well as revenue lines. That budget would go to the city for approval. He also began designing a system to schedule the building around the symphony's needs, because the Dallas Symphony was to be primary tenant. "Before the building opened, calls were already coming in from groups wanting to book the space," MacPherson remembers. "They didn't even know themselves what was going to be here. All they knew was what they'd read in the papers. I had to assemble and deal with a scheduling system immediately and create contracts, documents, forms, a system of checks and balances. It meant getting to know the players and conducting site visits galore for potential groups that wanted to use the building but had no idea what to expect."[16]

DeDee and MacPherson also worked on developing an identity for the Meyerson that would identify it as a city building, but different from the City of Dallas. The building needed to assume its own persona as a performing arts center and a downtown architectural landmark in the evolving Arts District. "We wanted to have some visual identity that could appear in an ad and have instant recognition: That's the Meyerson," says MacPherson. Working through the established city procedure for soliciting proposals from graphic artists, they

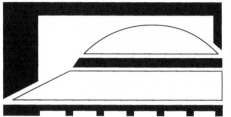

The Morton H. Meyerson Symphony Center

Adrienne Allen's logo for the Morton H. Meyerson Symphony Center.

selected Adrienne Allen. Her logo design was adopted for letterhead, envelopes, and anything else bearing an official emblem for the Meyerson.

MacPherson was assigned further responsibility for working with the fledgling docent program. "One of the things Ted emphasized when I arrived was that a major component of the opening would be making the building as accessible as possible to anyone and everyone," MacPherson recalls. The program had already graduated from its embryonic stages. As the city's representative, MacPherson assumed responsibility for scheduling and coordinating the tour program, walking the building with the volunteers, and devising itineraries and systems that would permit multiple tours to occur simultaneously. He met with Sharan Goldstein and her team, acquainting himself with the training manual as he got to know every nook and cranny of the unfinished building.

Goldstein recalls, "We refused to script the tour, because we felt that it was very important for each of the docents to be himself, but we ran into trouble with that. We tried to have the docents present the facts in their own way. It was very difficult, because some of our docents are very much involved with the symphony. We needed to emphasize that the symphony was the primary tenant of the hall and had a tremendous role in seeing that the hall happened—but the hall belongs to the City of Dallas. Especially given the political climate of the time, that was critical. We stressed that we want everybody to feel welcome in the hall."[17]

"Sharan was able to enlist people from all over the city to join us and be docents," explains Holahan. "Those docents were trained by people from the symphony and the Meyerson staff. I think I. M. Pei actually gave them a tour at one point. They became the spokespersons to the public for the hall."[18]

The DSO's director of volunteer services, Sydney Reid-Hedge, was a powerful ally for the program. She encouraged several Dallas Symphony League volunteers to join the docent group, spearheading the effort by signing up herself. As the docent group grew, they worked through practice tours for each other, critiquing each others' presentations. The first formal docent training session took place in the unfinished musicians' lounge. Goldstein says, "It was covered with dust and sheet rock. We made tables out of sawhorses. Of course there was no air conditioning at the time, and it was the dead heat of summer. The conditions were brutal, but all of us were just delighted to be there." The group continued to practice hard-hat tours in the building until the opening drew close. At that point, the crunch to get things finished meant that the docents were *personae non gratae* in the building.

Docent training sessions then relocated to the lower pavilion areas of nearby Trammell Crow Center, the building where the DSO maintained its marketing center. "We would break up into groups," remembers Goldstein. "We'd have to imagine that we were standing at the door to the building, and talk through a tour. Truly, we gave the first tours of the building without ever having seen it, which was really nerve-wracking! Our docents had never been through it in its complete state. That first weekend, I remember a group of architects asking me, 'Where is the wonderful spiral staircase that we've heard about?' I wasn't actually certain what the answer was. We started walking up, and as we ascended to the grand tier, I heaved a sigh of relief as the architects exclaimed over the spiral. Thank goodness that spiral staircase hadn't sneaked by!"[19]

At the time of the opening in September 1989, Goldstein had ninety volunteers prepared to guide visitors through the building. She warned them that they would have to be flexible, because they had no way of predicting how many visitors the hall would attract. "We couldn't all start at position number one in our tour book. They always understood that somebody would have to start up in the choral terrace, somebody else would start at the front door, a third in Betty Marcus Park."[20]

At Goldstein's insistence, every docent had memorized the telephone number of the Meyerson staff office, so that they could refer any hostile questions to Ted DeDee or Bruce MacPherson. "We told them it was not their responsibility to discuss or justify anything related to the building's high cost. There was no point in denying it. The building cost $81.5 million; it was over budget. We didn't want them to feel threatened. We instructed them that, if they had a problem with anybody, please give them the management number. Interestingly enough, it never happened. People were walking in the front door, and we'd hear a sharp intake of breath. Then, they'd enter the hall and exclaim, 'Aaah!' We referred to it as the 'oooh-aaah' response. Nobody had a negative comment."[21] Ten years after the opening, Goldstein still coordinates a group of more than thirty volunteers who meet regularly to learn more about the hall and hone their guiding skills. They have plenty of business; visitors flock to the hall. Official records of the Meyerson Symphony Center provided by MacPherson in 1999 tell the story. Over its first ten years, the docent program conducted more than 2,400 tours serving more than 150,000 visitors. Volunteer docents contributed approximately 7,000 hours of service. The City of Dallas has never charged a fee to the public for these tours.

Part Five

1989 AND BEYOND

Chapter Twenty-Seven

MAJOR GIFTS II

As the Dallas community realized that the hall was drawing close to completion, money continued to stream into the symphony center. "Everything that had been taken out, people wanted to add back in," recalls Joe Walker of Bateson. "We had changed the travertine marble in the lobby to carpet. Now that money was flowing in from contributions, everyone wanted travertine marble back in the lobby." It seemed that everyone who took a hard-hat tour of the building was making a donation. According to Walker, these monies were predicated on all enhancements being installed and complete by the time of the opening. "I kept saying to the city, 'We can't take any more of these add-ons or changes! If you want us to finish by September, you have got to cease making changes.' They said, 'You've got to do it, or we lose the money!' We said, 'Well, we can't lose any contributions, so we'll get it done one way or another.'"[1]

The project continued to run in the red in spring 1989. A series of large donations brightened the summer, with waves of money rolling in. The fund-raising bonanza did much to ease the symphony's financial anxiety. Some of it was public funding. In June, Dallas City Council approved funding for Artist Square, a block of land on the east side of the symphony site. Other significant donations came from individuals. Louise Kahn, who had already donated $1 million to the hall to name the orchestra's music library, endowed the music directorship in early August 1989, with another $3 million.[2] Jack Roach, her attorney and executor, also included Nancy Hamon and Greer Garson among his clients. Roach's philosophy with these wealthy widows was to disburse their resources during their lifetime when they could get some enjoyment out of seeing what their gifts could do. Roach remembers Louise Kahn telling him, after her husband's death in 1984, that she wanted to "provide the baton," *i.e.,* endow the conductor's chair. In her will, Kahn, who died in 1995, directed that sufficient funds be added from her estate to bring the assets of the Kahn Symphony Foundation to $7 million. Most of the corpus of the foundation was funded at its creation.[3]

Wendy Reves Gift

During the months leading up to the opening, efforts intensified to finish various facets of the building so that it would open in as complete a state as possible. Dolores Barzune, Stanley Marcus, Leonard Stone, Liener Temerlin, and others identified several locations that would require funding if they were to be finished, such as the restaurant and the musicians' quarters. As if playing a game of connect-the-dots, they tried to match up each prospective area with a donor who might have a special affinity for it. Especially at this late date, with local resources largely exhausted, their collective brainstorming led to some creative and offbeat fund-raising proposals.

Wendy Reves, the widow of Hungarian journalist and philanthropist Emery Reves, had catapulted into Dallas news in 1981, when she donated a substantial collection of paintings, furniture, and *objets d'art,* all drawn from her villa in Southern France, to the Dallas Museum of Art. The collection, valued at the time at $40 million, more than doubled the value of the museum's existing holdings; however, Reves came under stringent criticism because of the terms of her gift. She insisted that the museum construct a replica of her villa and exhibit all the furnishings and art as they had been situated in her and Emery Reves's French home. This stipulation meant that, in particular, many of the paintings were not easily visible to patrons, students, and scholars who wished to observe them at close range. Reves was adamant, and the museum complied. The press, in its turn, was harsh in its criticism.

One day in early 1988, Leonard Stone was touring the Reves rooms at the Dallas Museum. He spotted Reves, whom he knew by sight from newspaper and television coverage. "I had only heard about this legendary lady, but I certainly recognized her when I saw her," says Stone, "because she always wore a band around her beautiful forehead. She was one of the great fashion models of her time. She ran with a very heavy crowd: Cary Grant, Errol Flynn, Franchot Tone. I have seen pictures of her as a younger woman, and she was stunningly beautiful. When I saw her at the museum, she was straightening out some of her gowns and slippers.

"I've always characterized myself as an opportunist. I knew that she was a lady of means, and of generous means. Look what she had given to the Dallas Museum! I approached her and introduced myself. 'Mrs. Reves, I'm Leonard Stone, executive director of the Dallas

Symphony Orchestra, and I want to apologize for the Dallas media for the rotten way they have treated you.' 'Oh! my dear boy! Can we have coffee? Can we talk? Can we meet? You're with the Dallas Symphony?' I nodded. 'You know, Solti was my husband's cousin.' Emery Reves was Hungarian; his name was pronounced 'Revish.' Solti, of course, was also Hungarian. They were apparently related. She said, 'Look, I don't have time today, my dear boy. I'm staying at the Adolphus. Can you call me and visit me? You're going to be opening up this wonderful building, and we must talk.'"[4]

Stone called on her at the Adolphus Hotel in downtown Dallas. "Wendy said, 'Now, my dear boy'—I don't know that she knows to this very day that my name is Leonard; I think she thinks my name is My Dear Boy—'My dear boy, I understand you don't have any money to do a grand opening of your concert hall, that your building has cost so much that you're simply broke.' I said, 'No, that's not true at all. We have a gentleman by the name of Liener Temerlin who is spearheading a very effective fund-raising campaign, and we're actively organizing for our grand opening fortnight next year.' She replied, 'Well, I want to help, and I would like to give you $150,000.'"[5]

Stone thanked her for her generosity. Eventually, they negotiated that the Dallas Symphony would, on an annual basis, dedicate a particular performance and include in that performance a piece of Hungarian music in honor of Emery Reves. Stone reported back to his board president, Liener Temerlin, what had transpired.

COINCIDENTALLY, the symphony had another link to Reves through Bette Mullins, a long-time symphony patron who was also president of the Museum League at the Dallas Museum of Art in 1984 and 1985. Mullins remembers, "The year I was president, Wendy came to the first league meeting we held in September. As I was included in all the events for her when she did come to town, we got accustomed to seeing each other and talking together."[6]

Their friendship was sealed during work on the Adolphus Hotel's seventy-fifth anniversary celebration in 1987. Reves, who regularly stayed at the Adolphus, decided that the hotel needed more publicity. According to Mullins, "She suggested that the Adolphus and the DMA do something together that would publicize the hotel and generate income for the DMA. Wendy wanted me to chair the event, and she was the honorary chairman. All the proceeds went to the museum. To this day, of all the things I've chaired, that was the most spectacular party, the party people still talk about. That put the two of us on a firm footing. Wendy and I became good friends."[7]

Mullins knew that Reves had been a generous donor to the College of William and Mary in Virginia, as well as to the Dallas Museum of Art, and believed that she might be persuaded to contribute to the Meyerson as well. Mullins broached the subject in conversation and let it drop. The next time the two women talked, Reves asked Mullins what she had in mind. "Oh, I don't know, but there are lots of naming opportunities, and Margaret"—Mullins knew that Reves adored Margaret McDermott—"Margaret is doing the concert chamber. This building is going to be such an important part of Dallas. Since it's in the arts district, I think it would be nice to have a Reves anchor at each end of the district, both at the Meyerson and at the DMA."

"How much do you think?" Reves asked.

"I don't know. I just wanted to mention it to you," Mullins replied.[8]

Temerlin and Stone both received the impression from Mullins that Reves had the capacity to do something far in excess of the $150,000 to which she had committed. "Liener, I think Wendy will give us money, but let's come up with something really attractive to induce her to donate a large amount," Mullins told Temerlin. "Also, you really ought to go to visit her in France, because she likes to have a face-to-face meeting."[9]

Mullins had provided Stone and Temerlin a copy of the book that Emery Reves had written, entitled *The Anatomy of Peace*. Although it had sold very well in its day for a political science book, after World War II the volume was out of print. One weekend, Temerlin called Stone excitedly and said, "Leonard, I've got it!"[10]

I. M. Pei's building design included a flying, angular arch in front of the Flora Street entrance. The symphony had approached two large Dallas corporations for a $2 million gift that would secure the right to name the arch. Neither company felt that the arch represented anything of significance for its organization. Temerlin said to Stone, "This is a lady who is building pyramids to her husband's memory. We should dedicate the arch as the Emery Reves Arch of Peace. It's a stunning architectural design. It can be a peace arch."[11]

Temerlin set about developing a presentation that would persuade Reves to make the major donation the symphony sought. The proposal included three principal components for the suggested gift of $2 million. The arch in front of the Meyerson would be named the Emery Reves Arch of Peace. The Dallas Symphony would commission a prominent composer to write a piece entitled *The Anatomy of Peace*, record it with the Dallas Symphony, and distribute five thousand recordings. Finally, the DSO would arrange for re-publication of fifty thousand soft-cover copies of Emery Reves's book and distribute them to universities, colleges, and libraries throughout the country. Temerlin was acquainted with the conductor and composer Marvin Hamlisch. "I thought it would be a terrific idea if we could commission Marvin to write this symphony, *The Anatomy of Peace*, as part of our thanks to Wendy for her gift. Marvin was delighted to do that."[12]

Mullins arranged the appointment, which would take place at Reves's home in Southern France on June 22, 1989. (Reves still resides in the home she shared with her late husband: Villa La Pausa, the former home of Coco Chanel in Roquebrune, across the bay from Monaco.) By coincidence, Temerlin and his partner, Dennis McClain, had agency business in France within days of the appointment. Liener and Karla Temerlin and Dennis and Claudia McClain traveled ahead. Stone and Mullins flew to Nice the day before the appointment to join them. They took a helicopter from Nice to Monte Carlo, where Reves's driver, Bario, picked them up to transport them to the Vista Palace Hotel.

"She telephoned me at the hotel; we talked for about an hour," Mullins remembers. "She was so excited we were there! We agreed she'd pick us up the next morning to go sightseeing."[13]

Stone recalls, "That night, before we met with her, we had a dress rehearsal in Liener's suite. Liener had each page of the proposal letter blown up to four feet by three feet. We went through the presentation with this gigantic letter displayed on an easel, along with stunning,

elaborate, and expensive I. M. Pei renderings of the arch. Liener had a copy of the letter, and I was the audio-visual aide, moving the oversize boards."[14]

Mullins recalls, "All of us were in casual, scruffy, almost-ready-for-bed attire. Dennis McClain sat in bed with his sketchpad, working out things we wanted to show Wendy. We each had a part in the program. Liener was very uptight. I said, 'Liener, she's going to give us two million. Don't worry! I know she is.' 'Well, *I* don't know she is. We can't be sure. I believe in being prepared. We've got to be prepared.' *We were prepared!*"[15]

The next morning, Wendy and her driver picked up Temerlin, Mullins, and Stone at ten

The Emery Reves Arch of Peace. (Photo by Richard DeWeese, courtesy Meyerson Symphony Center)

o'clock. They went to La Réserve in Beaulieu for Bloody Marys at 11:00 A.M. "I think she wanted to look us all over before we went to her home," says Temerlin. "We passed the test, and she had her car and driver pick us up again that evening. When we arrived, she gave us a wonderful tour of the villa. I know she gave 'everything' from her house to the Dallas Museum of Art, which is amazing to me because the house is still full!"[16] Leonard Stone agrees that Villa la Pausa was a treat. "It still had a great number of artifacts, great pieces of art, and a great button and ring collection. It was fascinating because the bedroom still had Emery's evening clothes, pajamas, and slippers laid out. His presence was still there and was meant to be maintained."

Before dinner, Wendy had mentioned that the south of France was experiencing a drought. It had been one of the driest springs on record, and the countryside was parched. The normally lush area was brown. Reves had the draperies spread wide, revealing floor-to-ceiling French doors in her dining room, so that what air was moving could circulate within. Her villa was not air-conditioned.

The conversation continued on such benign topics as weather through the meal. Wendy Reves presided at one end of a long refectory dining table. Mullins sat to her right; the men sat across from one another. The presentation and the food were memorable. At one end of the table was a magnificent display, a cornucopia of orchids and fruit. Temerlin says, "Of all the dinners I've had over the years in France, my all-time great meal was without a doubt at Wendy's house that night. Emery was a great wine connoisseur. I have no idea how many different varieties of champagne and wine she served, but they had the kind of labels you see at auction from time to time!"[17]

Reves held Mullins's hand during the meal. Mullins remembers, "We made polite conversation and finished the meal. I thought Liener was going to have a heart attack, he was so cranked up! He wanted to walk in the front door and say, 'Wendy, we're here; let's talk about what you're going to do for the symphony.' Leonard was sitting next to me, fidgety beyond belief, saying in an undertone, 'What d'you think?'"[18]

After the meal, Temerlin opened up the conversation after dinner by saying, "Now, Wendy, we've come to visit you with a purpose."

"All right. I'd like to hear what you have to say."

Temerlin sat to Wendy's left and began his carefully rehearsed presentation. Wendy sat at the table with one hand on her forehead, the other hand in Bette Mullins's, ready to listen—but not to look. "Wendy had her hand on her brow the whole time I was reading," declares Temerlin. "She *never* looked up."

Stone set up the easel and ascertained that the five pages of blowups were in order. Temerlin started reading. "Here we have it on a board." Reves interrupted. "I don't want to see that. You just tell me what you have in mind." Temerlin went through the proposal: the

Arch of Peace, the reprints of Emery's book, the musical composition and recording. As he drew to the end of the presentation, he concluded by saying, "From everything I've read about Emery, I believe this is something that Emery would be very pleased to see happen."

"So this would be the Wendy and Emery Reves Arch of Peace?"

"That's right," agreed Temerlin.

"Well, I don't want my name on it. I just want it to be Emery's."

In a chorus, they all protested, "No, Wendy, your name needs to be on there, too. This arch will greet everyone who comes to the hall. This is the face of the Meyerson. It will look to the museum."

Reves pondered for a moment. "All that sounds interesting. For two million dollars?"

"Yes," said Temerlin, "and we'll do all these—"

"I don't want to hear that!" Reves interrupted again. For a moment she didn't move, then she squeezed Mullins's hand and said, "I will do it."

At that instant, a deafening clap of thunder split the summer night as lightning cracked outside. For a split second, everything was illuminated as if it were daytime. "It was like a Cecil B. DeMille movie!" Temerlin remembers. "The French doors were open, and winds blew the curtains parallel to the floors. And it rained like hell. It was as if the whole thing was staged. I had goosebumps. I got caught up in the whole mystique and magic of the evening, as did we all. I wouldn't tell that story to people if there hadn't been other people there! It sounds phony!"[19]

Wendy glanced upward, lifting her arms, and beamed, "Poochie is pleased." (Poochie is her nickname for Emery.) Leonard Stone echoed her sentiments and those of the rest of the table. "God in His Heaven is approving, too." Wendy Reves rose to close the windows and protect the room from the rain, which was coming down in sheets. She called for another bottle of Dom Pérignon, and they toasted the occasion again.

—◦⁊◦—

WHEN they returned to the hotel, they sought out Karla Temerlin and Claudia McClain, who had gone to dinner in town, and told them the good news. "Was it raining over there?" they inquired. "We saw this huge cloud in that direction." The thunderstorm had been an isolated cloudburst in just the few square kilometers around Villa la Pausa.[20]

—◦⁊◦—

REVES later told the press, "They brought a proposal so perfectly laid out. We were over brandy at the dinner table. I had my head down in my hands because I was staggered. I said to myself, 'I'm going to do it. I don't care how much it costs. I may not have enough to eat. I may eat black-eyed peas for the rest of my life . . . to hell with it, this I have to do for Emery.'"[21]

Upon their return to Dallas, Temerlin and Stone issued a formal announcement that Wendy Reves was making a $2 million gift to name the Emery Reves Arch of Peace at the front entrance to the hall.[22] The symphony commissioned Marvin Hamlisch to compose *Anatomy of Peace*. Because Reves's husband had such an affinity and friendship with Winston Churchill, Stone engaged Abba Eban to speak at the prologue to the evening where the symphony premiered the composition. Eban quoted from Reves's book. Stone remembers, "Abba Eban was the closest to a Churchillian-style talker: beautiful phrasing, beautiful use of the language. Wendy was very moved."[23]

In September, at the time of the dedication ceremony, Wendy Reves declared, "We're standing here because of one man. This man could sell the Brooklyn Bridge to anybody, because he sold the arch to me, and his name is Liener Temerlin."[24]

Greer Garson Fogelson Gift

Dolores Barzune and Stanley Marcus had both recommended that Greer Garson Fogelson be included on the major prospect list. The Irish-born actress had zoomed to Hollywood fame in her first film, *Goodbye, Mr. Chips* (1939), which earned her an Academy Award nomination. Her career included six additional nominations, and she won the Best Actress award in 1943 for *Mrs. Miniver*. Garson married Texas oil magnate Buddy Fogelson in 1949 and retired from the screen in the early 1960s.

While on vacation in Spain, Barzune had a dream that Garson would be a major contributor to the symphony for the still unnamed restaurant area. She returned to Dallas from her holiday determined to make the dream a reality. She told Leonard Stone, "I had this dream," and related its substance. He chuckled, "My goodness, Dolores, I always thought you were a witch; now I *know* it!" They discussed strategy and decided that Barzune would call Louise Kahn to arrange a lunch with Jack Roach, who was both Kahn's and Garson's attorney. They met at the Crescent Club to discuss the best way to approach Garson. "The difference is who makes the approach," Roach counseled them. They agreed that someone from her generation would be best, and decided on Stanley Marcus, who had known Fogelson and Garson for forty years.[25] "Buddy was a very generous man," Marcus recalls. "He loved to sing and play the piano at midnight. Otherwise, he didn't give a goddamn about music! We had Greer on our list of potential donors because she had money and a deep sense of public responsibility."[26]

The trick was catching Garson when she was in town, because she also maintained homes in New Mexico and California. Louise Kahn, who resided in the same Turtle Creek luxury high rise as Garson, was the lookout, monitoring Garson's visits to her Dallas home. As it turned out, the opportunity to ask her occurred not in Dallas, but in New Mexico.

The dedication of the Fogelson Pavilion occurred after the center opened. (*Courtesy Meyerson Symphony Center*)

During a visit to his second home in Santa Fe, Marcus made an appointment to visit Garson at her ranch in Pecos, outside Santa Fe. "Greer, I've come to see you on a cause. Actually, it's very important for Dallas. It involves a memorial to Buddy, who, as you and I both know, didn't give a damn about symphony orchestras. But I think that he would like the scope of this orchestra and what it does for children. I want to propose that you dedicate the south side of the building, which is our location for the restaurant, and name it in memory of Buddy." Marcus knew that Buddy loved to eat.

She didn't buy it. "That would be silly," she told Marcus. "People would remember that Buddy didn't even like classical music!"

Marcus suggested, "Well, we could call it Buddy's Delicatessen, or Buddy's Spot."

She reflected for a moment. "What will it cost?"

"Two million dollars."

"Let me think about it." A few days later, she called Marcus to say, "I think I'm going to have to do what you asked me to do."

Marcus was delighted. "That's wonderful!" He and his wife were still in Santa Fe. He called Dallas to leave the good news with Leonard Stone and DSA Board President Dolores Barzune.

———— ❧ ————

About two weeks later, Garson telephoned Marcus in Santa Fe again. "I want to see you," she announced. He went to her home. She said, "You know, it's written in the books that women have a right to change their mind."

Marcus knew what was coming. He said, "I'm not sure they have the right, but women *do* change their mind, and I'm very sympathetic. What's the problem?"

"I've been thinking about this thing, and it's been worrying me, because I just don't think it's the right gift. I'd like to withdraw from being a donor."

Marcus told her, "I think the worst thing you could do would be to live with something that you didn't like. Of course you can withdraw."

"Who will take my place?"

"Don't worry. We'll find somebody. It may take us a year or two to do it; we may miss the opening, but anyway, you should do it [withdraw] with an open conscience, and know that I love you just as much with or without the two million."

Less than six weeks later, she called him again, right before the hall was scheduled to open. "I want to see you again." They got together. "Remember I told you a lady had the prerogative to change her mind?"

Marcus remembered.

She said, "Everybody at the symphony was so nice to me when I reneged, that I just haven't felt right since then. I want to reinstate my gift."

"We're not going to give you a chance to change your mind again!" Marcus warned her, smiling through his admonition. "We're going to start work *today!*"[27]

—❦—

GREER Garson's attorney and executor, Jack Roach, confirms Marcus's story, with some additional details. "Ms. Fogelson was approached by Stanley Marcus to contribute $2 million to the symphony in connection with the Meyerson. Greer had no interest whatever in contributing the $2 million to the symphony. She came to me and said, 'Jack, I just don't know what to do. Stanley has been such a dear friend for so long, and this project means so much to him, but Buddy never had any interest in the symphony. That wasn't his type of music. We've never had any involvement in it.' Greer was keenly aware that all these large resources she had available to give away were the result of Buddy's endeavors."

Fogelson's fortune came from oil. After he died, Garson wanted to use his money toward projects in which she felt Buddy would have been interested. According to Roach, "It was fixed in her mind that the Meyerson donation was *not* something that Buddy would have done. I told her, 'Greer, Stanley is a very close friend of yours. He will certainly understand. If you explain it to Stanley just like you've explained it to me, Stanley will not be offended.' She came back to me shortly thereafter and said, 'I did talk to Stanley, and I still don't know what to do. He told me I should never give money to a project simply because a friend asked me to. Do not contribute funds to anything other than things that I'm interested in.' She said, 'Jack, he was so gracious I *had* to give him the two million dollars!' And she did."[28]

Leonard Stone remembers one additional circumstance he believes was key. When Garson withdrew her gift, the design team was at work on the Wall of Honor, the circular engraved limestone area to the left of the stairway that emerges from the lower level to the main lobby. "Of course her decision was a deep disappointment, because $2 million gifts are not easy to find," says Stone. "A couple of weeks later, I called Stanley to tell him we were working with the graphics people at the Pei office about type style and proportions for that wall. Once everything was carved into that wall, alphabetically and within its donation range, it would be too late to redo. I suggested we appeal to Greer once more, this time using a picture." The Pei group mocked up what the wall would look like fully engraved, including the Fogelson name. Stone remembers routing the photograph to Marcus to show to Garson. "I think it showed her what it would look like," declares Stone. "Was it the defining piece? I don't know, but I believe it played a role, because shortly thereafter, she changed her mind."[29]

The Greer Garson pledge was delivered to the Dallas Symphony with the first of three installments in August 1989 and announced publicly on Tuesday, September 5, 1989, the day before the first concert in the Meyerson Symphony Center. Like so many other aspects of the hall, the future Fogelson Pavilion would not be complete until after the official opening.

—❧—

SHORTLY after the Meyerson opened, the DSO held a reception to dedicate the Fogelson Pavilion. Greer Garson Fogelson was too ill to attend. According to Jack Roach, she had intended to be present, but her health did not permit. Stanley Marcus made some remarks on her behalf.[30]

Chapter Twenty-Eight

CRANKING UP

I
N JANUARY 1989, City Auditor Daniel Paul issued a special report evaluating costs of the new symphony center. He had undertaken his inquiry initially at the behest of City Councilman Al Lipscomb, who objected to interest earnings from the bonds being allocated to concert hall enhancements rather than being used for debt retirement. A formal request for the audit came via Mayor Pro Tem John Evans. First Assistant City Manager Jan Hart cosigned the report. Paul's figures added up to $157 million, and the local press emblazoned that figure in giant, front-page headlines.[1] Paul's figures included the cost of land at $14 million, the parking garage at $8.7 million, and the Betty Marcus Park at $2.1 million. None of those items had been figured into prior totals. The kicker, however, was debt service, which Paul calculated at $50.7 million. Park Board Vice President Gerald Henigsman protested that inclusion of the debt service was misleading. "I don't think we ever look at municipal projects by rolling in the interest. I think the whole thing got blown out of proportion, when he started adding apples and oranges."[2]

The next day, an editorial appeared in *The Dallas Morning News* taking Paul to task and debunking many of his figures. "Silliest of all is the inclusion of $51 million in debt service. When you buy a home for $100,000, the cost of the home is just that—$100,000. The interest isn't included in the cost. Don't change the rules of accounting in the middle of the game."[3]

Meyerson and the symphony were furious. One article quoted Meyerson disputing the results of the auditor's study, but the damage was done. Joe Walker of Bateson remembers the fallout from the city audit yielding the $157 million total. "When you think about all the things that went on prior to Bateson getting on board, I should have expected to have a lot of heartache before we ever got started. The external problems concerned the press. Some press was good, some was bad. They tracked this job so closely that anything that was done down here was going to be on the front page, or at least some page, in the paper. We had to be extremely careful all the time that we said precisely the right thing."[4]

Canopy Problems

Just a few weeks later, another major flap erupted concerning the acoustic canopy over the stage. In March 1989, only six months prior to the scheduled opening in September, the canopy builders, Hoffend & Sons, insisted that the apparatus, as designed by Artec, would be

The large canopy, measuring 40 feet by 70 feet and installed in summer 1989, is suspended by an elaborate cable suspension system. *(Courtesy Hoffend & Sons, Inc. Stage Equipment)*

unsafe. The forty-foot by seventy-foot piece of equipment made of steel and wood, which had irritated I. M. Pei since the early stages of design, was scheduled to arrive in June from Canada and New York. The symphony insisted that the elaborate cable suspension system for the canopy was safe. Hoffend disagreed.[5] The press continued its feeding frenzy, delighted with this latest squabble. The steady stream of change orders, each of which required city council approval, came under increasing scrutiny. When the acoustical canopy system was finally approved, Councilman Jerry Bartos fumed to the press, "I have seen change orders on this job that I do not believe a Dallas firm would have had the gall to submit."[6]

Mayor Strauss, a staunch supporter of the arts, placed herself in a potentially vulnerable position politically through her outspoken championship of the Meyerson Symphony Center. Pete Lesser, a populist/activist attorney, challenged her in the biannual spring mayoral election. Lesser viewed the Meyerson as Strauss's Achilles' heel and attacked the hall's extravagance at every opportunity. In late April, *The Dallas Morning News* reported: "Mr. Lesser, clad in a hard hat and rented tuxedo, used the uncompleted Morton H. Meyerson Symphony Center as the backdrop for a news conference in which he called on the city to end its funding of the hall's construction and future operating costs. . . . He targeted what he called excessive features, such as $82,000 for African teakwood doors, a box office and a cloakroom 'for the wealthiest few to hang their fur coats in.'"[7] Dallas voters apparently did not buy his argument, for they returned Strauss to office for a second term on May 6, 1989, thereby assuring that she would preside over the Meyerson's opening festivities that September.

Six weeks prior to opening, in late July, *The Dallas Morning News* rattled the cage again with a story exploring the geographical distribution of symphony patrons. Thirty-six percent of subscribers lived outside the city limits, thus they were not contributing their fair share to the tax burden, the paper alleged. The annual cost of operating the center was now estimated at $1.3 million per annum. City council members Jerry Bartos, Diane Ragsdale, and Al Lipscomb all recommended that a surcharge be added to nonresident ticket prices.[8]

By then, things were so frantic at the Meyerson that the impact of this latest attack was diluted. With the opening imminent, and the Meyerson in the local news on a daily basis anyway, the Dallas Symphony had other matters to worry about.

During the summer of 1989, Mort Meyerson was at the hall every other day. "We had committee meetings in the Bateson trailer at the site. Very bad coffee, the way I remember it! George Schrader, Louise Reuben, and the city were monitoring progress from day to day, week to week. I'd walk around with the Bateson people, with Cliff Keheley, with Louise Reuben, with Leonard Stone, I. M., Liener Temerlin, everybody's in the act now, because you've got so many things happening. We have to make decisions on the fly. Do we finish the corporate suites downstairs or not finish them and do something else? As problems popped up, we had to assess priorities and act. It was a pretty exciting time through late July."

Bateson's Bob Lemke had taken a brief vacation over Memorial Day weekend. He did not have another day off until mid-September. "It was just crazy. I. M. Pei was there all the time. He was partly directing getting the building finished. It became obvious that some things were not going to be complete for the gala. He was identifying what was critical, what mattered from an architectural standpoint, what was most important to him, what we needed to focus on."[9]

For everyone associated with the hall, things went to a steeper pitch. The political heat rose in early August when, in the middle of all the frenetic activity surrounding the last stages of construction, both local dailies, *The Dallas Morning News* and the *Dallas Times Herald,* published three-part series largely critical of the hall. At that point, Mort Meyerson questioned why he had taken this job. "Everybody wanted to get in to be a critic. I was being interviewed, but the stories were written before I was interviewed. They would drop a quotation in to suit their own needs and quote me out of context. I resented what the newspapers did, because they had a viewpoint, they were going to publish that viewpoint, and there was no talking to them. I still have bad feelings about that. However, my mother used to say, 'Sticks and stones can break your bones, but names can never hurt you.' The way I resolved not having a hemorrhage over it, was: Ultimately the hall would be judged on whether it was filled, what was the quality of the orchestra, and how the acoustics sounded. How it worked and felt. Was it a vibrant part of the city? Was it an asset? Did people move here because of it? Did the orchestra sound better? Did the quality get better? Could you sell the crowds out? I knew the ultimate answer would have nothing to do with what the newspapers were saying. With that thought in mind, I said, 'I'll just wait.'"[10]

It was a wise decision.

———— ❧ ————

MATTERS escalated to fever pitch as three major problems erupted. First: the seats. Meyerson remembers, "I was working intensively on the hall in preparation for the grand opening fortnight, because it looked like we weren't going to open. We couldn't get delivery of the seats from Germany. Without seats, we couldn't open." The matter of the seats was resolved by going with an American company that could guarantee delivery.

Then there was the marble. Italians normally take vacation during August—the entire month of August. The only exceptions are those individuals whose livelihood depends on tourism, such as hotel owners and restaurateurs, and retail businesses that also benefit from seasonal tourists. Blue-collar workers take all of August as a holiday. That included the stone cutters who were quarrying the marble in Tivoli. "We didn't have any way to get the marble here," remembers Meyerson. "That meant that we would have to have [temporary] carpeting in the lobbies, which we knew would be disastrous. But worse than a disaster was that it cost a million dollars to make the fundamental change for the difference in the depth of the concrete pourings we had already made."

The construction crew had built the lobby floor at a certain depth to accommodate marble travertine. If they installed carpeting instead, they would have to pour more concrete in to raise the level. Installing the carpet, then removing added concrete and carpet later on and replacing it with marble would cost another million dollars. Presented with that cost estimate, Meyerson and his group rejected it altogether. "We said, 'We're not going to do that. Number one, we don't have a million dollars, and number two, that's not going to happen.' That's when I called in some cards and got Ross, Bob Crandall, and Les Alberthal to help us."

The first order of business was to obtain the marble by early August, because once it arrived in the United States, it would take time for workers to lay it. That meant dispatching an ambassador to Italy who could negotiate with the supplier to fill the symphony's order by the end of July. Paul Lyons and George Miller, who speaks excellent Italian, flew to Italy in late June to try to expedite the marble. The special shapes such as railings were being cut in Tivoli, east of Rome. The travertine pieces for the lobby floor were being cut in Verona, midway between Milan and Venice. If not all the marble could be secured, Meyerson made it clear that the flooring was to be the first priority. Miller and Lyons contacted a young Pei architect who, coincidentally, was vacationing in Italy. According to Lyons, "George found him and put him in Verona for a month. I had a floor plan of the building on my wall in the Bateson trailer. After we returned, every morning he would fax me what pieces were cut and going onto the container to go on the boat."[11] Additionally, Meyerson called his friend, Les Alberthal, the CEO of EDS. Meyerson says, "When I left EDS, I recommended Les to succeed me as CEO. He used to be my assistant. I had known him for twenty years. Because I had left the company, however, I wasn't exactly on great terms with EDS. But, by 1989, I was retired; I didn't have a company. I needed a project manager who spoke Italian to go to Italy to break the deadlock. I didn't know what to do, so I called Les and explained our quandary. I said, 'Les, this is a job for an EDS kind of person. I need a can-do project manager who speaks Italian, and I need him for a week or two to help me break the back of this problem.' He said, 'Sure.' Next day he gave me the name of an EDS employee who spoke Italian. The day after that, the guy was on a plane to Italy. He went from Rome to Tivoli and, within days, had an agreement that the marble cutters would work overtime and cut the marble we needed."[12]

At the symphony offices, nervous staff members exhaled with relief when they heard the results. Leonard Stone remembers, "The fax report from the EDS operative was unbelievable, pure EDS, like a military operation. It read something like this: 'Arrived at the quarry such and such date, such and such hour. Met with head of quarry such and such hour. Convinced Italians to get job accomplished by so and so. Future report to deal with U.S. Customs and Immigration.' Just like *veni vidi vici*. And they cut the marble."[13]

The next challenge was transport. As the middle of July approached, Paul Lyons knew he was running out of time. "Because the end of July was the deadline, we had a fighting chance. We could have used another week or two of fabrication. We would have been in much better shape. As it was, we had to decide which pieces we were leaving behind."[14] The main lobby floor would go in; the upper lobby handrails would have to wait. Shipping the marble by the more affordable method, ocean freighter, was no longer an option. Meyerson called American Airlines CEO Bob Crandall to ask if American had any empty 747s or other large planes that flew back and forth. Could he slip this marble in the aircraft belly? Crandall came through. For the next several weeks, American Airlines Flight 73, nonstop from Frankfurt to Dallas, carried from 3 to 17 tons of marble every day. "We flew 220 or 230 metric tons of marble out of Italy," remembers Lyons. As Meyerson recalls, American did it *pro bono*. "And," he adds, "they had already given half a million for the opening. American Airlines absolutely saved the day on that."[15]

The third phase was clearing the marble through customs upon its arrival in the United States. Meyerson prevailed on H. Ross Perot to run interference with the customs officials at D/FW airport in order to expedite clearance of the imported stone. According to Meyerson, "The original argument was with INS at D/FW Airport. Immigration wouldn't let the marble land without quarantine because it might contain beetles and bugs! They treat it like wood. So Ross got us through immigration at the airport."[16] Enough marble cleared customs to complete major public areas, but not the entire building. Light carpet infill went in on portions of the upper lobby floor.

Declares Meyerson: "If Les Alberthal hadn't identified the EDS employee who spoke Italian to travel to Italy for us, we couldn't have gotten it out of the quarry. If American Airlines hadn't flown it in, we couldn't have gotten it here in time. If Perot hadn't gotten it prematurely cleared through customs, then we couldn't have gotten it here and gotten use of it. As it is, people were working twenty-four hours a day under lights laying that stuff the night before the opening! The fact that we had an opening with marble in there—I still, to this day, don't know how that happened. It's just amazing. It really is a fabulous thing, that so many people helped."[17]

—❧—

THE millwork supplier for the Meyerson Symphony Center was a Canadian company, Valley City Manufacturing, in Hamilton, Ontario. They specialized in fine newel woodwork, wood supply, and installation. In early August 1989, a few parts of the wood were still missing in the upper areas above the stage. At one of the daily meetings, Bateson announced that Valley City couldn't deliver the wood to finish off the upper areas on the stage, therefore they would have to use paint. Meyerson remembers, "The Bateson people said, 'We've got this big problem. Our wood supplier is not going to deliver enough on time. We're going to have to paint.' I said, 'Look, you guys don't understand. I'm going to have to raise extra funds to pay for the wood, and I'm not going to have people who put up millions of dollars to do things walk into a hall and have white painted sheet rock walls." They said, 'Well, we can't get the wood.' I said, 'Wait a minute. I was told we couldn't get the marble.'"

Of course, by this time they all knew about the Herculean team effort to get the marble in time for the opening. Meyerson continued, "Now here's what I'm willing to do. I am willing to get people to go to the freaking woods, chop it down, plane it, sand it, color it, ship it, and get it here. Now, I don't want to do that, so you've got two choices. You either get it here, or I'm going to take command and we're going to do it."

They got the wood.

Mort Meyerson says, "We had encountered problems with the glass people, because each panel is a unique size, and they were having trouble casting, hanging. But those were what I consider the normal construction issues on a big project. The wood, the marble, and the seats, though, were extraordinary. Those three cases could have devastated us. The seats were the only one that could prevent us from opening. The marble was a million dollars difference plus it would look tacky if we didn't have it. We couldn't get the product we wanted within the budget. That's when I told Schrader, 'Just do it, and I'll raise the money. We'll get it done somehow.'"[18]

THE countdown to opening night was little more than two weeks. Bateson's crew, which had been working ten- and twelve-hour days, seven days a week for three months, began round-the-clock shifts. "We were working twenty-four hours a day," asserts Bob Lemke. "Every night, about 9:00 P.M., all the crew that worked for Bateson, about fourteen of us, would walk the building together, noting everything we could find that was unfinished: a missing part, a missing piece. Anything that wasn't done, we would establish who was going to take care of it and when. The next night we'd walk it and repeat the process."[19]

Large pipes for the organ façade were going up as paneling was affixed to the walls. Elsewhere in the concert room, with no seats yet installed, canopy assembly was taking place on the orchestra-level floor. Out in the lobbies, more workers were laying marble flooring and temporary carpet.

Louise Reuben Elam, the city's architect, was spending most of her waking hours at the hall. "A couple of weeks before the opening, the flooring wasn't in, the wall panels weren't on, the seats weren't installed," she says. "There was a lot of work remaining to be completed in a very short period of time. Just days before the first concert, I. M. saw the plaza trees and did not believe their proportions were correct in relations to the Chillida sculpture. He requested that they be replaced with larger trees that had a more horizontal canopy. So George Miller, Steve Hamway [of Sasaki Associates], and I went to a tree farm to select new trees. Over Labor Day weekend, the new trees were being installed. While I watched the planting, I. M. Pei walked up to me and said that he had visited city hall and looked at the tree grates in the plaza. He felt that we needed to change the tree grates over there! I asked him jokingly, 'Can we finish this building first?' These are examples of I. M. Pei's attention to detail. Eleven years after the completion of one of his buildings, he was still looking for ways to improve it. When he visited the site during construction, we could expect that he would make a change to perfect something. His attention to every detail and his striving for perfection are reasons the Meyerson is such a wonderful building!"[20]

—❧—

INEVITABLY, some things had to be forfeited. There simply wasn't enough time to get everything complete. One particular sticking point was the restaurant, intended for the west lobby area. Meyerson Manager Ted DeDee and the city had planned the contract so that the concessionaire was to pay the cost of finishing out the kitchen. City estimators figured that it would cost an organization $400,000 to $500,000 to purchase and install equipment to suit the caterer's needs. The contract looked like a plum: The winner would also operate the building's lobby bars, catering for special events beyond regular restaurant meals on concert days, coat check, and the valet parking service.

When the bids came in, DeDee and his supervisors at the city were astonished to see kitchen finish-out estimates of $900,000. The gap between their estimates and the bids coming in was enormous. Potential concessionaires claimed they could not make a profit the way the city proposed the contract. With so many other pressing matters requiring attention, DeDee and his supervisors reluctantly agreed to shelve the restaurant until two months after the opening. It would take considerably longer.

Chapter Twenty-Nine

REHEARSALS AND OPENING NIGHT

EDUARDO Mata and the symphony's operations staff were becoming anxious about rehearsal time. With a massive international press contingent set to descend upon Dallas over Labor Day weekend, media coverage would be extensive. The orchestra required time to adjust to the space and become acquainted with its acoustics. The hall was new and untested, and the Dallas Symphony was preparing an extremely ambitious series of concerts during the grand opening fortnight, including performances of the Verdi *Requiem* and the Mahler *Resurrection* Symphony.

On Monday, August 28, office furniture was being moved into the DSO third- and fourth-floor administrative offices at the rear of the hall, flanking Woodall Rodgers Freeway. The offices were officially closed for the day. That morning, representatives from Bateson, Meyerson management, the city, and the symphony met. The Meyerson management announced that the hall would not be ready in time for the August 30 rehearsal, and maybe not on August 31. Mark Melson, who had been promoted from public relations manager to head the orchestra operations department in February 1988, had been holding an alternate site, the fellowship hall at Highland Park Presbyterian Church, just in case. Eduardo Mata decided that rehearsals in an alternate location would be useless and vetoed the idea."[1] The DSO moved the schedule back a day, beginning on August 31 and adding a rehearsal for Sunday, September 3, which was to have been a free day over the Labor Day holiday weekend. Free days were no longer possible.

On Tuesday afternoon, August 29, the DSO gave its musicians a get-acquainted tour of the building. According to Melson, "Everything was incomplete, under construction, and utterly disheveled. Construction workers let us show very little, and that only briefly." On the way out, a skeptical orchestra member asked him, "*When* did you say the first concert was?" Those within earshot laughed nervously, but clearly most of them shared the same incredulous thought.

The next morning, Wednesday, August 30, the implementation group convened for a 7:30 A.M. meeting with the subcontractors at the Bateson trailer. Coy Porter, the Bateson supervisor, asked for one more day, August 31, before the orchestra rehearsed in the building. "We gotta have it," he insisted. "Our boys are killing themselves. Can't you move the next rehearsal to September first?" As orchestra operations manager, Melson was placed in the uncomfortable position of refusing. "I was getting a lot of pressure from Eduardo to rehearse in the building. I was the liaison between the musicians and the construction crew. The subcontractor reaffirmed his need for time to finish, and then I made a note in my diary: 'August 31 rehearsals promise to be interesting.'"[2]

That Thursday, August 31, the orchestra arrived for its rehearsal to find its risers not yet in place. Conditions were like camping out. Mata conducted the rehearsal on the flat stage, much to the consternation of Russell Johnson and the Artec staff, who had spent considerable time in developing an acoustic riser system. The front two rows of the choral risers were also missing.[3] The side and rear stage doors were not yet in place, so the orchestra sound escaped backward and sideways from the stage. Backstage construction noise resonated onto the stage and into the hall.

Everything hinged on the acoustics. Yuri Anshelevich, the DSO's associate principal cellist, was the first to walk out onto the stage. Leonard Stone was out on the audience floor, watching and listening. "He sat down, pulled his bow across the cello. I could feel the sound come through the floor, up my feet, into my guts. I knew then that we had a world-class music chamber, if not one of the three or four greatest music chambers in the world. The next time I really had that feeling was at an evening rehearsal. There were fewer workmen in the building. They were pouring most of their energies, everything they could, in the daytime. Isaac [Stern] stood with me at the rear of the hall while Eduardo was rehearsing Beethoven's *Consecration of the House* Overture. Isaac looked at the stage, turned left and looked at me, then backed to the back wall of the main floor, under the horseshoe, as far as he could. Here's what I read on his face: 'This sounds better than Carnegie Hall. I can't stand it!' He was the savior of Carnegie Hall, which went from a great acoustic through the renovation to a not-so-great acoustic. He grudgingly honored the Meyerson in a subsequent television interview. He said, 'You wanted a great hall; you've got one,' as if to say, 'I'm just going to say as little as I have to, and I'm not going to say any more.' I sensed that he was momentarily pained that someone was able to achieve what I believe they didn't achieve in the renovation of Carnegie Hall."[4]

First violinist Mary Reynolds remembers the orchestra's first reaction in rehearsal. "Maestro Mata raised his baton and gave the first downbeat for the Verdi *Requiem*. He stopped, and we heard the reverberation, about three seconds of decay. Everyone was just amazed. We knew; it was live. But from my standpoint—I could *hear* myself individually. It was this combination of individual clarity right under your chin with the violin, and the entire ambience of the orchestra."[5]

For Mort Meyerson, those chords were the pinnacle of a decade-long experience. "When the music stopped, I heard the tail of the sound. When I heard that decay, I said, 'Oh my God!' —because I knew. It was awesome. It was really moving. This is like your wife giving birth to a child after a nine-month interval. There's great drama, particularly if you're a first-time parent. This is all new, and you're all excited. When you have a birth, it's a great time of celebration. Here we had a ten-year gestation. We had a preview before anybody else would know what was going on. So we were able to judge. The public and the critics would hear at the opening, but we got to sample it early. It was pretty exciting. I walked on air that day."[6]

EXCITING or not, there remained a superhuman amount of work to be done, both musically and in terms of construction. After the initial elation, the orchestra began rehearsing in earnest. Battles erupted between Eduardo Mata and the construction workers. He would ask for quiet during rehearsal. Silence would last for a scant twenty or thirty seconds, then a drill would resume from up in the grand tier, a hammer would thwack in the loge boxes, an electric saw would buzz in the rear orchestra. Mata finally lost his temper in annoyance and frustration. A small army of symphony personnel hastily convened an emergency meeting with the Bateson supervisors to devise a schedule that would accommodate both musicians and construction crew.

General dishevelment verging on chaos was apparent throughout the building. Because the overhead lights were still lacking on stage, the musicians used music stand lights. Mata was asked to wear a white shirt so he could be better seen at rehearsal. Bathrooms were incomplete throughout most of the building and elevators were not yet functional. During rehearsal breaks, the orchestra musicians had to climb two flights of stairs to the office level to use the staff rest rooms. The musicians had no place to leave instrument cases, purses, and other personal effects. They appropriated the first-floor orchestra library, despite the fact that the room was bare and had not yet been released to them by Bateson. With no lock on the door, the Meyerson security staff posted a round-the-clock guard.

Battles resumed between Maestro Mata and the construction workers. Melson asked a large man in a torn T-shirt working on main floor seats to turn off his drill during rehearsal. He said, "Can't. Not done yet," and resumed working. Melson tried a philosophical approach. "You know how painters paint on canvas? Well, musicians paint on silence." The workman stared at Melson for about ten seconds, then spat tobacco juice into a coffee can without comment and resumed drilling.[7]

Out in the hall, various symphony staff members, board VIPs, and members of the Pei and Artec design teams audited each rehearsal intently, continuing to gauge the environment for music making. Fortnight Chairman Temerlin remembers asking Johnson a couple of days before the opening, "Russell, how are the acoustics?" Johnson, short-tempered and doubtless worried about that very question, snapped, "Goddamn it, Liener, if you stop listening for the acoustics and start listening to the music, you can judge for yourself!" Temerlin calls it one of the best put-downs he ever received. "I thought it was a hell of a funny line, and a very accurate one! First of all, it took me years to learn to pronounce the word!"[8]

❧

OUT IN the lobby areas, I. M. Pei led a walk-through of the building with all individuals responsible for opening events, including catering staff. They discussed the elaborate buffets planned for the grand opening fortnight, and they realized that there was no place for gala patrons to sit. It might be wise, they concluded, to jumpstart the restaurant and procure furniture for the opening. The task fell to Abby Suckle, a member of the Pei team, to acquire in short order the furnishings for a convincing-looking restaurant. Suckle had done extensive work on other aspects of the interior, including color coordination of paints, selection of fabrics and carpets, and design and detailing of subsidiary spaces such as box office and dressing rooms. She plunged into her new assignment in the same overdrive mode that now prevailed throughout the building. "I started with the restaurant tables," she recalls, "because in the best of all possible worlds they should be travertine to match the floor. Someone recommended the Triad Travertine Company of Dallas who happened to have a supply of similar travertine, which they cut into table tops and delivered to the symphony a couple of days later. The bases were in stock at Gordon International, a New Jersey company. They were duly air-freighted, and our furniture contractor assembled them."[9]

Next was chairs. Suckle located a company in Grand Prairie, a southwest suburb halfway to Fort Worth, that had about forty metal chairs in its warehouse in a finish that resembled the brushed aluminum of the skylights. She persuaded them to deliver a sample to the Meyerson to secure Pei's approval. "He looked at it, and approved it with one proviso," says Suckle. "The metal was a little too cold to sit on; he thought a seat pad would improve its comfort." She went shopping again, this time to Crate & Barrel, then at NorthPark Shopping

Center. They had the perfect seat pad, but an insufficient number in stock. "Luckily, Crate & Barrel has a lot of stores!" laughs Suckle. "None alone had enough seat pads in stock, but together they could provide the quantity we needed. This took a long time—so long that I had plenty of time to look through the store. This worked out well, because they also had a good selection of votive candles and bud vases, which were the next items on my restaurant fit-out list. I maxed out my credit card!"[10]

Once the tables and chairs had been delivered to the hall and set up in the restaurant area, Pei requested pale orange rosebuds to fill the vases. Suckle was apprehensive. Dallas was experiencing typical late summer heat, with temperatures in the upper 90s. The hall's HVAC system was still being tuned, and no one knew yet how it would fare with two thousand patrons in the lobby areas. Further, the roses had to last several days. To be safe, she contacted two sources. "I went to the person recommended to be the best florist in town and ordered the roses, from a picture, to be shipped to the hall late that week. I also called my office in New York and asked that they send some roses down with the next person flying to Dallas. Between them, there was a chance we'd have what Mr. Pei wanted."[11]

Between rehearsals, meetings continued in the Bateson trailer. Bateson asked the orchestra to move its scheduled Saturday, September 2, morning rehearsal to evening, in order to give the workers more time in the hall. The change could only be made if the orchestra voted to do so. Under union rules, once the schedule was set contractually, within five weeks of a scheduled service, no rehearsal or performance could be changed without specific orchestra approval. The orchestra voted at the conclusion of the evening rehearsal on August 31 as to whether it would move the morning rehearsal on September 2 to evening. The change passed, but not unanimously.

The evening of August 31, members of the chorus showed up to rehearse the Mahler *Resurrection* Symphony. Two rows of chorus risers were still missing. Two hundred singers squeezed into space intended for one hundred. Because no chairs were in place, the choristers stood for the duration of the rehearsal. Fortunately, the benches were not yet installed in the choral terrace either, so they at least had more standing room than they would have otherwise.

Mark Melson, the DSO's operations manager, was standing at the rear of the hall with Chorus Director Ronald Shirey. "Some of the chorus had flashlights," Melson recalls. "Somebody had suspended a naked light bulb right above them, and there was a soft glow from the music stand lamps that the orchestra had to use, because there were no stage lights yet. Only the back two rows of the choral terrace were in place.

"Eduardo wanted to let the chorus go, because he knew they had a big week, so he rehearsed them first. The first thing we heard was a place near the end of the Mahler Second where the chorus enters very quietly. We heard this warm, resonating, organ-like sound, and we realized it was the men in the chorus. I turned to Ron [Shirey]. Tears were streaming down his face. I know that my eyes were kind of misty, too, because it was at that precise moment that we knew that the hall worked acoustically, as incomplete as it was."[12]

Principal percussionist Doug Howard remembers the same moment. "The first entrance of the chorus in the Mahler Second, at rehearsal, not only gave me goosebumps, but I also had tears in my eyes. I looked around the orchestra. Just about everybody was wiping away tears. That was really an amazing moment, because I never in my entire life heard sound like that. It was a special thing."[13]

Countdown

Friday, September 1. Only five days until the first concert. Mata was continually frustrated by construction noise at rehearsal. At one point, a workman was on a ladder in the choral terrace with a hammer and drill, installing one of the last pieces of wood. Mata stopped the orchestra and called, "How are we supposed to play? How can we rehearse with all this banging going on?"

The workman shrugged. "What do you want to do? You want to finish this thing or you want to rehearse?"

Mata, of course, wanted both. Valiantly, he lifted his baton. "Again, from rehearsal No. 48." Two minutes later, he stopped the orchestra again and exploded, "Tell that man up there to stop hammering," he shouted. "If he doesn't stop, tell him we'll kill him."

Mark Melson ascended three flights to where the offender was working. He found twelve laborers instead of the two who had been there earlier. One of them said, "We heard something about somebody killing someone and we came over to watch him try."

Later that day, after hours of such exchanges, Bateson's Coy Porter asked for two days of work in the hall with no musical interruption. Reluctantly, the DSO agreed to move a chorus-only rehearsal scheduled for Labor Day—Monday, September 4. Scrambling, the chorus finally found an alternative site that was large enough to accommodate them: the choir room at Park Cities Baptist Church.[14]

———— ✧ ————

THAT same morning, at 11:00 A.M., Melson took a telephone call from the organ dealer in Philadelphia who had the only available portable electronic organ in America large enough for the Mahler Second. (The Meyerson organ would not be operative for some time.) He told Melson that the cheapest shipping on a reliable carrier he could find would cost $5,000. "That was just to *ship* it," recalled Melson. "It didn't include the rental. He needed an answer within an hour in order to have time to load the organ, or it would arrive in Dallas too late for rehearsals and performance. Adele Demler [the DSO's operations manager for pops concerts] and I called other movers frantically. None could do it for less. I called my brothers in suburban

Philadelphia, in New Jersey, to see if they knew any movers in the area, but they didn't. So, within the hour time limit that we had, we called back and gave the company in Philadelphia the go ahead to move that organ for $5,000."[15]

Saturday, September 2. One of the musicians dubbed Mark Melson "the noise police" at rehearsal. Mata reported that noisy conditions had put rehearsals far behind schedule. He would require an additional rehearsal for the Verdi *Requiem*. After scrutinizing the schedule, Melson determined that Saturday morning, September 9, would be the best time. "We notified the Meyerson management, Ted DeDee and Bruce MacPherson, who reacted in horror. They had been advertising tours of the building for days and expected ten thousand people to pass through that Saturday morning! They refused to keep the McDermott Hall off limits for the tour, which would make a Saturday morning rehearsal impossible. The only other available time was Sunday morning [September 10]. Unfortunately, we would lose half the chorus, because so many of the chorus members have church jobs or church choir commitments. So we took the daring step of scheduling an 8:00 A.M. Sunday rehearsal for the Verdi *Requiem*. Our contract with the orchestra musicians forbids beginning any service before 9:30 A.M. There is, however, a seldom-used clause permitting an emergency rescheduling for reasons 'beyond the control of the employer.' We invoked that clause for that 8:00 A.M. Sunday rehearsal, the first and probably the last time in the Dallas Symphony's history."[16]

The orchestra was under enormous pressure because of the broad spectrum of repertoire they had to deliver over the next two weeks. "In retrospect," Melson later observed, "We bit off a little more than we could reasonably chew, although we had expected to have the hall for a few more days without noise and interruptions. If we had had the hall those extra days and there hadn't been construction noise, it would have worked better."

That evening, as Mata worked with the orchestra, workmen labored furiously around the hall. A drill whined from above the choral terrace. Mata asked the driller to stop, but he didn't. Mark Melson remembers, "I wandered out onto the choral terrace to engage the driller in a dialogue. He respectfully refused to stop. Losing his temper for really the first time, Eduardo said, 'Mark, I want you to physically restrain him from making noise.' I looked at Mata and said, 'Eduardo, if I do that, you'll have a practical use for the Verdi *Requiem* this weekend.' That broke the tension, because the orchestra was sitting there listening, and they all burst out laughing."[17]

Monday September 4, Labor Day. Mark Melson drove to Park Cities Baptist Church to persuade the two hundred chorus members to attend the 8:00 A.M. rehearsal the following Sunday morning. "I praised their dedication and rhapsodized about the marvelous way they sounded in the new hall. I read them the long list of national and foreign press who were in attendance. I assured them that this would be a week they would remember for the rest of their lives. I asked them to go the extra mile for Eduardo, the orchestra, Dallas, Verdi, and their own pride. All but fifteen of the two hundred agreed to attend."

Tuesday, September 5. Tuesday was a crucial day for the arrival of needed materials. Within a span of two hours, seven different shipments were scheduled to arrive at the hall's loading dock: the organ from Philadelphia; Van Cliburn's Steinway, also coming from Philadelphia, but separately; thirty cello chairs that arrived later than the rest of the orchestra chairs because of modifications requested by the musicians; leather sofas and other furniture for the dressing rooms; Eduardo Mata's new podium; boxes of *Stagebills* for the opening week of concerts, and the benches for the choral risers. Miraculously, they all arrived, without damage or further delay. "It was *very* crowded at that little dock," remarked Mark Melson.

Marble had not arrived in time for the lobby banisters. Liener Temerlin cornered Gale Sliger, who had been working with the fortnight committee to ensure smooth production of all fortnight activities. "Gale, can we do something about these banisters?" She told him, "You can put any type of temporary top on here. We have even taken Styrofoam and glued it down, because it's easy to tear off when you get your marble in. If you put a coating of fiber paint on it, it will hold."[18] She got her green light to proceed. The architects made the molded, painted plastic foam look like faux marble, and another stop-gap measure was checked off the list.

During rehearsal that day, Meyerson and Stone grabbed Melson to ask him to ensure that the acoustical canopy would be raised all the way to the ceiling, exposing the organ pipes for an official orchestra portrait. The canopy was not yet fully operational. Instead of pushing a button, the process of raising or lowering it involved manual physical labor and could take six to eight hours. The portrait was scheduled for immediately before the September 6 concert, when the canopy would have to be in a lower position in order to have optimal acoustics for the "Salute to Dallas" performance. In theory, the canopy position would have little effect on the sound of the organ because the instrument was not yet fully installed; however, its largest pipes would be called upon in the Mahler *Resurrection* Symphony. More to the point, with the façade fully in place, the visual impact of the organ would be considerable, even if the instrument's full glory lay in the future.

Charles Young of the Pei firm says, "We felt that the organ looked peculiar when you're covering the top of it with the canopy, partly lowered. In fact, Ross Perot was perturbed about that, because Mimi Lay [Amelia Lay Hodges] was a great friend of his, and she donated the money for the organ in honor of her late husband."[19]

Leonard Stone confirms Perot's consternation. "Ross was concerned that the photographs taken at the opening would be the ones that the world would recognize for years to come. When I say raising the canopy was a manual process, I mean you didn't have 5,000 Hebrew slaves pulling the ropes, but it took hours for this thing to be raised, because the rigging was incomplete. Then it had to be dropped back into place, where Russell wanted it for optimum acoustical results, because we had the world press there. Russell's concern was not the look; it was the sound. Ross, I. M., and Mort's concern at that point was the look. I thought that Mort was in a somewhat uncomfortable position. This great benefactor, his great friend, and his boss and mentor wanted it one way, and yet he in his heart of hearts knew that acoustically it had to be another way."[20]

Meyerson was adamant about accommodating Perot's request. The only other possibility for the orchestra portrait was Thursday morning. Once again, the orchestra was asked to vote for a schedule change. Again, they approved it. "I really have to hand it to the orchestra," Melson says. "They were magnificent in terms of cooperating. They knew the problems; they knew the stress. We invoked the emergency clause for the 8:00 A.M. Sunday rehearsal, but just to show up and do it, and then approve these other changes was a really noble effort."[21]

Melson hastily set about rescheduling the photo shoot for first thing Thursday morning and arranging for the canopy to be raised to its uppermost position. According to Charles Young, "The night before, we had twenty guys up there, manually hoisting this forty-ton canopy with winches to get it up as high as it had been designed to be." Young and Melson located a photo studio that could enlarge the photographs in four hours, because Perot wanted them posted in the lobby in time for Friday night's first grand opening fortnight concert, so that visitors could see the hall with the organ visible in its full glory.

Wednesday, September 6. D-Day had arrived: the first public performance in the Meyerson. The hall would be inaugurated by a free concert, featuring soloist Isaac Stern performing the Beethoven Violin Concerto. The invitation-only event was styled "A Salute to Dallas."

Melson arrived at the hall early for rehearsal to find mismatched scraps of carpet all over the stage. "Artec was suddenly concerned that the hall would be too reverberant. They were trying to dampen the sound. You could not easily move the canopy at this point; they had it all the way up because of the morning photo shoot. That meant the sound was more reverberant. Eduardo was not at all pleased, but he continued with rehearsal. Afterward, he quietly asked me to have the stagehands remove all the carpet. We realized later that Artec had miscalculated, because there were no people in the hall. Based on the rehearsals, Russell Johnson expected that the hall would be too reverberant, so he put carpet on the stage. Subsequently, he found out that, with two thousand people in the hall, the carpet was unnecessary; in fact it made for a sound that was too dry."[22] Artec's Robert Wolff maintains that the acousticians' concern did not stem from reverberance but from balance, because the brasses, particularly trombones, were having a difficult time adjusting to the new environment. "We felt they had not yet reached a good balance with the rest of the orchestra," Wolff explains.[23]

In any case, Mata told Melson, "We don't want carpet on the stage; take it off." One hour after rehearsal ended, Melson observed Wolff and his assistants moving in lengths of carpet for the top two tiers of orchestra risers. He leapt onto the risers and ordered Johnny Gutierrez, the DSO's stagehand, to remove the carpet. "Bob Wolff started screaming right into my face, and we almost came to blows! I left Wolff thinking he had won the dispute, but Johnny Gutierrez removed most of the carpet by concert time."[24] Wolff acknowledges that he and Melson had a heated exchange but denies that they approached exchanging blows. His recollection is that, during the intervening time, the orchestra was able to achieve the right balance, and the issue became moot.[25]

In the main lobby, Gale Sliger had been waiting since noon for the construction crew to finish its assembly and installation of the bar. She had a group of waiters from the Sheraton Park Central who would be tending bar and serving *hors d'oeuvres* that evening. Finally, she went over and leaned on the bar. "Guys, you know, it's two o'clock in the afternoon, and I've owned this bar since twelve. I thought maybe sometime you were going to get through. You see those twelve or fifteen men out there in that tent?" Sliger gestured outside, where the temperature was in the upper 90s, and a group of men stood beneath a catering tent. "They're waiting to set up this bar."

"Oh! Why didn't you say something?" came the answer. "We just need to finish off this front edge, but we don't have our stainless steel band here yet."

Sliger took charge. "Get some aluminum tape and tape it down, so nobody gets snagged or hurt," she instructed. They ran a little bead of special electrical tape around the problem area. The next day, when the stainless steel arrived, they removed the temporary fix and finished the bar as planned.[26]

By mid-afternoon, not all the seats had been installed; many of them were still encased in plastic shrink wrap. Most of the building was in place, but some of the lighting fixtures had not yet been mounted and wired. Last-minute arrangements still had to be made to place temporary carpet through much of the upper lobby, where the travertine installation remained incomplete.

DSO Artistic Administrator Victor Marshall left work at 5:00 P.M. to go home and change into dress clothes for the evening concert. "When I left for home, there were still huge piles of refuse and dirt, fifteen, twenty feet high, still in the lobby. I thought to myself, 'There's no way!' People were showing up in less than two hours! Workmen were crawling all over the building like ants. It was just unbelievable. When I came back at about 6:30, I was amazed. It was spotless."

Dallas in early September is still very hot. The temperature on September 6, 1989, crested at 100 degrees. The Meyerson was swarming with workmen all afternoon and into the early evening. Its air-conditioning system would have a baptism by fire: a full house in extreme conditions. Doors to the building were to open at 6:30; the auditorium would open for seating at 7:30. Workers used that last precious hour within the Eugene McDermott Concert Hall to screw in the last of the seats and complete the removal of shrink wrap. As the city's invited guests flocked to admire I. M. Pei's sweeping, radiant lobbies, outside the hall about fifty picketers had gathered to protest the unchecked expenditures and alleged extravagance of the building.

Opening Night

Inside, the crowd was clearly enthralled by the beauty, grandeur, and incomparable play of light streaming through the panels of Pei's glass conoid and lenses. The palpable excitement increased when the doors to the Eugene McDermott Concert Hall opened. As people walked in to locate their seats in a venue no one yet knew, one could hear sharp intakes of breath as they caught their first glimpse of the concert room. From the austere, bold drama and expanse of the lobby spaces, they were transported into warmth and intimacy. Earth tones prevailed: in the African makore and American cherry wood of the walls, in the rich upholstery of the seats. At the front of the hall, behind the musicians, the splendid façade of the still-incomplete organ dominated the room, providing a magnificent backdrop to the orchestra. Incandescent light glowed from onyx sconces on the sides of the music chamber. The effect was dazzling.

Mark Melson was standing in the lobby, watching people flood into the hall. He felt a tap on his shoulder. "Mark, can you find someone to remove the paint can from my box?" It was a loge patron who had come back downstairs from the box seat level.[27]

—❧—

THUS FAR, all the audience had heard was the hubbub of an eager crowd and the familiar sound of an orchestra tuning. They listened through a series of welcoming and congratulatory speeches by city and symphony dignitaries, including Mayor Strauss. Seconds before Maestro Mata lifted his baton to conduct the national anthem and Beethoven's *Consecration of the House* Overture, an orchestra member adjusted his chair, scraping the wooden floor of the stage. The sound was clearly audible, carrying to the back row of the uppermost grand tier, where people looked at each other in awe and astonishment, wondering for an instant if a chair inches from them had made the noise.

That night, styled by the symphony as "Prelude to Greatness," Isaac Stern was the guest soloist, playing Beethoven. On this momentous occasion, both soloist and repertoire took a back seat to the hall itself. The audience was enthralled, not only by the unique event, but also, especially, by the quality of the sound. Even those who did not know music well—and this was not a subscription audience; this was a cross-section of the city of Dallas—seemed to sense that they were hearing something extraordinary.

Over the course of the next two weeks, the audience's intuitive response was confirmed again, and then again. From local, national, and international press, the verdict was unanimous: The new symphony hall in Dallas was more than a success. It was a triumph.

Chapter Thirty

FORTNIGHT AND CRITICAL ACCLAIM

WITH "A Tribute to Dallas" having inaugurated the hall in its free concert for the citizens of Dallas, the elaborately planned fortnight began to unfold. Around Dallas, the Meyerson opening was the lead news story. Its attendant events drew their own media attention.

The national and international press descended on Dallas. London-based Dvora Lewis escorted a group of two dozen European journalists from seven countries to cover the opening. "I looked for major national papers in the major target territories. We had representatives from the UK, Germany, France, Spain, Austria, Switzerland, and the Netherlands," she remembers. "It was a remarkable group. They were very interested in going to Dallas. There was the link of I. M. Pei, who is a very high-profile figure in Europe because of the Pyramid at the Louvre. The one thing that was very much appreciated from the word go was the kind of hospitality which was offered to them."[1]

That hospitality included professional support. The symphony persuaded Trammell Crow Company to provide additional finished-out space on the third floor of the nearby LTV Center. About a week before the opening, the symphony had transformed that space into a massive temporary press center. They brought in fax and telex machines, copiers, word-processing computers with printers and office supplies, and installed several additional telephone lines. The symphony's development and marketing departments had worked with Bozell & Jacobs to assemble an enormous international list of press representatives who would be in Dallas at some point during the fortnight to cover the opening. The center was available to press representatives for ten hours a day. Staffing responsibilities for the center were shared by the Dallas Symphony and by Bozell & Jacobs. A full complement of press kits was available, not only for the Meyerson, but also for the Dallas Chamber of Commerce and Dallas Convention and Visitors Bureau, and for Artec Consultants and I. M. Pei & Partners. Translators from Southern Methodist University's foreign language departments were on call.[2]

The LTV press center provided a venue for communications, coffee breaks, impromptu interviews, and easy proximity to the Meyerson. Jane Holahan chuckles, "Russell Johnson used to come and just lurk in the press center, waiting to talk to people. We'd glance up and he would have approached a journalist and started chatting. They would find out who he was, put him in a corner and capture all his thoughts for the next hour! He had multiple interviews during that time. Everyone from the major European newspapers in Germany, Italy, Spain, all got equal time with Russell Johnson because he made himself so available. That was a big hit, and the press coverage was great."[3]

Dvora Lewis coordinated activities for the European and Asian press representatives; Clara Hinojosa, a member of Temerlin's fortnight committee, attended to the needs of a major press contingent from Mexico. "Naturally they were very interested in Eduardo [Mata] and what he thought of the hall," recalls Holahan. "One young man from the television group in Mexico City went to Love Field with Eduardo and filmed him in his private plane. They discussed flying as well as the new hall, in a sequence that was produced for Mexican television."

From Thursday, September 7, through Tuesday, September 12, visiting media representatives attended a whirlwind of nearly non-stop events from 8:30 A.M. to midnight. Continuous shuttle service to all concerts, receptions, and other special events such as dedication ceremonies, was available to major downtown hotels where visiting press were housed. Eduardo Chillida's sculpture, *De Musica*, was formally dedicated in Betty B. Marcus Park on the morning of September 7. A ceremony took place in the Grand Foyer overlooking the Reves Arch of Peace that evening at 6:00, dedicating the arch to the memory of Emery Reves and the international language of music. It was followed by a welcome reception and dinner for visiting media representatives at an elegant Highland Park residence.

Friday evening, September 8, was the first concert of the fortnight package. Official events were to begin with the dedication of Ellsworth Kelly's *Dallas Panels* on the east lobby wall outside the Meyerson's Green Room. Meyerson, Pei, and Johnson presided over a luncheon at the Fairmont Hotel. A pre-concert cocktail reception at the hall was to precede the gala opening concert. That afternoon, Gale Sliger had to move her buffet table in the Meyerson's east lobby three times. "It was twenty-one feet long, five feet wide, padded, and already full," she says. "I got a call from Mort Meyerson saying, 'We have got to move this. There's one flower you can see if you stand here that hits the edge of one of the Kelly panels.' It didn't touch it, but visually it blocked one of the panels. It took about a dozen men to move that table, because we didn't have time to reset it. I finally said, 'I either need to quit moving tables or we're not going to have an opening. You've got to get out of here. No more opinions!'"[4]

Meyerson was tense. Going into that unforgettable evening, his nerves were wracked. "We drove to the hall in my car, our kids and Marlene, my mother and my dad, and a reporter, the woman who wrote the American Airlines [magazine] article, 'The House that Mort Built.'[5] We parked underneath the building, where the players park. We were in tuxes. Everyone was tittering and pretty nervous. We were early, of course. We went up the elevator, then through the valet parking area into the lower lobby where the box office is. They had pictures of the musicians on the walls, and natural light was streaming down from upstairs. The crowd was buzzing. I was keyed up for the evening, and more than a little embarrassed, because I didn't know how to handle this. Marlene and the kids were very excited. I think my mother was very proud. We walked to the base of the stairs, and looked up at the limestone wall where the major donors are inscribed. At the top, it says 'Morton H. Meyerson Symphony Center.' Dad said, 'This is a great day for our family, and this is a wonderful thing for you, Morton. But I always knew I should have named you Junior!' Of course everybody cracked up. That broke the tension. We went on upstairs and to the reception."

————— ❧ —————

EACH of the patrons attending opening night had paid from $500 to $5,000 per ticket to attend the black-tie event. Their tickets included a lavish cocktail/dinner reception at the hall beginning at 6:30 P.M., with elaborate *hors d'oeuvres* and a dessert buffet following the performance. The pre-concert menu included salmon mousse, vegetable canapés, and lobster. Bartenders served champagne and Perrier.

Shortly after 8:15 P.M., when the gala audience had found its way to its seats, Liener Temerlin strode onto the stage to deliver a welcoming address. Adding to the excitement of the evening, he was able to announce that the DSA had received another round of donations and secured a line of credit. Together, those monies would enable repayment of the outstanding $32 million in debt that the city had underwritten.[6] Temerlin also asked the crowd to acknowledge H. Ross Perot, who was in attendance, seated in his center loge box.

Following Temerlin's remarks and the appreciative ovation for Perot, Maestro Mata and piano soloist Van Cliburn came onstage for the national anthem and Cliburn's performance of the Tchaikovsky First Piano Concerto. An ecstatic audience applauded enthusiastically after the first movement, then brought Cliburn and Mata back for five cheering curtain calls at the conclusion. For most of the audience, that was probably enough for one evening of listening, but the Dallas Symphony had bitten off another enormous chunk of repertoire. The second half was the Mahler *Resurrection* Symphony, which had so moved those present at the first rehearsals two weeks prior.

—⁓—

THE FORTNIGHT committee had engineered a wealth of free community events for persons not well-heeled or well-connected enough to participate in any of the exclusive, high-profile events surrounding the opening. With the assistance of the DSO's Victor Marshall, the Dallas Public Library mounted a special exhibit outlining the history of the Dallas Symphony. Southern Methodist University presented a lecture series. The Adams-Middleton Gallery in Dallas' trendy Oak Lawn neighborhood presented an exhibition of sculptor Eduardo Chillida's work. The Five Hundred, Inc., a local volunteer organization devoted to raising money for the cultural arts in Dallas, presented an early autumn street festival called Montage, staged within the Arts District on the still-undeveloped land between the Dallas Museum of Art and the Meyerson. With lectures, dances, exhibits, previews, and retrospectives, the Arts District boasted events in, adjacent to, and removed from the Meyerson Symphony Center. No one had any doubt where was the epicenter of all the celebratory activity.

Public tours of the hall also began on Saturday, September 9. The docents were thronged with crowds eager to tour the new building. Sharan Goldstein's full complement of more than 100 volunteers worked nonstop. Meyerson Manager Ted DeDee monitored building traffic, confirming that Goldstein and her group showed more than 10,000 visitors through the hall that first day. Between 10,000 and 20,000 more were expected on Sunday.

For visiting members of the press, Saturday morning began with a coffee at Southern Methodist University, preceding a symposium, "The Orchestra in the 21st Century." Maestro Mata was guest speaker at a luncheon briefing in the Sheraton-Dallas North Ballroom. At the Meyerson residence, the converted power station on Armstrong Avenue, Mort and Marlene Meyerson were hosts for a luncheon honoring the two chief corporate sponsors of the fortnight: Robert L. Crandall, chairman and president of American Airlines, and James D. Robinson III, chairman of the board of American Express.

That evening Mata had a breather from the podium, as the Kronos Quartet performed the first chamber music concert in the Meyerson. Before the concert, Neiman Marcus presented "American Fanfare," a salute to the patrons of the grand opening fortnight and honorary chairmen, Mr. & Mrs. Robert Crandall and Mr. & Mrs. James D. Robinson III. The party took place at the Neiman Marcus flagship store downtown. The pace was catching up with Leonard Stone. "I was so tired," he remembers, "that on the Saturday night that Neiman Marcus threw that fabulous party, I was in my apartment. I showered. I laid my black tie on the bed. I felt my knees crumbling and thought, 'I'll just take a fifteen-minute nap.' I woke up the next morning, still in my robe. I just collapsed. I cratered. I couldn't handle it any more. Later, people asked, 'Why didn't you show up?'"[7]

—⁓—

SUNDAY, September 10, began with a special breakfast at the Dallas Museum of Art, with Dallas developer and sculpture collector Raymond Nasher and Museum Director Richard Brettell guiding a tour of the I. M. Pei exhibit that had been mounted in honor of the hall opening. An architectural tour of Dallas followed. Members of the press had the option to attend a late-afternoon performance in the Cathedral Santuario de Guadalupe on Ross Avenue, one block south of the Meyerson. Some of the curious attended to hear that concert, which included the American premiere of Spanish Baroque music in a program called "Queen's Collection." Most, however, were glad for a break to catch a nap or a quick meal before the Dallas Symphony performance of the Verdi *Requiem* that evening in the Meyerson.

The society press had another midday party to cover. Mort and Marlene Meyerson were hosts again that day, this time for a luncheon honoring Henry Miller and the Cornerstone campaign committee, members of Meyerson's smaller unit, and patrons of the grand opening fortnight.

Somehow during that jam-packed weekend, public relations consultant Dvora Lewis arranged for Antony Thorncroft of the London *Financial Times* to have tea with Meyerson. "Tony writes on the business of the arts: sponsorship and funding," she explains. "To a European, the whole circumstance of how Ross Perot named the hall through this business connection as a tribute was of enormous interest. We always have culture gaps with European coverage of an American arts event. The way money is handled is quite different. We had an extraordinary and productive time with Mort. He put it across in a very civilized way."[8]

By Monday, September 11, the parties were easing up, but two significant musical events remained to display the full range of the hall's acoustical properties. Cellist Mstislav Rostropovich performed a solo recital that night. On Tuesday evening, September 12, soprano Leontyne Price sang the first solo vocal music in the Meyerson.

Rildia Bee Cliburn's seat collapsed during the Rostropovich recital, adding an unexpected note of embarrassment for the symphony center and provoking humorous reports from the press. According to British critic Russell Davies, who was in Dallas on behalf of London's *The Daily Telegraph:* "Backstage, [Rostropovich] pronounces the new hall '*fantastik!*' and indeed there has been one strange vindication of its acoustic when, in mid-performance, Van Cliburn's aged Mom fell off her prime dress-circle seat, achieving a most complex, yet well-rounded thump. As Russell Johnson admits, acoustics work in both directions. A little cough will go a long way."[9] Even the construction staff was honored during the fortnight. The Eugene McDermott Foundation and Mort and Marlene Meyerson underwrote a picnic luncheon for the workmen and the musicians in conjunction with a DSO rehearsal on Thursday, September 14.

Chapter Thirty-One

THE PUNCH LIST

Very few buildings are done when they officially open. Consider the private residence. If you build a house, you may be able to take occupancy on, say, the first of October. Throughout the autumn, however, you continue with finishes on flooring and walls, adding a decorative molding in a formal room, completing the landscaping. The chances are excellent that you have weekly punch lists for the contractor extending a month or two beyond your formal change of address.

For a large civic building, the punch lists are extensive. In the case of the Meyerson Symphony Center, September 1989 and the grand opening fortnight were major milestones, but not the end of the journey. During the months right after the opening, the emphasis was on dotting the "i's" and crossing the "t's" that had been left incomplete during the frantic weeks leading up to the fortnight. The punch lists turned out to be the easy part. Eventually, the delayed marble arrived. The painted Styrofoam, now pock-marked by finger holes from curious, tactile patrons, was removed in favor of the marble for the railings. The temporary carpet came out from various levels of the building and the last of the travertine went in.

While most of the press reaction was extremely positive, a few residual attempts at grousing dogged the building. Less than a week after the opening, some city council members questioned the rates the Meyerson was charging outside organizations. For eight hours of commercial rent, the fee was $3,000. The comparable fee at Fair Park Music Hall was $3,155. Nonprofit ensembles could rent the Meyerson at a reduced rate of $2,250 or, if they were city-supported, $1,500 for that same eight-hour period. At the Music Hall, comparable rates were

$2,438 and, for city-supported groups, $1,723. Attackers now challenged that the new hall should be generating more income. Defenders of the hall argued that the rent structure was scaled so as not to price local nonprofit organizations out of the Meyerson. Local press attacks had not entirely abated, but at least they appeared to be on the wane. The unquestioned acoustical and architectural success of the building appeared to have achieved what supporters had hoped.

The DSO discovered during the opening weeks that a set of stairs at the main Flora Street entrance was a serious hazard. Removing the stairs and replacing them with a gradual sloped area of marble travertine was an issue that was not addressed until summer 1990. At the conclusion of the Dallas Symphony's first season in the Meyerson, the restaurant remained unfinished because the building management was still negotiating with prospective concessionaires to operate it. Other unfinished spaces, including the choral rehearsal room, storage rooms, and the so-called corporate entertainment suites, were pushed farther back on the calendar in favor of more pressing and visible projects.

One was the glorious semicircular staircase leading from the lobby to the McDermott Concert Hall, which experienced some casualties with patrons slipping and falling. The City of Dallas put its foot down eventually and insisted that railings be installed as a safety feature. City code mandated that railings could not end abruptly in mid-air; otherwise, the railing termination could be construed as a hazard. Consequently, in 1995, railings with curlicues went in that terminated at an interior curve, theoretically removing any real or imagined physical danger that a patron might be impaled. Unfortunately, the designer of the railings had no aesthetic sense of cohesion with the balance of the Pei design. The railings created a minor uproar among Dallas aesthetes and had still not been replaced by mid-1999. The railings have, however, reduced the hall's liability exposure significantly, because patrons are no longer falling on the stairs.

The Onyx Lamps

When the hall opened, only temporary lamps had been installed in the lobby areas. Those could not be replaced until a donor was identified for the onyx lamps that I. M. Pei had designed. The subject had first come up in late 1988, when Pei suggested to George Schrader, "The hall lacks glitter. We need something . . . I've personally designed some onyx lamps that will give it the glitter it needs."

"How much money is it going to take?" Schrader asked, already suspicious. His long experience with Pei had taught him well.

"We can do it for $285,000. That's for lamps on the bars, and lamps on the posts."

"OK, let's talk to two or three people, but if we raise the money, I don't want it to be *one penny* above that figure!"[1] Other matters took precedence, and no donor was identified for the lamps. Pei tried again a few months later.

Stanley Marcus remembers receiving a phone call from the architect about two months before the hall opened. "I need to see you," Pei declared. They met for lunch in Dallas.

He told Marcus, "I'm having great trouble satisfying myself that everything is just as it should be. I think our lobby lacks sparkle. I have only myself to blame on that. It's not festive enough."

"I. M., if you can fix it without it costing anything, you've got full backing. But we don't have any money left, period."

"Oh," he said, "It won't take much money."

Marcus had heard that before. (Today, he says, "He is *the best* salesman I've ever run into in my life! He never takes issue with you. He always skirts the issue. And you end up in his lap!") Pei continued to explain his idea. "I can just visualize a few lamps that would give us a lot of sparkle. Then I think we have a perfect building."

"OK." The perfect building part sounded good. "How much is that going to cost?" Marcus asked.

"Oh, probably about two hundred thousand dollars." In his mind, Marcus automatically doubled that figure. He had enough experience with Pei to know that no estimate had a guaranteed maximum. But he agreed to seek a donor.

In conjunction with the preparations for the grand opening fortnight, Liener Temerlin had worked with Marcus and others to secure funding for various details in the hall. Temerlin suggested, "Why not approach Nancy?" Nancy Hamon was a major donor both to the Dallas Museum of Art and the Meadows School of the Arts at Southern Methodist University. Her interest lay in art, and she had declined to support the DSO before, on the ground that her late husband, Jake, disliked classical music.

Marcus was dubious about Temerlin's suggestion. He had solicited Jake Hamon many years before to serve on the board of the symphony. Hamon had declined in no uncertain terms. He told Marcus, "I don't like the symphony." Attempting to sway him, Marcus persisted, "Well, that's just the trouble. Too many parents in the past didn't like symphony, and their children didn't get the benefit of symphonic education. You can be a great benefactor."

I. M. Pei's onyx lamps. (*Photo by James E. Langford*)

Hamon didn't buy it. "Don't tell *me* that I never knew anything about symphony, because my mother dragged me to the Chicago Symphony for two years when I was nine or ten years old. I had to go every goddamn Saturday afternoon of the season! I got more symphony education than I wanted, and I've hated it ever since!" he told Marcus.

"He turned me down flat," Marcus recalled. "Of course, Nancy was trying to do what her husband would have liked."[2]

Temerlin came up with the idea that, because Pei had designed the onyx lamps, they could be presented to Nancy Hamon as art. He and Marcus invited Nancy Hamon to lunch. "The interesting thing was that she didn't like the symphony at all," Marcus chuckles. "She never goes to it, except pops concerts. We knew she didn't like music, but we knew she liked art." He and Temerlin debated about the optimal approach.

"Maybe we should try to have some fun with this," Temerlin finally suggested. "Tell her, 'We are approaching you as music lovers wearing the false costume of being artists,' or something like that."

Marcus was skeptical. "She'll laugh you right out of the room! You can't put anything over on Nancy. She used to be in show business, back in the days when they threw vegetables!"[3] That reminder of Nancy Hamon's youth gave Temerlin another idea. "I sent someone to the Farmers Market to pick up a basket of fresh tomatoes," he recalls. "We took her to lunch at the Mansion on Turtle Creek and prefaced our presentation by placing the tomatoes in the center of the table. 'If you want to, you can reach in and throw tomatoes at us any time you want!' From time to time as we outlined our proposal about the lamps, she reached toward the basket as if to throw one at us, but she listened through. At the end, she said, 'That's the biggest crock I've ever heard in my life!—but I loved the entertainment, so I'll give you the money for the lamps.'"[4]

According to Marcus, Nancy Hamon remains very proud of her contribution to the Meyerson. Ironically, even $400,000 was not enough to cover the cost of the onyx lamps. After Marcus and Temerlin secured the Hamon donation, Schrader repeatedly reminded Pei's project architect, George Miller, "Keep in mind, that's all the money there is. *No more money!* $285,000, that's it."

Of course, when Pei's people obtained firm prices on the lamps, the cost exceeded $285,000. George Schrader demanded to know what they were going to do to bring the figure back within budget. Pei told him, "We'll take the bar lights out."

Some months later, Schrader had lunch with Pei, Ted Amberg, and George Miller at the Mansion on Turtle Creek. I. M. said, "George, I've just come back from California, and I've looked at the lamps, and they're spectacular. But you won't believe what happened."

Schrader thought to himself, *Yeah, I won't*. He said, "Yes, I would."

Pei continued, "The man showed me the slices of onyx, and I said they're too small. He insisted they were according to my plans. I said, they're not. And you won't believe what happened!"

Schrader shook his head. He'd been dealing with I. M. Pei now for more than twenty years. He had no idea what Pei was going to tell him, but he knew it was going to cost.

Pei beamed. "He's made the bar lamps too!"

Schrader said, "Well, we can only pay for the lamps covered by the $285,000 we committed to."

Pei said, "I'll help raise the money, or I'll pay for it myself."

According to Schrader, the DSA was able to raise some of the additional funds. "In the final settlement, however," he says, "we refused to pay. He agreed to pick up half the cost for the bar lamps, and we paid for the other half. I. M.'s partners got a big kick out of it!"[5]

NationsBank and EDS Gifts

Two major corporate gifts came in on the heels of the Meyerson's opening. The first, from NationsBank (the bank has since become Bank of America), was $2 million for capital construction for the building, to be paid out at $200,000 *per annum* for ten years. The gift was solicited by Dolores Barzune, Stanley Marcus, and Liener Temerlin. Temerlin made the formal presentation. "I went to see Ken Lewis, who was at the time the president of Nations-Bank, to ask him for $2 million. I had put this enormous presentation together. I began by telling him what this would do for NationsBank and for the symphony. He said, 'I'll do it.' I hadn't been in there two minutes. Maybe one minute, and he said, 'We'll do it.' I said, 'Oh no you don't! You're taking all the fun out of it! You've got to let me do my spiel!' He laughed and said, 'OK, we'll listen.' For fun and games, I went through it."[6] The bank's pledge was officially announced in October 1989, and the first payment was received in February 1990. NationsBank made an early payment of $400,000 in August 1993 to assist the Dallas Symphony in meeting its obligation to the City of Dallas.

The second corporate gift came from EDS. After General Motors took over EDS, the DSO thought of them as off limits, because the Perot gift naming the hall for Meyerson was deemed to have been an EDS gift, even though it came from the Perot Family Foundation. According to Leonard Stone, "Once Ross Perot was disassociated from EDS, we thought that EDS in its own right might be approached. A senior executive of EDS, and one of the finest gentlemen I have ever known, was Davis Hamlin. He loved music, and had been a member of the DSA Executive Board for many years. Mort Meyerson brought him to our attention. Hamlin once said to me that the most appropriate time to approach EDS for a gift was after they had two superb consecutive quarter financial results. I never forgot that. I kept watching the business pages.

"Right after the Meyerson opened, EDS had two remarkable quarters. In spring 1990, I called Davis. He apprised me of some interesting intelligence. Les Alberthal, who was then the head of EDS, had played trombone in a marching band in his student days, so he had a feel for music. As a result of the less-than-amicable departure of Perot and Meyerson from the GM/EDS relationship, we asked Stanley Marcus if he would visit Les Alberthal, based upon my understanding that the timing was right as a result of the clue that Davis Hamlin had given me.

"Stanley was now very actively committed to helping us raise the final amounts of money to pay for this building. He had taken over the role that Henry Miller had played. Stanley laid out the following predicate to Les Alberthal: The two most important gifts are the first gift to launch a project and the final gift to meet the goal. A gift of $2 million from EDS could close the campaign."[7]

EDS was twenty-five years old, and the approach was successful. Seven months after the Meyerson opened, the EDS gift was announced, allowing the Dallas Symphony to clear its hall-related debt.[8]

Use Agreement

Until the Dallas Symphony moved into the hall, for a period of years most of its energies and focus were on building the hall, paying for it, and getting the orchestra settled in its new home. Nine months after the grand opening fortnight, Richard Freling assumed the DSA Board presidency in May 1990, and the focus shifted from the past and present to the future. "We had, by then, understood that we had one of the great concert halls of the world," says Freling. "What were we going to do? Certainly the orchestra was a good orchestra, but it had lots of room to grow. How would we get from here to there? How would we 'grow' an orchestra that was comparable in quality and prestige to the hall?

"We began scrutinizing every aspect of our operations and tried to focus on our future goals. Ultimately we engaged [the management consulting firm of] Booz Allen to undertake a *pro bono* study for us and to help us develop a vision statement. The engagement of Andrew Litton as music director, the hiring of Gene Bonelli as president, our focus on education and technology as a means of catapulting the orchestra to national recognition—they've all been pieces of the puzzle. The genesis of this took place during my presidency. It continued and was brought to fruition under Howard [Hallam, DSA president, 1992–94] and remains an ongoing process."[9]

After the hall opened to such universal critical acclaim, criticism receded to the background. "You hardly heard anyone say anything negative about the Meyerson after that," recalls Howard Hallam. "But it did remain an issue at city hall, because operating the Meyerson turned out to be an enormous burden for the city. When I was the president, I used to worry about them all the time. The Meyerson was taking in slightly less than $1 million per year, and it cost about $2 million a year for operating expenses: utilities, maintenance. The city had to pick up that annual million dollar shortfall. I believe that the city staff realized that the revenue from the building would never match the expenses. The building was conceived and approved at a time when the City of Dallas was rich. By the time the Meyerson was completed, Dallas was in a depression. The city was scraping for every dollar it could. Anything that was losing money stood out like a red light."[10]

The annual operation agreement between the city and the symphony was the most complex issue to be resolved after 1989. Four city managers were involved between the mid-1980s and mid-1990s: Charles Anderson, Richard Knight, Jan Hart, and Charles Ware. At the time of the opening in September 1989, the Dallas Symphony gave the building back to the City of Dallas as thanks for the city's contribution. In its capacity as principal tenant, the symphony was to pay a nominal amount to the city as rent.

When the hall opened, with the Dallas economy still in recession, property values declined and the city's tax base decreased. The DSO was committed to giving the city its share of the rent, but the city was unable to maintain its percentage of upkeep costs. Fred Hoster, the DSO's general manager, called Rufus Shaw, a political consultant with whom he had worked at SMU before joining the symphony staff in 1982. Shaw was a prominent member of the African-American community with clout in city politics. "We've got a problem, and we believe we need your help," Hoster said. "Would you consider joining the symphony board to help us out? Or, alternatively, we will pay you as a consultant to get this situation resolved."

Rufus Shaw replied, "Well, I don't give a damn about the symphony, *but* my wife does. If you put her on the board, then I will help you out. She brings some politics along with mine."[11] Shortly thereafter, in May 1992, Lynn Flint Shaw was voted to the DSA Board of Governors. Her appointment coincided with Leonard Stone's departure from Dallas to return to his native Canada to assume the executive directorship of the Calgary Philharmonic and Eugene Bonelli's departure from the deanship of the Meadows School of the Arts at SMU to succeed Stone at the helm of the symphony.

During the managerial transfer, the issue of the use agreement temporarily took a back seat. In fairly short order, it floated to the top of Bonelli's stack of things to be done. Bonelli says, "When I assumed the position [of symphony president], there was a big dispute with the city over the implementation of the original operating agreement. The original procedure set up was that the Cultural Affairs Commission would make an annual grant to the symphony to cover the rent. When we went to a 14-1 council, some of the minority members felt that this was an elitist organization, and they wanted more of the cultural dollars to be absolutely guaranteed to minority groups—so a percentage of the cultural budget would automatically go only to minority groups. As a result, the Cultural Affairs Commission appropriation to the DSO was no longer equaling the rent being charged to us by the city. We refused to pay the difference, saying that it was a violation of our agreement. That went on for a couple of years, so that the city was carrying a debt from the symphony on its books. The auditors began to raise Cain about that, which finally put pressure on the city to settle. We were prepared to see this go to court, because we felt it was legally and morally right. We had this agreement with the city, and it wasn't our fault that their procedure to implement it wasn't working."[12]

Two months prior to Bonelli's assumption of the DSA presidency on July 1, 1993, Howard Hallam moved into the chairmanship of the DSA Board of Governors. Bonelli and Hallam enlisted Lynn Flint Shaw's assistance almost immediately, because she knew many members of the city council and other persons in the minority community. The first thing she told Hallam was that the symphony had a serious image problem with the city that needed to be rectified. According to Shaw, "Three years after the hall opened, the ancient elitist accusation was still there. The symphony played dead white men's music. It was 'only the rich go to the symphony,' 'only the rich support the symphony,' 'only the whites support the symphony.' The minority community didn't feel welcome."[13]

Shaw proved to be a savvy contributor to the DSA Board, recognizing that its various task forces assigned to the problem were ineffective. She suggested to Bonelli and Hallam that a direct, personal approach to City Manager Jan Hart was in order. The process of ironing out various aspects of the use agreement took nearly two years, during which time Hart left the city to return to the private sector, and John Ware succeeded her as city manager.

Ware was a personal friend of the Shaws. Lynn Flint Shaw was able to convince him, diplomatically, that the two assistant city managers assigned to the Meyerson use agreement negotiations were not conversant with the arts. Ware did some internal juggling and assigned Mary Suhm to oversee the Cultural Affairs Commission. As Shaw remembers, "Mary Suhm, Frank Poe, who's with the city over events and facilities, Gene Bonelli, Al Meitz, Christina Zertuche [then the DSO's director of public relations and public affairs], and I got together every two to three weeks to iron out all the difficulties. Then we brought in Dave Morrison, an attorney with Thompson & Knight who was the DSA Board secretary, to discuss the legal matters. It took Dave and Tracy Pounder, a City of Dallas attorney, about four months to resolve all the legal definitions."[14]

The legal complications arose because a city rule stating that its contracts are binding was largely negated by the fact that no city council can bind an upcoming city council. Because the makeup of the Dallas City Council changes every two years, any contract is in a near-constant state of flux. "That was one of the political problems we had to look at," Shaw says. "The city naturally wants to do what's in its best interest."[15]

Bonelli recalls working very closely with the city to find a common ground. "We worked on the political side to convince the minority council members of the value of the symphony to all the citizens of Dallas. Finally, we worked out a revision of the use agreement where we paid $1 a year rent. That passed unanimously through city council."[16]

Shaw helped develop the use agreement stipulating the $1 annual rent, in return for which the symphony provided the city with free parks concerts, SundayFest concerts, and the annual African-American and Hispanic festival concerts: a cool $1.6 million in programming and performances. Shaw explains, "We wanted to get out of the loop whereby we had to go before the Cultural Affairs Commission each year to ask them for money." Under the terms of the new agreement, the DSO had use of the building virtually rent-free in exchange for its gift of free concerts to the city. Shaw also encouraged a structure whereby specific changes in number of concerts from year to year could be negotiated through the assistant city manager staff, rather than through appearances before city council or council subcommittees. The reason was that, while the council is in an almost perpetual state of flux, the city manager staff customarily has longer tenure, frequently approaching or exceeding twenty years.

The contract between the city and the symphony was renegotiated early in 1995.

—❧—

BECAUSE the City of Dallas is responsible for the Meyerson's maintenance and upkeep, and because of the city's contractual arrangement with the DSO, the likelihood that the hall will ever become a profit center is slim. The deficit is far less than anyone had anticipated, because the building is used for so many functions beyond what was initially forecast. In fiscal 1997–98, for example, Bruce MacPherson, now serving as the Meyerson's overall manager, booked more than 500 events at the hall in addition to rehearsals and setup/takedown hours. "The first year, 1989–1990, was a good year with 296 events, but I don't think anyone ever truly expected it to continue growing as it has," MacPherson commented in 1996. "We have not experienced a year yet where the amount of activity in this building did not increase over the previous year. Despite this increased usage, our staff, for all intents and purposes, is still the same size."[17]

As manager, MacPherson oversees a staff of twelve full-time persons, including an operations manager, a technical director, and three stage technicians. "One of the Dallas Symphony's rights, as the primary tenant, is first selection of dates for any given season. By the end of September every year, they have to give us their schedule for the year that follows. Once they submit that schedule, we are free to book and rent the spaces to anyone who wants it." There is no cancellation penalty. MacPherson has found that anything released is done so early that the available slot is taken up by another group or event. But he does keep busy.

"I consider myself a flight controller," he says, "because I'm the one who determines how to line up the planes [user groups], and how to let them take off in the proper order to maximize our scheduling options. My busiest time of the year is October. I've got fifty groups who've now been performing here since the year we opened and have returned every year since, whether for one event, two events a year, or a series. As a result, I've had to come up with a system that's fair to all. They are mostly arts groups; they want to start their planning for the following year, to prepare their marketing brochures. They're all biting the bullet each year come September to find out what dates they can get.

"If the Symphony wants something else, they have to come back to me to see if it's available, because my regulars are hitting me up now for two seasons ahead. I'm happy to say, every group that's wanted to perform or have a function here has done so. Despite the fact that we've gotten so many more frequent users, we've found a way to do it. Our staff bends over backwards to make that happen. That's what the building is here for. It's not here to sit dark; it's here to be used."[18]

By the late 1990s, the annual budget to operate and maintain the building had leveled out at $2.6 million. Because of Dallas' climate, utilities comprise thirty-seven percent of that figure, an unusually high proportion. The cost of air conditioning is exacerbated by the size of the building and the extensive glass surfaces that admit sunlight on the hot days—up to six months a year in North Texas—and by the increase in events each year. Those factors all play big roles in the cost. "I honestly don't think people envisioned it being used for trade shows, receptions, banquets, wedding ceremonies, photo and film shoots," MacPherson declares. "It's a very user-friendly environment, a great thing for the city."[19]

Choral Rehearsal Room

Early plans for the hall had included administrative and rehearsal space for the Dallas Symphony Chorus. Those areas were early casualties of the 1982 redesign that reduced the number of above-ground lobby levels from two to one, and of the budget constraints that led to so many enhancements being cut in the lean years of the mid-1980s.

A couple of years after construction began, the chorus made another appeal to the Dallas Symphony Association. They had identified space beneath the concert room that had originally been allocated to the hydraulic piano lift. The chorus was able to strengthen its plea by suggesting internal resources: architect Brenda Stubel, a DSO chorus member since 1978. Stubel conducted some planning studies to determine the feasibility of finishing out the piano lift space as a choral rehearsal room. The area was still dirt in a subterranean cavity. As J. W. Bateson began to place piers in the mid-1980s, Stubel was able to refine her layout and demonstrate that, architecturally, the choral rehearsal room was a plausible option. In the interim, the DSO Chorus rehearsed at First Baptist Church in downtown Dallas.

Stubel collaborated with Bill Johnson (he is unrelated to Russell Johnson of Artec), an acoustical consultant with whom her architectural firm had dealt on prior projects. Ideally, they wanted to approximate the acoustic qualities of the McDermott Concert Hall. Equally important was sound isolation, so that if the chorus were warming up during the orchestral first half of a program, it would not interfere with the performance taking place upstairs.

In 1985, the estimated budget for finishing out a choral rehearsal room was $100,000. Inevitably that figure rose because of delays analogous to those that affected the hall, combined with inflation. Also, the original budget did not take risers into account. Fortunately, the chorus received seed money from several donors, including two members of the board of governors. The final cost was approximately $200,000, after some adjustments in the HVAC system. The choral rehearsal room was inaugurated on October 31, 1994. The room is the property of the Dallas Symphony Association. The DSO Chorus has priority use.

Chapter Thirty-Two

OPUS 100: THE LAY FAMILY CONCERT ORGAN

I would argue that the Meyerson Symphony Center and its new Fisk organ are alone worth a trip to Dallas just for the visual and architectural splendor of both the organ and the room. . . . the Fisk organ is, by all accounts, an enormous success. Some who have come to hear it regard it as the finest organ in the world. This is, of course, a matter of taste and opinion, but by any reckoning, this is one of the most important organs to have been built in this or any century.[1]

JAMES C. MOESER, PRESIDENT,
AMERICAN GUILD OF ORGANISTS

FROM the earliest discussions and sketches in 1981, an organ was part of the plan for Dallas' concert hall. Artec wanted an organ because it is an integral part of every great concert hall. From an acoustical standpoint, an organ presented both advantages and disadvantages. A massive façade could provide additional reflective surfaces beneficial to room acoustics, helping to disperse sound even when the organ was not being played. On the other hand, Russell Johnson thought the organ might also absorb sound in orchestral performances, and he considered a shutter to close it off when it was not in use.[2] In the final analysis, the hall Artec was planning would provide a splendid environment in which to hear an organ, whether solo or as part of the orchestra. Meyerson's committee members had seen impressive organs on their European tour in London, Amsterdam, and Vienna, and they recognized the importance a major instrument would have as a component of the concert hall.

Logically, the members of the smaller unit turned to Eugene Bonelli, their preeminent musician, for advice about how to obtain an organ. He assembled an organ subcommittee in April 1981, enlisting Dr. Robert T. Anderson, distinguished professor of organ and sacred music at Southern Methodist University. "I was really the *de facto* 'chair' of the organ committee," says Anderson. "When Gene Bonelli needed information, he asked me." Anderson tapped a number of his colleagues in the community: Howard Ross, director of music ministries and organist at Dallas' Episcopal Church of the Transfiguration; Jody Lindh, director of music ministries at University Park United Methodist Church; Jim Livengood, organist and choirmaster at St. Mark's School of Texas and Holy Nativity Episcopal Church in Plano, Texas; and Canon Dr. Paul Lindsley Thomas, music director (now emeritus) and then composer-in-residence at St. Michael and All Angels Episcopal Church.

Anderson's group had three principal tasks. The first was to select a builder. The second was to work through the design parameters of the instrument, in collaboration with that builder, Artec Consultants, and I. M. Pei. Finally, when the instrument was ready for installation and voicing, Anderson and his group would oversee that process.

The builder selection process was nearly as exhaustive as the search for an architect and acoustician had been. Anderson's plan was to investigate the style and capabilities of various organ builders, then recommend a small group of candidates who would be invited to submit a proposal for the concert hall organ. Russell Johnson presented Anderson's organ committee with a group of proposals, ideas and literature he had solicited from various European organ builders: Schuke, a Berlin builder; Beckerath of Hamburg; Marcussen, from Aabenraa, Denmark; Brunzema, an organ builder from North Germany; and Flentrop of Zaandam, the Netherlands.

"It was wonderful to have an acoustics expert who knew and liked organs!" recalls Bob Anderson. "Russell's list of builders showed that he was informed, but he presented his list with no strings attached. The organ builder for the concert hall was to be chosen by the organ committee. We proceeded the same way I customarily do: ask the builders to submit proposals—but do not tell them what to do. You won't know what *they* know if you have them bid on a set proposal. We recommended Marcussen [Denmark], Rieger [Austria], Schuke [Berlin], Klais [Bonn], and C. B. Fisk [Gloucester, Massachusetts]."[3]

Fisk was the only American builder on the list. Anderson believed this was important. "You see, we all wanted a tracker organ," he later said. (Tracker action is the traditional key action of the pipe organ, in which a thin wooden strip called a tracker connects the key mechanically to a valve beneath the pipe. When the player depresses a key, air enters the pipe, giving him more control over attacks and releases than with the electronic action used for the same purpose in many twentieth-century organs. Fisk improved on this principle, as we shall see.) According to Anderson, tracker action provides better communication for the player and often takes up less space. Gregory Bover of C. B. Fisk elaborates: "There are fewer things to go wrong in a tracker instrument. It's easier to fix. And aside from the musical question of the feedback that the organist gets from the feel of the keyboard, nothing beats a tracker for longevity."[4] Bover notes that the oldest extant playing organ in the world, a tracker instrument in Sion, Switzerland, was built in 1390.

Anderson and his organ subcommittee acknowledged that the European companies had more experience building large tracker organs, whereas the Americans had limited exposure.

But Anderson was stubborn in his support of Charles Fisk, his good friend for many years, whom he considered a brilliant organ builder and a fine engineer. Anderson was convinced that Fisk could plan and build a magnificent instrument that would suit the needs of a major concert hall.

Anderson's conviction was strengthened on the basis of Charles Fisk's plans for an organ in San Francisco's Louise Davies Hall. Fisk had been invited to be organ consultant for the job. According to Steven Dieck, then project manager in charge of production in the workshop at C. B. Fisk and now its president, there was no promise that an organ would go in, but the planners wanted to ensure that the hall was designed to accommodate an organ, should the opportunity materialize. Ironically, San Francisco opted not to go with the Fisk design, choosing instead one with an electropneumatic action from an Italian builder, Fratelli Ruffatti of Padua. "Charles [Fisk] thought that he had an edge," says Dieck. "He was tremendously disappointed that none of his ideas were carried through. He felt as if he had wasted his time."[5] All the same, that disappointment strengthened his commitment to the concept he had developed. Charles Nazarian, Fisk's visual designer, explains, "The Davies Hall experience made Charles [Fisk] feel very determined that if he had a chance to do a hall right and an organ right at the same time, *that* would be the project of a lifetime."[6]

Although discussions about an organ in Dallas had taken place since the earliest stages of the concert hall project, no organ builder would have been able to commence design without knowing the nature of the room in which the organ would reside. Consequently, the Johnson/Pei plans for the audience chamber had to reach a certain point before formal solicitation of organ proposals could get underway. Specifically, the DSO requested, in September 1981, that Artec Consultants isolate the area of the concert hall relating to the organ, providing a full description of the systems associated with its performance areas, a cost projection for those systems, and estimated square footage.

Robert Wolff of Artec responded with a summary of space and equipment required to support performances including organ, enumerating acoustic walls (a shutter in front of the organ), rigging, and other items requiring wiring, plus special organ lighting and acoustic adjustment banners and curtains.[7] His space and dollar figures allowed Stewart Donnell of Hanscomb Roy to proceed with formal cost estimates.

Eugene Bonelli's letters inviting proposals for the Dallas organ went out January 26, 1982. Responses arrived promptly from Marcussen, Rieger, Schuke, and Klais, but not from Fisk. Anderson was convinced that Charles Fisk was not responding because of the disappointment in San Francisco. (Louise Davies Hall opened in September 1980. The decision to go with the Ruffatti organ there followed that autumn.) "I saw Gene Bonelli every day because we worked in the same building at SMU," Anderson remembers. "I told him, 'We prefer the concept of Fisk's designs. Let's not waste time. Why don't you call Charles and tell him that we're at the point of making the decision, we're most interested in what he has to say, we're serious about working with him, and we hope he'll present something in a timely fashion so that we will have what we need.' His ingenious concept for San Francisco, fresh and American —not 'old world'—impressed us greatly. I had never seen a design such as Charles's from an American builder—I could almost say from any builder in the world."[8]

Bonelli acted on Anderson's suggestion, telephoning Fisk in March 1982. "We've gotten responses from everybody except you," he told Fisk. "Are you interested in this?" Dieck remembers, "Bonelli managed to generate some enthusiasm on Charles's part to pick up his [Bonelli's] letter, which had been sitting in his in-box, and submit a response about a week later." Fisk's proposal was dated March 18, 1982.[9]

Dieck had considerable personal reservations about building an organ in a symphony hall. "Our present-day history does not show that an organ is used much in a concert hall. Conductors don't seem to favor them. When Charles was feeling me out about building this organ, my question was, 'Why should we invest more than two years of fifteen people's time, on a project in which the organ is going to sit there and look pretty?' He told me, 'The people in Dallas want to build the best organ they can, and they want it used. They're going to put the pieces together, financially, through endowment, so that the organ *will* be used.' He had to work on me quite a bit to get me enthused about the project, but he persuaded me."

The primary difference between a concert hall instrument and a church organ is volume of sound, because a concert instrument must both blend and be heard when it is played with full orchestra. Dieck says, "We had never heard an organ in the United States that we thought worked successfully with the orchestra. We realized that we had to develop an organ capable of producing sound a couple of notches louder than anything we had ever worked with before. We didn't want an instrument that was *always* extremely loud, however, because it often needs to be quiet. Our challenge was to design an instrument with flexibility: to be very soft, very loud, and yet blend with the orchestra."[10]

Anderson remembers, "Fisk's was the smallest organ and the most expensive proposal that we received. We were talking, initially, about a cost of $713,000. Steve Dieck had written to Leonard Stone that the instrument would cost between $625,000 and $825,000. With the information he had at that time, that was correct. At that point, we thought the hall would open in 1986." As with many other aspects of the hall affected by the delay, the cost of the organ was to increase significantly.

By the time the organ subcommittee completed its evaluation of builders in June 1982, Bonelli anticipated that the cost of the organ would be approximately $800,000, including a movable electric console.[11] Allowing for the cost of the additional organ-related equipment that Artec had specified, the symphony believed that a $1 million donation would be adequate to cover the cost of the organ.

The organ subcommittee evaluated proposals submitted by the four European builders and Fisk. As chair, Bonelli reported to the smaller unit, on June 23, 1982, its recommendation of C. B. Fisk as the builder for the organ, asserting that it had no second choice. If Fisk did not accept the offer, or if the committee rejected the selection, Bonelli's committee was going to have to start from scratch. The instrument would take approximately four years to build and install. The smaller unit voted unanimously in favor of accepting the subcommittee's recommendation. They agreed that after the bond election scheduled for August 3, a search should begin for a donor to underwrite the cost of the organ.

The large concert hall committee formally voted in favor to appoint Fisk as the organ builder in February 1983. The City of Dallas was to contract with C. B. Fisk as a consultant responsible for the integration of the organ design within the audience chamber design. Initially, an agreement for preliminary design services was executed in April 1983 between C. B. Fisk, Inc., and the City of Dallas. Project Manager George Miller of I. M. Pei & Partners requested information from Dieck concerning the structural requirements of the organ.[12]

The final contract, executed more than five years later, specified a guaranteed maximum dollar figure of $1 million. Inevitably, that figure was exceeded, because the organ was subject to as many delays and design modifications as the building in which it would eventually reside.

—⁊⁊—

CHARLES Fisk developed the design with the assistance of Robert Cornell, senior design engineer, and Charles Nazarian, his long-time visual designer. They submitted their plan to the Dallas Symphony in spring 1983, spelling out the tonal design of the organ: itemizing the pipes, what stops the instrument would have, what colors (meaning musical timbres) would be available. They also proposed a preliminary visual design based upon the tonal concept at that time. Dieck explains, "The two aren't totally divorced; they have to be integrated. If you have a large number of pipes, a certain size case is necessary to accommodate those pipes. You wouldn't want to have a large case with just two or three pipes behind." Fisk specified a central organ console on a balcony-like projection above the stage's choral terrace.

The initial design specified a sixteen-foot façade. As the interior of the hall grew, so did the instrument. The concept evolved to a larger façade—with thirty-two-foot pipes rather than sixteen-foot—in April 1983, when Fisk personnel became aware of the unusual height of the proposed concert room. The thirty-two-foot façade seemed essential to deliver the visual grandeur and splendor of the organ. C. B. Fisk realized that many of the pipes were too large to be built in its facility, and the company subcontracted seventy pipes to August Laukhuff GmbH of Weikersheim, a West German specialty pipe organ supplier. Laukhuff was one of only three companies in the world that could manufacture such large pipes.

The original plans called for the organ case to be painted. After funding came through for the interior of the McDermott Concert Hall to be finished with African makore and

American cherry rather than plaster, the organ case was also changed to cherry. Inevitably, both changes meant increases in the cost.

—⁂—

AT THE time of C. B. Fisk's selection as the builder for the Dallas organ, Charles Fisk was terminally ill. When he died in December 1983, the concert hall committee was understandably concerned that, without his leadership, the organ might not match the quality of prior Fisk instruments. Bonelli dispatched Anderson to hear and play new instruments that were completed after Fisk's declining health precluded his direct supervision. In April 1984, Bonelli issued a reassuring memo to the smaller unit with a ringing endorsement of the Fisk legacy and team. "All of the staff which Mr. Fisk gathered over the years and his wife, Virginia, are continuing to operate the company. Recently, the Fisk Company has completed a four-manual organ for the gallery of the chapel at Stanford University in California. The head of our organ department, Dr. Robert Anderson . . . is absolutely convinced after seeing and playing this organ and talking with the technicians that the Fisk Company is indeed capable of continuing the excellent work for which the firm is noted. . . . Virginia Fisk verified that Charles had personally spent more time and involvement on the Dallas project than on any other work during the last year and a half of his life. We believe that he executed a brilliant design for the instrument which will be a great asset to the Symphony in the years ahead."[13] Bonelli further pointed out that without an executed contract and receipt of a down payment, Fisk would not schedule the Dallas organ in its official timetable. He urged identification of a donor to underwrite the cost of the instrument as soon as possible.

Prospects were being approached, but the DSA still had no commitment to underwrite the instrument. In February 1985, the association paid a deposit to C. B. Fisk, Inc., to ensure placement in Fisk's production schedule. One happy coincidence of that phase of the contract occurring when it did was the number that C. B. Fisk assigned to it: Opus 100. The company assigns its numbers in the order that contracts are executed. The Palmer Episcopal Church in Houston signed for C. B. Fisk's Opus 99 shortly before Dallas committed. Dieck pointed out to Anderson and Bonelli, "We need to get our contract signed so that Dallas gets the next number." Bonelli and Anderson were able to accelerate the process. Not only was Opus 100 secured for the Meyerson, but also Opus 101 was reserved for a new organ at Southern Methodist University, in Caruth Auditorium at the Meadows School of the Arts.

C. B. Fisk officials ultimately negotiated a cost-plus contract—actual cost plus ten percent profit—because they recognized that the building design was still evolving. That meant uncertainties, changes, and unforeseeable circumstances. "Because this was our first concert hall instrument, we realized that, if we didn't price it right, it could easily be our last," Dieck explains. "We insisted on the cost-plus contract, which had some flexibility. Usually you'd go to an organ builder and ask, 'OK, we've got a million dollars. What can you build me for it?' We would specify what pipes, what it would look like. In this project, there were so many unknowns that we felt we could not do that."[14]

The donation for the organ came from Amelia Lay Hodges, the widow of Herman Lay, a co-founder of Frito-Lay who later became chairman of PepsiCo. Herman Lay had loved organ music. Henry Miller approached Hodges about a gift to fund the Meyerson instrument, and in October 1985, she offered $1 million to the Dallas Symphony Association for design, construction, and installation of an organ honoring the Lay family. Under the terms of her offer, she would pay $100,000 in two installments by January 1986, and $100,000 semi-annually thereafter.[15] The symphony expected that the organ would be installed and working by the time the building opened.

—❦—

AFTER Charles Fisk's death, his widow, Virginia Lee Fisk, and Steve Dieck assumed the managerial reins at the company. "At the time, we were all devastated," says Dieck. "But, we had a very determined band of people here. The last thing we wanted was to stop doing what we were doing! We had no choice but to plow forward without Charles. I knew his excitement for the project. Once he was gone, I realized that it was going to be my responsibility to keep this up and make it happen. I wanted to do that in his memory. We realized we had this one shot, and we were entrusted with the future of the organ in the concert hall. Nothing else was going on as far as new organs in concert halls. If we blew this, there might not be any more organs in concert halls. We convinced ourselves if we could do a really good job in Dallas, the instrument would draw its own audience and the organ would be used. The public would become much more interested in the organ. A lot of people go to a concert in a concert hall who would never go to performances in churches. It's a whole different aesthetic. It put the organ in a new context, a new light, which we all thought very exciting."[16]

The fact that Artec was promising the Fisk team favorable acoustics provided additional impetus. "We hoped for something with an adjustable acoustic that would give us four or five seconds [of reverberation], yet could also be toned down for the symphony to be happy," Dieck says. "That seemed all very appealing, and it turned out well."

One of his first actions was to contact I. M. Pei's office to determine the overall status of the Dallas project. He was referred to Charles Young, who invited the Fisk staff down to have a look at what Pei & Partners was doing with the organ design. "That was telltale in itself," recalls Dieck, who traveled to New York on June 7, 1984, with Bob Cornell and Charles

Right A late interior model from the I. M. Pei & Partners model shop shows the compromise reached between the Fisk and Pei visions of the façade. (*Photo by Richard DeWeese, courtesy Meyerson Symphony Center*)

Nazarian. "We thought *we* were designing the organ! We went down to find that they had built a model and designed an organ which we thought was ghastly. It was taken from organ building in the 1960s, a style that we didn't particularly identify with. Charles Young indicated they could change this, that, and the other thing; they just needed to be educated about what goes on in an organ."

There was little question in Dieck's mind that Young thought *he* should be designing the organ and that the Fisk staff should be teaching him what he needed to know in order to do that. "Of course, it's not that simple," Dieck explains. "We would have had to spend five years to get him to that point! He didn't have that sort of time. Anyway, we moved ahead, feeling our way. At that point, we started our model and developing a design, sort of in competition with what Charles Young was doing in New York."[17]

Dieck invited Young to visit Boston and look at three Fisk organs. "We went through and explained what everything was about: what was important to us and why things had to be the way they were and—specifically—why one of our organs couldn't work behind the façade they had designed," Dieck remembers. Charles Nazarian, Fisk's visual designer and the person there ultimately responsible for the façade of the Dallas instrument, explains: "The pipe array in an organ façade is like the skeleton of the human body. The woodwork is like a suit of clothes. We have quite a lot of latitude in how we place the 'bones' and how we develop the 'bone structure.' We manipulate the arrangement of the pipes to form a pleasing skeleton, and the woodwork is secondary: the clothing that makes the formal ensemble. If the pipe arrangement is wrong to start with, no amount of woodwork will fix it. This principle extends back to seventeenth-century instruments that we studied as models—as every good organ builder does—in which the arrangement of the front pipes actually tells you something about the instrument itself."[18]

Charles Young maintains that the Pei group realized from the beginning that C. B. Fisk had great expertise in organ building and that the disposition of the pipes and other functional components of the organ was their responsibility. Their difficulty with the Fisk design lay in the realm of aesthetics. "It was apparent to us [I. M. Pei & Partners] from Fisk's brochures that Charles Nazarian had not previously designed a façade in the style of the McDermott Hall and that he was not inclined to conceive a casework design in that architectural language," Young later stated. "The initial designs Nazarian showed us proved our concerns. In our opinion, they were Victorian and inappropriate for the hall, with large cornices and ornate fretwork shades reminiscent of the nineteenth-century organ façade. That is why we began proposing designs attempting to incorporate the Fisk placement of pipes within a casework façade compatible with the room."[19]

To the Fisk group's relief, the Pei team backed down from its first design, but not for long. According to Dieck, "Rather than letting us [Fisk] proceed with the design and get input from them, they insisted on continuing to design and work on a model. The next time we went to New York, there was a completely different organ façade in the Pei model!"[20]

Fisk made its own presentation to DSA representatives in early February 1985 and subsequently sent drawings of various possible designs to Dallas. Referring to one of these, George Schrader commented, "It looked like it belonged in a medieval church. I. M. Pei saw it and was gracious, but he said, 'We can't have that.'" Within days, Schrader received a color photograph of a model that the Pei group had prepared with a picture of the organ. The architect called to explain: "That's the front of my hall. There's three other sides to the hall, but that's the one people are going to see. It's important to me that I have something to say about it!" The Fisk people were not happy upon receipt of the Pei drawings. "Absolutely not!" came the unequivocal reaction. Schrader sensed that he had a dispute brewing similar to others he had mediated on the building.

The organ design was in high gear by late 1986. Schrader reported to the board that Pei and the Fisk organ designers had met to ensure that the instrument was both visually pleasing and of high acoustical quality. As had been the case with the building proper, the organ design underwent several revisions, at least three sets of changes by April 1987, when a presentation to the concert hall committee finally took place.[21]

Discussions continued without satisfactory resolution. By early 1987, Dieck and the Fisk team were frustrated enough to request a formal review from Bonelli and the concert hall committee. Virginia Fisk, Steve Dieck, and Charles Nazarian flew to Dallas to make a presentation on April 22, 1987, to the smaller unit about the direction of the Fisk design. Pei and members of his team flew in from New York. How did the committee want them to proceed? "We needed a referee, a mediator," explains Dieck. "[The symphony people] weren't entirely happy with our design and wanted to see it developed further—but advised us to proceed along those lines rather than taking Pei's ideas and going forward. From that point on, our communication with Pei and his group began to improve."

I. M. Pei, George Miller, and George Schrader flew to Boston to meet with the Fisk staff in Gloucester in July 1987. Their intent was to review plans for the organ and iron out any remaining differences.[22] Schrader was to mediate between the two parties. They discussed aspects of visual design and compared drawings, but a final decision was not forthcoming. The design remained at an impasse for more than two years.

Dieck and Virginia Fisk flew to Dallas again in May 1988 to make a formal presentation at a meeting of the smaller unit. Virginia Fisk reported that the design was now complete except for details of case decoration, which were still to be worked out.[23] C. B. Fisk had placed the order for the largest pipes and was already thinking ahead to construction of the actual instrument, which would follow the formal opening of the Meyerson Symphony Center.

First, however, all parties had to ensure that a façade would be in place for the grand opening fortnight in September 1989. With the urgency of that deadline weighing upon them, C. B. Fisk, I. M. Pei & Partners, and the Dallas Symphony exchanged a flurry of drawings and comments for several weeks, attempting to enlarge their areas of common ground. The Pei group continued to express reservations about the presence of spaces in the Swell façade and asked if the central rounded tower of the Great division might be widened further. (A division is a set of pipes playable from a keyboard or from the pedals. The Lay Family Concert Organ has four keyboards. The keyboard of the Great, the main division in English and American organs, commands the larger pipes. The Swell division pipes, commonly more specialized, *i.e.,* imitative of other instruments, are housed in a large wooden box, in this case with Venetian louvers at the front to facilitate gradation of sound. In the twentieth century, Great pipes have generally not been enclosed.)

George Schrader and George Miller flew to Boston to meet with the Fisk staff in Gloucester on June 20, 1988. They hoped to make a final decision on the instrument's visual design. While the architects and organ builders were inching toward agreement, eight areas of concern remained. Two that clearly required further compromise were the vertical posts— wider in the Fisk design than the Pei design—and the presence or absence of a frame member above the great center grouping of pipes.[24]

In September 1988, with the opening of the hall only one year away, George Schrader decided to force the issue to finalize the design. "I finally called I. M. and said, 'We need to get this resolved,'" he says. "I flew to New York to have dinner with I. M. and stayed overnight. The next morning we flew up to Boston's Logan Airport, the nearest major airport to Gloucester. I had asked I. M. to bring along the plans. We met the Fisk people in the [American Airlines] Admirals Club. I said, 'Now we're going to decide here just what the issues are.' There were twenty of them. We were going to get them resolved that day. 'Y'all just work on them, and what I want you to do is just mark up this set of plans.'"

Virginia Fisk remembers the September 14, 1988, meeting vividly. "George Schrader is a very good get-down-to-business person. He announced, 'I've circled the areas in the drawings of the façade where you disagree. We are going to resolve these one by one. Make a note as to what's important to you and what's not so important.' We went through them one at a time. Pei was gracious and charming."[25]

The Fisk contingent acquiesced on the pipe shades. "Those are wooden forms at the top of the towers that hold back some of the sound," explains Virginia Fisk. "They permit the sound to develop within the case before it goes out into the hall, and they are also an important element of the visual design. Pei was dissatisfied with our pipe shade design. We easily came up with something else." The Fisk group also conceded to Pei on the onyx columns in the façade, succumbing to his plea, "Oh, permit me these indulgences!"[26]

They worked their way systematically through Schrader's list. Pei was under greater time pressure than the Fisk representatives. Although the pyramid at the Louvre would not be officially inaugurated for six more months, previews of the structure had been under way since early July 1988, and Pei was much in demand in the French capital. He was scheduled to fly to Paris for an event the next day and had a dinner meeting in Manhattan that evening. About two o'clock, he looked at his watch and announced, "I've got a flight tomorrow out of Kennedy, and I've got to get back for this engagement tonight. We've got all but a handful of these issues decided, and we're way along with those six or eight. We'll get those solved pretty quickly."

George Schrader replied, pleasantly but firmly, "No. You're not leaving. You're going to mark up that set of plans for Mrs. Fisk, a set of plans for you, and a set of plans for the city, and a set of plans for me. Four sets. Mark them all, and date them, and sign them. We're not leaving until you do that."[27]

"And Pei *did* stay!" Dieck remembers. He perceives that meeting as a turning point for resolution of design issues. "Actually, we got quite a ways with Pei. Charles Young was not at that meeting, as I recall, but George Miller and Pei were. I have a great deal of respect for Pei because he immediately said, 'OK, here's what's important to me. Here's what I don't like about your design.' All the haggling ceased. He just cut to the quick and told us what he could deal with." Nazarian adds, "Any case work that wasn't rectilinear was out of the language that I. M. was comfortable with. He also surprised us by overruling Charles [Young] on a number of details. It was clear that Pei allows his select staff to go through all the machinations, but at the end he comes along and says, 'I like that, and I like that, and I like that.' Ultimately, I. M. makes the choices."[28] After that, the parties rapidly came to an agreement on all points. "It worked," says Dieck. "That's basically what you see now."[29]

Charles Young maintains, "In the end, even after all the compromises, the casework façade that was built was, in fact, a variation on the design we [I. M. Pei & Partners] had shown in renderings, drawings, and model. While we regret any tensions caused by the ensuing design negotiations, we and the audience would have regretted still more having as the focal point of the McDermott Concert Hall an organ façade casework in a post-modern, Victorian style."[30]

Because the façade pipes are an integral part of the audience's visual experience in the McDermott Concert Hall, the appearance of the organ was a prime consideration. All of Pei's early models showed brass pipes—a material that was doubtless easier to fabricate in the Pei & Partner's model shop. "They didn't have any strong leaning toward brass," Dieck believes. "We had suggested if they wanted that color that we could make the pipes out of copper. They were afraid the pipes would turn green. They really wanted to see the pipes silver, which is the natural color for pipes made of tin. We were all in agreement then, because tin was the natural metal to use."[31]

A tin façade meant an increase of $142,000 in the cost. Other enhancements that would raise the price tag included veneer casework (rather than painted) at $95,000 and professional redesign fees of an additional $60,000.[32] In order to preserve the not-to-be-exceeded cost of $1,000,000, the smaller unit found itself in the same position with the organ that it had been in with the building: looking for items to cut. Alternatively, they could defer certain components

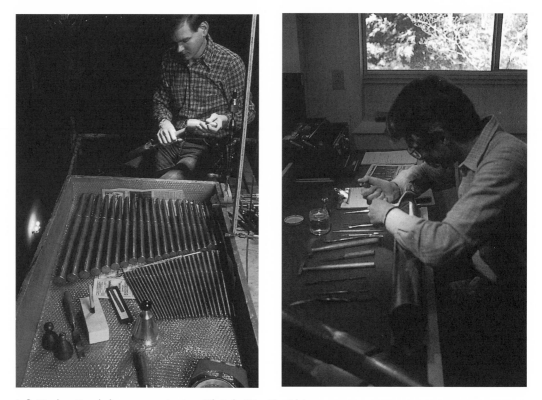

Left Stephen Kowalyshyn cones a pipe toe. (*Photo by Peter Henricks*)
Right David Pike prepares a newly made pipe for voicing. (*Photo by Steve Dieck*)

of the organ, to be added later if funding became available. In a May 1988 meeting attended by Virginia Fisk and Steve Dieck, Ted Amberg of the Pei & Partners Dallas office, and Louise Reuben of the City of Dallas, the smaller unit voted to eliminate a remote electric console, which meant a savings of $152,000. They also elected to defer the instrument's Positive (the lowest keyboard), Great, and Solo (for French Romantic music) divisions, all important to the organ's flexibility and use as a solo instrument but able to be reinstated into the design without penalty as late as June 1989. They were eventually reinstated. In the interim, the deferrals pared the budget by another $485,000.[33]

———&———

IN AN ideal situation, an organ is installed in a dust-free atmosphere. C. B. Fisk did not have that luxury in advance of the Meyerson opening. When they began to install the organ façade and casework in June 1989, construction activity at the Meyerson was at fever pitch. Conditions were not just less than ideal; they were appalling. "Our contract said that we would install the façade after all other [construction] work was done," says Dieck. "That

Left Pipemaker Forrest Dillon ladles molten metal into the casting trough. (*Photo by Steve Dieck*)
Right Charles Nazarian poses with his model of Opus 100. (*Photo by Robert Cornell*)

didn't work out at all! Rather than sticking to the contract and insisting that, 'OK, you're just not going to have a façade for the opening,' we went ahead and put it in. Everything had to be cleaned again after the opening. There were some tense moments in the construction of the façade, because a little bit of dust in the wrong place can stop a pipe from 'speaking.' For example, in a reed pipe, which has a vibrating tongue, if you get dust underneath the tongue, it just won't speak. Many of the organ's mechanisms will malfunction if grit gets into them. So, the safest thing is to install the organ in an environment that is not under construction."

The decision to proceed with the façade was made primarily for aesthetic reasons. The hall had to *look* complete by opening night. In order to accommodate the Dallas Symphony's schedule for the organ, Fisk also elected to subcontract much of the woodwork. "We originally approached Valley City Manufacturing, the Toronto company that did the woodwork interior of the hall," Dieck recalls. "They were very keen on doing the organ case. But at the last minute, the upgrade for the woodwork in the interior of the hall came through. All of a sudden, the people at Valley City found themselves swamped. They felt they could not do the upgrade and the organ at the same time. They recommended that we go to Gillanders, their competitors down the street, and Gillanders built the case for us. The two companies shared veneers and cooperated to make sure that everything meshed on the project."[34]

C. B. Fisk dispatched at least one staff member to Dallas, usually Dieck or senior design engineer Bob Cornell, to oversee each phase of the construction of the façade, including woodwork. American Airlines flew the Laukhuff pipes from Frankfurt to Dallas. "Those pipes were a tremendous length," recalls Virginia Fisk. "Only certain planes could accommodate the pipes in the cargo hold. It took planning for American to do that. They were extremely cooperative."[35]

"Six-foot Joe" stands in Fisk's model of Opus 100. (*Photo by Robert Cornell*)

A crew of eight Fisk people installed the pipework in August 1989, right before the hall opened. "As we were putting the façade pipes up, the construction crew still had people welding on the canopy above us!" Dieck recalls. The instrument was not planned to be functional until two or three years later. Therefore, a substitute organ had to be located and installed temporarily for use during the grand opening fortnight performances, specifically for the Mahler *Resurrection* Symphony.

DSO Artistic Administrator Victor Marshall remembers, "The organ console wasn't finished. There was a blank wall where it was going to be. The façade pipes were in, so it sort of looked like the organ was there even though it wasn't really there. I remember Paul Riedo [then the DSO's organist] scurrying around Oak Cliff trying to find an electric wind chest. He located one in an old church that wasn't being used and hooked it up through an electric switch to the thirty-two-foot pipes to augment the electronic organ we had to use for the Mahler Second [the *Resurrection* Symphony]. In the symphony's finale, he played most of the notes on the electronic organ, but when it came time for the big thirty-two-foot pipes, he would reach over and press this button that activated the chest, forcing air through the big pipes. It certainly added to the bass response! We had at least a couple of the pipes working for that concert."[36]

—☙—

AFTER the Meyerson opened, Fisk continued its work in Gloucester on the remainder of the organ's 4,535 pipes and the multitude of other parts. Significant innovations that had been developed in the Fisk shop were to be used in Opus 100. The servopneumatic machine, developed by Fisk's Stephen Paul Kowalyshyn to enhance the already smooth tracker action, was modeled after the Barker machine used in French instruments of the nineteenth century. Organ scholar David Fuller has called it the most important innovation in organ action in the last hundred years. "The Servopneumatic Lever is as different from a Barker machine as a rheostat is from an ordinary light switch: As the finger depresses the key, the valve under the pipe (or 'pallet') follows its motion, opening as slowly or quickly as the finger descends, stopping wherever the finger stops, and closing only as rapidly as the finger releases the key—all this with no added effort no matter how many stops are drawn or how many manuals coupled together."[37] Another first for Fisk was the use of dual wind pressures, with the higher wind pressures feeding the treble chests (the boxes containing the smaller pipe divisions) of several divisions to fortify both flues and reeds in their sound production. The Tuba division, with its twenty-inch wind pressure and batteries of English tubas, fully accommodates the extreme demands of the literature for organ and orchestra.[38]

The process of installation and voicing began in August 1991, and continued for thirteen months. Mechanical installation was substantially complete by October. The voicing process took considerably longer. "It's not that we're slow," explains Dieck. "We want to be sure that every pipe in the organ does exactly what it needs to do and does it to the best of its ability. That's C. B. Fisk's trademark."

David Pike, the tonal designer at C. B. Fisk, describes the process, which begins in the Fisk workshop and continues during installation. "Simply stated, the voicer's task is to coax each pipe into making a musical tone," he says. "Most of the voicing process centers around the mouth of the pipe. It's a matter of manipulating metal around the mouth area to enable the pipe to speak. Once a pipe has its voice, it must work within the context of an entire stop, that is, be adjusted to its neighbors so that the set of pipes as a whole makes musical sense. When the organ is set up in its final residence, each pipe is revisited and adjustments are made so that each rank of pipes relates properly to all others and the overall sound structure fits well with the acoustic of the room. The Meyerson organ has more than 4,500 pipes, ranging in size from three-quarters of an inch to thirty-two feet. Every single one of those pipes had to be listened to carefully, inspected visually, and made to sound its best in that acoustic and within the context of the entire instrument. That takes time. It takes a *lot* of time.

"We rotated our shifts, each three to four weeks long, throughout the year," Pike continues. "We spent a lot of time listening to the organ from out in the room. There's nothing like 'living' in a space over a long period of time to get to know it well and to understand what one needs to do to get the organ to sound its best."[39]

Like pianos and other instruments using wood, organs are subject to the vagaries of temperature and humidity fluctuations and require periodic tuning. The tuning process does not affect the voicing and is handled locally in Dallas, including a check prior to each concert involving the organ.

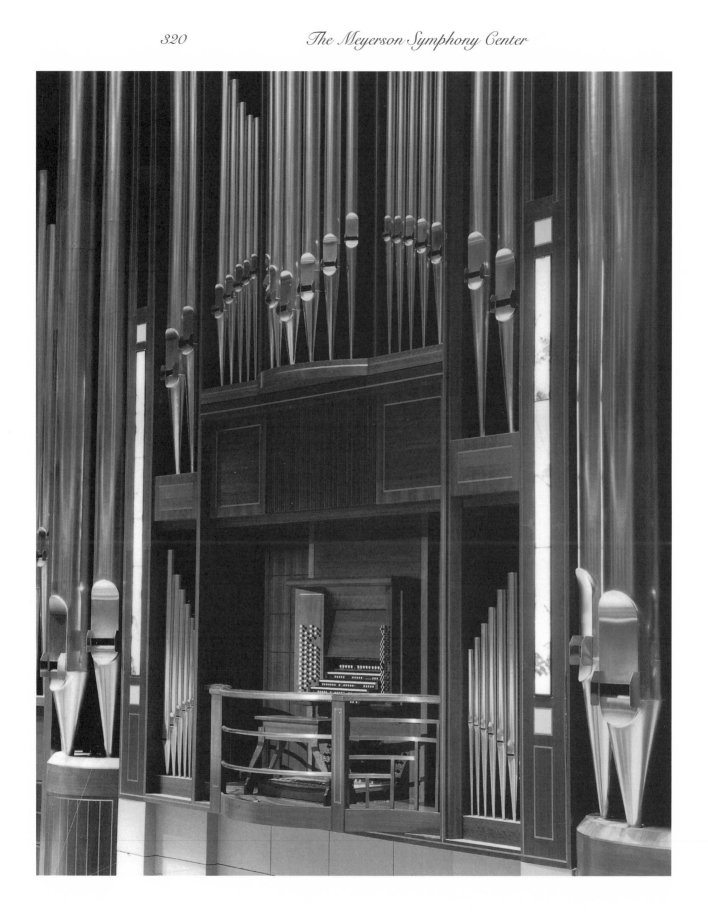

Formal dedication of the Herman W. and Amelia H. Lay Family Concert Organ took place on Wednesday evening, September 2, 1992. For the gala inaugural program, Maestro Eduardo Mata led organist Michael Murray and the Dallas Symphony Orchestra in a performance of Strauss's *Festival Prelude,* the Poulenc Concerto for Organ, Strings, and Timpani, and the ever-popular Saint-Saëns Symphony No. 3, Op. 78 ("Organ"). The premiere organ recital followed on September 28, 1992, featuring organist David Higgs. He demonstrated Opus 100's extraordinary versatility in a program of music by Bach, Daquin, Franck, Schumann, Conte, Hampton, Mozart, and Liszt.

A more private inauguration took place on Thursday, September 3, when the staff of C. B. Fisk presented their own concert. Most Fisk employees are musicians, and fully one-third are organists. Courtesy of American Airlines, about twenty staff members who had built Opus 100 were flown to Dallas for the gala together with their family and friends. Fisk staffers Steve Dieck, Casey Dunaway, Michael Kraft, Stephen Kowalyshyn, Stephen Malionek, Charles Nazarian, Mark Melson, David Pike, John Schreiner, and Ted Stoddard all played the organ, and Kathleen Adams sang with organ accompaniment by Nelson. A small, select audience attended: members of Meyerson's smaller unit and the organ committee, other C. B. Fisk personnel and their families, some DSO players and staff members. Once the music was underway, even the Meyerson housekeeping crew parked their cleaning carts in the outside corridors and entered the concert room to listen. "We had a great audience," recalls Virginia Fisk. "At the end, a lot of wild applause, whistles, everything! It was very informal—*not* your normal organ recital. It was wonderful."

Lenora McCroskey, professor of organ and harpsichord at the University of North Texas, reported in the company's newsletter: "The room sizzled with excitement and joy, and the deep pride of the men and women who had built the organ permeated the atmosphere. The community of organists is grateful for this instrument, and those of us who were able to be there will remember the day for a long time."[40]

———— ❧ ————

ORGANIST, conductor, and pianist Wayne Marshall is one of the instrument's most enthusiastic fans. "The organ is one of the finest in the world, without exception. I'm amazed by how this instrument works. It's mechanical, yet it doesn't feel or sound like a mechanical instrument. It feels like a vast romantic instrument, which is unusual for a mechanical action. It is a prime joy to play. From the organ loft, you get a completely different perspective [on sound] from the orchestra. You hear the whole spectrum, right across the board, in a way that's probably not quite as evident out front, I found."[41]

Facing page The Lay Family Concert Organ (*Photo by Donald Fuller, courtesy Meyerson Symphony Center*)

Bob Anderson relishes his subscription seats in the hall's grand tier, because he believes the organ is best appreciated from that high level. He is delighted with the Fisk instrument. "I think that there is no other mechanical [tracker] action organ of this quality in the United States for an orchestra organ. Opus 100 shows what a major orchestra must focus on in its planning in order to design for today, for our orchestras and our repertoire."[42]

The impact of Opus 100 on the Meyerson has been manifold. Visually, the organ is stunning, contributing significantly to the grandeur and beauty of the hall's interior. As a musical instrument, it has the flexibility and the power to sound magnificent both as a member of the orchestral ensemble and as a solo instrument. The presence of the organ allowed the Dallas Symphony to establish a Triennial International Organ Competition that was inaugurated in April 1997. The competition boasted an initial purse of $45,000, underwritten by H. Ward Lay, president of Lay Capital Group (and the son of Amelia Lay Hodges and the late Herman W. Lay) and by the Dallas Foundation. The competition immediately became one of the most prestigious in the world, drawing outstanding international competitors. A second competition was scheduled for March 2000.

S. Wayne Foster, who was gold medalist at the inaugural organ competition in 1997, is another enthusiastic proponent of Opus 100. "This instrument was built with all the state-of-the-art technology, but it also reflects historical principles in organ building that were neglected in the 1940s, '50s and '60s," he says. "The Meyerson organ has an electronic system that enables the organist to make rapid changes in both registration and volume. Yet the [traditional tracker] action, the mechanical linkage between the actual keys and pedals to the pipes, allows for the sensitivity and control [needed] to play expressively."[43]

Among the Fisk innovations in Opus 100, Foster cites the unique layout of the pipes in the organ case. "When you look at the inside of the instrument, it is revolutionary the way C. B. Fisk laid out the divisions. You really get the feeling that they were intent on creating an instrument unlike any other in the world. I think they succeeded, because, for once, they had an almost perfect acoustical environment. Here at the Meyerson, acoustics were the number one priority from the beginning. Coming into a situation like this, I'm sure the organ builders felt that, for once, everything was perfect for them to create exactly the sound that they wanted."[44]

The superlative quality of both the Fisk instrument and the McDermott Concert Hall make the competition exceptionally attractive to gifted young organists and aficionados of organ music who wish to hear those outstanding players. Dallas' Triennial Organ Competition should eventually achieve a stature in the organ world like that of the Van Cliburn Competition in the piano world.

ART

MARGARET McDermott made her \$5 million gift naming the audience chamber for her late husband early in 1983, stipulating that interest earned from the funds prior to their expenditure for capital construction costs be allocated to art for the building. By September 1983, the art fund had already grown to \$174,363.[1] By the time the funds were disbursed for art acquisitions in 1989, the monies exceeded \$1 million. Beginning in April 1985, the McDermott Art Fund was managed by the Dallas Symphony Foundation. The committee, chaired by Margaret McDermott, consisted of Stanley Marcus, Linda Marcus, Mort Meyerson, Marlene Meyerson, Raymond Nasher, George Schrader, Leonard Stone, Karla Temerlin, Liener Temerlin, and, *ex officio,* I. M. Pei. Dallas architect Bill Booziotis joined the committee in 1990, after Linda Marcus succeeded Margaret McDermott as chair.

The art committee had powers to select and approve art for the building. "We chose to keep the spaces clean," says Stanley Marcus, "instead of letting the building become overdecorated with art. We also realized that the most important contribution we could make was to keep peoples' hands off trying to redecorate the place themselves! Believe me, that is a tough thing in any public building. If you have a thousand members, you have a thousand potential interior designers."[2]

The committee began meeting late in 1985, shortly after groundbreaking for the building occurred. Working with Pei, they established three locations to exhibit major works: the top of the central staircase, the large interior east wall of the lobby, and Betty Marcus Park. "We had grand ambitions," recalls Linda Marcus. "We had that grand staircase with the limestone wall above it and asked ourselves, 'What artist would we like to see be given that space?' We felt that wall presented a challenge, an unsurpassed opportunity, and that artists would jump at the chance to have a monumental-scale piece placed there."[3]

The art committee's perception of the large space above the staircase was doubtless influenced by the various building models coming out of the Pei & Partners model shop in New York. Ian Bader, a member of Pei's design team, says, "I. M. and I 'invented' a [Roy] Lichtenstein mural that was going to be arrayed on the great wall above the staircase. The idea was to emphasize the transparency of the [building] exterior and suggest the life of the interior. It was an amusement that we concocted. Its specific design had a lot to do with the geometry of the building."[4] James Langford, another architect formerly of the Pei staff, adds, "Almost from the first models and drawings, we used to cut up reproductions of Roy Lichtenstein paintings and piece them together as a colorful piece of tapestry over that wide expanse of limestone."[5]

The early models of the hall also showed an Anthony Caro sculpture outside the hall, near where Pearl and Flora Streets intersect. Bader recalls, "The sculpture was to be a counterweight to the building. We had speculated about an Anthony Caro piece for a long time. He did a series of ledge pieces, which had to do with balancing on edge. It seemed to be potentially a good accompaniment to the concert hall. In fact, we adapted one of his pieces in a series of models."[6] At the time of the design unveiling in May 1982, long before the art acquisition committee existed, Pei told *The Dallas Morning News* architecture critic David Dillon, "We don't have the money for these, but we're looking for donors. We just have to be careful not to compete with the museum."[7]

ONCE formed, the art committee remained close-mouthed about its deliberations. Even to the DSA Board, they intimated only that several prominent American artists had expressed interest in painting or sculpting for the symphony center, based on the perception that Dallas' new concert hall would be a building of major architectural significance.[8] Pei's reputation and personal acquaintance with many American artists doubtless contributed to the prestige associated with the project outside Dallas.

The art committee drew up its list of candidates and ultimately interviewed several prominent American artists, including David Hockney, Frank Stella, Jasper Johns, and Ellsworth Kelly. Each of the artists interviewed was enthusiastic about the project, and Stella even sent a six-foot maquette of a proposed sculpture for the committee's consideration. "During the development phase, we tried to arrange our meetings when I. M. was in town," Linda Marcus recalls. "With Pei's keen hand in all of this, we finally took another long look at

Ellsworth Kelly, who had not been considered initially. I. M. suggested that we leave the wall above the grand staircase clean, concentrate instead on the large limestone wall, forty-five feet wide by forty-three feet high, on the east side of the building, and think in terms of Ellsworth Kelly."[9]

Pei had worked with Kelly on the Raffles Center Hotel in Singapore and was enthusiastic about his work. Kelly was certainly no stranger to North Texas. He had a piece in the new Dallas Museum of Art sculpture garden, and the Modern Art Museum in Fort Worth owned a Kelly multi-canvas painting. Kelly submitted sketches for the wall in question, outside the Meyerson's Green Room, opting for a work that expressed "clarity, optimism and joyful good spirits." In 1986, he was awarded the commission for the hall's first major work of art. No public announcement was made.

—✧—

THE ART committee continued to work actively with Pei through 1987 and 1988 to discuss other locations for paintings and sculptures. The amounts under consideration for art acquisition and the artists whose names were being bandied about by the committee continued to be kept under very close wraps.[10]

Word of an Ellsworth Kelly commission leaked in May 1989; however, even when *The Dallas Morning News* ran a story, DSA and City of Dallas officials declined to disclose any details. Not until one week before the opening in September 1989, did city officials confirm that four painted aluminum panels by Kelly would hang on the east lobby wall, and that the artist was driving the panels to Dallas himself to supervise two and one-half days of installation.[11] The process leading to the announcement was complex. Although the art committee made recommendations, because the city owned the building, all works of art required approval by the city's art in public places committee and the Cultural Affairs Commission— even though the private sector had funded the art in its entirety.

Dallas Panels (Blue Green Black Red; acrylic enamel on composite) was Ellsworth Kelly's largest painting at the time. Each panel measures thirty-four feet high by fifty inches wide. The artist oversaw the panels' installation in 1989 at the time of the Meyerson's opening. "The piece does have a relationship with my association with music, the seasons and human temperaments," he said at the time. "I consider the whole wall the painting and the interspaces as important as the color itself."[12]

Chillida sculpture

By means of his firm's model shop and in his remarks to the art committee, Pei had also made it clear that he favored placing a significant sculpture in the plaza outside the main street-level entrance to the Meyerson. Asked whom he would recommend, Pei told Stanley Marcus, "Now that [Henry] Moore is dead, and you already have several important Moores in Dallas, there's only one living person who'd be appropriate for this building: my friend from the Basque country, Eduardo Chillida."

Shortly afterward, Linda and Stanley Marcus encountered Frank Ribelin in Santa Fe. They had met Ribelin at a party in Dallas and learned that he was a collector of Chillida's work who had made gifts to the Dallas Museum of Art, the Guggenheim Museum, and the Metropolitan Museum of Art. "I suggested to Frank that the new symphony hall would be a great place for a sculpture," Stanley Marcus remembers. "I told him, 'Pei feels Chillida is the only sculptor he would want.' Frank responded very generously and asked what it would cost. We told him. There was an estimate for a Chillida, but Chillida hadn't been to Dallas at that time. Once Chillida visited Dallas and saw the site, the sculpture grew, as they always do. Instead of being seven feet, it became nine feet, then twelve feet, then fifteen, and the price went up with it."[13]

Ribelin already owned a number of Chillida works in various media. He also knew that Chillida and Pei had been friends for some thirty years. The prospect of the Dallas commission meant an opportunity to heighten awareness of Chillida in the United States, where at the time he was far less known than in Europe. Chillida traveled to Dallas to assess the site

Eduardo Chillida's sculpture *De Musica* dominates the plaza in front of the Meyerson Symphony Center. (*Courtesy Frank Ribelin*)

and discussed the project with Pei. Ribelin's gift was announced on January 26, 1989, by Park Board President Ida Papert and Meyerson Art Committee Chairman Margaret McDermott.

Architect and art committee member Bill Booziotis remembers that Ribelin agreed to donate the sculpture if the symphony's art committee would underwrite its installation. "The art committee thought they ought to at least put up the money to install it," Booziotis says. "Neither party had a clue as to how much that would mean. The sculpture had not yet been designed, let alone enlarged and made so heavy. It turned out to weigh sixty-eight tons, which necessitated strengthening the building infrastructure to support it! Plus, the shipping costs from overseas and then from Houston were very high. They spent over $100,000 installing it!"[14]

Chillida's completed piece, *De Musica,* was his first major outdoor public sculpture in the United States. Standing fifteen feet high, *De Musica* now dominates Betty Marcus Park. The structure, consisting of two massive corten steel cylinders resting on steel slabs, is an arresting visual complement to the Meyerson's west facade.

FOR THE grand opening fortnight, the art committee prevailed upon Dallas developer and sculpture collector Raymond Nasher to lend several pieces on a temporary basis. Pei worked

The Meyerson boasts unusual spaciousness in its lobby areas. (*DSO Archives*)

with Nasher to select which sculptures would best enhance the lobby areas during the festivities. They chose Jean Arp's *Torso with Buds* and Aristide Maillol's *La Nuit*. A longer-term loan came from Gwen Weiner of Dallas and Lake Tahoe, in memory of her father, Fort Worth arts patron Ted Weiner. Those two pieces, Jacques Lipchitz's *Sacrifice III* (1949–57) and Henri Laurens's *Les Ondines* (1932), are in Betty Marcus Park and are visible both from the musicians' lounge and the Fogelson Pavilion. They were lent for an initial period of six years. In 1998, Weiner extended her loan for an additional six years.[15]

—❧—

THE MEYERSON Symphony Center is a public building, and its most prominent art may be viewed in the public spaces. The building, however, also includes a number of areas that most of the general public does not visit: the music director's and guest artists' dressing rooms, the musicians' lounge, and the Dallas Symphony administrative offices.

After the hall opened in September 1989, Margaret McDermott asked Linda Marcus to assume the chairmanship of the art committee. Even after she relinquished her chairmanship, McDermott remained actively involved and committed to enriching the building with art. "The art committee has been funded primarily by Margaret McDermott," declares Bill Booziotis. "Her ongoing generosity provided funds for numerous projects. A couple of years after the hall opened, she auctioned some Chinese screens that she recognized were inappropriate for the hall, but still quite valuable, and made the proceeds from that sale available to the art committee. That money funded all sort of things: backstage redecoration, the bases for the installation of the Laurens and Lipchitz sculptures, the proper labeling of the Chillida, cut into the granite that supports it, and the night lighting for all the sculptures."[16]

—❧—

ONE OF Linda Marcus's first projects as the new chairman of the art committee was the musicians' lounge. "Coming out of Fair Park, the orchestra members were thrilled, of course, to have that space," she remembers. "We thought it important to try to please them and make that room as attractive as possible. It's a large room. We were faced with very large walls, and we wanted something rather graphic as well as large. We chose Navajo textiles."[17]

In the Green Room hangs an Andy Warhol lithograph, *George Gershwin,* that was a gift of Laurel Ornish in 1989. The north wall of the backstage atrium leading from the artists' dressing rooms to the stage door sports an oversize reproduction of a Ben Shahn ink drawing, *Silent Music.*

During the grand opening fortnight, DSO Artistic Administrator Victor Marshall had assembled a historical survey of the Dallas Symphony that was exhibited at the Dallas Public

Library. Linda Marcus toured the exhibit with great interest and asked questions of the librarians concerning additional archival sources. "I was able to locate historical negatives of the symphony, starting with a full shot of the first DSO from 1900," she remembers. "Then we found negatives for portraits of every conductor!"[18]

Library officials granted permission for the archival materials to be removed temporarily from the J. Erik Jonsson central facility. Linda Marcus entrusted them to Andy Reisberg at Photographic Archives. "I thought he did a magnificent job of making blowups for us of those pictures. We framed shots of the full orchestra from approximately ten-year intervals and placed them on one of the walls in the musicians' lounge."[19] The conductor portraits were placed in the fourth-floor administrative offices on the wall outside the executive director's office.

Working with these historic photographs, Marcus was reminded of old Dallas Symphony recordings on 33 1/3 LPs, with brightly colored album covers. "Victor [Marshall] had pulled together two or three jackets from those old recordings," she says. "I searched through used record shops around the city. Bill Wisener at Bill's Records helped a great deal in locating some of the older albums for me. We then framed these wonderful, colorful record jackets." The artwork from Dallas Symphony LP recordings now hangs in the hallway flanking the music director's, concertmaster's and visiting artists' dressing rooms.

When Andrew Litton became music director of the Dallas Symphony in 1994, Marcus approached him on behalf of the art committee to inquire if he would like some special art in his dressing room, a two-room suite across the corridor behind the Green Room. "He was kind enough to let us choose something for him," she reports. "We found a chromolithograph in New York by Harnett called *The Old Violin.*"

The art committee made one significant additional contribution that was unrelated to the visual aesthetics of the building. Linda Marcus explains: "Leonard Stone made a strong plea to us at one point to help backstage. The area lacked carpeting and other finish-outs for spaces that were left incomplete when the hall was opened. We were anxious to have the symphony orchestra members feel good about the hall. They badly needed lockers in which they could store instruments and personal effects after performances and between rehearsals. We finally decided that this need was sufficiently important that we would go a little bit out of bounds to accommodate the musicians. Even though, strictly speaking, that expenditure was beyond the purview of the art committee, we had a little money left in our budget, and we voted to spend those monies."[20]

LONG-RANGE plans for art at the Meyerson include paintings for the corporate entertainment and education complex that opened in October 1998, and additional sculpture for the public areas outside the hall. "Four artists have work on public display at the hall: Kelly, Chillida, Laurens, and Lipchitz," notes architect Booziotis. "All of them have undisputed international reputations of the highest order. Is it necessary to maintain that policy or can there be a policy of slightly more risk in future art that comes into the Meyerson? If so, should art with the higher risk factor be considered in the large public spaces or in the smaller, new spaces such as the Symphony Suites?"[21]

During the next decade, the art committee will wrestle with these issues. It took its first step in March 1999, with the announcement that Dallas-based sculptor David Bates had been commissioned to create two painted cast bronze floral arrangements for permanent display in the atrium of the Hart Symphony Suites. The art works, which Bates calls "still lifes," were installed in September 1999.

Chapter Thirty-Four

ACOUSTICS FROM AN OPERATIONS STANDPOINT

A majority of an acoustician's time on a project is spent keeping the room quiet. This is not the glamorous part of the job, but it is more important than you might think. Research has shown that the quieter the hall, the quieter the audience. An audience will hold its breath if necessary during an extremely quiet passage or a dramatic pause. Musicians sense this, too, and will often play much more quietly in a very quiet room. This adds to the dynamic range of the performance, therefore adding to the excitement.[1]

ACOUSTICIAN DAVID KAHN

THE EUGENE McDermott Concert Hall at the Morton H. Meyerson Symphony Center consists of an audience chamber encircled by a reverberation chamber above the concert hall. On either side of the stage, the reverberation chamber begins about thirty feet up. In the rear of the hall, above the curved wall of the uppermost level (the grand tier), the reverberation chamber is substantially higher.

The reverberation chamber features a series of movable concrete doors, each of which weighs approximately two and a half tons. They are controlled by a series of electrical actuators from the stage left area. The doors are used to control the amount of reverberance. With the doors completely closed, sound travels exclusively within the music chamber proper, resulting in the most intimate acoustic. If the doors are fully opened, the acoustical effect is like one enormous room, with significantly greater cubic footage than it actually has. Acoustically, the effect is akin to a cathedral sound but without the muddiness that can occur in a large structure (such as a medieval church). Through control of the aperture between the concrete doors, the sound technician can accommodate a conductor's desire to make the space more intimate or give the sound more room to "breathe."

Because the concrete doors have the capacity for adjustment, the hall can achieve various degrees of reverberation decay. When closed, the doors allow for maximum clarity. As they are opened, the degree of reverberance increases. A conductor thus has considerable latitude for settings to suit the size of the ensemble and the character of the music being performed.

This concept of room coupling is the result of years of trial and error by Johnson and subsequent testing and analysis by several of his former colleagues, including Nicholas Edwards, Robert Essert, and John Walsh. Lamar Livingston, the Meyerson's technical director since 1991, describes the result this way: "We have an incredible amount of clarity within the Eugene McDermott Concert Hall because of the care that Artec took with the materials, shape, and dimensions of the room. As a result, every listener receives the impact of early sound reflections at almost the same time that he receives direct sound from the stage. Later reflections follow from farther back in the room. The beauty of this room is that we have this second room: the reverberation chamber. It's a coupled room design, two rooms working together. This design allows the sound to travel upward, bounce around, and 'wash' back out into the concert room at the same time. We have the best of both worlds. We have clarity *and* reverberance."[2]

Livingston explains: "When we open these groups of doors, sound energy is routed or *transferred* from the concert room to the reverberation chamber. Two separate rooms are working in different ways to benefit each other. That process is called 'decoupling.' If the doors are only opened partially, what occurs is a *delayed* sound decay, because the sound is being 'held' in the reverb chamber for a longer time. For example, if a conductor wants lengthy reverberation, we can achieve that by opening all the doors just a few inches. That setting is optimal for the organ."[3]

Within the music chamber, the most dramatic and visible component of adjustable sound is the forty-two-ton acoustical canopy above the stage. The large canopy functions as a ceiling whose level rises or descends according to the scale of the music being performed. The Meyerson Symphony Center actually has a series of four canopies. Like the concrete doors, the canopy system may be manipulated. The large canopy may be raised, lowered, or tilted to alter the acoustical properties of the room. The lower the canopy is, the more clarity is possible. Further, the lower canopy increases a visual and psychological sense of intimacy within the music chamber. The main canopy's capacity to tilt results in reflecting some of the sound out to the rear of the room, particularly at orchestra level. Equally important is that, when tilted, its position improves the sight lines from the uppermost tiers.

The canopies serve several functions. Their principal value is to the musicians on stage, because it allows them to hear themselves better. The canopies also enhance intimacy and the immediacy of the sound experience for the audience. The height of the side canopies can also dictate how much sound will be allowed into the lower reverberation chamber, the area closest

Facing page The doors of reverberation chamber, which runs above the curved wall of the uppermost level (the grand tier), are opened or closed to control the amount of reverberance. (*Photo by Richard DeWeese, courtesy Meyerson Symphony Center*)

to the stage. For large orchestras, solo organ performances, orchestral works including organ and works with chorus, the large canopy is raised higher. Conversely, for a chamber orchestra or a violin/piano recital, the canopy is lowered, resulting in a drier, crisper sound with less reverberance.

When the orchestra is rehearsing and working out its optimal acoustical settings of the canopy system and reverberation chamber doors, it must take into consideration that the hall will sound different with an audience of 2,062. In order to approximate the absorptive power of bodies, hair, and clothing, Artec designed a system of mechanically controlled draperies. These heavy acoustic curtains are present on three levels of the concert room: the uppermost grand tier, the dress circle, and the orchestra terrace. When fully extended, the curtains provide a fabric backdrop to most of the wall surfaces of the concert room, allowing the music director to better gauge how the orchestra will sound with an audience present. The curtains are also regularly employed in pops concerts that entail electric amplification. (The curtains presented a design challenge to the architects responsible for the hall interior. According to Abby Suckle of I. M. Pei & Partners, each set of draperies had to fit into special closets when it was not in use. "This meant that there are all sorts of hidden cabinets in the hall. These were tricky to figure out, because the curtains are bulky." The curtains are dyed brown or beige to match the wood or limestone.)[4]

A basic architectural element Artec adopted from earlier halls is horizontal soffits cantilevered from the walls. In the Meyerson, these are the dress circle and grand tier boxes. These "shelves" reflect sound energy down to audience members seated on the main floor. Analogous levels exist in Vienna's Musikvereinssaal and Amsterdam's Concertgebouw, the two principal halls that Meyerson's committee strove to emulate. Artec knew that, in order to make these acoustical shelves function effectively, the side walls should have very few people seated along them. In the Meyerson, these two tiers of boxes have only one row of seats. The one-row limit is equally important for good sight lines.

A favorite tenet of Artec Consultants is the idea that one begins with silence. That is, excluding unwanted noise is a prerequisite to ensuring optimal acoustics for the sound one does want. The site of the Morton H. Meyerson Symphony Center had two distinct disadvantages from the standpoint of acoustics. The first was its proximity to a major freeway; the second was its situation on the flight path for incoming Southwest Airlines jets headed for Love Field. These were not insurmountable problems, but they presented special challenges to Artec. The heart of the building is the concert room. Artec's early design called for insulating the room with a double envelope of concrete. "Originally, we specified separate steel trusses supporting an outer fourteen-inch concrete roof slab and an inner eight-inch ceiling slab," says acoustician Nicholas Edwards. "Later, we agreed to the use of a single set of trusses to reduce the cost."[5] Inner pieces of concrete block were filled with grout to ensure that no outside noise—whether a thunderclap, an aircraft, or an air-conditioning compressor cycling on—would interfere with the music. Artec and I. M. Pei & Partners determined to separate the various mechanical systems from the concert room as much as possible. The air-conditioning system was placed under Betty Marcus Park, adjacent to the hall, rather than underneath the main structure.

David Kahn was recruited by Russell Johnson in 1985 from another small acoustics consulting firm in New York City in 1985. During the next four years, while the Meyerson was under construction, he was Artec's primary on-site person. "That required that I learn more about the details of the construction documents," he remembers, "in terms of the structural separation between the mechanical room in the building and some of the special sound-isolating construction to deal with aircraft flyovers and things of that nature."[6]

Kahn became Artec's sound isolation and noise control specialist for the Meyerson. "Our design criterion for this hall was absolute silence, or the threshold of human hearing," he recalls. "In other words, there would be no audible difference if the mechanical system was running." Kahn points out an unusual element in the Dallas hall to that end: places where the air is delivered into the hall. When the building opened, they were unobstructed ducts, with no diffusers or grilles in front of the openings. "The air shot directly into the hall," he explains. "That's quite unusual. There are several advantages. If you don't have anything obstructing the air stream, you can blow the air much faster without making noise. That allowed for a lower number of duct openings than in other halls. We were pushing the envelope, in that we wanted to push air into the hall as fast as possible while keeping the openings as small as possible to avoid losing sound down the duct openings—but not force the air so quickly that it generated any noise."[7]

Elevators in the public spaces of the Meyerson and backstage areas have sound-insulated doors. Artec insisted that all heating, ventilating, and air-conditioning equipment be situated independent from the building with the music chamber: off-site, so that air handling noise would not interfere with sound. Plumbing noise was minimized by installing oversize copper tubing for water lines and cantilevered, wall-mounted toilets rather than floor-mounted. Neoprene rubber seals back the tile walls in the rest rooms.

All these details of construction and materials are components of a comprehensive design package that ensures superior acoustics within the Eugene McDermott Concert Hall and isolation of extraneous noise from without. In its capacity as the hall's theatre and performance equipment consultant, Artec also designed basic sound and lighting systems that allow the Meyerson Symphony Center to be used with maximum flexibility. In planning these systems, Artec considered both the day-to-day needs of the hall's principal tenant, the Dallas Symphony Orchestra, and the requirements of non-symphony users. Unfortunately many of its recommendations were cut in 1982 and 1984, when the budget for the hall was being pared back so ruthlessly.

The system that exists today includes loudspeaker and microphone systems and versatile patching, as well as the invention of a performance lighting/dimming system that was specifically designed to minimize lamp filament noise and reduce it to inaudible levels. During the development process for the special dimmers, the acoustical/engineering team rented outside space to test the system. "We located a quiet recording studio space," recalls Kahn. "About ten of us from the city, the symphony, Bateson, and Artec convened there one morning. We were intent upon gathering around one of the lights to try to listen for any noise as it was turned up and dimmed back down. All we could hear were people's stomachs growling as the lunch hour approached! We all eventually lost our composure, and all these very serious grown adults dissolved into laughter."[8] Ultimately, the dimmer system proved inaudible.

THE MEYERSON'S acoustics succeed so brilliantly because of a combination of structural and design factors, including the shape of the room, materials used within the room, the reverberation chamber, and the canopy system. Acoustician Kahn recalls his impressions listening in the hall during the first weeks of rehearsals and performances in 1989. "One of the most dramatic elements of the sound is the feeling of envelopment, like the sound is all around you. I've heard comparable sound in Boston Symphony Hall, but only in front of the cross aisle in the middle of the main floor. As you move back on the main floor there, or up to the balconies, you lose that incredible feeling of being surrounded by the sound. The sound becomes more frontal, less enveloping. In Dallas, you get that wonderful feeling of being surrounded *everywhere* on the main floor, and even in the balconies."[9]

An aspect of traditional design that Artec consciously avoided during its design phase was the principle of sound scattering. In the early stages of Johnson's career, a characteristic of older halls that caught his eye and ear was the decorative elements of traditional architecture. "I noticed lots of sound-diffusing elements on the ceilings and walls: vines and flowers modeled in plaster, cherubs, gryphons, grapes, geometric patterns. Then there were all the Greek-inspired architectural details such as pilasters and cornices, all of which diffuse the sound. They scatter frequencies just enough to enhance good musical sound in the room."[10]

Small statuary and other decorative surfaces on the walls and ceiling of a hall were deemed acoustically advantageous because they increased the amount of small sound reflections. The idea was that sound would scatter in different directions because of these architectural decorations and, through scattering, would deliver reflected sound to the listener. Such ornamental items creating irregular surfaces, including columns, were a standard component of music chambers in the high baroque and classic eras. Because so many of these older rooms were admired for their acoustics, analysts inferred that their elaborate decoration must be an additional factor in their success. Some of the perceived decoration, however, was actually only paint or gilt on flat plaster. This is the case in Vienna's legendary Musikvereinssaal.

Edwards notes, "I was taught at university about the importance of scattering on side walls and ceilings on concert halls. That was my training. Certainly that is what everyone has believed in England, probably since the 1930s. When I got to New York, Russell challenged that. Where did that all come from? He felt, at that time, that scattering from the surfaces would reduce the audibility of the reflections that contribute to your sensation of loudness or envelopment. I listened to what he was saying. It's very difficult when you're trained by teachers whom you have to respect to accept the opposite of what you've been taught. But I did, in the end." Edwards points out that when the Artec team was working with the Pei group on the shaping of the wood on the side walls, Artec declined the option to "model" the sections highlighting the differences between cherry and African makore by raising one surface by half an inch. The walls have two veneers that are closely attached where they join, so that they are absolutely flat, with nothing to scatter sound. There is thus *no* high-frequency diffusion in the Meyerson, according to Edwards, who believes that the success of the room proves that it is not necessary.[11] (Ironically, Johnson changed his thinking again in the late 1990s, when he began putting a moderate amount of high-frequency diffusion into his newer rooms. "The McDermott Concert Hall room does not have much of that detail, but the rooms we'll open in the year 2001 and 2002, some of them will have as much high frequency rolloff diffusion as halls built in 1885," he stated in 1996.)[12]

Using the newly conceived reverse-fan shape was clearly the biggest risk for the Artec team. "The reverse-fan shaping was unknown territory," acknowledges the room's principal designer, Nicholas Edwards. "What the Meyerson shows is that this shape works. Reverse fan shaping *does* bring in strong lateral sound; it *does* create a sense of envelopment and acoustical intimacy, along with clarity and loudness. This was all very scary when we were still in the design phase, because we were so uncertain about the outcome of doing something so revolutionary, rather than evolutionary. And we had already taken risks with the first reverberation chambers in a concert hall and the unprecedented height of the concert room!"

Despite the acoustical success of the Meyerson, its design team is aware that the hall could have been even better. "It was always our intention to have much more flexibility for the concert platform," Edwards states. "The ability to go easily from a flat floor to a steeply-raked floor, the ability to shift from two rows to four in the chorus to enlarge the concert platform, or extend a stage extension lift that would allow the orchestra to move forward—all these things were in our original plans. Regrettably, we were instructed to remove them, when the budget was being cut."[13]

Chapter Thirty-Five

WHAT THE
MUSICIANS SAY

PERFORMING in a hall is entirely different from attending a musical event there. The Dallas Symphony musicians and visiting conductors and performers offer another perspective not only on the specifics of the McDermott Concert Hall, but also on the issues that performers face. Paramount among these is the need to hear oneself and the other musicians with whom one plays. Second is the ability to see. Musicians must be able, of course, to perceive cues and nuances from the conductor. They also see upbows and downbows from string section leaders, intakes of breath and preparation for attack from wind and brass players, and the like. A third consideration is space, both physical and psychological. How much room do the cello and bass sections require to make that big sound audiences so love in, say, the finale of Beethoven's Ninth?

These needs, at least the first two, appear to be similar to those that an audience expects or at least hopes for: good acoustics and good sight lines. Achieving those goals both on the stage and in the audience presents a conundrum for the acoustician and architect. What works on stage to enhance the players' ability to hear one another may work less well in the audience. For example, at Fair Park Music Hall, the Dallas Symphony musicians could hear each other, but the sound was traveling across the edge of the stage to the audience in a severely diluted fashion. Principal horn Gregory Hustis says, "In Fair Park Music Hall, you could just bust your tail forever, and hardly anything got out. It was demoralizing. I think sometimes the players didn't put out because it just didn't matter what they did; it wasn't heard."[1]

Conversely, at the Meyerson, where the audience has an extraordinary listening experience from virtually every seat in the house, the musicians have problems on stage, particularly with physical space and with sound. "Our stage is one of the most difficult stages I've ever played on," asserts principal bassoon Wilfred Roberts. "It's both challenging and frustrating. From the middle of the stage, where the woodwinds sit, I can't hear the first violins or the celli when I'm playing. If I'm not playing, I can hear them. That's actually not uncommon in concert halls, if you're principal bassoon, not to hear the first violins or the cellos. What I find uncommon is when I'm playing I have a lot of trouble hearing the flutes and the oboes, and they're right in front of me. Yet when I hear the sound coming back at me after I play, I can tell the sound is really good. One of the first things I noticed is that this hall has one of the most beautiful pianissimo sounds of any hall in the world.[2]

"It's a very naked feeling playing on stage," Roberts continues. "It's not just a matter of being exposed. You want to be exposed. In this particular hall, if anything is the least bit wrong, it's magnified. If something doesn't gel, if your high notes that night are not quite as great as they were the night before, if there's a little 'dirt' on your attack on a certain note that night, it's magnified."[3]

Opinions among orchestra members vary widely, depending upon where on the stage a player sits. In general those on the outer perimeter—the front of the stage and the semicircle to the rear—are better able to hear themselves and others than players in the center of the stage. Those who sit in the center, particularly the woodwinds, have to rely heavily on visual cues. "The stage is dead where I sit, and the hall is live where the audience sits," says principal oboe Eric Barr. "Neither one is a realistic observation of the other. If I could, I would lower the height of the risers by half. It would get the bells of the clarinets out of the back of my head. It's just noisy! To me, we sound more like a band than an orchestra most of the time, because you take the loudest instruments [brass and percussion] and put them up in the air." He also cites visibility problems from the center of the stage. "I don't know how the people on the outer edge of the cellos and violins cope. I can't even see them from where I am! It's like they're in another room."[4]

Principal horn Hustis faces a similar challenge. "All the way up the middle is what we call the Bermuda Triangle. Many of us who sit in the middle of the stage find that things get lost there as we're playing. The audience may hear them, but we don't get a sense of self. I can move to my right three or four feet and hear myself much better, closer to the wall. It's difficult to monitor yourself on stage because you don't get immediate feedback. I have to play so much on trust."

Still, Hustis believes the Meyerson is the crown jewel of Dallas' cultural venues and that it has been beneficial for the city and the orchestra in several respects. "Initially, it brought better conductors here," he says. "It's made the orchestra more responsible, more accountable in terms of personal playing."[5]

On the infrequent occasions when he sits out in the Meyerson listening to the orchestra, Hustis thinks his colleagues sound good, but he still has some reservations. "I always have this sense that I'd like to feel closer to the orchestra when I hear it, even if I can hear everything.

Some musicians may have trouble hearing one another play, but for the audience, there isn't a bad seat in the hall. (*DSO archives*)

Maybe that's part of the era of compact discs. I like the sound around on the side, in dress circle boxes, because you're close enough to get more of the immediacy that I like."[6]

Eric Barr acknowledges that he has always been more tuned in to the way players felt playing than the way the audience experiences music as a listener. "I don't think any player likes to play where [he feels] it sounds bad and it's uncomfortable, even if the audience thinks it's the greatest thing that ever happened," he notes. "You spend all day, hours, just trying to sound OK to yourself in the Meyerson. This is a totally different environment from Fair Park, and it has taken me ever since we have been here, coping with it, trying to work with it. I think the lower the instrument, the less uncomfortable it is. The higher frequency instruments where we sit [in the woodwind section] start to become more uncomfortable."

When the orchestra first played in the hall in 1989, they were on the flat performance platform, without risers. Second violinist Janet Cherry says, "We thought it was wonderful; then they put the risers in and everyone was disappointed. Now I like the risers better. In fact, I'm the fourth or fifth person to ask to be moved back in my section because I like sitting farther back and higher up on the risers. It's cooler. You see better. You have more room. Down the middle, where I used to sit, you don't get any air, and you don't get any sound. It's too crowded. You don't hear as much. You can't see anybody, and nobody can see you. I used to get terrible cramping and backaches, getting in contorted positions not to hit anything. We had to avoid each other's stands and bows. With woodwinds behind you, there are more stands because each player has a stand."[7] (String players share music stands.)

On the opposite side of the stage, the cello section faces the same problems of space as the front desks of the second violin section. Cellist Michael Coren remembers, during the design phase, using a tape measure to determine the minimum amount of space that a cellist needs on the outside of the bow to be able to play. "The minimum amount of space between your elbow and the edge of the riser was another question," he says. "There is such a thing as psychological space, too. An extra couple of feet on the stage would eliminate what has become, I won't say an albatross, but I will say certainly a quality of life which is problematic. We'll have to live with it forever."[8]

From the first violin section, making music in the Meyerson is a completely different experience from the woodwinds. Mary Reynolds says, "We're sitting *in* a great instrument, and I think it's gotten better with age. I love Russell Johnson's idea of the canopy and its many uses. I can tell when the canopy is at its highest extension. It's a whole different acoustic than when it's lowered even a few feet. But of course, when we do the huge pieces with organ or full brass, and extra musicians, it has to be raised all the way up. There are times when we string players use ear plugs just for protection. That's not just in pops concerts where there is always amplification. When we have very big pieces with the chorus, and if the brass is specifically orchestrated, and the percussion—usually we wear earplugs. A lot of people do because it's a very live hall, and the sound level can do damage to the ears. As a string player, I would change the risers if I could. The risers have been difficult. I sit on the floor, with the risers to my immediate left. My bow tip is oftentimes in danger of hitting the riser edge. If your freedom to bow is cramped, and you're fearful of running into a piece of furniture, there's a tightening of muscles. Muscularly, I don't have room to play. That used to be a problem in the pit at the [Fair Park] Music Hall, playing the opera. It's that same feeling, and it shouldn't be, in a symphony hall of this grandeur."[9]

From the front of the viola section, directly facing the conductor, associate principal viola

Barbara Hustis believes she has one of the best seats in the house because she doesn't have to be on a riser. She is keenly aware of the space constraints on her colleagues, however. "I don't have to worry about hearing, because I've got the sound falling in on me all the time. It's great; I can't complain. I can only feel my colleagues' frustration, and close to me!" For her, the biggest disappointment is that so few of the players' suggestions solicited during the design phase seemed to have been implemented. "We told them we needed space to get instruments on and off, space so people don't fall. We had played on many other stages, so we knew the problems. String players know that you don't want your bow hitting somebody else's scroll, and you don't want to get hit in the head. We have to be on our toes all the time."[10]

Principal trombone John Kitzman, who plays from the rear center right of the stage, says, "I think I have the best seat in the building. I hear everything! When we're on risers, the trombones are the highest section in the orchestra. The only thing that's difficult is that, because we're so high, we must play quiet, exposed passages very softly, sometimes softer than is comfortable. But the hall has great bass response. Of course, you have to be sensitive that, when you play loudly, it's not ugly, because if you play ugly on stage, it will sound ugly in the audience."[11]

At front stage left, principal bass Clifford Spohr has good sight lines to the conductor and the rest of the orchestra, but he cannot hear himself so well on the riser system as when his instrument's end pin is on the flat stage. Like most of the DSO musicians, he has mixed feelings about the stage but is quick to praise one of the hall's unsung attributes: how quiet it is. "When we hear a plane go over, which we do very occasionally, or we hear some rumbling from the freight elevators, we all turn to look at each other. At [Fair Park] Music Hall, all we heard was the hiss of white noise from the air conditioning, street noise, and airplane drones. People don't put that quality high enough on the list of reasons that the Meyerson is so good. You still hear a little outside noise, but you can really listen."[12]

Nearly all the orchestra musicians, even those with space constraints or problems hearing themselves on stage, acknowledge that audiences assure them how wonderful the sound is in the hall. Eugene Bonelli points out that, if one were to err, it was better to err in favor of the sound that listeners hear. Even those players who are critical of the on-stage acoustics and space acknowledge that the hall is both a comfortable and aesthetically beautiful place in which to work.

Visiting performers to the hall, both soloists and conductors, are delighted with the responsiveness and warmth of the space. Gunther Herbig, who has conducted regularly in Dallas since the late 1970s, believes that a hall like the Meyerson makes an enormous difference in performances. "A hall is, so to speak, an additional instrument of the orchestra. It's not just an architectural thing: It is a musical instrument through which the sound that the orchestra produces is filtered, improved, or made worse than what actually comes from the players. In this respect, the Dallas Symphony is incredibly fortunate to have a hall with these characteristics that enhance the quality of an orchestra. What comes back to you, what you hear, is very encouraging. You have the feeling, 'We are performing well.' This is true in rehearsal as well as performance."[13]

Herbig is enthusiastic about the Meyerson's capabilities for adjusting sound, for example using the acoustic curtains to simulate the presence of an audience. "There are no surprises in the evening when you come on stage. With some halls, you have a short acoustical rehearsal in the empty hall. You say, 'Aha, so that's how it sounds here.' Then one hour later you come on stage with the audience in the hall, and you start, and you suddenly realize, 'Oh my God, this is completely different from what it was before!' This characteristic [flexibility] of the Meyerson is very helpful for the performer." Herbig believes there are very few halls in the United States that compare to the Meyerson. "Among contemporary halls, there are not any which equal this hall." What makes it so distinctive? "Simply the quality of sound," he says. "The possibility of flexibility, according to the repertoire you are playing."[14]

Andrew Litton, the Dallas Symphony's music director since 1994, has favored large works for large performing forces that produce big sound. He has reveled in the acoustic options that are available to him and the orchestra in the Meyerson. Litton has been sensitive to his players' difficulty in hearing one another. Shortly after his arrival, he lowered the back two tiers of risers. "I noticed from the podium that I wasn't hearing much percussion or brass, when in fact, out in the hall, they were decimating the rest of the orchestra!" he says.[15] His initial solution was to place percussion and brass lower, to direct their sound toward the podium. In 1999, he began experiments with rearranging the woodwind section, moving each row back to improve their ability to hear.

Litton considers that he is in a constant state of evolution with respect to the acoustic possibilities of the stage and the hall. The biggest problem, he agrees, is the space: the stage is too small. He and the players struggle constantly with where to fit everybody, a problem that increases with works requiring a large orchestra. The size of the stage is further compromised by the inflexibility of the riser configuration. When recording, Litton opts for a flat floor, abandoning the risers altogether. For most performances that the DSO plays in the Meyerson, however, the risers are a fact of life. Litton and the musicians try to work out improved, if not ideal, arrangements. "Of course,' he chuckles, "I've never worked with an orchestra resident in a hall that *didn't* have complaints about playing in that hall! I am convinced that, if you can hear yourselves too well, that means somebody else is not—like the audience." He agrees that ensuring a superb listening experience for the audience is the primary goal.

"To keep live music alive, we must make the concert-going experience as incredible as possible," he declares. "The hall does that on many different levels. It is a gorgeous place to make music, and a very attractive place to go, but it's also a great place to hear music, because the sound in the Meyerson is so visceral. No matter how many thousands of dollars you spend on a home sound system, you cannot replicate the sound of a hundred people going full tilt—or three hundred when we have the chorus—on loudspeakers. What makes it so exceptional is that the analogue acoustic sound is ideal in this setting."[16] With the Meyerson as recording studio as well as concert venue, Litton has committed to capturing the magical sound of the hall on recordings. He has become an outspoken proponent of live recordings. "In some small way," he says, "it makes the shared experience of attending a concert in the Meyerson available for posterity."

EPILOGUE

I am, frankly, very much in love with the building. It has such refinement. That's a quality you see in very few buildings any more because it costs money to refine a building.[1]

STANLEY MARCUS, 1998

THROUGHOUT the ten years preceding its inauguration in September 1989, the Meyerson Symphony Center was regularly criticized for its high cost, officially stated as $81.5 million at the time of the opening. That figure has since fallen into an entirely different perspective. In October 1997, Newark's New Jersey Performing Arts Center (NJPAC) opened with total expenditure of $187 million. That figure included land acquisition, design, early administrative staffing, and an anticipated operating deficit in the first fiscal year. Seattle's Benaroya Hall, inaugurated in September 1998, carried a price tag of $118.1 million, which also included the cost of the site. Renovations of existing halls are costing even more. London's Royal Opera House in Covent Garden completed a $360 million redevelopment at the end of 1999. New York's Lincoln Center has embarked on fund-raising for a face-lift that could cost as much as half a *billion* dollars, with $200 million estimated for Avery Fisher Hall alone.[2]

From a strictly monetary standpoint, Dallas' expenditure hardly seems excessive in comparison, even if one accepts the high figure of $157 million that includes the cost of land acquisition, infrastructure, and debt service. The Meyerson Symphony Center's superiority, both architecturally and acoustically, makes its price tag, so controversial during the 1980s, seem reasonable. The building has proven to be a win-win proposition. The Dallas Symphony Orchestra has a home that is the envy of major orchestras throughout the world. The City of Dallas and its citizens have a magnificent landmark to anchor the Arts District and grace a renewing urban center.

The Meyerson Symphony Center has become one of Dallas' principal tourist attractions, supplanting the Southfork Ranch and superseded only by the Sixth Floor Museum (formerly known as the Texas School Book Depository Building), chronicling the Kennedy assassination. An active group of thirty volunteer docents continues to guide visitors through the hall.

Between 1989 and 1998, the Dallas Symphony enjoyed nine consecutive sold-out seasons for both its classical and pops series, a record matched in the United States only by the Chicago Symphony. In its capacity as the Meyerson's principal tenant, the orchestra has increased its use of the hall every year since the opening. Yet, its annual percentage of the hall's total use is declining because so many other organizations are using the facility.

The City of Dallas and the Dallas Symphony have forged an excellent working partnership that benefits both entities. From the earliest planning stages of the Arts District, the City of Dallas committed itself to infrastructure to support and enhance the arts facilities: Flora Street, the district's "spine," the parking garage, sidewalks, and landscaping. The symphony continues to provide the city with a substantial number of free concerts: a SundayFest series of matinee performances, outdoor parks concerts in the warm months, and annual Hispanic and African-American festival programs specifically geared to the city's ethnic communities. All these events are free and open to the public, emphasizing the initial philosophy that the hall belongs to the citizens of Dallas.

One reason that the Meyerson Symphony Center has been such an enormous success is the unusual spaciousness of its lobby areas. Prior to the completion of the Meyerson, according to Artec's Robert Wolff, the largest lobby facilities in North America, proportionally, were in Centennial Hall in Winnipeg, at 19.5 square feet per person. By comparison, the Meyerson has 39.5 square feet per person. The vast space gives the audience room to circulate and mingle prior to concerts and at intermission.

"Most venues don't have the kind of space that will allow you to do that comfortably," observes Bruce MacPherson, facility manager at the Meyerson. "In this building, you never experience any sense of crowding or congestion. The lobby will hold over 3,000 people, and we have proven it! The hall's capacity is 2,062 with the choral terrace filled. With every sold-out concert we have, if the entire audience wants to mill in the lobby at intermission, there's still room to move."[3]

The Meyerson remains a favorite of Scott Cantrell, who was music and architecture critic of the *Kansas City Star* before becoming music critic of *The Dallas Morning News* in fall 1999. "One of the Meyerson's strokes of genius is the enormous public space. It's so comfortable and grand and inspiring to be there, even before you enter the concert hall. I also like the fact that it's sort of grand in a very austere way. Then you go into the hall, and it's opulent. The whole thing is such a wonderful piece of theatre, from the time you see the building outside to the time you get to your seat. I wish more halls were like that. It really enhances the musical experience. From that standpoint, I think the Meyerson is unparalleled. I know of no other hall that is quite such a thrilling experience to be in."[4]

The hall's greatest glory, however, remains its extraordinary acoustics. The Morton H. Meyerson Symphony Center has received widespread and consistent acclaim from conductors, soloists, audience members, and critics. Today, Leonard Stone says, "In the final analysis, I. M. was absolutely the right architect to create this building. The firm, with its great sense of style and design and engineering, clearly served this project very, very well. Although I agree that Pei is certainly the architect of the era, there may have been many other brilliant architects to design this building. There was only one acoustician who could have gotten the results in that building. That was Russell Johnson. The one thing that I accomplished for that building of which I am most proud was my unending support of Russell."[5]

Architect Charles Young praises Mort Meyerson's smaller unit for its commitment to excellence and quality throughout the project. "An architect can only make a building as good as his client will let him make it. As the Dallas committee came to each hurdle, not only in the decision-making and building process, but also when they had to come up with the money for the enhancements they wanted, they always rose to the challenge. That's one of the things I would really laud them for as clients."[6]

Johnson himself acknowledges the unusual series of partnerships that brought the Meyerson to fruition. "The Meyerson is unique in that the families that provided the money were also determined not only to achieve absolute top-notch acoustics but also top-notch architecture. Those two things together don't happen very often. The committee had that initial resolve, and they stuck to it through years of budget adjustments and fund-raising. They never faltered in their determination to see the best quality designed and built in Dallas. Certainly, in that sense it stands out among all the projects I've done since 1950."[7]

JoLynne Jensen was the DSO's in-house general contractor for several of the finish-out projects that took place in the 1990s. She was impressed by the ongoing commitment the Meyerson Symphony Center inspired in its participants at all levels. "We had many of the original subcontractors working on the building in summer 1997 and 1998," she points out. "The guy who did the cinderblock walls within the percussion warmup room was the same man who laid most of the limestone blocks in the building. The company that engraved the granite wall outside the Green Room is the same one that engraved the circular Wall of Honor above the curved staircase coming up from the box office and parking garage level. They all feel a connection to this building. They take incredible pride in it. I guess Pei started it: He wanted to build a concert hall because he hadn't built one in his career. His attitude was contagious, and eventually everyone caught it: 'This is probably the only concert hall I will ever work on. I may build another building; I'll probably design another house. I'll *never* have another opportunity in my entire life to build a concert hall, and we want this one to be perfect.'"[8]

At the turn of the twenty-first century, people have come to think of the Arts District and the immediately surrounding area as "downtown Dallas." In the 1960s and 1970s, the Elm, Commerce, Main area extending from Dealey Plaza and the site of the Kennedy assassination to the Baker and Adolphus Hotels would have been thought of as downtown. As the area around the Arts District has been developed, that has changed. Tourists and young people flock to the West End, but that part of greater downtown flourishes more as an entertainment area than as a center for business (excepting restaurants, of course). The area around the symphony hall has become the most prestigious area for corporate offices. Ross Avenue, the southern boundary of the Arts District, now boasts several major business towers. It has become the Main Street of Dallas.

A thorn in many sides was the Cullen-Frost motor bank building on a part of the symphony site that by all aesthetic rights should have been part of the jigsaw puzzle of land on which Pei would situate the building. The bank stubbornly refused to sell in the 1980s when the land issue was being hammered out. By the mid-1990s, the facility was abandoned. An observer from a nearby office tower likened it to an old filling station.

The Dallas Symphony was able to acquire the land and the empty bank building in 1998 for $1.5 million, with assistance from Chase Bank. Raymond Nasher, the developer and noted sculpture collector, agreed to provide a major sculpture for the space if the bank could be torn down. It was razed in October 1998. The symphony's sculpture garden will further enhance an Arts District that stands to benefit also from the Nasher Sculpture Garden two blocks west, adjacent to the Dallas Museum of Art. No doubt spurred by the increased attraction of the area promised by the Nasher gift, developers announced plans in 1998 to build adjacent high-rise housing in the same blocks.

Also in 1998, Dallas voters approved a bond issue to purchase land for a new multi-facility performing arts center that will serve as a permanent home for the Dallas Opera and the Dallas Theater Center downtown, as well as provide a Dallas home for the Fort Worth-Dallas Ballet and a venue for smaller arts organizations. The approval of the 1998 bond initiative placed the projected opera/ballet facility at the same point that the Meyerson Symphony Center was two decades prior. The plan for a downtown arts district has taken considerably longer than Carr, Lynch Associates envisioned when they made their recommendations to the City of Dallas in 1977. But it has made considerable progress, and the prognosis is good for it to reach full fruition in the first decade of the twenty-first century.

The Meyerson Symphony Center has given the Dallas Symphony a permanent home that is the envy of orchestras throughout North America and internationally. Visiting performers are delighted by its acoustical superiority, flexibility, visual beauty, and practical amenities. The universal acclaim and prestige accorded to the building are a continuing source of pride to Dallas citizens. Once derided as a cow town, Dallas has redefined its image. The presence and prestige of the Meyerson declare Dallas to be a city that takes its culture seriously. DSO President Eugene Bonelli often quotes from Winston Churchill: *"We shape our buildings, and then they shape us."* "That is so true about what happened here," Bonelli says. "The decisions we made, the whole way we approached it—we knew that we were doing something that would shape the cultural life and the soul of this city well into the next century." The hall is aging gracefully. As the next millennium dawns, the symphony faces the challenge to match artistically the quality of the building that is its home. Similarly, the city and the Dallas community must commit to maintain the Meyerson Symphony Center so that it endures for the generations to come.

APPENDIX

SPECIFICATIONS OF THE LAY FAMILY CONCERT ORGAN

T HE FOLLOWING information was printed in the commemorative program booklet for the fortnight dedication concert in September 1992 and is reprinted with the permission of C. B. Fisk, Inc.

—⁂—

RISING the full height of the concert chamber behind the stage, the Herman W. and Amelia H. Lay Family Concert Organ serves as the visual focal point of the Eugene McDermott Concert Hall at the Morton H. Meyerson Symphony Center. One of the largest mechanical action organs ever built for a concert hall, the instrument is Opus 100 of C. B. Fisk, Inc., of Gloucester, Massachusetts.

C. B. Fisk, Inc., was founded in 1961 by Charles Brenton Fisk (1925–1983). It was Fisk who made the initial proposal to the Meyerson Symphony Center Organ Committee in 1982. Throughout his career, Fisk sought to recapture the sound, touch and enduring qualities of historical instruments in creating new instruments on which a wide variety of organ literature could be performed. C. B. Fisk, Inc., is internationally recognized for its innovation, exceptional level of craftsmanship, architectural sensitivity and the tonal quality of its instruments, achieved by the meticulous voicing of each pipe. It is for these reasons that the firm was selected by the Meyerson Symphony Center Organ Committee, chaired by Dr. Eugene Bonelli, then Dean of the Meadows School of the Arts at Southern Methodist University.

The design of the instrument evolved from consultations among architect I. M. Pei, acoustician Russell Johnson, and principals from Fisk. The team of designers included Robert Cornell, Senior Design Engineer; Charles Nazarian, Visual Designer, and 32 artists and crafts-men who played an integral role in the design, construction, installation, tuning and voicing of this, the 32-year-old firm's *magnum opus*. Nazarian designed a free-standing case of warm-hued cherry wood to house the 4,535 pipes and interior mechanisms of the instrument. Others involved in its creation include Jas. Gillanders, Ltd., of Toronto, who crafted the mill-work on the massive cherry wood case, and August Laukhuff of Germany, who had one of the few pipe shops large enough to manufacture the 32-foot polished tin pipes.

The completed instrument draws its tonal inspiration from many different styles and peri-ods of organ building, enabling it to showcase as much of the organ literature as possible. The key action is mechanical, directly linking each key to a valve controlling wind to the pipe and imparting sensitive control to the player's touch. The action includes a Fisk-designed servo-pneumatic lever that assists the key action to the large Résonance division. The stop action is electrically controlled with a solid-state combination action to permit instant access to nearly limitless combinations of preset registrations.

The instrument is composed of six divisions which are played on four manual keyboards and one pedal keyboard. The Great, Swell, Positive and Pedal divisions form the Classical core of the organ. The Résonance division, played on either manual or pedal keyboard, is a power-ful division of French Romantic influence designed to be used with orchestra. An English-inspired Tuba division, also played on either manual or pedal keyboard, is voiced on high wind pressure and is especially suited for crescendos in music for organ and orchestra.

Centuries of craftsmanship and artistry have been married with modern technology to create the Lay Family Concert Organ. It now stands as a tribute to a city that does not settle for second best—a city that continues to set standards in musical excellence. The organ speaks proudly in a concert hall that is the architectural and acoustical benchmark by which others are judged and a great legacy that Dallas will leave to many generations of music lovers.

Lay Family Concert Organ Stop List

Résonance I and/or IV
Prestant 32′
Montre 16′
Montre 8′
Violoncelle 8′
Flûte harmonique 8′
Bourdon 8′
Quinte 5 ⅓′
Prestant 4′
Octave 4′
Quinte 2 ⅔′
les Octaves III
les Quintes VI
Plein jeu VIII
Bombarde 16′
Trompette 8′
Clairon 4′

Great I
Principal 16′
Quintadehn 16′
Octava 8′
Spillpfeife 8′
Octava 4′
Rohrflöte 4′
Superoctava 2′
Mixtur VIII–XII
Trommeten 16′
Trommeten 8′

Positive II
Bourdon 16′
Principal 8′
Dulciane 8′
Gedackt 8′
Octave 4′
Baarpijp 4′
Nazard 2 ⅔′
Doublette 2′
Tierce 2′ & 1 ⅗′
Sharp VI–VIII
Trompette 8′
Cromorne 8′
Trechterregal 8′

Swell III
Flûte traversière 8′
Viole de gambe 8′
Voix céleste 8′
Bourdon 8′
Prestant 4′
Flûte octaviante 4′
Octavin 2′
Cornet III
Basson 16′
Trompette 8′
Hautbois 8′
Voix humaine 8′
Clairon 4′

Tuba IV
Tuba Magna 16′
Tuba 8′
Royal Trumpet 8′
Tuba Clarion 4′

Pedal
Prestant 32′
Untersatz 32′
Prestant 16′
Contrebasse 16′
Montre 16′
Bourdon 16′
Quinte 10 ⅔′
Montre 8′
Flûte 8′
Flûte harmonique 8′
Violoncelle 8′
Bourdon 8′
Quinte 5 ⅓′
Prestant 4′
Octave 4′
Quinte 2 ⅔′
Mixture VI
Tuba Profunda 32′
Bombarde 16′
Tuba Magna 16′
Posaune 16′
Trompette 8′
Tuba 8′
Royal Trumpet 8′
Clairon 4′

Couplers
Great to Résonance
Positive to Résonance
Swell to Résonance
Tuba to Résonance
Résonance octaves graves
Positive to Great
Swell to Great
Tuba to Great
Swell to Positive
Résonance to Pedal
Great to Pedal
Positive to Pedal
Swell to Pedal
Swell 4′ to Pedal

Ventils
Pedal reeds off
Résonance reeds off
Great reeds off
Positive reeds off
Swell reeds off
Résonance off

General Tremulant
Résonance Flue Tremulant
Nachtigal
Cymbelstern

Eighty-four ranks,
Four manuals and pedal:
Manual key compass 61 notes,
Pedal compass 32 notes
Mechanical key action

C. B. Fisk Company Workers for the Herman W. and Amelia H. Lay Family Concert Organ

Kathleen Hallman Adams

Stephen A. Boody

Gregory R. Bover

Robert Cornell

Linda Cook Dieck

Steven Dieck

R. Forrest Dillon

D. Casey Dunaway

Robert Finley

Virginia Lee Fisk

Andrew Xury Gingery

Erik Grausam

Robert L. Hazard

Terry L. Joris

Carol S. Judd

Kees Kos

Stephen Paul Kowalyshyn

Michael B. Kraft

Jerry W. Lewis

Stephen F. Malionek

Charles L. Nazarian

Mark Edward Nelson

Diane M. Oliver

Brian A. Pike

David C. Pike

Patricia Pike

Michael P. Rathke

John E. Schreiner

David M. Sedlak

Peter Pindar Stearns

Theodore Stoddard

Akimasa Tokito

David W. Waddell

NOTES

Prologue

1 Michael Coren, interview with author, Dallas, Oct. 3, 1996.

2 John Corigliano, letter to Russell Johnson, Apr. 15, 1993. Quoted by permission of Mr. Corigliano.

3 Robert Finklea, "What Sank the Dallas Symphony Orchestra?" *The New York Times,* June 9, 1974.

Chapter One

1 Anshel Brusilow, interview with author, Addison, Tex., Aug. 24, 1998.

2 John Merwin, "High Culture, Low Politics: The Death of the Dallas Symphony," *D Magazine,* November 1974, 44. Ralph Rogers's book, *Splendid Torch* (West Kennebunk, Maine: Phoenix Publishers, 1993) states it was the Marine Corps Band. "[The orchestra musicians] said their union contract called for the hall to be heated to not less than 68 degrees, but the Cotton Bowl was not—that night! Fortunately, the Marine Corps Band did play so it wasn't a complete disaster. I explained to the musicians that this was no way to show their appreciation to the people of Dallas. I suggested that they apologize. They refused. I resigned." (p. 207)

3 Brusilow interview.

4 *Ibid.*

5 Kalman Cherry, interview with author, Dallas, Aug. 19, 1998.

6 Dorothea Kelley, interview with author, Dallas, Apr. 9, 1998.

7 DSA Executive Board minutes, Feb. 14 and Mar. 20, 1973; each includes copies of the financial resolutions.

8 Henry S. Miller, Jr., letter to author, June 10, 1999.

9 Clifford Spohr, interview with author, Dallas, Oct. 14, 1998.

10 Brusilow interview.

11 *Ibid.* Stretch died March 23, 1972.

12 *Ibid.*

13 Patricia Evridge Hill, *Dallas: The Making of a Modern City* (Austin: University of Texas Press, 1996), 109.

14 *Ibid.,* 165.

15 Henry S. Miller, Jr., interview with author, Oct. 30, 1996.

16 William L. Schilling, interview with author, Dallas, Aug. 6, 1997.

17 *Ibid.*

18 John Merwin, "High Culture, Low Politics: The Death of the Dallas Symphony," *D Magazine,* Vol. I, No. 2 (November 1974), 47.

19 William A. Payne, "Dallas Orchestra Halts Operations," *The Dallas Morning News,* Mar. 13, 1974, 1A.

20 Dallas Chamber of Commerce News Release, Mar 18, 1974. DSO archives.

21 DSA Board minutes, closed session, Mar. 25, 1974.

22 Musicians' committee statement, Apr. 12, 1974. Courtesy of Henry S. Miller, Jr.

23 Terry Kliewer, "DSO Plays, Passes Hat," *The Dallas Morning News,* Apr. 15, 1974, 1A.

24 Janet Cherry, interview with author, Dallas, Aug. 18, 1998.

25 Miller interview.

26 Philip Jonsson, interview with author,

Addison, Tex., July 21, 1997.

27　Editors of *D*, "Power in Dallas: Who Holds the Cards?" *D, The Magazine of Dallas*, Vol. I, No. 1 (October 1974), 52.

28　Jonsson interview.

29　*Idem.*

30　*Idem.*

31　Robert Glaze, interview with author, Dallas, Aug. 7, 1997.

32　Henry S. Miller interview.

33　Richard I. Galland, interview with author, Dallas, Dec. 23, 1996.

34　Jonsson interview.

35　Quoted in John Ardoin, "Musicians to Sue DSO over Wages," *The Dallas Morning News*, June 5, 1974, 9B.

36　DSA Press release, "DSA and Players' Committee will Continue Negotiations Next Week," July 19, 1974. Courtesy of Henry S. Miller, Jr.

37　John Ardoin, "DSO Negotiations Break Off," *The Dallas Morning News*, July 28, 1974, 21A.

38　Francis Raffetto, "Musicians Blacklist DSO," *The Dallas Morning News*, Aug. 6, 1974, 12A, and Olin Chism, "Action strikes symphony," *Dallas Times Herald*, Aug. 6, 1974, B-4.

39　DSA Press release, "Miller expresses surprise at musicians' blacklist move," August 6, 1974. Courtesy of Henry S. Miller, Jr.

40　Janet Cherry interview.

41　DSA Press release, "Arbitrator Rules Symphony Musicians to Receive Full Salaries," Aug. 13, 1974. Courtesy of Henry S. Miller, Jr.

42　DSA Press release, "DSA to begin Subscription Drive," Oct. 4, 1974. Courtesy of Henry S. Miller, Jr.

Chapter Two

1　John Ardoin, "The Saving of the Dallas Symphony," *The New York Times*, Oct. 4, 1981, arts & leisure, 25.

2　John Ardoin, "Haldeman Given Top DSO Posts," *The Dallas Morning News*, Nov. 6, 1974; Olin Chism, "Symphony signs on new manager," *Dallas Times Herald*, Nov. 6, 1974.

3　Henry S. Miller and Jonsson interviews.

4　John Ardoin, "Haldeman Given Top DSO Posts."

5　The memo, dated January 8, 1975, is in the

Dallas Symphony archives.

6　Jonsson and Miller interviews.

7　Jonsson interview.

8　Douglas Howard, interview with author, Dallas, Sept. 5, 1996.

9　Gregory Hustis, interview with author, Dallas, Aug. 17, 1997.

10　Al Milano, interview with author, by telephone from Newport Beach, Calif., June 29, 1998.

11　Janet Haldeman Moore, interview with author, by telephone from Houston, Oct. 5, 1998.

12　Leonard Stone interview.

13　Haldeman's original intent was to appoint Masur as principal guest conductor. Although Masur did lead a couple of subscription concerts in Dallas, the formal appointment did not materialize.

14　Hustis interview.

15　Lloyd Haldeman, memorandum to facilities committee, July 14, 1977. DSO archives.

16　Minutes of facilities committee meeting, July 28, 1977. DSO archives.

17　Minutes of facilities committee meeting, Aug. 16, 1977. DSO archives.

18　Jonsson interview.

19　"Family" in the corporate sense; actually a composite of the Dealey, Decherd, and Moroney biological families.

20　Robert Decherd, interview with author, Dallas, Oct. 4, 1997.

Chapter Three

1　Robert Folsom, interview with author, Addison, Tex., June 1, 1998.

2　Decherd interview.

3　Galland interview.

4　Decherd interview.

5　George R. Schrader, interview with author, Addison, Tex., Mar. 25, 1997.

6　*Ibid.*

7　Folsom interview.

8　Schrader interview.

9　Unsigned, "Leedom convinced arts aid available," *The Dallas Morning News*, Nov. 19, 1976, 13B.

10　Folsom interview.

11　Schrader interview.

12　The City of Dallas contracted with Carr,

Lynch on May 2, 1977. Interim reports submitted to participating arts organizations in June, July, and September chronicled the firm's preliminary findings, including criteria for site selection and exploration of general policy alternatives. City of Dallas Resolution 77-3503, dated November 23, 1977, formally accepted the final version of the Carr, Lynch report.

13 Carr, Lynch report, A-1, "Brief Summary of Findings and Recommendations." City of Dallas Archives.

14 DSA Board minutes, July 26, 1977.

15 Schrader interview, July 21, 1998.

16 *Ibid.*

17 City of Dallas Resolution #79-3739. City Archives.

18 DSA Board Executive Committee meeting minutes, Nov. 1, 1977.

19 *Ibid.* In fact, the original arts district plan included a surface (as opposed to underground) parking garage, based on the assumption that the City of Dallas would provide parking as part of the infrastructure for the area.

20 Folsom interview.

21 DSA Board Executive Committee meeting minutes, Jan. 10, 1978.

22 Promotional literature issued by the Citizens' Information Committee listed seventeen proposals for a total of $285,173,000. City of Dallas Resolution 78-1614, "Report of Canvassing Committee Resolution and Order Adopting Report," June 12, 1978, was adopted two days after the election.

23 Schilling says that Morris Hite was the author of the slogan.

24 Schilling interview.

25 Jim Schutze, "Effect of Proposition 13 on bond vote uncertain," *Dallas Times Herald,* June 8, 1978, C-1.

26 Howard interview.

27 Michael Coren, interview with author, Dallas, Oct. 3, 1996.

28 David Dillon, interview with author, by telephone from Amherst, Mass., Dec. 14, 1998.

29 Leonard David Stone, interview with author, Calgary, Alberta, Aug. 30, 1997.

30 Kalman Cherry interview.

31 Eric Barr, interview with author, Dallas, June 11, 1998.

32 Leonard Stone interview.

33 *Ibid.*

34 Cherry interview.

35 Leonard Stone interview.

36 *Ibid.*

37 Milano interview.

38 Schrader interview, July 21, 1998.

39 *Ibid.*

40 Decherd interview.

41 Howard interview.

42 Schrader interview, July 21, 1998.

Chapter Four

1 Morton H. Meyerson, interview with author, Dallas, Aug. 18, 1997.

2 Decherd interview.

3 *Ibid.*

4 *Ibid.*

5 *Ibid.*

6 *Ibid.*

7 A Facilities committee memorandum to the DSA Executive Board, Dec. 12, 1978, summarizes a meeting with Crow on Dec. 11. Crow reiterated his wish to proceed with the proposed symphony hall and his refusal to relinquish the tract bounded by Ross, Olive, Harwood, and Flora streets because of his intent to build an office tower on the site. Crow insisted that he, as builder, would have final say over every aspect of the symphony hall, including the architects. The facilities committee concluded that "should we accept this hall, we would be excluded from any further city planning for the next quarter to half century, even though the hall might prove to be inadequate." DSO archives.

8 DSA Board minutes, May 16, 1979.

9 Meyerson interview, July 9, 1997.

10 *Ibid.*

11 Decherd interview.

12 Meyerson interview, July 9, 1997.

13 *Ibid.* DSA Executive Board meeting minutes from Nov. 28, 1979, indicate that Meyerson "has accepted the chairmanship of the Facilities Committee and is forming its membership."

14 *Ibid.*

15 *Ibid.*

16 Meyerson interview, Aug. 18, 1997.

17 *Ibid.*

18 Penn was Nancy Penson's maiden name. Her

mother, Mrs. Elizabeth Hudson Penn, was
also a long-time donor to the symphony and a
major early supporter of the concert hall.

19 Meyerson interview, July 9, 1997.

20 *Ibid.*, Aug. 18, 1997.

21 *Ibid.*, Aug. 18, 1997, and Sept. 10, 1998.

22 Al Milano, interview with author, by
telephone from Newport Beach, Calif.,
June 29, 1998.

23 Meyerson interview, July 9, 1997.

24 Dolores Barzune, interview with author,
Dallas, Sept. 4, 1998.

25 Meyerson interview, Sept. 10, 1998.

26 Stone interview, Aug. 30, 1997.

27 Milano interview.

28 Meyerson interview, July 9, 1997.

29 Peter Wexler, interview with author, New
York City, Oct. 21, 1997.

30 Wexler interview.

31 Meyerson interview, July 9, 1997.

32 Howard interview.

33 Mary McDermott Cook, interview with
author, Dallas, Oct. 21, 1996.

34 *Ibid.*

Chapter Five

1 Wexler interview.

2 Meyerson interview, July 9, 1997. Meyerson
made a second trip to Davies Hall shortly
after it opened.

3 Stone interview, Aug. 30, 1997.

4 Mort Meyerson sent letters to each member
of the concert hall committee on March 20,
1981, announcing McNeil's appointment.
Cook archives.

5 Wexler interview.

6 DSA Board minutes, October 9, 1979.

7 Milano interview.

8 Melissa McNeil, interview with author,
Dallas, Sept. 17, 1998.

9 Howard interview.

10 Eugene Bonelli, interview with author, Dallas,
Jan. 8, 1997.

11 Meyerson interview, July 9, 1997.

12 Leonard Stone interview, Aug. 30, 1997.

13 Meyerson interview.

14 Nancy Penson, interview with author, Dallas,
Oct. 28, 1996.

15 Meyerson interview.

16 Bonelli interview, July 9, 1998.

17 Meyerson interview.

18 *Ibid.*, July 9, 1997.

19 DSA Board minutes, Nov. 13, 1980.

20 Meyerson interview.

21 The Musikvereinssaal's seat count of 1,680 is
deceptive, because the seats are physically
small and do not conform to modern fire
codes. If its audience seating space were fitted
with chairs the size of those in contemporary
concert halls, in conformance with accepted
safety parameters, the seat count would
shrink to only 1,250.

22 Donald J. Stone, interview with author,
Dallas, Feb. 3, 1997.

23 Meyerson interview.

Chapter Six

1 Louise Kahn, memo to Morton H. Meyerson,
June 11, 1980. DSO archives.

2 Leonard Stone interview, Aug. 30, 1997.

3 George Miller, interview with author, New
York City, Jan. 16, 1997.

4 Leonard Stone interview.

5 *Ibid.*

6 Marcus interview, Aug. 7, 1998.

7 Stone interview.

8 Mary McDermott, handwritten notes from
architecture interviews, Nov. 14, 1980.
Cook archives.

9 Stone interview.

10 Marcus interview.

11 *Ibid.*

12 Stone interview.

13 Mary McDermott, handwritten notes, Nov. 14,
1980. Cook archives.

14 *Ibid.*, and Stone interview.

15 Stone interview.

16 Marcus interview, Oct. 16, 1996.

17 Stone interview.

18 Richard C. Levin, memo to concert hall committee, Nov. 19, 1980. DSO archives.

19 Richard Levin, interview with author, Dallas,
Nov. 1, 1996.

20 Marcus interviews, Oct. 16, 1996, and Aug. 7,
1998.

21 Amberg interview.

22 Marcus interview, Aug. 7, 1998.

23 *Ibid.*

24 Levin interview.

25 Marcus interview, Aug. 7, 1998.

26 Levin interview.

27 Stone interview.

28 Marcus interview, Aug. 8, 1998.

29 Cook interview, Sept. 11, 1998.

30 Stone interview.

31 Don Stone, interview with author, Dallas, Feb. 3, 1997.

32 Charles Young, interview with author, New York City, Jan. 16, 1997.

33 Cheryl Taylor, "Pei to design Dallas concert hall," *The Dallas Morning News,* Dec. 31, 1980.

Chapter Seven

1 John Kitzman, interview with author, Dallas, Oct. 25, 1996.

2 Bonelli interview, July 9, 1998.

3 Melzer was later the acoustical consultant for the 1986 renovation of Carnegie Hall.

4 Quoted in Leonard Stone interview. Stone recalls no major element in the room that Mata influenced. According to him, Mata initially opposed the height of the orchestra risers but later became very supportive both of the acoustic riser system and of Johnson. (Ironically, the riser system was eventually eliminated.) Mata's "conversion" represented a major change, because he had been a Chris Jaffe proponent. Mata had not conducted in any of the halls that Johnson was using to try to win the position as the acoustician of the Dallas concert hall. Johnson appears to have won Mata over in their conversations. At least one lengthy letter from Mata to the DSO Board summarizing a meeting with Johnson is in the DSO archives. A letter from Johnson to Melissa McNeil of June 15, 1982, mentions "two very useful meetings with Eduardo Mata" the previous week in London. Cook archives.

5 Stone interview, Aug. 30, 1997.

6 Meyerson interview, July 9, 1997; the substance of the story is corroborated in the Stone interview, Aug. 30, 1997.

7 Stone interview.

8 Bonelli interview.

9 *Ibid.*

10 *Ibid.*

11 Levin interview.

12 Bonelli interview.

13 *Ibid.*

14 Howard interview.

15 Kitzman interview.

16 Clifford Spohr, interview with author, Dallas, Oct. 14, 1998.

17 Douglas Howard, letter to Eugene Bonelli, Jan. 13, 1981. Cook archives.

18 Eugene Bonelli, memo to working group, Dallas Symphony concert hall committee, Jan. 15, 1981. Cook archives.

19 Bonelli interview, Jan. 8, 1997.

20 Stone interview, Aug. 30, 1997.

21 *Ibid.*

22 DSA Executive Board minutes, Feb. 20 and May 22, 1981.

23 The initial letter of agreement, dated April 6, 1981, specified that Artec would review the concert hall committee's brief, prepare a written response to the brief, work with Hanscomb Roy Associates, the cost consultant engaged by the Dallas Symphony Association in March 1981, on the first estimates, prepare information on the acoustics aspect of the seat count and prepare a preliminary report on seat count, list facilities spaces, and assess the acoustics implications of various independent reports the DSA had commissioned from Shaver and McKinsey. The last of those initial reports was submitted in August 1982. City of Dallas Resolution 84-1385 summarizes the history of the Artec contract prior to its assumption by the city. City of Dallas archives. See also Cook archives, letter of even date.

24 Cook interview, Oct. 21, 1996.

25 Both Meyerson and Cook confirm the exchanges.

26 Meyerson interview, July 9, 1997.

27 Meyerson interview, Sept. 10, 1998.

28 *Ibid.*

Chapter Eight

1 Wallace Clement Sabine, "Reverberation," in *Collected Papers on Acoustics* (Cambridge: Harvard University Press, 1927), 4.

2 Sabine, "Architectural Acoustics," *Op. cit.,* 221.

3 Hope Bagenal and Alexander Wood, *Planning for Good Acoustics* (London: Methuen & Co., Ltd., 1931), 129.

4 George C. Izenour, *Theater Design* (New York: McGraw-Hill, 1977). See, for example,

Izenour's discussion of the Bayreuth Festspielhaus, a facility that he considers marks the beginning of contemporary theatre design, 282–84.

5 Leo Beranek, *Music, Acoustics and Architecture* (New York: John Wiley & Sons, 1962).

6 Yoichi Ando, *Concert Hall Acoustics* (Berlin and New York: Springer Verlag, 1985); see also Manfred R. Schroeder, "Toward better acoustics for concert halls," *Physics Today,* Oct. 1980, 30.

7 Manfred R. Schroeder, Foreword to Ando, *Op. cit.,* vii. Italics in original.

8 Leo Beranek, *How They Sound: Concert and Opera Halls* (Woodbury, N.Y.: Acoustical Society of America, 1996), 23 and 428.

9 Russell Johnson, interview with Alexandra Witze, Dallas, Oct. 21, 1976.

Chapter Nine

1 Quoted in John Ardoin, "Eduardo Mata: Music Director wants 'feeling of happening' in new concert hall," *The Dallas Morning News,* Sept. 6, 1981, 1C.

2 Decherd interview.

3 DSA Board minutes, Dec. 19, 1978.

4 Schrader interview, May 20, 1998.

5 Schrader and Folsom interviews.

6 One site had been purchased by a developer; another would have to go through condemnation court; and the third was owned by the Dallas Independent School District, which would not relinquish the land for five years. One month later hope had revived for the DISD-owned site, strategically situated on Ross Avenue. DSA Executive Committee Board minutes, Sept. 19, 1980.

7 DSA Executive Board minutes, Feb. 20, 1981.

8 Ted Amberg, interview with author, by telephone from Chicago, Ill., Mar. 7, 1997.

9 Schrader interview, July 21, 1998.

10 A copy of the Tishman proposal, with plats, summary analyses, *pro forma* statement of income and expenses forecasting July 1985 occupancy, and area maps, is in the Cook archives.

11 DSA Board minutes, June 19, 1981.

12 Steve Gunn and Olin Chism, "Symphony abandons plan to relocate near museum," *Dallas Times Herald,* June 20, 1981; see also

Scott McCartney, "DSA abandons land purchase," *The Dallas Morning News,* June 20, 1981.

13 DSA Executive Board minutes, July 24, 1981.

14 Leonard Stone interview.

15 Schrader interview, July 21, 1998.

16 Skip Hollandsworth, "A Funny Thing Happened on the Way to the Symphony," *D Magazine,* September 1986, 68 ff. George Schrader says that the meeting was dinner, not breakfast, and that Sullivan was the host.

17 Frank Kauffman, "Symphony hall to be built in arts district," *Dallas Times Herald,* Sept. 18, 1981.

18 Galland interview and letter to author, June 1, 1999.

19 Stone interview, Aug. 30, 1997.

20 Victor C. Suhm, interview with author, Dallas, Aug. 8, 1997.

21 *Idem.* Dr. Montgomery is the father of 1982 bond campaign chairman Phil Montgomery.

22 David Dillon, "Arts District Plan to be Presented," *The Dallas Morning News,* Aug. 19, 1982. A "Dallas Arts District Urban Design Plan" from August 1982, submitted to Dr. Philip O'Bryan Montgomery, the Dallas Arts District Consortium, and the City of Dallas by Sasaki Associates, Halcyon Ltd., and Lockwood, Andrews & Newnam, Inc., outlines the program in more detail. The report is incorporated into City of Dallas Resolution 83-0596 as Exhibit B.

23 Stone interview, Aug. 31, 1997.

Chapter Ten

1 Bonelli interview, July 9, 1998.

2 Robert Wolff, interview with author, New York City, Jan. 16, 1997.

3 Meyerson interview, July 9, 1997.

4 Martha Blaine, interview with author, Dallas, Mar. 24, 1997.

5 Blaine interview.

6 Melissa McNeil, "An Economic Analysis of The Dallas Symphony's Concert Hall FY 1985/86," July 27, 1981. Cook archives.

7 McNeil interview.

8 Stone interview, Aug. 30, 1997.

9 Meyerson interview, July 9, 1997. That distance in the Meyerson Symphony Center, from the podium to the uppermost seat in the

grand tier, is approximately 130 feet. Mata was a proponent of Christopher Jaffe's room designs, particularly the Sala Nezahualcoyotl in Mexico City, which is a modified surround hall. The 90-foot parameter, strictly construed, leads to a full surround hall.

10 Meyerson interview.

11 *Ibid.*

12 Bonelli interview, July 9, 1998.

13 Meyerson interview.

14 Don Stone, interview with author, Dallas, Feb. 3, 1997.

15 *Ibid.*

16 Mort Meyerson, memo to members of the concert hall committee, Oct. 23, 1981. See also DSA Executive Board minutes, Dec. 18, 1981.

17 Meyerson interview, Aug. 18, 1997.

18 Joe Walker, presentation to Meyerson Symphony Center docents, Dallas, Dec. 14, 1996. The author was present and taped the presentation. Walker subsequently reviewed the transcript. Hereafter cited as Walker address to docents.

Chapter Eleven

1 Travis Selmier, letter to Leonard Stone, June 1, 1981; and Morton H. Meyerson, letter to concert hall committee members, June 15, 1981. Cook archives.

2 Artec Consultants, "Dallas Concert Hall Project. Preliminary Report, Phase I (6 April 1981–12 July 1981)." Cook archives.

3 Artec Consultants, "Space Portion of our Response to the Dallas Concert Hall Draft Brief," July 6, 1981. Cook archives.

4 Nicholas Edwards, interview with author, Dallas, Apr. 30, 1999.

5 Michael Barron, "The Effects of Early Reflections on Subjective Acoustical Quality in Concert Halls," Ph.D. thesis, University of Southampton, 1974; Dieter Gottlob, "Comparison of Objective Acoustic Parameters in Concert Halls with Results of Subjective Experiments," Ph.D. thesis, University of Göttingen, 1973; and a technical paper by Yoichi Ando, subsequently published as *Concert Hall Acoustics* (Berlin and New York: Springer Verlag, 1985).

6 Edwards interview, Apr. 30, 1999.

7 *Ibid.*

8 *Ibid.*

9 I am indebted to Nicholas Edwards for providing me with a photocopy of the memorandum.

10 Edwards interview, May 3, 1999.

11 Edwards interview, Apr. 30, 1999.

12 Carol Allen, memorandum to Russell Johnson, Robert Wolff, Nicholas Edwards, Robert Essert, and Jeremie Franks, Feb. 19, 1982.

13 Memorandum of meeting, smaller unit of the concert hall committee, Jan. 26, 1982. Cook archives.

14 Memorandum of meeting, smaller unit of the concert hall committee, May 11, 1982. Cook archives.

15 Ralph Heisel, interview with author, New York City, Jan. 14, 1999.

16 Bonelli interview, Jan. 8, 1997.

17 Robert Wolff, interview with author, New York City, Jan. 16, 1997.

18 Ian Bader, interview with author, New York City, Jan. 15, 1999.

19 *Ibid.*

20 *Ibid.*

21 Bader interview and letter to author, May 28, 1999.

22 *Ibid.*

23 George Miller interview.

24 James Langford, interview with author, Dallas, Oct. 13, 1996.

25 Stone interview, Aug. 30, 1997; also Bader interview.

Chapter Twelve

1 Blaine interview.

2 *Ibid.*

3 *Ibid.*

4 Russell Johnson, letter to Eduardo Mata, Mar. 29, 1982; see also memorandum of meeting, smaller unit of concert hall committee, June 17, 1982. Cook archives.

5 Blaine interview.

6 Marshall interview.

7 Blaine interview.

8 Leonard Stone interview, Aug. 30, 1997.

9 *Ibid.*

10 *Ibid.*

11 Henry S. Miller and Leonard Stone interviews.

12 Liener Temerlin, interview with author, Irving, Tex., July 15, 1998.

Chapter Thirteen

1 Philip O'B. Montgomery III, interview with author, Dallas, Oct. 2, 1996.

2 Sydney Reid-Hedge, interview with author, Dallas, Oct. 17, 1996.

3 Suhm interview.

4 Stone interview, Aug. 30, 1997.

5 *Ibid.*

6 George Rodrigue, "The Arts District," *D Magazine,* May 1982, 103.

7 Scott Parks, "Study backs arts district concert hall," *The Dallas Morning News,* Apr. 23, 1982.

8 "Pei Unveils Design for Concert Hall," The Dallas Concert Hall press release, May 12, 1982 DSO archives.

9 David Dillon, "Pei hits high notes with concert hall," *The Dallas Morning News,* May 16, 1982.

10 Montgomery interview.

11 Nela Wells Moore, interview with author, Dallas, Mar. 19, 1999.

12 DSA Executive Board meeting minutes, May 20, 1982.

13 Enid Gray, interview with author, Dallas, Apr. 8, 1999.

14 Moore interview.

15 Montgomery interview.

16 DSA Executive Board minutes, June 14, 1982.

17 Henry Tatum, "City hears music hall cost plan," *The Dallas Morning News,* June 15, 1982; also David Dillon, "Want to buy a concert hall?" *The Dallas Morning News,* June 27, 1982.

18 Montgomery interview.

19 Henry Tatum, "Bond backers fear appraisal backlash," *The Dallas Morning News,* June 20, 1982.

20 Diane Flowers, interview with author, Dallas, July 18, 1997.

21 John Ardoin, "What will it do for Dallas?" *The Dallas Morning News,* Aug. 1, 1982.

22 David Dillon, "Want to buy a concert hall?" *The Dallas Morning News,* June 27, 1982.

23 Gray interview.

24 DSA Executive Committee meeting minutes, July 22, 1982.

25 Howard interview.

26 Montgomery interview.

27 Terry Maxon, "Dallas voters approve entire bond package," *Dallas Times Herald,* Aug. 4, 1982.

28 Montgomery interview.

Chapter Fourteen

1 Leonard Stone, interview with author, Calgary, Alberta, Aug. 30, 1997.

2 *Ibid.*

3 The firm changed its name to Hanscomb Consultants, Inc., in December 1981 Stewart Donnell founded Donnell Associates Incorporated in 1986 in Tampa, Florida. His firm now specializes in cost consulting for performing and visual arts facilities.

4 Stewart Donnell, interview with author, Dallas, July 2, 1998.

5 Donnell interview. His meeting with Meyerson took place on Feb. 27, 1981. His letter of proposal to Meyerson is dated March 4, 1981. Hanscomb Roy completed an initial program budget report for the DSA Executive Board in July 1981, and submitted its formal proposal for cost consulting services on Oct. 30, 1981. Cook archives.

6 Donnell interview.

7 After Artec's selection as the acoustical consultant in late February 1981, Robert Wolff provided some input regarding performance platform support areas. Melissa McNeil's second and third drafts of the brief, both dated April 1981, reflect his suggestions.

8 Minutes of the smaller group of the concert hall committee, Sept. 11, 1981. See also summary of early Hanscomb budgets in minutes of the Nov. 24, 1981, meeting. Cook archives.

9 Donnell interview.

10 Artec Consultants, Inc., Project No. 2893, "Areas of Impact on Dallas Symphony Orchestra Concert Hall," Apr. 16, 1982. Cook archives.

11 Hanscomb Consultants, "$45.0 Million Project Budget and List of Options," Apr. 28, 1982 Cook archives.

12 Hanscomb Consultants, "Dallas Symphony Orchestra Concert Hall, Project Budget Summary," May 11, 1982. DSO archives.

13 Meyerson interview, Aug. 18, 1997.

14 The meetings would take place immediately *after* the bond election.

15 Mort Meyerson, letter to I. M. Pei and Russell Johnson, July 12, 1982. DSO archives.

16 Leonard Stone, memo to Mort Meyerson, July 16, 1982. DSO archives.

17 Minutes of Cornerstone campaign steering committee meeting, Aug. 24, 1982. Cook archives.

18 Hanscomb, "The Dallas Symphony Hall Project Budget #8," Nov. 1982. Cook archives.

19 Memorandum, dated February 3, 1983, with minutes of smaller unit meeting from Dec. 15, 1982, and DSA Executive Board meeting minutes, Dec. 16, 1982

20 *Ibid.*

21 Amberg interview.

22 Louise Reuben Elam, interview with author, Dallas, Aug. 20, 1996.

23 Amberg interview.

24 Donnell interview.

25 Ordinance No. 17719, dated Feb. 8, 1983, incorporated into City of Dallas Resolution 83-0596. This mandate has held for major Arts District structures: the Dallas Museum of Art, Trammell Crow Center, and the Meyerson, but not for areas that remained undeveloped. In mid-1999, the stretch between the museum and the symphony from one block north of Ross Avenue to Woodall Rodgers remained an unsightly swath of street-level parking lots, a symbol of a vision still incomplete.

26 Memorandum, dated Aug. 26, 1982, summarizing meeting, smaller unit of concert hall committee on August 18, 1982.

27 Donnell interview.

28 DSA Executive Board meeting minutes, Sept. 20, 1984.

Chapter Fifteen

1 Levin interview.

2 Bader interview.

3 Cliff Keheley, interview with author, Dallas, Jan. 9, 1997.

4 DSA Executive Board meeting minutes, Aug. 23, 1984.

5 Keheley interview.

6 *Ibid.*

7 Meyerson interview, Aug. 18, 1997.

8 Edwards interview, Apr. 30, 1999.

9 *Ibid.*

10 Langford interview.

11 Young interview.

12 Stone interview, Aug. 30, 1997.

13 Bonelli interview, Sept. 8, 1998.

14 *Ibid.*

15 Edwards interview, May 3, 1999.

16 Stone interview.

17 Bonelli interview, Sept. 8, 1998.

18 Schrader interview, July 21, 1998.

19 Stone interview.

20 Young interview.

21 Leonard Stone, memorandum, "First Report to Unify I. M. Pei and Partners and Artec Consultants," Apr. 22, 1983. The document was considered sufficiently sensitive to be hand-delivered and marked "Private and Confidential." Cook archives.

22 Meyerson interview, Aug. 18, 1997.

23 Mort Meyerson, letter to Mary McDermott, Oct. 24, 1983. Cook archives.

24 Young interview.

25 Barzune interview, Sept. 4, 1998.

26 Edwards interview, July 7, 1999.

27 Don Stone interview. George Schrader observes that, in the end, Pei did influence many of the materials choices within the audience chamber.

28 Barzune interview, Sept. 4, 1998.

Chapter Sixteen

1 Willem Brans, interview with author, New York City, Oct. 21, 1997. Brans recalled the figure as "nearly fifty percent." Henry S. Miller announced the forty-two percent figure to the board of governors at its quarterly meeting on January 20, 1983.

2 Brans interview.

3 *Ibid.*

4 *Ibid.*

5 *Ibid.*

6 Brans interview; also, Liener Temerlin, interview with author, Irving, Tex., July 15, 1998.

7 Isaac Stern, transcript of Cornerstone kickoff luncheon remarks. DSO Archives.

8 Brans interview.

9 Stone interview, Aug. 30, 1997.

10 Margaret McDermott, interview with author, Dallas, June 27, 1998.

11 *Ibid.*

12 Margie Seay, interview with author, May 24, 1999.

13 McDermott interview.

14 Stone interview, Aug. 30, 1997.

15 Henry S. Miller, Jr., memorandum to the Cornerstone steering committee, Nov. 3, 1983 Cook archives.

16 DSO archives, Cornerstone files; see also Terry Maxon, "Dallas Symphony asks city to let hall bear donor's name," *The Dallas Morning News*, June 1, 1984, 25A.

17 Penson interview.

18 Stone interview, Aug. 31, 1997.

19 The DSA Executive Board minutes of June 3, 1984, mention a "gift of Ray Nasher for $10 million . . . to be enthusiastically accepted, pending legal review."

20 Stone interview, Aug. 31, 1997.

21 *Ibid.*

22 Stone interview, Aug. 31, 1997.

23 Terry Maxon, "Concert hall park plan Ok'd, rocks rejected," *The Dallas Morning News*, June 8, 1984, 21A, for example, states that "sources have said" that Ray and Patsy Nasher had promised the $10 million, but that the DSO declined to confirm the rumor and that Nasher was unavailable for comment.

24 Meyerson interview, Aug. 18, 1997.

25 *Ibid.*

26 *Ibid.*

27 Liener Temerlin, interview with author, Irving, Tex., July 15, 1998.

28 Henry Miller interview.

29 Henry S. Miller, Jr., letter to author, June 10, 1999.

30 Stone interview, Aug. 31, 1997.

31 Henry Miller interview.

32 Temerlin interview.

33 Meyerson interview, Aug. 18, 1997.

34 Stone interview, Aug. 30, 1997.

35 DSA Executive Board meeting minutes, Dec. 19, 1984.

Chapter Seventeen

1 DSA Executive Board meeting minutes, Feb. 17, 1983.

2 Schrader interviews, Feb. 5 and Mar. 25, 1997.

3 Quoted in *The Dallas Morning News,* Aug. 6, 1989, 29A.

4 *Ibid.* According to DSA Executive Board meet-

ing minutes, Schrader formally agreed to serve as the association's liaison to the city and the construction manager on June 28, 1984. The board approved an annual honorarium for him. On July 19, 1984, he submitted his formal resignation from the DSA Board, which was accepted.

5 Meyerson interview, Aug. 18, 1997.

6 Schrader interview, Mar. 25, 1997.

7 *Ibid.*

8 *Ibid.*

9 Melissa McNeil, memorandum dated June 2, 1983, summarizing meeting of smaller unit of the concert hall committee on Apr. 6, 1983. Cook archives.

10 McNeil interview.

11 Donnell interview.

12 Melissa McNeil, "Concert Hall Operational Agreement: Summary of Points," Mar. 8, 1983. Cook archives.

13 Stone interview, Aug. 30, 1997.

14 *Ibid.*

15 Walker address to docents.

16 DSA Executive Board meeting minutes, July 19, 1984.

17 Donnell interview.

18 Joe Walker, interview with author, Dallas, June 20, 1999.

19 McNeil interview.

20 Warren Gould, interview with author, Dallas, Jan. 30, 1997.

21 Elam interview.

22 Walker interview.

23 *Ibid.*

24 David Dillon and Terry Box, "The Meyerson Center: Saga of a Symphony hall," *The Dallas Morning News,* Aug. 6, 1989, 1.

25 Walker address to docents.

26 Schrader interview, Mar. 25, 1997.

27 Terry Maxon and Allen R. Myerson, "Officials say concert hall extras predate '82 vote," *The Dallas Morning News,* Jan. 19, 1985, 33A.

28 Terry Maxon, "Contracts for concert hall approved; City Council action clears way for construction of $75 million project," *The Dallas Morning News,* Jan. 31, 1985, 46A.

29 City of Dallas Resolution 85-0703, dated February 27, 1985, states "Notice of intent to issue Combination Tax and Revenue Certificates of Obligation, Series 1985 in the principal amount of $32,000,000, for the

purpose of paying contractual obligations to be incurred for the construction and equipping of public works, to-wit: the Dallas Symphony Hall, and paying all or a portion of the contractual obligations for professional services of engineers, attorneys and financial advisors in connection with said public works and Certificates of Obligation." The resolution further states intent to pass the ordinance on March 20, 1985, *i.e.*, the date the certificates would be available for sale. Max Goldblatt was the only councilman to vote against the resolution. At this point, the Dallas Symphony Association's share of funding had risen to fifty-two percent of the $75 million total.

30 Gregory Curtis, "Behind the Lines," *Texas Monthly,* March 1985, 5.

31 Suhm interview.

32 Temerlin interview.

33 Terry Maxon, "City will be urged to start building Symphony center," *The Dallas Morning News,* Jan. 26, 1985.

34 Mark Edgar, "Council revises contract for symphony hall," *The Dallas Morning News,* Aug. 1, 1985, 29A.

35 Elam interview.

Chapter Eighteen

1 Schrader interview, July 21, 1998. "I love to work with Pei because he stretches my ambition—then I can pull him back!" Schrader told the author in June 1999. "We get a lot more for our money that way." See also Morton H. Meyerson, letter to members of the concert hall committee, Feb. 3, 1982. Cook archives.

2 Henry Tatum, "Land swap proposal to double arts site," *The Dallas Morning News,* Jan. 23, 1982, 1A. One acre is 43,560 square feet.

3 Melissa McNeil, memorandum, summarizing Mar. 10, 1982, meeting of smaller unit, Mar. 22, 1982.

4 Henry Tatum, "Dallas needs to buy 5 tracts for music hall," *The Dallas Morning News,* Mar. 23, 1982. See also City of Dallas Council Communication No. 245-82 from Assistant City Manager James R. Fountain, Jr., regarding Site Acquisition, Symphony Hall; Five Tracts of Land in Block 531 and 532, Mar. 24, 1982, filed with City of Dallas Resolution 82-1090.

5 DSA Executive Board meeting minutes, Oct. 21, 1982.

6 Cornerstone campaign steering committee meeting notes, Nov. 4, 1982. Cook archives.

7 Terry Maxon, "Land problems stall concert hall project," *Dallas Times Herald,* Dec. 7, 1982.

8 Melissa McNeil, memorandum detailing minutes of meeting of the smaller unit of the concert hall committee, Feb. 3, 1983. Cook archives.

9 Minutes of Jan. 11, 1983, design team meeting. DSO archives.

10 Quoted in George Rodrigue, "Evans hopes to end concert hall roadblock," *The Dallas Morning News,* Jan. 5, 1983.

11 Melissa McNeil, Memorandum dated June 2, 1983, summarizing meeting of the small unit of the concert hall committee on Apr. 6, 1983. Cook archives.

12 George Rodrigue, "Concert hall land deals to go before council," *The Dallas Morning News,* Feb. 26, 1983, 1A. Negotiators worked out the final swap with Borden, which still owned substantial patches of the quilt, toward the end of April. See Cliff Foster and Bill Turque, "Land swap approved for concert hall site," *Dallas Times Herald,* Apr. 21, 1983, A-1.

13 The agency is now called the Texas Department of Transportation.

14 Cliff Foster, "Evans expects land suit accord," *Dallas Times Herald,* Mar. 11, 1983, 1A.

15 Suhm interview.

16 Cliff Foster, "Ground broken for concert hall," *Dallas Times Herald,* Apr. 30, 1983, A-1.

17 According to Vic Suhm, they resolved it by buying the land back from Triland's Nick di Giuseppe at a premium. "Nick didn't get his development site. Of course by then, I think he knew that the economy was going in the tank, and he wasn't going to be able to develop that land anyway. We paid a little bit more money, I imagine, than otherwise we would have had to, but it was the only way, at that point, to site the hall." Suhm interview.

18 Cliff Foster, "Arts garage gets support of council," *Dallas Times Herald,* Jan. 12, 1984, A-1.

19 Minutes of Dallas CBD Enterprises Board Meeting, June 3, 1983. I am indebted to E. Larry Fonts of the Central Dallas Association for making this and other related documents available to me for research purposes.

20 Minutes of Dallas CBD Enterprises Board Meeting, Sept. 2, 1983.

21 Notes from Steering Committee Meeting of Sept. 9, 1983, dated Oct. 12, 1983. Stone (or the note-taker) mistakenly referred to CBD Enterprises as the Central Business District Foundation. Cook archives.

22 DSA Executive Board minutes, Jan. 17, 1985.

23 Dallas CBD Enterprises Board Minutes, May 3, 1985. See also Allen R. Myerson, "Legal talks delay start of concert hall construction," *The Dallas Morning News*, Apr. 10, 1985, 29A.

24 Allen R. Myerson, "Land swap may allow building of concert hall," *The Dallas Morning News*, May 2, 1985, H2.

25 Dallas CBD Enterprises Board Minutes, Aug. 2, 1985. CBD then still owed approximately $20 million on its original $28.1 million loan. The land it had purchased was valued at $43 million.

26 City of Dallas Resolution 85-2878.

27 City of Dallas Resolution 85-4010.

28 Dallas CBD Enterprises. *Sale of the Arts District Property to the City of Dallas, December 23, 1985*, contains all the closing documents. Central Dallas Association archives.

29 Suhm interview.

Chapter Nineteen

1 Blaine interview.

2 Dvora Lewis, interview with author, by telephone from London, Aug. 25, 1998.

3 Temerlin interview.

4 Tim Graham, "Symphony hall accord approved," *Dallas Times Herald*, Sept. 19, 1985.

5 George Rodrigue, "Symphony board OKs lease pact," *The Dallas Morning News*, Sept. 20, 1985, 20A.

6 Richard Freling, interview with author, Dallas, Feb. 26, 1997.

7 Mark Melson, memorandum to Leonard David Stone, Jan. 15, 1986. DSO archives.

8 *Idem.*

9 Meyerson interview, Aug. 18, 1997. Meyerson retired in December 1986 and resumed active participation in the smaller unit in 1987.

10 Bonelli interview, July 9, 1998.

11 Sherry Jacobson, "$3 million hike in concert hall fees may force cutbacks," *The Dallas Morning News*, Apr. 10, 1986.

12 Cliff Keheley, letter to the editor of *The Dallas Morning News*, Apr. 16, 1986.

13 Sherry Jacobson, "Heralded hall half-finished; symphony center labeled as 'jewel,'" *The Dallas Morning News*, June 14, 1987, 33A.

Chapter Twenty

1 Bob Lemke, interview with author, Dallas, May 24, 1999.

2 DSA Executive Board minutes, Dec. 19, 1985.

3 Paul Lyons, interview with author, by telephone from Las Vegas, Nev., June 17, 1999.

4 Lyons interview.

5 *Ibid.*

6 Lemke interview.

7 Perry Chin, interview with author, by telephone from New York City, June 17, 1999.

8 Lyons interview.

9 Keheley interview.

10 According to Redmond, some of the aesthetically deficient columns in the lower lobby were allowed to remain because I. M. Pei agreed to let them be finished in plaster. *The Dallas Morning News*, Sept. 6, 1989, 30–31A, summarizes the concrete saga. The information is further substantiated in the Langford, Redmond, and Walker interviews.

11 Langford interview.

12 Redmond interview.

13 DSA Board minutes, July 23, 1987.

14 DSA Board minutes, Aug. 27, 1987.

15 Reuben interview.

16 Glenn Redmond, memorandum to author, June 22, 1999.

17 Bonelli interview.

18 Chin interview.

19 *Ibid.*

20 Lyons interview.

21 Lemke interview.

22 Redmond interview.

23 Reynolds interview.

24 *Ibid.*

25 Kalman Cherry interview.

26 Barbara Hustis, interview with author, Aug. 17, 1997.

27 Ed Housewright, "City urged to OK $2.5 million more for symphony hall," *The Dallas Morning News*, June 7, 1988, 21A. See also Sally Giddens, "The Sound of Money: Explaining

the Symphony's Price Tag," *D Magazine,*
Aug. 1988, 23.

28 Walker address to docents.

29 Walker interview, June 20, 1999.

30 Lemke interview.

31 Redmond interview.

32 Coy Porter, letter to author, July 31, 1998.

33 Redmond interview.

34 Walker interview, June 20, 1999.

35 Keheley interview.

Chapter Twenty-One

1 Ed Housewright, "The vision takes shape: a hard-hat tour of Dallas' lavish new concert hall," *The Dallas Morning News,* Apr. 30, 1989, C-1.

2 Schilling interview.

3 Keheley interview.

4 Bonelli interview, July 9, 1998.

5 Fred Hoster, interview with author, Dallas, Jan. 30, 1997.

6 Keheley interview.

7 Dillon interview.

8 Warren Gould, interview with author, Dallas, Jan. 31, 1997.

9 Donnell interview.

10 Stone interview, Aug. 30, 1997.

Chapter Twenty-Two

1 Barzune interview, Sept. 4, 1998.

2 Stone interview, Aug. 31, 1997.

3 Barzune interview, Oct. 7, 1996.

4 Domenick Ietto, telephone interview with author, from San Diego, Calif., Sept. 11, 1998.

5 *Ibid.*

6 *Ibid.*

7 Jensen interview.

8 Ietto interview.

9 Jensen interview. The donor for the Praetorian Building space was SPG International, according to DSA Executive Board meeting minutes, July 19, 1984. The donated space enabled the development department, previously housed in InterFirst Properties space, to move. DSO departments were still scattered among various locations and would not be centralized until the opening of the Meyerson Symphony Center in September 1989.

10 Jensen interview.

11 Barzune interview.

12 Jensen interview.

13 *Ibid.*

14 Reid-Hedge interview.

Chapter Twenty-Three

1 Dan Ellinor, interview with author, Dallas, May 25, 1999.

2 Stone interview, Aug. 31, 1997.

3 DSA Executive Board meeting minutes, June 28, 1984.

4 DSA Executive Board meeting minutes, July 19, 1984.

5 Stone interview, Aug. 31, 1997. Peter Wolf Concepts, specialists in marketing centers, theatre sets and interior design, designed the marketing center interior, with special effects consultation by Peter Wexler.

6 Wexler interview.

7 Stone interview.

8 Freling interview.

9 *Ibid.*

10 Ellinor interview.

11 *Ibid.*

12 Robert Miller, "Concert hall starts with boxes on way to building full house," *The Dallas Morning News,* Aug. 14, 1987.

13 Freling interview.

14 Minutes of the DSA annual meeting, May 13, 1987.

15 DSA Executive Board minutes, June 25, 1987.

16 Freling interview.

17 Stone interview, Aug. 31, 1997.

18 Freling interview.

19 Kinzey interview.

20 Stone interview.

21 *Ibid.*

Chapter Twenty-Four

1 John L. Adams, Preface to "A Report on the Meyerson Symphony Center Project Budgets Within the Context of a Project Chronology, 1977–1988," Oct. 19, 1988.

2 Sherry Jacobson, "Symphony gets more donations," *The Dallas Morning News,* Sept. 10, 1987.

3 Stone interview, Aug. 30, 1997.

4 DSA Executive Board minutes, Aug. 17, 1987.

5 *Ibid.*

6   DSA Executive Board minutes, Sept. 10, 1987.

7   *Ibid.*

8   *Ibid.*

9   Schrader interview, Mar. 25, 1997.

10 First Republic was the amalgamation of InterFirst and RepublicBank. It was subsequently taken over by NCNB, which ultimately became NationsBank.

11 Stone interview, Aug. 30, 1997.

12 *Ibid.*

13 David Jackson, "2 hurt in crane collapse at symphony center site," *The Dallas Morning News,* Feb. 21, 1988.

14 Ed Housewright, "Concert hall draws fire," *The Dallas Morning News,* May 6, 1988, 1A.

15 Schrader interview, July 21, 1998.

16 Catalina Camia, "Some question cost of A-1 concert hall," *Dallas Times Herald,* June 26, 1988, B-1.

17 Catalina Camia, "Council wants plan for concert hall costs," *Dallas Times Herald,* July 21, 1988, B-1.

18 Howard Hallam, interview with author, Dallas, Feb. 14, 1997.

19 LWFW's 1989 forecast stated: "Economic impact is calculated based upon the 'multiplier' effect of the Hall's construction and ongoing financial activity [*e.g.* ticket sales, employment, services and purchases]. For example, a ticket sale leads to the purchase of labor which leads to the purchase of food, lodging, etc. and the process continues."

20 Catalina Camia and Kara Kunkel, "Council OKs $2 million more for symphony hall," *Dallas Times Herald,* July 28, 1988, B-1.

21 Walker interview.

22 Walker address to docents.

23 Robert V. Camuto, "Drug search angers symphony site labor," *Dallas Times Herald,* Aug. 26, 1988, A1.

24 Catalina Camia, "Parks agency to run symphony center," *Dallas Times Herald,* Sept. 2, 1988, A28.

25 Robert V. Camuto, "Symphony center chief begins job next week," *Dallas Times Herald,* Nov. 29, 1988.

Chapter Twenty-Five

1   Temerlin interview.

2   Meeting report, of Meyerson Symphony Center press entertainment subcommittee, Jan. 29, 1988, DSO archives.

3   Walker interview.

4   Keheley interview.

5   Holahan interview.

6   Wolford McCue, interview with author, Dallas, Jan. 24, 1997.

7   McCue interview.

8   Lewis interview.

9   Meeting report, Meyerson Symphony Center press entertainment subcommittee, Feb. 22, 1988, DSO archives.

10 McCue interview.

11 Ietto interview.

12 McCue interview.

13 Holahan interview.

14 *Ibid.*

15 David Fritze, "Symphony nears sellout at new home," *Dallas Times Herald,* May 27, 1989, A-1.

Chapter Twenty-Six

1   Jensen interview.

2   Barzune interview, Sept. 4, 1998.

3   Barzune interview, Oct. 7, 1996.

4   Ted DeDee, interview with author, by telephone from Nashville, Tenn., Nov. 22, 1996.

5   *Ibid.*

6   Catalina Camia, "Council wants plan for concert hall costs," *Dallas Times Herald,* July 21, 1988, B-1.

7   Jeff Collins, "Meyerson restaurant delayed," *Dallas Times Herald,* Aug. 26, 1989. According to Bruce MacPherson, the actual budget for the first full year of operation, 1989–90, was $1.8 million.

8   Sharan Goldstein, interview with author, Dallas, Oct. 11, 1996.

9   A copy of the original docent manual, dated May 21, 1989, is the Dallas Public Library Meyerson clippings files. The volume has been supplemented and updated since then.

10 DeDee interview.

11 Louise Elam, letter to author, May 24, 1999.

12 Jensen interview.

13 DeDee interview.

14 Bruce MacPherson, interview with author, Dallas, Aug. 21, 1996.

15 MacPherson interview.

16 *Ibid.*

17 Goldstein interview.

18 Holahan interview.

19 *Ibid.*

20 *Ibid.*

21 *Ibid.*

Chapter Twenty-Seven

1 Walker interview.

2 Robert Miller, "Symphony gift gets business support," *The Dallas Morning News,* Aug. 9, 1989.

3 Jack Roach, letter to author, July 1, 1998.

4 Stone interview, Aug. 31, 1997.

5 *Ibid.*

6 Bette Mullins, interview with author, Dallas, July 23, 1998.

7 Mullins interview.

8 *Ibid.*

9 Temerlin and Mullins interviews.

10 Stone interview.

11 *Ibid.*

12 Temerlin interview.

13 Mullins interview.

14 Stone interview.

15 Mullins interview.

16 Temerlin interview.

17 *Ibid.*

18 Mullins interview.

19 Temerlin interview.

20 *Ibid.*

21 Ron Ruggless, "Reves' gifts honor late husband," *Dallas Times Herald,* Sept. 8, 1989, A-1.

22 DSA Press release, "Dallas Symphony to Receive $2 million in honor of Emery Reves and World Peace," July 6, 1989. DSO archives.

23 Stone interview.

24 Alan Peppard, "So much for reserve; crowd gives five standing ovations," *The Dallas Morning News,* Sept. 9, 1989, 27A.

25 Barzune interview.

26 Marcus interview.

27 Marcus interview, Aug. 7, 1998.

28 Jack Roach, interview with author, Dallas, June 25, 1998.

29 Stone interview, May 25, 1999.

30 Jack Roach, letter to author, July 1, 1998.

Chapter Twenty-Eight

1 David Dillon, "Hall's cost put at $157 million," *The Dallas Morning News,* Jan. 25, 1989, 1A.

2 Ed Housewright, "Officials express shock over cost of concert hall," *The Dallas Morning News,* Jan. 27, 1989, 25A.

3 Editorial, "Unfair Figures: Auditor misstated symphony hall costs," *The Dallas Morning News,* Jan. 28, 1989.

4 Walker address to docents.

5 Ed Housewright, "City told canopy at hall safe; Symphony center contractor disagrees," *The Dallas Morning News,* Mar. 16, 1989, 33A.

6 Jeffrey Weiss, "Council OKs music hall canopy plan," *The Dallas Morning News,* May 2, 1989, 1A.

7 Mark Edgar, "Lesser rips symphony hall funding," *The Dallas Morning News,* Apr. 26, 1989.

8 Ed Housewright, "Not all symphony patrons footing the bill for hall," *The Dallas Morning News,* July 23, 1989, 33A.

9 Lemke interview.

10 Meyerson interview, Aug. 18, 1997.

11 Lyons interview.

12 Meyerson interview.

13 Stone interview, Aug. 31, 1997.

14 Lyons interview.

15 Meyerson interview.

16 *Ibid.*

17 *Ibid.*

18 *Ibid.*

19 Lemke interview.

20 Elam interview.

Chapter Twenty-Nine

1 Melson interview.

2 *Ibid.*

3 The front two rows of the Meyerson riser system are portable. The rear two rows are stationary.

4 Stone interview, Aug. 31, 1997.

5 Reynolds interview.

6 Meyerson interview, Aug. 18, 1997.

7 Melson kept a day-to-day diary during the last weeks in August and through the grand opening fortnight. He reconstructed from the diary during his interview.

8 Temerlin interview.

9 Abby Suckle, interview with author, by

telephone from New York City, May 20, 1999; and memo to author, May 25, 1999.

10 Suckle interview.

11 *Ibid.*

12 Melson interview.

13 Howard interview.

14 Melson interview.

15 *Ibid.*

16 *Ibid.*

17 *Ibid.*

18 Gale Sliger, telephone interview with author, May 26, 1999.

19 Young interview.

20 Stone interview, Aug. 31, 1997.

21 Melson interview.

22 *Ibid.*

23 Wolff interview.

24 Melson interview.

25 Wolff interview.

26 Sliger interview.

27 Melson interview.

Chapter Thirty

1 Lewis interview.

2 Media Relations Plan for the Opening of the Morton H. Meyerson Symphony Center, Draft #5, June 10, 1988. DSO archives. Also, Holahan and Kinzey interviews.

3 Holahan interview.

4 Sliger interview.

5 Gayle Golden, "The House that Mort Built," *American Way Magazine,* Sept. 1, 1989, 82 ff.

6 *Idem.* See also Terry Box, "Symphony group says it can cover hall debt," *The Dallas Morning News,* Sept. 9, 1989, 1A.

7 Stone interview, Aug. 31, 1997.

8 Lewis interview.

9 Russell Davies, "A Symphony of Dollars," *Daily Telegraph Magazine,* Oct. 7, 1989, 49.

Chapter Thirty-One

1 Schrader interview, July 21, 1998.

2 Marcus interview, Aug. 7, 1998.

3 Temerlin interview.

4 *Ibid.*

5 Schrader interview.

6 Temerlin interview.

7 Stone interview, Aug. 31, 1997.

8 Terry Box, "Gift to let Symphony clear

Meyerson Debt," *The Dallas Morning News,* Apr. 10, 1990, 15A.

9 Freling interview.

10 Hallam interview.

11 Lynn Flint Shaw, interview with author, Dallas, July 7, 1997.

12 Bonelli interview, July 9, 1998.

13 Shaw interview.

14 *Ibid.*

15 *Ibid.*

16 Bonelli interview.

17 MacPherson interview.

18 *Ibid.*

19 *Ibid.*

Chapter Thirty-Two

1 James C. Moeser, "From the President," *The American Organist,* Mar. 1994, 5.

2 According to Nicholas Edwards, the proposed organ shutter was to prevent absorption of sound by the deep organ cases. Charles Fisk persuaded Russell Johnson to drop the requirement for the shutter because Fisk organ cases are traditionally shallow. Edwards interview, May 3, 1999.

3 Robert T. Anderson, interview with author, Aug. 25, 1998.

4 Gregory Bover, interview with author, Gloucester, Mass., Nov. 23, 1998.

5 Steven Dieck, interview with author, by telephone from Gloucester, Mass., Aug. 10, 1998.

6 Charles L. Nazarian, interview with author, Gloucester, Mass., Nov. 23, 1998.

7 Robert W. Wolff, letter to Leonard Stone, Oct. 19, 1981. DSO archives.

8 Anderson interview.

9 Dieck interview.

10 *Ibid.*

11 Eugene Bonelli, memorandum to Leonard Stone, June 10, 1982. DSO archives.

12 Melissa McNeil, memorandum dated Feb. 9, 1983, minutes of design team meeting of Feb. 3, 1983. DSO archives.

13 Eugene Bonelli, memo to concert hall committee, smaller unit, Apr. 3, 1984. Cook archives.

14 Dieck interview.

15 DSA Executive Board minutes, Oct. 17, 1985.

16 Dieck interview.

17 *Ibid.*

18 Charles Nazarian, interview with author, Gloucester, Mass., Nov. 23, 1998.

19 Charles Young, letter to author, July 9, 1999.

20 Dieck interview. Dieck visited I. M. Pei & Partners on October 30, 1984, with Charles Nazarian. The following month, Virginia Lee Fisk accompanied Dieck and Nazarian on another visit to New York. This time, they visited the Pei & Partners model shop.

21 DSA Executive Board minutes, Apr. 23, 1987.

22 DSA Board minutes, July 23, 1987, indicate the meeting was scheduled for July 30; Virginia Lee Fisk's records indicate it took place on July 29. The Schrader and Dieck interviews confirm the content of the meeting.

23 Virginia Lee Fisk, handwritten outline for presentation to smaller unit, May 26, 1988.

24 C. B. Fisk, Inc., minutes of meeting at the Fisk workshop on June 20, 1988.

25 Fisk interview.

26 *Ibid.*

27 The exchange is documented both in the Schrader and the Fisk interviews.

28 Nazarian interview.

29 Dieck interview.

30 Charles Young, letter to author, July 9, 1999.

31 Dieck interview.

32 George Schrader, cost analysis for organ, May 26, 1988; attachment to John L. Adams, memorandum of meeting of smaller unit, June 9, 1988. Cook archives.

33 John L. Adams, memorandum dated June 9, 1988, summarizing meeting of smaller unit May 26, 1988. Cook archives.

34 Dieck interview.

35 Fisk interview.

36 Victor Marshall interview.

37 David Fuller, "The Slee Hall Organ and its History," paper published by the State University of New York at Buffalo, April 1990, 3–4.

38 Virginia Lee Fisk provided the information about these innovations.

39 David Pike, interview with author, Gloucester, Mass., Nov. 23, 1998.

40 Lenora McCroskey, "C. B. Fisk Presents Opus 100," *The Pipeline, a newsletter from C. B. Fisk, Inc.,* Vol. 3, No. 2 (Dec. 1992).

41 Wayne Marshall, interview with author, Dallas, Jan. 17, 1997.

42 Anderson interview.

43 S. Wayne Foster, interview with author, Dallas, Feb. 14, 1999.

44 *Ibid.*

Chapter Thirty-Three

1   Pamela A. Guinn, DSA chief financial officer, letter to Margaret McDermott, Sept. 19, 1983 Cook archives.

2   Stanley Marcus interview, Oct. 16, 1996.

3   Linda Marcus, interview with author, Dallas, Aug. 20, 1998.

4   Bader interview.

5   Langford interview.

6   Bader interview.

7   "Pei Hits High Note with Concert Hall," *The Dallas Morning News,* May 16, 1982.

8   DSA Board minutes, Oct. 23, 1986.

9   Linda Marcus interview.

10 Bill Marvel, "DSO to announce symphony artist," *The Dallas Morning News,* Oct. 10, 1988.

11 Janet Kutner, "Meyerson art deal confirmed," *The Dallas Morning News,* Aug. 31, 1989, 31A.

12 Information sheet issued by the grand opening fortnight committee, Sept. 1989. DSO archives.

13 Stanley Marcus interview, Oct. 16, 1996.

14 Bill Booziotis, interview with author, Dallas, Jan. 6, 1999.

15 Linda Marcus interview; and Margaret Robinette, public art coordinator, City of Dallas Office of Cultural Affairs, telephone conversation with author, Mar. 3, 1999.

16 Booziotis interview.

17 Linda Marcus interview.

18 *Ibid.*

19 *Ibid.*

20 *Ibid.*

21 Booziotis interview.

Chapter Thirty-Four

1   David Kahn, letter to author, Mar. 16, 1999.

2   Lamar Livingston, interview with author, Dallas, Oct. 21, 1996.

3   *Ibid.*

4   Suckle interview.

5   Edwards interview, Apr. 30, 1999.

6   David Kahn, interview with author, by telephone from Larchmont, N.Y., Feb. 23, 1999.

7 Kahn interview. According to the technical staff at the Meyerson, some diffusers were added in the mid-1990s to route the air differently after the DSA received complaints about draftiness on the main floor. Kahn maintains that the drafts resulted from the HVAC contractor not balancing the system properly and failing to install dampers.

8 Johnson interview.

9 Kahn interview.

10 Johnson interview with Witze, Sept. 21, 1996.

11 Edwards interview, by telephone from Coventry, England, July 7, 1999.

12 Johnson interview, Sept. 21, 1996.

13 Edwards interview, July 7, 1999.

Chapter Thirty-Five

1 Hustis interview.

2 Wilfred Roberts, interview with author, Dallas, Oct. 13, 1996.

3 *Ibid.*

4 Barr interview.

5 *Ibid.*

6 *Ibid.*

7 Janet Cherry interview.

8 Coren interview.

9 Reynolds interview.

10 Barbara Hustis interview.

11 Kitzman interview.

12 Spohr interview.

13 Gunther Herbig, interview with author, Dallas, Nov. 22, 1997.

14 Herbig interview.

15 Andrew Litton, interview with author, by telephone from Los Angeles, Calif., July 14, 1999.

16 *Ibid.*

Epilogue

1 Marcus interview, Aug. 7, 1998.

2 Ralph Blumenthal, "Midlife Hits Lincoln Center With Calls for Rich Face Lift," *The New York Times*, June 1, 1999.

3 MacPherson interview.

4 Scott Cantrell, interview with author, St. Louis, Mo., June 20, 1997.

5 Leonard Stone interview.

6 Young interview.

7 Johnson interview.

8 Jensen interview.

BIBLIOGRAPHY

BOOKS AND ARTICLES

Allison, Wick. "End of the Yes-and-No Men," *D Magazine,* Vol. 22, No. 10 (October 1995), 26–29.

———, and other editors of *D,* "Power in Dallas: Who holds the cards?" *D Magazine,* Vol. 1, No. 1 (October 1974), 47–55.

Ames, Katrine. "But . . . How Does it Play? Pei's New Dallas Concert Hall Traces the True Test," *Newsweek,* September 25, 1989, 64.

Ando, Yoichi. *Concert Hall Acoustics.* Berlin & New York: Springer Verlag, 1985.

———, ed. *Music and Concert Hall Acoustics.* London and San Diego: Academic Press, 1997.

Bagenal, Hope, and Alexander Wood. *Planning for Good Acoustics.* London: Methuen & Co., Ltd., 1931.

Barna, Joel Warren, "Meyerson Symphony Center: A Preview of I. M. Pei's New Twist." *Texas Architect,* September–October 1989, 40–41.

Barnett, Margaret. "An Art in Acoustics," *Sky,* June 1990, 32–40.

Barron, Michael. *Auditorium Acoustics and Architectural Design.* London and New York: E&FN Spon, 1993.

Beranek, Leo. *How They Sound: Concert and Opera Halls.* Woodbury, N.Y.: Acoustical Society of America, 1996.

———. *Music, Acoustics, and Architecture.* New York and London: John Wiley & Sons, Inc., 1962.

Branch, Mark Alden. "The Artful Science of Acoustical Design," *Yale Magazine,* October 1990, 44 ff.

Butler, H. Joseph. "Competition Fever." *Choir & Organ,* July–August 1997, 45–46.

Cannell, Michael. *I. M. Pei: Mandarin of Modernism.* New York: Carol Southern Books, 1995.

Cantrell, Scott. "How Dallas Did It," *Symphony Magazine,* September–October 1989, 34–37.

———. "Pipe Organs, not Dreams," *Symphony Magazine,* July–August 1991, 44–49.

Chism, Olin. "New Home for the Dallas Symphony," *Musical America,* January 1990, 27–29.

Curtis, Gregory. "Behind the Lines," *Texas Monthly,* March 1985.

Dallas Symphony Orchestra Staff. "The Morton H. Meyerson Symphony Center: Dallas' Cultural Renaissance," advertorial section in *Texas Monthly,* September 1989, 57–65.

Davies, Russell. "A Symphony of Dollars," *Telegraph Weekly Magazine [The Daily Telegraph,* London], October 7, 1989, 38–49.

DeDee, Ted. "Beauty and the Beast: A Contract Looks Good Only in the Eye of the Beholder," *Facility Manager Magazine,* July–August 1995.

Fairweather, Virginia. "Sound Structure." *Civil Engineering,* May 1987, 56–58.

Fantel, Hans. "Travel By Ear," *Condé Nast Traveler,* July 1992, 141–45.

———. "The World's Greatest Concert Halls," *Delta Sky Magazine,* February 1999, 15–19.

Filler, Martin. "Power Pei," *Vanity Fair,* September 1989, 260–78, 291 ff.

Forsyth, Michael. *Buildings for Music: The Architect, the Musician, and the Listener from the Seventeenth Century to the Present Day.* Cambridge, Mass.: The MIT Press, 1985.

Giddens, Sally, "The Sound of Money: Explaining the Symphony's Price Tag," *D Magazine,* August 1988, 23.

Golden, Gayle. "The House that Mort Built," *American Way Magazine,* September 1, 1989, 82 ff.

Hill, Patricia Evridge. *Dallas: The Making of a Modern City.* Austin: University of Texas Press, 1996.

Hollandsworth, Skip, "A Funny Thing Happened on the Way to the Symphony," *D Magazine,* September 1986, 68 ff.

Holmes, Maxine, and Gerald D. Saxon, eds. *The WPA Dallas Guide and History.* Introduction by Gerald D. Saxon. Dallas: Dallas Public Library, Texas Center for the Book, University of North Texas Press, 1992.

"How Do Our Spaces Perform?" *Symphony Magazine,* October–November 1986, 36–66 Includes views of ten experts: R. Lawrence Kierkegaard, Rein Prin, Peter J. George, David Lasker, Chris Jaffe, Richard Cormier, Richard B. Bauschard, Tom Beaman, Nicholas Goldsmith, and Glenn E. Seger.

Izenour, George C. *Theater Design.* New York: McGraw-Hill, 1977.

Johnson, Russell. "An Answer to the Enigma of Flexibility for Music and Theater," *Architectural Record,* mid-August 1981, 68–73.

———. "Concert Halls: Designing By Ear. Acoustics in the Meyerson Symphony Center," *The Construction Specifier,* April 1990, 88–97.

———. "Acoustics: Halls of Sound." *Canada's Contract Magazine,* February–March and April–May 1990.

Korman, Richard. "Sound and Fury: Noise level rises over acoustics," *ENR,* April 9, 1987, 22–27.

Marcus, Stanley. *Minding the Store.* Denton: University of North Texas Press, 1998.

McGuigan, Cathleen. "The Perfectionist: At 72, modernist master builder I. M. Pei reaches the top of his game," *Newsweek,* September 25, 1989, 60–62.

Mehta, Madan, Jim Johnson, and Jorge Rocafort. *Architectural Acoustics: Principles and Design.* Upper Saddle River, N.J.: Prentice Hall, 1999.

Merwin, John. "High Culture, Low Politics: The Death of the Dallas Symphony." *D Magazine,* November 1974, 43–52.

Pfeiffer, Norman. "A Tale of Two Concert Halls," *Symphony News,* August 1975 [excerpts from presentation about Minneapolis and Denver halls at American Symphony Orchestra League National Conference], 12–13, 32–34.

Pike, David C., Robert T. Anderson, and Paul Riedo. "Meyerson Symphony Center, Dallas, Texas." *The American Organist,* Vol. 28, No. 5 (May 1994), 50–54.

Porter, Andrew. "How it Played in Peoria (and Elsewhere)," *The New Yorker,* October 18, 1982 [on opening of six large concert halls within two weeks in New Orleans, Baltimore, Peoria, Eugene, East Lansing, and Toronto], 163–70.

Rodrigue, George. "The Arts District," *D Magazine,* May 1982, 103 ff.

———. "I. M. Pei's Superhall: A Marriage of Design and Acoustics," *D Magazine,* August 1982, 46 ff.

Rogers, Ralph B. *Splendid Torch.* West Kennebunk, Maine: Phoenix Publishers, 1993.

Sabine, Wallace Clement. *Collected Papers on Acoustics.* Cambridge: Harvard University Press, 1932.

Salter, Charles M., ed. *Acoustics: Architecture, Engineering, the Environment.* San Francisco: William Stout Publishers, 1998.

Schroeder, Manfred. "Toward Better Acoustics for Concert Halls," *Physics Today,* October 1980, 24–30.

Smith, Lorraine. "Concert Hall Wrapped in Curves," *Engineering News Record [ENR],* November 6, 1986, 58 ff.

———, and Janice Tuchman. "A Fantasy in Concrete and Glass," *ENR* [The McGraw-Hill Construction Weekly], July 20, 1989.

Snedcof, Harold R. "Cultural Facilities in Mixed-Use Development," *ULI—The Urban Land Institute,* 1985.

Spiegelman, Willard. "Sights & Sounds of the Dallas Symphony Orchestra 1900–1989." History brochure published by the Dallas Public Library in conjunction with an exhibit observing the opening of the Morton H. Meyerson Symphony Center, September 6–November 30, 1989.

Stovall, Lisa M. "The Morton H. Meyerson Symphony Center. A Dream Becomes Reality," unpublished paper dated November 23, 1988, submitted as coursework in SMU Center for Arts Administration program; in Dallas Public Library.

Whyte, Bert. "Halls for All," *Audio,* July 1993.

Wiseman, Carter. *I. M. Pei: A Profile in American Architecture.* New York: Harry N. Abrams, 1990.

NEWSPAPERS

Dallas CityLife
Dallas Downtown News
The Dallas Morning News
Dallas Times Herald
Fort Worth Star-Telegram
The New York Times

ARCHIVAL SOURCES

Central Dallas Association
City of Dallas
Mary McDermott Cook
Dallas Symphony Orchestra

INTERVIEWS

[Interviews took place in Dallas, except as noted otherwise.]

Adams, John Luther—former DSO concert hall coordinator, August 21, 1996.

Allison, Wick—publisher of *D Magazine,* June 23, 1998.

Amberg, Ted—architect, former head of I. M. Pei & Partners Dallas office, by telephone from Chicago, Ill., March 7, 1997.

Anderson, Robert—chairman of organ subcommittee, August 25, 1998.

Bader, Ian—architect with I. M. Pei & Partners [now Pei, Cobb, Freed & Partners], New York City, January 15, 1999.

Barr, Eric—DSO principal oboe, member of players' committee, June 11, 1998.

Barzune, Dolores—DSA Board member, former DSA president, October 7, 1996, May 11, 1998, and September 4, 1998.

Berkow, Sam—acoustician, New York City, May 10, 1999.

Black, Jan Hart—former Dallas city manager, October 8, 1998.

Blaine, Martha—former DSA orchestra manager, March 24, 1997.

Bonelli, Eugene—member of Mort Meyerson's smaller unit and chair of acoustics subcommittee, later president of DSA, January 8, 1997, July 9 and September 8, 1998.

Booziotis, Bill—architect of Symphony Suites/corporate entertainment space and member of art committee, January 6, 1999.

Bover, Gregory—Vice President for Operations, C. B. Fisk Company, Gloucester, Mass., November 23, 1998.

Brans, Willem—DSO development director 1981–85, now with Artec Consultants, New York City, October 21, 1997.

Brusilow, Anshel—former music director of DSO, Addison, Tex., August 24, 1998.

Cantrell, Scott—music critic of the *Kansas City Star,* now of *The Dallas Morning News,* St. Louis, Mo., June 20, 1997.

Cherry, Janet—DSO second violinist, August 19, 1998.

Cherry, Kalman—DSO principal timpanist and member of players' committee, August 19, 1998.

Chin, Perry—architect with I. M. Pei & Partners, now an architect/consultant specializing in building façades, by telephone from New York City, May 20, 1999.

Cook, Mary McDermott—DSA Board member, member of DSO building committee smaller unit, October 21, 1996, and September 11, 1998.

Coren, Michael—DSO cellist, October 3, 1996.

Decherd, Robert W.—DSA Board member and former DSA president, February 4, 1997.

DeDee, Ted—former MHMSC director (facility manager), by telephone from Nashville, Tenn., November 22, 1996.

Dieck, Steven—project manager for C. B. Fisk Company, now president, by telephone from Gloucester, Mass., August 10, 1998.

Dillon, David—architecture critic of *The Dallas Morning News,* by telephone from Amherst, Mass., December 14, 1998.

Donnell, Stewart—cost consultant, formerly with Hanscomb Roy Associates, July 2, 1998.

Edwards, Nicholas—acoustician with Artec, 1979–91, now with Acoustic Dimensions, April 30 and May 3, 1999; by telephone from Coventry, England, July 7, 1999.

Elam, Louise Reuben—City of Dallas architect, August 20, 1996.

Ellinor, Dan—DSO staff member in charge of box seat sales, 1986–90, May 25, 1999.

Fisk, Virginia Lee—owner, C. B. Fisk Company, by telephone from Gloucester, Mass., April 12, 1999.

Flowers, Diane—secretary to Ted Amberg in I. M. Pei & Partners Dallas office, July 18, 1997.

Folsom, Robert—former mayor of Dallas, June 1, 1998.

Foster, S. Wayne—organist, winner of first Triennial Organ Competition, February 14, 1999.

Freling, Richard A.—attorney with Jones, Day, Reavis & Pogue, former president of DSA Board, February 26, 1997.

Galland, Richard—former CEO of American Petrofina, former president of DSA Board, December 23, 1996.

Girko, Betty—DSO double bass player, December 9, 1996.

Girko, Steve—former DSO principal clarinet, December 9, 1996.

Glaze, Robert—former chairman and treasurer of DSA Board, August 7, 1997.

Goldstein, Sharan—National Council of Jewish Women, developer and volunteer coordinator of MHMSC docent program, October 11, 1996.

Gould, Warren—former DSA development director, January 31, 1997.

Gray, Enid—political consultant, April 8, 1999.

Hallam, Howard—former DSA Board president, February 14, 1997.

Heisel, Ralph—architect, by telephone from New York City, February 25, 1997; in New York City, January 14, 1999.

Herbig, Gunther—DSO guest conductor, November 22, 1997.

Holahan, Jane—MHMSC coordinator for symphony grand opening fortnight, January 4, 1997.

Hoster, Fred—DSO general manager of, 1982–93, January 30, 1997.

Howard, Douglas—DSO principal percussion, chair of MHMSC players' committee, September 5, 1996.

Hustis, Barbara—DSO associate principal viola, August 17, 1997.

Hustis, Gregory—DSO principal horn, August 17, 1997.

Ietto, Domenick—former DSO development director, by telephone from San Diego, Calif., September 11, 1998.

Jensen, JoLynne—DSO associate director of development, September 25, 1997.

Johnson, Russell—Artec consultants, MHMSC acoustician, interview conducted by Alexandra Witze of *The Dallas Morning News,* October 21, 1996; videotaped interview conducted by Katina Simmons, September 1989; and interview with author, April 10, 1999.

Jonsson, Philip—former chairman of Dallas Symphony Board and member of DSA Council to the Chairman, Addison, Tex., July 21, 1997.

Kahn, David—acoustician with Artec Consultants, 1985–91, now with Acoustic Dimensions, by telephone from Larchmont, N.Y., February 23, 1999.

Karayanis, Plato—Dallas Opera executive director, March 27, 1997.

Keheley, Cliff—engineer, former City of Dallas director of public works, January 8, 1997.

Kelley, Dorothea—former DSO associate principal viola, April 9, 1998.

Kinzey, Douglas—former DSO marketing director, August 6, 1996.

Kitzman, Diane—DSO first violinist, October 25, 1996.

Kitzman, John—DSO principal trombone, October 25, 1996.

Langford, Jim—architect with I. M. Pei & Partners, 1981–85, now practicing as James E. Langford, Architects & Planners, October 13, 1996.

Lemke, Bob—project engineer with J. W. Bateson Co. [now Centex Construction], May 24, 1999.

Levin, Richard—board member and attorney, member of DSO building committee smaller unit, November 1, 1996.

Lewis, Dvora—public relations consultant, by telephone from London, England, August 25, 1998.

Litton, Andrew—DSO music director, by telephone from Los Angeles, July 14, 1999.

Livingston, Lamar—MHMSC sound engineer, October 21, 1996.

Lyons, Paul—architect, quality control supervisor for J. W. Bateson Co., Inc., during construction, by telephone from Las Vegas, Nev., June 17, 1999.

MacPherson, Bruce C.—MHMSC facility manager, August 21, 1996.

Marcus, Linda—art committee member, committee chair since 1989, August 20, 1998.

Marcus, Stanley—board member, member of DSO building committee smaller unit, October 16, 1996, and August 7, 1998.

Marshall, Victor—DSO artistic administrator, August 7, 1996.

Marshall, Wayne—organist, pianist, and conductor, January 24, 1997.

McCue, Wolford—former public relations director at Bozell & Jacobs, developed marketing and press plan for MHMSC opening, January 24, 1997.

McDermott, Margaret—arts patron, art committee member, and major donor, June 27, 1998.

McNeil, Melissa—DSO concert hall planning coordinator, 1980–86, September 17, 1998.

Melson, Mark—DSO director of orchestra operations, August 13, 1996.

Meyerson, Morton H.—chairman of building committee and smaller unit, July 9 and August 18, 1997, and by telephone, September 10, 1998.

Milano, Al—former DSO development director and general manager, by telephone from Newport Beach, Calif., June 29, 1998.

Miller, George—project architect I. M. Pei & Partners [now Pei, Cobb, Freed & Partners], New York City, January 16, 1997.

Miller, Henry S.—DSA board member and former president, headed Cornerstone campaign, October 30, 1996.

Montgomery, Philip O'B. III—chairman of 1982 bond campaign, October 2, 1996.

Moore, Janet Haldeman—daughter of former DSA President Lloyd Haldeman, by telephone from Houston, Tex., October 5, 1998.

Moore, Nela Wells—staff of 1982 bond campaign headquarters, March 19, 1999.

Mullins, Bette—member of fortnight committee, assisted with Wendy Reves gift, July 23, 1998.

Nazarian, Charles—visual designer, C. B. Fisk Company, Gloucester, Mass., November 23, 1998.

Ohga, Norio—chairman of Sony Corporation and conductor, November 14, 1996.

Oue, Eiji—music director of Minnesota Orchestra, November 2, 1996.

Pei, I. M.—videotaped interview conducted by Katina Simmons, September 1989.

Penson, Nancy—DSA Board member, member of building committee smaller unit, October 28, 1996.

Pike, David—tonal designer, C. B. Fisk Company, Gloucester, Mass., November 23, 1998.

Porter, Coy—construction manager for J. W. Bateson Co., July 14, 1998.

Redmond, Glenn—architect's on-site representative, October 23, 1996.

Reid-Hedge, Sydney—DSO director of volunteer activities, October 17, 1996.

Reynolds, Mary—DSO first violinist, November 14, 1996.

Richardson, Mike—former president of DSO Chorus, October 26, 1996.

Roach, John [Jack], Esq.—attorney and later executor for Greer Garson Fogelson and Louise Wolff Kahn, June 25, 1998.

Roberts, Wilfred—DSO principal bassoon and orchestra manager, October 13, 1996.

Robertson, Leslie—Leslie E. Robertson Associates, consulting structural engineers, New York City, January 17, 1997, and May 10, 1999.

Schilling, William L.—former president of DSA Board, August 6, 1997.

Schrader, George—former city manager, consultant/liaison between DSO and City of Dallas, Addison, Tex., February 5 and March 25, 1997, May 20 and July 21, 1998.

Seay, Margie—widow of William H. Seay, DSA Board president, 1982–84, May 24, 1999.

Seelig, Timothy—director of Turtle Creek Chorale, has recorded fifteen albums in the MHMSC, December 6, 1996.

Shaw, Lynn Flint—chairman, community affairs/DSA Board, July 7, 1997.

Shirey, Ron—former director of DSO Chorus, Fort Worth, Tex., October 10, 1996.

Sliger, Gale—Gale Sliger Productions, produced special events for the grand opening fortnight, by telephone, May 26, 1999.

Spohr, Clifford—DSO principal bass and member of players' committee, October 14, 1998.

Stone, Don—former president of DSA Board of Governors, February 3, 1997, and June 22, 1998.

Stone, Leonard—former DSO executive director, Calgary, Alberta, August 30 and 31, 1997; by telephone from Calgary, May 25, 1999.

Stubel, Brenda—president of DSO Chorus, architect of MHMSC choral rehearsal room, November 26, 1996.

Suckle, Abby—architect with I. M. Pei & Partners [now Pei, Cobb, Freed & Partners], by telephone from New York City, May 20, 1999.

Suhm, Victor C.—former Dallas assistant city manager, August 8, 1997.

Temerlin, Liener, former DSA Board president and chairman of grand opening fortnight committee, Irving, Tex., July 15, 1998.

Walker, Joe—retired president and CEO of J. W. Bateson Company, construction manager for MHMSC, informal address to volunteer docents at MHMSC, December 14, 1996; interview June 20, 1999.

Wexler, Peter—designer, consultant to DSO during planning stages, New York City, October 21, 1997.

Wolff, Robert—theatre planning consultant, Artec Consultants, New York City, January 16, 1997; and by telephone from New York City, May 27, 1999.

Young, Charles—architect with I. M. Pei & Partners [now practicing independently as Charles Young, P.C.] and principal designer of MHMSC concert room, New York City, January 16, 1997.

INDEX

NOTE: "Meyerson" refers to Morton H. Meyerson. "MSC" refers to the Meyerson Symphony Center. Page numbers in **bold** refer to illustrations.

ABOUT THE TYPE

The text of this book has been composed in a digitized version of Dante, a typeface designed by scholar-printer Giovanni Mardersteig (1892–1977). An active book printer and proprietor of the Officina Bodoni, Mardersteig's typographic creed stressed service to the author, followed by service to the reader and concluded with the tertiary aim of producing an elegant page without the trappings of idiosyncrasy. After many years studying and using the great Venetian and Aldine types, Mardersteig began work on his own interpretation of the renaissance form. His efforts culminated in the drawings for Dante, which Mardersteig completed in 1954. To render his letterforms in metal type, Mardersteig commissioned Charles Malin, a renowned punchcutter with whom he had worked for many years. By 1955 the types were complete and Mardersteig eagerly used them for an edition of Boccaccio's *Trattatello in Laude di Dante*, from which the his type derived its name.

Book design and composition by Mark McGarry

Texas Type & Book Works, Dallas, Texas